THE FILMS OF FRANKENHEIMER

ERRATA

p. 141, right column, line 21: "4fl hours" should read "4½ hours".
p. 141, right column, line 30: "1/ hours" should read "1½ hours".
p. 164, left column, line 40: "7fi million" should read "7 million five".
p. 275, left column, line 2: "225 to 1" should read "2.55 to 1".

THE FILMS
OF FRANKENHEIMER

● ● ●

FORTY YEARS IN FILM

● ● ●

**John Frankenheimer talks
about his life in the cinema
to Gerald Pratley**

Bethlehem **Lehigh University Press**
London **Cygnus Arts**

PUBLISHED IN THE UNITED KINGDOM BY

Cygnus Arts, a division of Golden Cockerel Press
16 Barter Street
London
WC1A 2AH

PUBLISHED IN THE UNITED STATES OF AMERICA BY

Lehigh University Press
440 Forsgate Drive
Cranbury
NJ 08512

First published 1998

ISBN 1 900541 40 8
ISBN 0 934223 47 5

LIBRARY OF CONGRESS CATALOGUING-IN-PUBLICATION DATA

Pratley, Gerald.
    The films of John Frankenheimer : forty years in film / Gerald Pratley.
        p.   cm.
    Filmography: p.
    Includes index.
    ISBN 0-934223-47-5 (alk. paper)
    1. Frankenheimer, John, 1930–   . I. Title.
PN1998.3.F7327P73 1998
791.43'0233'092—dc21   97-50118
                                                CIP

Printed in the United Kingdom by Martins the Printers

For Orize, Denise and Jocelyn

CONTENTS

John and Evans Frankenheimer in 1997, with two of JF's Emmy awards.

FOREWORD by John Frankenheimer

Gerald Pratley has been a very important part of my life for over thirty-five years He has been on practically every film location since *The Train* in 1963. No one, except my wife Evans, has spent as much time watching me work as Gerald.

I trust and respect him. Therefore, I felt free to express myself. We have talked at great length about my films and my life. The result is here in these pages—my career has been a long one—it is all here for better or worse, the triumphs and the defeats.

I have been extremely lucky—by that I mean, I have been able to make a living in a profession that I truly love. I never had to decide between various occupations—from a very early age I wanted to be a movie director. As a result of that choice, I have travelled to incredible places, met extraordinary people and led a life that exceeds my wildest dreams.

I consider myself a professional movie director and I define the difference between a professional and an amateur as follows: an amateur only does things that he/she wants to do; a professional does things even when he/she doesn't want to do them. There have been times during the last forty-two years that I have not wanted to be on a movie set, nevertheless, I carried on. Fortunately, the good times have far outnumbered the bad.

Recently, I was asked how I wanted to be remembered. After a lot of thought, the answer was that I wanted people to remember me as being better at the end than at the beginning.

Finally, I would like to close by saying that the most important person in my life is my wife of thirty-five years, Evans Evans. She has always been there for me. She has inspired me, encouraged me, and supported me. She has made it possible for me to have a lasting career.

Los Angeles, November 1997.

Acknowledgments

Grateful acknowledgment is made to Peter Cowie, International Publishing Director, *Variety* (London); Patricia Thompson, Publisher and Editor, *Film Canada Yearbook* (Toronto); Penelope Houston, British Film Institute, *Sight and Sound* (London); Sylvia Frank, Reference Library, Cinémathèque Ontario (Toronto); Risa Shuman, Producer, TV Ontario's "Saturday Night at the Movies" and "Film International" (Toronto); Nanette Siegert (LA), and Joan Boyd (Toronto) for their services, support and willing co-operation.

We also acknowledge with thanks the co-operation of the following: Turner Pictures, HBO Pictures, United Artists, MGM, 20th Century-Fox, Paramount Pictures, Columbia Pictures, Embassy Pictures, Universal Pictures, Warner Bros., and Cannon Pictures.

The author thanks the John and Evans Frankenheimer Archive for providing so many of the photographs used in this book.

Above all, the author's thanks are due to John Frankenheimer for the time he has given me over the years to make this book possible.

INTRODUCTION

Los Angeles. 1995 marks the centenary of the cinema. Once again, the *Year in Review* surveys of what happened, what was attempted, what succeeded and what failed, what was best and what was worst in art, entertainment, industry and politics during 1994 are flooding the media. There are few references to the anniversary. Facts and figures, opinions and generalizations all make the headlines and are voiced by over-excited presenters on television and radio, their main concern being the Hollywood studios—the films, the deals, the good intentions of the deceitful and the deposed, the fortunes made and lost, and, above all, what the weekly box office returns amounted to over the year: *Hollywood Films Draw Record Crowds in 1994* and *Hollywood Sells Record $5.4 Billion Tickets* but turn the pages and we find: *For Hollywood Flops Are a Way of Life* and *Creative Bewilderment Leads to Paralyzing Self-doubt* and *Movie Budgets are Out of Control.*

In Beverly Hills, shortly before Christmas 1994, John Frankenheimer and his actress wife, Evans Evans, returned from an exhausting location at Sharpsburg some thirty miles south of Atlanta, where he had been filming *Andersonville,* his thirty-first picture. For over forty of the hundred years that motion pictures have existed, he has worked steadily and consistently making films in which the conviction of his feelings transform the subject matter of his work into profound experiences. His grasp of all aspects of film creativity—from script to camera, acting, editing, music and sound—have made him a master of the cinema.

Frankenheimer is well aware of what goes on in the world of film surrounding him and of which he is very much a part; yet he distances himself from it. A brilliant and extraordinary film-maker—imaginative, tenacious and determined, somewhat aloof from the crowd—he is not to be found with the social set, nor attending awards ceremonies, parties and premières. Seldom is he mentioned in the trade papers and he keeps out of the conversation columns. He does not comment on what the media is saying, at the closing of the year or at any other time, about the state of Hollywood—its lack of quality, the financial disturbances, the constant rotation of studio heads, the losses, the profits, the huge budgets and the immense sums paid to certain stars. He is loyal to, but not uncritical of his profession. He is pleased with what American film-makers, particularly the rising tide of young independents, are doing, but also concerned about the excesses of studio management and its often ill-considered decisions. He is genuine in his admiration of good films from other countries. He speaks thoughtfully on any aspect of film-making and what it entails, both philosophically and intellectually, but shuns pretentiousness and tends to view the scene around him with ironic detachment. He would rather think about his next film than ponder over Hollywood's production trends, its political and financial uncertainties. He goes his own way, letting all these vicissitudes drift past, and remaining positive in his outlook and true to himself. All that matters to him is to continue making films he believes in, reflecting the human condition within informed narratives which strike a thoughtful balance between form and content. He has remained true to his calling as a film-maker over the years, from the heights of acclaim to the depths of despair, from certainty to the unknown, yet always giving himself wholeheartedly to the demanding art of cinema.

I first met John Frankenheimer with Evans Evans at the Acapulco Film Festival in Mexico in December 1962 after the showing of *Birdman of Alcatraz.* A beautiful actress and a handsome director, they made an attractive couple among the glamorous crowds of film people once drawn to film festivals but now largely surplanted by a more informal generation. Ever on the move, then as now, he was to return to Los Angeles almost immediately, leaving little time to talk about his work. In 1956, in my capacity of film critic and commentator for the CBC's Trans-Canada radio network, I had seen *The Young Stranger* followed several years later by *The Young Savages.* Although he was far from satisfied with either of them, I was, along with other critics, impressed by what the films had to say, by their vigor, style and photography, and the immediacy of the acting. The stories were concerned with contemporary society, they took a different look at familiar situations and showed an intelligence, an inquiring mind and a refreshing disdain for tired, formulaic approaches. Above all, they contained the first indication of Frankenheimer's remarkable film sense which emerged in *Birdman of Alcatraz* and his second film, *All Fall Down,* a defining characteristic of his work which has remained strongly in evidence throughout the years.

I knew at that time in Acapulco that he was highly acclaimed for his work as a director in "live" television drama but, as I seldom had time to watch television in these early days, being fully occupied by the cinema, I saw none of them until years later when he gave me kinescopes of certain titles. As he spoke at the festival of returning to television, I had not expected to see him again. But with the ever-changing technology and pattern of popular entertainment, the cinema became his life and work, indeed his entire world, both in art and politics. As I watched successive films, I was gripped by their realism, their graphic yet poetic depiction of many lives and the individuals who lived them at different times and in many places. There is something powerfully compelling about Frankenheimer's films that is difficult to describe. It forms an inherent part of his creativity, and shows an instinctive expressionism in his cinema that is an art in itself.

Although we have never been close friends, and there were years when we never met, Frankenheimer and I always kept in touch on location as often as possible. As his work progressed, I came to like and admire this tall, somewhat shy individual, who was such a commanding figure on the set and who, through the years, has changed from a striking young man to the older, much weathered artist he is today. No matter what the years have done to Hollywood, and what the system has at times done to him, he has worked on steadily. Over the past forty years, John Frankenheimer, through good and difficult times, has maintained his dominant position in that recognized center of important film-makers. As one of the small and impressive groups of television directors from the "live" days of drama on CBS, NBC, ABC—Delbert Mann, Arthur Hiller, Daniel Petrie, Sidney Lumet, Sydney Pollack, Franklin Shaffner, Norman Jewison—who first entered the cinema (the first wave of a new generation of film-makers who had not worked their way up through the major studios) Frankenheimer has always been a name to reckon with.

• • •

In 1956, the names of new directors were rare and when the opening credits for *The Young Stranger* ended with "directed by John Frankenheimer," many critics, and audiences who followed developments in the cinema, showed immediate interest. During the film, they sensed an unexpected achievement, and at the conclusion they knew they had seen the work of a promising, skilled and concerned film-maker.

To audiences outside the USA and Canada, he was a complete newcomer, but to many North American television audiences he was already known and admired for his imaginative CBS *Playhouse 90* shows. However, movie-goers who hoped soon to see another film from him were disappointed, and had to wait until 1961 for his second film, *The Young Savages*. Having been so discouraged by the making of his first film, he had returned to the satisfactions of live television.

Since then he has made more than thirty films. Unlike many other now great and distinguished film-makers, he has never gone through a period of making indifferent films in order to earn the right to future freedom—the just reward for proving oneself in the factory or as a hired director. It could be said that his television years constituted such a period, but this he would deny in view of the importance of the shows he directed.

Frankenheimer believed in freedom right from the beginning and his efforts played a large part in bringing about the changes in Hollywood which saw the collapse of the old studio system and the emergence of the independent film-maker in partnership with the studio. The independent film-maker, in most cases, was the new, inspired and youthful graduate from television, who was at that time more closely attuned to the life of America than the older generation of film-makers who seldom knew what was happening in Los Angeles.

After his first disappointment with *The Young Stranger*, he was determined not to take on any other commitments without the freedom to be the moving and decisive force behind the picture. He was compelled to agree not to work entirely on location for *The Young Savages* and *Birdman of Alcatraz*, but with *All Fall Down* he achieved the freedom to do everything his own way.

Frankenheimer has rarely made a poor, indifferent or unsatisfying film, and all have shown a profit. Indeed, most have been both artistic and commercial successes. He is a committed realist with a deep concern for humanity. His body of work has been personal and of a consistently high standard, demonstrating variable structures, imaginative techniques, a documentary realism brought to life with the drama and conflict of human participation, and with extreme formal and thematic continuity. With visual truth and frequently outspoken dialogue, his films reflect political issues, and the corruption of moral and artistic ideals. They are living social documents within highly dramatized narratives and filmed with a striking visual skill.

Although he works in the best traditions of British-American narrative cinema, and acknowledges David Lean and William Wyler as his ideals, he owes little to any other film-maker, having established himself as a creative and perceptive individual, always aware of the complexity of people and the problems and decisions which beset them.

● ● ●

His career actually began in the summer of 1953 on the day when, alone and unknown, he walked into the offices of CBS in New York City.

John Frankenheimer begins his career in television, 1953.

FRANKENHEIMER ON HIS EARLY DAYS

"I was always a very introverted child, and I recall finding great escape in films. I remember being seven years old, going to the movies every Saturday. I recall *The Lone Ranger* was being shown in serialized form, fifteen-minute episodes every Saturday. The day before Christmas I think, when I was eight years old, I read that all twenty-five episodes were going to be shown at once, and my old maiden aunt who was at that time sixty-eight or sixty-nine and who loved movies too, took me to see every episode, lasting something like seven and a half hours in the theatre. But, in all seriousness, I have always been terribly interested in films and it was not something that happened to me later in life.

"I was born in New York City in 1930 and raised there. My father was a stockbroker, a partner actually in a Stock Exchange firm called LeBair, Stout, Eisler and King. I have a brother four years younger and a sister six years younger. I had gone to the Catholic LaSalle Military Academy in Oakdale, Long Island.

"My mother was Irish, my father German-Jewish and I was brought up a Catholic until the age of seventeen when I could no longer believe in religion. I graduated from the Military Academy in 1947 and then I went to Williams College in Williamstown, Massachusetts, and I graduated from there in 1951 with a B.A. major in English because we did not have a Drama major. I spent a great deal of time with the theatre company at Williams in a beautiful theatre designed by Stanley McCandless called the Adams Memorial Theatre. Strangely my wife, my wife now, did summer stock there eight years later.

"My father wanted me to be a good tennis player and I was. I started playing when I was eleven. I was captain of the tennis team at school, at LaSalle, and the outstanding graduate of the class. I later on became a rank player in the East. But I gave that up when I really started acting at eighteen, nineteen, because there just wasn't time to do both. Although I had always wondered how movies were made, my interest was more toward acting in those days and an actor was what I wanted to be. I did act at college and in summer stock for a year. But I was really not very good. I was quite shy and quite stiff, and it wasn't until I got into the Air Force that I really started to think seriously about directing.

"I left home shortly before I graduated from college when my father and I had a disagreement about acting as a profession. He didn't feel that was what he wanted his son to do. I was going to college and I was doing summer stock in the summer so really there wasn't any time to be home. I got married as soon as I got out of college to a girl who had gone to Bennington which is a women's college right near Williams. Quite frankly, the only reason we got married was that we were living together and I had no money, and when I was called into the Air Force the only way I could take her with me was to marry her so that the Government would pay for it. We had an understanding that when I got out of the Air Force we'd get a divorce which we did, because neither one of us wanted to be married. It was a very pleasant relationship. Both of us knew that we were not ready to be married nor did we want to be married—it was like playing house for a year and a half."

The Air Force

"My thoughts turned to making films when I found my-self assigned to the Reserve Officers Training Corps, to a job in the mail room in the Pentagon. This was just atrocious, it was awful. One day a letter came in saying the Air Force was forming a film squadron and anyone who had any kind of qualification please apply. You didn't even have to go through the channels. Well, at that time I was taking a few courses at the American University in Washington, one of them on speech and the other on television production, because this too was interesting me. I applied to the film squadron and I was accepted and sent out to Burbank, California. It was there that I really started getting interested in films, cameras and everything else. There were no union problems, and I found I could do anything I wanted because nobody there really cared what you did.

"The first thing I ever shot, aside from using a home movie camera, was a film about the making of asphalt in Sherman Oaks, California. I went out there and discovered this whole photographic squadron was a real sham. They had two cameras and about 150 men and about six officers, none of whom had any experience in motion pictures at all. The head of the motion picture squadron was a Major who had been in the Warner Bros. special effects department and he said to me, 'Well, our

Frankenheimer (second from left) in the Air Force film squadron.

big problem here is discipline. We've got to have something to do with the men, and I'm going to give you a camera and just go out and shoot anything.' And that's just what I did. My director of photography was a man named Bill Kazumplick, a New York taxi driver who had been recalled into the Air Force for this occasion. He knew nothing about photography. The only meter he'd ever read had been on a taxi cab. The only reason he'd joined this photographic squadron was to avoid going to Korea and he admitted that quite freely and couldn't have cared less what I did as far as the camera and everything was concerned just as long as he was covered. I had men in the squadron who had absolutely no interest in photography. I'd let them go to lunch starting at nine-thirty in the morning and I would just film the whole thing myself—light it, operate the camera, and edit the film.

"Of course I made some terrible movies, but I did learn what I was doing, and all at the Government's expense. They let me take cameras home on weekends with all kinds of films and I'd go out and shoot all manner of stuff. I shot a whole short subject about my automobile. I guess that was the forerunner of *Grand Prix*. I tied the camera on to it

and tried all kinds of angles. I started to read a lot. I read about Eisenstein's work and all the basic how-to-do-it film books. Then I went on from the making of asphalt to a TV show about cows. There was a farm in Northridge, California, where a man raised registered cattle. His method was like a chain letter—he had the bulls and then what you would do was buy the females, the cows, and they in turn would be mated to his bull. Then you would sell the calf to someone else and that calf would eventually come back to his bulls and you would get a share of the profits. What he had devised was a kind of rotating gang bang. We went out one day to his farm supposedly to keep the men busy again and shoot a film about cows. Now the only cow I'd ever seen in my life, coming from New York as I did, was a cow in a field when I was going by in my father's car on the Parkway. So getting within three feet of cows was very strange.

"This fellow had a television show on one of the local stations in Los Angeles and while I was shooting this epic film he fired his producers who were also his writers, and he said to me 'Listen, Lieutenant, do you write?' I said I did but of course I had never written anything except some short

stories in college. He said 'Well I want you to write my television show for me and I'll pay you $40 a week in cash,' which was fine with me. I was making about $250 a month. I sat down and wrote *Harvey Howard's Ranch Roundup*. I'd get the *Encyclopedia Britannica* out and look up cows and things like that and write all kinds of nonsense. The show featured popular western singers. Then he'd go on and give a pitch about the cows. You can imagine what it was like, bringing these big cows into the television studio. The smell was overpowering, and the local television director couldn't have cared less about the program. He had two cameras and he was drunk most of the time, so I would do it. I would direct the show and Harvey would get up there and make a pitch for his cows. Finally, the FCC took us off the air after about fifteen weeks because they said 'in a one-hour show you are allowed to have six minutes of commercials and fifty-two minutes of show, and what you gentlemen have is fifty-two minutes of commercials and six minutes of show—so you're off the air.' And that was my television *début*."

The Television Years

"Our film unit was at Lockheed Air Terminal at Burbank, what is now Burbank Airport. We had no proper film studio, this was the latter part of '51, the entire year of 1952 and early '53. I left the Air Force in 1953. At that time I wanted so much to enter films and had done so since being stationed in California. I tried to get a job in a studio but I couldn't. That was the year they were firing everyone. Then I tried to get a job in television in Los Angeles and I couldn't get one there either. And, going back to New York with only about $150 to my name, I found out that quite a few of my friends whom I'd known before I went into the Air Force and who had been actors, were now working in television production. Well, of course, they seemed terribly glad to see me until they found out what I wanted, which was a job, and there was nothing. I didn't know anyone at CBS and when I went in to ask for a job as an assistant director I even entered the wrong building. The receptionist laughed at me and the man in charge of personnel said, 'Well, send that man back here,' and I came back and he said 'I just wanted to see what somebody looked like who was such a damned fool as to come up here and ask for a job as an assistant director. You're even in the wrong damned building. But you sound like you've got a lot of guts to even try it.' (His name was Dick Stanley and we got along very well—I saw him many times over the years.) He said, 'You're in the wrong place. There's a guy you should be seeing down at Grand Central Station, named Hal Meier.' He set up an appointment, I went down there and gave the secretary my *résumé* and she said, 'Mr. Meier will call you.' And I said, 'That's not good enough. I have to go back to California in two days.' Of course, I was bluffing desperately. She said, 'Oh, well, you can come in at ten o'clock tomorrow morning.' I went in at ten o'clock and she said, before I went in, 'Listen, if he doesn't spend much time with you, don't worry because he's very busy.' I went in and it turns out that he had also been in the Air Force during the Second World War and he'd been in the photographic squadron. We talked a lot and we got along very well. He pointed to a pile of applications about four feet high, and he said 'What makes you think you can do it any better than these fellows here who have much more experience that you do?' I said 'I think I probably could do it better and also you wouldn't have to get rid of any of my bad habits because I don't have any yet.'

"All humor aside, he did like me and I liked him and he said 'Don't do anything for a while and I'll call you within two weeks if anything happens.' I was running out of money now and I took a job as an extra on a couple of television programs. At the end of the second week Meier called me saying 'We have a vacancy for an assistant director for about eight weeks. We are promoting one of our assistant directors to director temporarily for the summer. Would you be interested?' I could hardly believe it. I said I certainly would, and that was the beginning of my years with CBS. I went and stayed and I became a director in 1954. I loved that time.

"The first day I reported for work my emotions were very high as they would be for a twenty-three year old boy having a job like that. They sent me to observe another assistant director and I watched him work. I watched what he did and I was very impressed. When I stop to look back on it, it was such a simple program, the *Gary Moore Show*. People were very nice to me at CBS, and I got along

very well there. I was particularly well suited for that job which was in a sense what the director of photography is in films. In other words, what you would do was prepare a shot for the director. He would tell you what he wanted and you would get it from the cameraman. Then you would warn each camera that this shot was coming up next and tell him where he should go after he finished the present shot he was on. You'd also be responsible for timing the show. But I think, well I know, I was born with a good eye for camera and so the job really was playing right into what I would call my own strength.

"This went on for a year. From the *Gary Moore Show* I quickly went on to do a dramatic-religious show on Sunday afternoon called *Lamp Unto My Feet*. The director took a liking to me because he thought I was good and he recommended me to other people. Sidney Lumet, who was directing *You Are There*, was about to lose his assistant director—he was being promoted—and I was interviewed for the job by Sidney Lumet and by Charles Russell, who was producing the show. They decided that I could do it. So I got the best dramatic show on CBS, *You Are There*, and then, right after that, Charlie Russell was also given *Danger* to produce so he was producing two shows a week and he asked me if I would be the assistant director on both. I said, yes I would. Then I was working with Ed Murrow on *Person to Person*, I was the assistant director at the remotes, at people's houses, so I really had the ideal existence. Saturday and Sunday on *You Are There*, Monday and Tuesday on *Danger*, I had Wednesday and Thursday off, and on Friday I didn't have to work until about five o'clock at night which would be the Ed Murrow *Person to Person*. I was directing the toothpaste commercials on *Danger*. I was doing a lot of overtime and was making about $300 a week which for me, at twenty-three, was an awful lot of money in those days. I never wanted it to end.

"In the meantime, I had met a girl and wanted to get married. One thinks about one's future—in those days being at CBS was very good job security and being about the best assistant director they had, the one most in demand, I didn't want to give it up to be a director. I was offered a few soap operas to direct and things like that but I didn't want to do them.

"Finally, Charlie Russell was about to lose Sidney Lumet on *You Are There* because he was going into films. By now there were only a few live shows left, so Charlie went to the powers-that-be at CBS and asked that I be made a director. I was very frightened. I'd never really directed anything with actors except a play at college. I was twenty-four then. It was November 7, 1954, as a matter of fact. The show was called *The Plot Against King Solomon* and the actors were Shepperd Strudwick and Marty Brooks, and the script was very good— it was actually written by Walter Bernstein under another name, as he was blacklisted at the time. The show came off pretty well. So they decided that they wanted to keep me as a director and then came the business of signing a contract at CBS, a five year contract where they could fire me with two weeks' notice but I'd have to work for them for five years. It was a standard director contract in those days, your base salary was $180 a week and then if you had a commercial show there were certain fees you received. For instance you would get $240 for a half-hour commercial show. I think it was $350 for an hour. From *You Are There* I went to *Danger* as a director and I directed *Danger* every two weeks. So at the beginning, I lost a lot of money by becoming a director.

"As a director, I was already familiar with the control room screens. I thought my great problem would be blocking the show and rehearsing. I didn't worry about the technical part of it at all, and when I did that first show I knew I could shoot it. We read the show, we had a week to rehearse and it all went terribly smoothly and terribly well. I remember sitting up for nights figuring out how I'm going to block this, how I'm going to have this fellow move from there to there, and, of course, when we got on our feet and started doing it, we didn't do any of those things at all. It took me quite a long time to get rid of that feeling of panic that I really didn't know how to stage a scene beforehand. It took many years actually, because I'd always think 'It's not going to happen today for you, that thing that happens won't happen.' Well, sometimes it doesn't, but sooner or later it does again. Needless to say the show went on at six-thirty on a Sunday afternoon and we began rehearsing on Tuesday, so we went Tuesday through Sunday. And by the time six-thirty came around on Sunday I was pretty much on edge.

Somehow or other I knew when it went on, I knew that it was going to be good. I don't know how I knew it was going to be good, but I knew it was going to be good. And it was.

"In the beginning I wasn't too much concerned with content or its significance. To tell you the truth I was so happy just to get my first television show on the air within the allotted time limit because nobody missed lines that I really couldn't start thinking like that. It wasn't until I got much more secure in what I was doing. Being young, I kept thinking that this is a terrible accident, that one day it was going to be found out that I really had no talent and be made to go back to being an assistant director. As a matter of fact, I said that to Hubbell Robinson at CBS when he promoted me to director. I said, 'Well, I'll really only do it, Mr. Robinson, under one condition, that if I'm no good I get my job back as assistant director,' because in those days perhaps the most precarious profession in the world was being a television director. If you were terribly good you were stuck with this contract, if you were no good you were canned, and there were only three places to go, CBS, NBC, and ABC. ABC was not much then, so it was only CBS and NBC. You ran out of networks very quickly and one was not about to hire you if you'd been fired by the other.

"So there was that worry. But, as I became more secure in what I was doing, I did want to start saying some things that I believed in at that time, that were important to me, and I think that it was evident in shows like *Days of Wine and Roses*, and *Journey to the Day*, which was about mental health. I wanted to do *Clash by Night*, and I did. I was very enamoured of Fitzgerald at the time, I think all young people are, and I did *Winter Dreams* (one of his short stories), and *The Last Tycoon*. Martin Manulis was the producer and I must say he was marvelous in that if you really wanted to do something he would see that it was done. I wanted to do Faulkner's *Old Man* and I did. I wanted to do quite a bit of Hemingway and I did: *Fifth Column, The Snows of Kilimanjaro, For Whom the Bell Tolls*.

"I think television gave me a tremendous confidence as far as the camera is concerned because I work with actors in a rather fluid way. In other words, if I have good actors I will not impose staging on them. I'll wait and see what they do in a scene, where they want to go, and then perhaps I'll correct it if I don't like it. But I have to get ideas from the actors. If you have good actors you might as well let them contribute, and you *must* let them contribute. If you cast the right people they can help you a lot. I did not want to be a director who would stifle the creative impulse in actors. What I tried to do was to give them a very comfortable climate to work in. In other words, they knew if they made a mistake nobody was going to be yelling at them. I had very close working relationships with most of the actors that I worked with. I would watch a scene developing and perhaps I would correct it a bit, and discuss with somebody whether it was right to cross on that particular line of dialogue. I found I could start photographing these things in my mind almost immediately and I do think that whatever camera style I have came about as a result of my television work. Television cameras are very fluid and I also had a marvelous crew, on *Playhouse 90* especially, which I trained because they had never done a dramatic show before. They were all young and they all wanted to work and we pulled together as a really homogenous unit.

"Working under Hubbell Robinson was one of the greatest things that ever happened to me. When it became clear to them and to me that I was just not another contract director, they immediately re-negotiated the contract. They were extremely generous in what they paid me. They didn't make me do five years at all. As a matter of fact, they were unbelievable. They had no reason to let me go freelance but they did because they didn't want me to be unhappy, with the understanding that I would work mainly for CBS, which I did, but they also allowed me to go and do shows at NBC which I think was very generous. I really did not have the problems you've heard about in television because of considerate people like Hubbell Robinson up on top and William Dozier who was the Executive Producer of Drama when I first became a director—as a matter of fact, he was instrumental in making me a director when he became head of CBS in California—and Martin Manulis, who was the producer of a vast number, I would say over eighty per cent, of the shows I did.

"By the time he left CBS I was in a strong enough position that I didn't have to worry. There was no sponsor interference or anything like that.

Oh, it happened a few times. One of the worst shows I ever did was called *The Death of Manolete*, but that was something we had to throw in with two weeks' notice because the sponsor of the show we were going to do for the opening of *Playhouse 90* for the second year refused to permit it. It was a show written by Rod Serling based on the Emmett Till case. We shot it later at the end of the season, but we had to change it to a western, set a hundred years ago. Even so, it was a very good show called *The Town Has Turned to Dust*, with Rod Steiger. Both he and I were nominated for the Emmy Award. I really enjoyed television. I enjoyed television more than I can really tell you and I think I owe everything I am today to it.

"It would be impossible for me, or anyone else, to do on television today what we did then, mainly because it has become such a big business. When I was doing *Danger*, *Playhouse*, *You Are There*, and even *Climax* these shows were not reviewed in the *New York Times* every week. If you made a mistake, you were not pasted from coast to coast. Television gave you a great chance to grow. It enables, or it certainly enabled me as a director, a person to take chances because I would be back on the air three weeks later with another show. If I fell on my rear end it really wasn't that bad. It wasn't like working on a film for three years of your life and having it come out and be a disaster with nothing else to show. I think that kind of thing deadens you and constricts you and I think we all have to fight against it. Don't be too careful, in other words, take a chance, do what you think is right. Sometimes you start to think that a film has got to be good because you're not going to have another film for two or however many years, and once you say it's got to be good it never is. You lose that freedom, you lose that flexibility. And if you lose the ability to just do what you feel, the moment you start mistrusting your instincts, I think you're finished. And the moment you try to play it safe I think you're finished too. I've seen that happen to so many people who made the transition from television to films. Their work has become very sterile and they do very ordinary things.

"But talking about television today, I can't say I'm against it. I got a lot of experience from five years as a television director, more I think than many film directors ever get in their entire career. I fully believe that. I've encountered more situations that required me to really apply my craft, which I could never have managed without my live TV experience.

"To come back to the present, I don't want to discuss at length what television is today because, in the first place, I have no time for run-of-the-mill programming. I think there's a big difference between watching it and doing it. For instance, we were never aware of the commercials on *Playhouse 90*, never aware of them. As a matter of fact, we liked them because they would give us a chance to have actors make a wardrobe change, to re-position our cameras, and things like that. I realize now that six commercials is an awful lot and it does destroy your concentration to a degree, but at least when I was doing television if somebody wanted to shut you off they would have to get up and walk across the room and turn the dial. Today they have all these electronic gadgets, they just press a button and you're finished and on comes the next program.

"Television today I think is much more highly competitive than it was when I was doing it, although ours was certainly not the only dramatic program on the air. Today they watch the ratings so closely, they keep canceling shows and putting new ones on, and making hasty decisions, it's all on film or tape—it's really not the same. But then we were just beginning, we were finding our way. On almost every show we worked in ways we had never done before. And it was live and I think that's really important—the word *live*. In other words, everyone knew that at six-thirty on Thursday night, because we did *Playhouse 90* from California (and I talk about *Playhouse 90* because that really is the bulk of my work), everyone knew we were in the studio there and then doing the show in person.

"Incidentally, everybody thinks I'm a New York director, but I moved from New York to California in 1955 after only directing about seven or eight shows in New York. Of about 125 shows I've done, about 110 of them were done from California. I suppose no-one really stops to think that we did all the *Playhouse 90*s and all of our *Climax* shows from California.

"Everyone then knew we were on the air. It lent a climate of excitement and anticipation to rehearsals very similar to the theatre. Not only that—it also served as a great leveler because there was never any time for temperament. We had three weeks of rehearsal. It was certainly to the actors' benefit, to be there on time and to get just as much rehearsal as he or she damn well could, because there they were, naked to the world; well, not to the world, but certainly to the entire country and there was no-one to help them once the show went on the air, they were out there all by themselves. There was none of this 'I want a Rolls Royce with a chauffeur,' and 'I want an air conditioned dressing-room' and 'I want my stand-in,' and all the nonsense that you have to put up with sometimes in film and TV. If someone didn't agree with something we'd talk it over peacefully. There was no place for temperamental behavior like that.

"Television made me very much aware of the need to adhere to a type of form—act one, two and three. Also, I think it tended to make me say 'Well, I've got to capture the audience within three minutes otherwise they're going to turn us off.' With film you've got a captive audience—they pay to get into the theatre and they will stay. You can take much more time with your narrative and you don't have the frantic atmosphere we had to have on television. I remember some shows would have a very slow beginning and we would deliberately take an exciting scene from say the middle of the second act and put it at the beginning of the show and then do the show in flashbacks up to that point just to keep the audience 'hooked' as we say.

"As a matter of fact, one particular show comes to mind, *Face of a Hero*, based on the Pierre Boulle novel. Jack Lemmon was in it. We did the whole thing in flashback because it had a languid beginning. Now I think this was bad. One of the things I had to overcome as a director was this adherence to form, this worry that the audience may walk out of the theatre in ten minutes. Then, like a condensed play, we had to end every act on a high note to lead into the commercial.

"Yes, we had to pace a television play quite differently from a film. Almost like the serials I used to see as a boy—with cliffhangers to make you come back next week. I would notice this particularly when I ran a kinescope of a show I had done, with the commercials cut out, with the parts ending up on a kind of hysterical note and then starting again and you would say, Good Lord, I wonder why, and then you remember the commercials, the need to keep the audience while the toilet paper commercial came on. (And we really did have a toilet paper sponsor on *Playhouse 90*.) Actually, it was a fascinating combination of theatre and film in a sense, except I never used any film. I used cameras and actors as it would be on the stage to a certain extent. It was a much more talkative medium than real film is. Someone once described it as 'summer stock in an iron lung.'

"Now all this time, I continued to see as many movies as I could in the cinemas, and, when I found that television was turning into a purely film and tape medium, I started thinking about leaving. I thought, if I'm to work on film, I'll work in the real film. I was convinced and confident that having done the number of television shows that I did, well, it was over 125, helped me in many ways to become a film director. It enabled me to work with a great variety of writers and actors. After all, I'd worked with 125 different casts, and I think it is very important for directors to work well with actors and that's what it's really all about. I began to know how to communicate with actors. At first I was hesitant and I think I grew in this area quite a bit. My self-confidence grew. I worked very closely with all our writers, especially on *Playhouse 90*. Sometimes we'd be working on two or three shows at once—there would be one in the formative stage, one going into the second or third draft, and one would be actually rehearsing.

"During the summers I would collaborate with writers on scripts that we were going to do the following year. I think this is also a very important function of being a film director. If you don't write yourself (which I don't) you have to be able to work extremely well and communicate closely with your writer, because if you're going to have any of your own personality in a film or in a television show it has to be there in the script. It cannot be done just with the camera."

This recollection took place in JF's office at the MGM Studios in May 1968.

"When a boy has to hit someone to get his father to believe him ...there's something wrong"

A NEW KIND OF MOTION PICTURE
BY YOUNG PEOPLE...
ABOUT YOUNG PEOPLE

RKO RADIO PICTURES presents

THE YOUNG STRANGER

STARRING **JAMES MacARTHUR**
KIM HUNTER • **JAMES DALY**

WITH **JAMES GREGORY**
WHIT BISSELL • **JEFF SILVER**

Written by ROBERT DOZIER • Produced by STUART MILLAR
Directed by JOHN FRANKENHEIMER

THE YOUNG STRANGER 1956

Director John Frankenheimer • *Producer* Stuart Miller • *Production Company* RKO • *Screenplay* Robert Dozier *based on the television play* Deal a Blow *by* Robert Dozier • *Photography* Robert Planck • *Art Directors* Albert D'Agostino, John B. Mansbridge • *Editors* Robert Swink, Edward Biery Jr. • *Music* Leonard Rosenman • *Release* December 1956 • 7,593 ft. • *Running Time* 84 minutes • *Location* filmed at the RKO Studios, July 9 to August 10, 1956 • *Cost* $350,000 • *Availability* VHS and LD.

CAST

Hal •	James MacArthur
Helen •	Kim Hunter
Tom Ditmar •	James Daly
Shipley •	James Gregory
Grubbs •	Whit Bissell
Jerry •	Jeff Silver
Confused Boy •	Jack Mullaney
Man in Theatre •	Eddie Ryder
Girl in Theatre •	Jean Corbett
Detective •	Charles Davis
Mrs. Morse •	Marian Seldes
Donald Morse •	Terry Kelman
Lotte •	Edith Evanson
Lynn •	Tom Pittman
Doorman •	Howard Price

SYNOPSIS

Hal is the sixteen-year-old son of Tom Ditmar, a film executive, who has little time to spare his son and is quite unsympathetic towards his careless dress and behavior. In a mood of undefined frustration, Hal and his friend go to the movies one evening. Hal puts his feet up on the seat in front of him, annoying a young man who is attempting to romance his girlfriend. Hal is ordered to leave, which he does. However, Grubbs, the manager, heartily disliking youths who appear to be undisciplined, deliberately provokes Hal into striking him.

Taken to the police station, Hal's insolent, sarcastic and uncooperative attitude loses him the sympathy of Shipley, the police officer. Ditmar uses his influence to get the theatre manager to withdraw his charge, but, much to Hal's dismay, refuses to listen to his son's side of the story or to believe him when he tells it. Hal returns to Grubbs in an attempt to get him to tell his father the truth. Grubbs refuses and tries to throw Hal out of his office, and, once again, Hal strikes him and is taken back to the police station. This time, Shipley, impressed by Hal's account of what happened, gets the truth from the manager. When Ditmar comes to realise the truth of the situation, he has taken the first steps towards establishing a proper relationship with Hal. And even the police officer is moved to think about his relationship with his own son.

Script conference: Frankenheimer with James MacArthur (second from left).

COMMENT

On the surface a very simple film, underneath it is complex, poignant and full of sympathy and understanding. At the time of its release, the lack of love and understanding between husbands and wives, children and parents, was losing its validity as a subject in cinema because of overstatement, repetition and unconvincing characters. "Lack of love" had become an easy device with which to put down social ills among people and the theories behind this had created a new phrase soon to become a cliché "the lack of communication." However, Frankenheimer, in his first film, steers clear of all such pitfalls and gives credibility to a very real problem. Against a subtle background of an affluent home with little warmth and character, where the husband has little to say to his wife and has forgotten how to love her, the writer and director examine the difficulties faced by the adolescent son. The boy has gradually become resentful towards his father who has no time for him, only

THE YOUNG STRANGER   MAT 2-J

HELEN HAYES gets set for a ride with her son, James Mac-Arthur, teen sensation of "The Young Stranger," which stars MacArthur, Kim Hunter and James Daly. The first lady of the American stage visited MacArthur on the RKO lot during filming of the .... Theatre drama about today's teen-agers and their problems.

From promotional material issued by RKO.

talks to him in a continually bantering tone, and who believes that in providing money, clothes and a home, he is taking good care of his son. In his loneliness, the boy's frustrations grow, expressing themselves in insolent wit and sharp, sometimes silly retorts. Yet he knows, miserably, that he always says the wrong things at the worst time and cannot reach an understanding with his father. He becomes a victim of his own inability to explain what is wrong with him. He sees everywhere, as in the cinema incident, a conspiracy devised by adults to crush his every endeavor.

This is all suggested in telling details and sequences of great force and psychological convictions in a spare and simple narrative. James MacArthur as Hal (this was his first film) plays with astonishing naturalness, awareness and feeling, and the entire cast is always convincing, particularly James Daly as the film producer, a character who never slips into caricature. The blame for his son's attitude and behaviour is not entirely the father's—Kim Hunter, as the mother, plays a weak woman who has grown remote from her son and who has let things slide but then tries, with little conviction, to point out to her husband where they have gone wrong. It is clear that Frankenheimer knew how to direct his actors, always keeping his frames pictorially and dramatically interesting and alive. Among several notable scenes is the one in which the father is dressing while talking to his son, which ends by him giving the boy one of his jackets pretending that it fits him.

A story or chapter from life such as this, is always difficult to resolve without resorting to a hopeless ending or a falsely happy outcome. Dozier and Frankenheimer achieve a familiar yet acceptable conclusion in which the father, now believing his son, walks away from the police station with him down the street. The implication is that time and attitude, not words and promises, will bring about a lasting change. Left behind in the police station is an unwanted delinquent youth, probably past the point of saving, a character written quite effectively into the film and not part of the television play.

The Young Stranger is, rightly, a world of fathers and sons, theatre managers and police officers, and while we are not made to suffer extraneous romantic sequences dragged in for box-office purposes, this inclination towards subjects strongly dominated by male activity has marked Frankenheimer's films ever since. A small but telling detail, (an indication of work still to come and showing that the director was not afraid of the then touchy political climate) is the line of dialogue in which Hal says sarcastically, "I'm a Communist." Despite the fact that all the interior scenes were done on studio sets, Frankenheimer here shows his insistence on realism in the lighting and *décor* and the beginning of what was to become a characteristic visual style. The music by Leonard Rosenman, generally a skilled composer, strikes the wrong tone at times. But even so, this is not enough to mar an impressive first film, filled with significant details, the treatment of which is as successful as it is interesting.

JF "*The Young Stranger* was based on a television show I'd done on *Climax* called *Deal a Blow*, written by Robert Dozier, who also wrote the screenplay. James MacArthur was in both the television show and the film. I personally much preferred the television show. I was asked to direct the film when William Dozier, the head of CBS in California, became head of RKO Radio Studios. His son, Robert, wrote the script. It was a good script and he bought it for RKO to make and then asked me to direct it because I had directed the same story on television.

"I was panic-stricken on my first day at the studio. I had two weeks' rehearsal before shooting in the way I did in television. This was a mistake. We rehearsed in continuity, and the actors began to use one scene to get into another. When we shot the film out of continuity they were lost and had to start all over again. I have a very high regard for my crews today because I hand pick them. On *The Young Stranger* I was given a crew, and I thought they were terrible and treated me very badly. It made me very bitter about the whole experience. I had a cameraman who really didn't want to do the film, who just wanted to slap it together. This attitude affected a great many of the other people on the crew, and the assistant director, who came from filmed TV, kept saying 'twelve by twelve,' which means twelve pages by noon. We had twenty-five days to make the film, and I heard remarks like 'trying to make an A movie on a C budget,' and so on. According to some, we did make an A movie, but to me we didn't. I felt confined, constricted and consequently a bad director.

"I thought the camerawork was very sloppy, very restricted. It was as if I was terribly afraid to do anything with the camera. There were so many things I thought I could have done that I didn't do. I wanted a very grainy effect in that police station. I wanted to use two different stocks of film. I wanted to use Plus X, which is a gentle type of film and you get a very pretty effect from it, in the house, and I wanted to use Tri-X, which at that time was very grainy, in the police station. I wanted a complete contrast. I never got it. There were a lot of things that I thought could have been a lot better. As a result of this experience I was fed up with films and went back to television. I went back and I did *Playhouse 90*. Yet film-making interested me—I wanted to do it but I wanted to do it under the right conditions.

"Several months later I read a story called *Breakfast at Tiffany's* which I liked very much, and the producer who bought it, Martin Jurow, was a friend of mine. He asked if I would like to do it, and I said I would love to. I worked very hard with George Axelrod on the script and out of it came a very good relationship, which later proved fruitful in *The Manchurian Candidate*. We worked about three months on that script and then the producer said, 'Well, what about Audrey Hepburn for the part?' And I said, 'That's hardly what Capote wrote.' Pressure was brought to bear, she wanted to do it and Paramount, who was financing the film, wanted her. The producer went to Europe to get her and she said she would do it, but not with me because she had never heard of me. She wanted a director with whom she had worked before. That was that.

"At the same time, live television was coming to a very rapid and dramatic close and being a live television director was like being the village blacksmith after the event of the automobile, because everything was now being done on tape. I never did anything on film for television. I knew that I had to get out, I knew I had to do something. There was a popular belief in Hollywood at that time, this being 1960, that anyone who directed live TV for the seventeen-inch screen could not direct a film on a forty-foot screen. And there were all these stories being told about live television directors who came in and were built beautiful sets, and they shot everything back in the corner, which I didn't believe."

Stanley Kristien, Burt Lancaster, Frankenheimer, and Shelley Winters discuss a difficult scene.

THE YOUNG SAVAGES 1961

Director John Frankenheimer • *Screenplay* Edward Anhalt, J.P. Miller *based on the novel* A Matter of Conviction *by* Evan Hunter • *Photography* Lionel Lyndon • *Art Director* Burr Smidt • *Set Decorator* James Crowe • *Editor* Eda Warren • *Sound* Harry Mills • *Assistant Director* Carter de Haven Jr • *Music* David Amram • *Executive Producer* Harold Hecht • *Producer* Pat Duggan • *Production/release* United Artists, April 1961 • *Running Time* 103 minutes • *Location* some scenes filmed in New York City • *Availability* LD • *Soundtrack* Columbia Records.

CAST

Hank Bell •	Burt Lancaster	*Soames* •	William Sargent
Karin Bell •	Dina Merrill	*Pretty Boy* •	Chris Robinson
Mary di Pace •	Shelley Winters	*Lt. Hardy* •	Stanley Adams
Dan Cole •	Edward Andrews	*Capt. Larsen* •	William Quinn
Mrs. Escalante •	Vivian Nathan	*Maria Amora* •	Linda Danzil
Randolph •	Larry Gates	*Jose* •	Raphael Lopez
Richard Gunnison •	Telly Savalas	*Pierce* •	Henry Norell
Louisa Escalante •	Pilar Seurat	*McNally* •	Jon Carlo
Angela Rugiello •	Jody Fair	*Turtleneck* •	Bob Biheller
Walsh •	Milton Selzer	*Diavalo* •	Mario Roccuzzo
Judge •	Robert Burton	*Doctor* •	Harry Holcombe
Barton •	David Stewart	*Mrs. Patton* •	Helen Kleeb
Danny di Pace •	Stanley Kristien	*Mr. Abbeney* •	Thom Conroy
Arthur Reardon •	John Davis Chandler	*Lonnie* •	John Walsh
Anthony Aposto •	Neil Nephew	*Officer Wohlman* •	Irving Steinberg
Zorro •	Luis Arroyo	*Whitey* •	Clegg Hoyt
Roberto Escalante •	Jose Perez	*Clerk of the Court* •	Joel Fluellen
Gargantua •	Richard Velez	*Sullivan* •	Robert Cleaves

SYNOPSIS

New York City. In a teeming tenement district where gangs of Puerto Rican and Italian youths are at war with each other, three members of the Italian gang, Reardon, Aposto and Danny di Pace, push their way along the crowded streets until they reach the steps of the apartment house where the blind Roberto Escalante lives. They then murder him in broad daylight and make a run for freedom. They fail to elude the police and are caught and taken to the precinct station. This is a between-titles-and-credits sequence, brilliantly filmed and edited, with moving close-ups of the boys' feet as they walk quickly along the streets accompanied by driving, staccato music on the soundtrack by David Amram. Long white lines enter the screen from each side introducing the credits for each frame.

Daniel Cole, the District Attorney, who is running for Governor in the coming elections, sees the case as an aid to his ambitions and assigns his assistant, Hank Bell, to investigate and get the youths convicted for the crime. Bell, who comes from an Italian slum family and was raised in the district where the crime was committed, also has political and social ambitions. He is married to a well-educated and wealthy socialite, prefers to forget his origins, and does not share his wife's sympathies for under-privileged youths whose environment has turned them to a life of crime.

At first he sees no difficulty in prosecuting what seems to be an obvious case of vicious gang murder. He discovers, however, that the victim was not so innocent, acting as a decoy for his gang and concealing their weapons beneath his coat when confronted by the police. Bell is criticised by his wife for his determination to prosecute the youths and send them to the electric chair, and is depicted as a monster by a sensational reporter. Bell also discovers that one of the boys, Danny di Pace, is the son of a woman he once loved. After listening to her defence of the boy, he learns that the boy was lying out of misguided loyalty and fear and did not himself stab the victim. This is revealed in the courtroom, where the film ends, at the trial of the three youths. Despite physical attacks on his wife and himself, censure by the victim's mother and pressure from his superior, Bell follows his own convictions once he finds there are extenuating circumstances, and does not allow personal considerations to influence the outcome of the trial. His political chances are lost for the time being, but he has won the respect of his wife and has the satisfaction of knowing that he has been true to his convictions.

COMMENT

The original title, *A Matter of Conviction*, is highly appropriate for a story dealing with the strong convictions of all the characters concerned. These convictions conflict with the pursuit of a legal ruling drawn up in accordance with society's terms of retribution for those members who have fallen away and broken the rules. But it is not a box-office title, and, much as Frankenheimer disliked the substitute, *The Young Savages* (which sounds like a cheaply-made second feature) he was not in a position, at the beginning of his second encounter with films, to oppose it. It is a tribute to his skill that this narrative, so over-crowded on paper, never seems, on film, contrived and complacent in its social concerns. It is not easy to keep all the threads running evenly throughout this broad tapestry of poverty, violence and despair, but the director has managed this so skilfully, and not at all episodically, that events and characters seem consistently believable.

With a film shot in strong black and white tones, with an arresting opening sequence (the influence of television), Frankenheimer returned to the cinema after an absence of more than four years with many of the ideas, events, places and themes that were part of in *The Young Stranger*. This film ended in a police station; *The Young Savages* begins in one (after the titles)—the difference being that here we feel it is far more real than in the first picture. (Frankenheimer took his New York set designer, Burr Smidt, to Hollywood to design the interiors and this marked the beginning of what was to be Frankenheimer's insistence on getting the right people to work with him.) The youths in this story might well be some of those we

Merrill conveys the 'better-born' wife with her intelligent, blonde sophistication, and Shelley Winters, as the house-worn mother, never bettered this performance. This is the first time we are to become aware of Frankenheimer's uncanny ability to cast actors who, even if not greatly gifted, will become or will suggest the characters they represent.

The ever-reliable Babbit, Edward Andrews, as Daniel Cole, presents his semi-comic political figure convincingly, but he does so in the only sub-plot which seems strained—because of the importance placed on the outcome of the trial as it affects his chances of becoming Governor. It is hard to believe, with the high incidence of crime and murder, that so much would depend on this one case. The obnoxious journalist also fails to ring true.

The screenplay by Anhalt and Miller takes the many issues raised involving juvenile delinquency, racial antagonisms and environmental influences and relates them fittingly to the squalid background from which they arise. The ending makes no attempt to show these issues resolved. When Bell tells the mother that 'many people killed her boy' it is a statement that has several meanings. What the film has done is to show what the issues are, and this Frankenheimer does with honesty and concern and a perceptive insight into the lives of all his characters.

met in the first film, but further down the road to delinquency.

The acting throughout is authoritative, with vivid portrayals by the Italian and Puerto Rican players, particularly the victim's mother (Vivian Nathan) whose scene on the steps of the funeral home when she talks about the death of her son is extremely moving and effective. This funeral sequence is impressively photographed by Lionel Lindon—in fact the photography throughout the film is alive with a strong, visual sense which is to characterize all of Frankenheimer's future work. Burt Lancaster, in the first of five films with Frankenheimer, is ideally cast as Bell, a part he plays quietly yet powerfully. Telly Savalas makes his screen début as the police sergeant, Dina

JF "In the early sixties, Harold Hecht offered me a script through my agent, called *A Matter of Conviction*, a script to which Burt Lancaster was committed. I thought the script was pretty bad, but I wanted to do it because I knew the locations terribly well. This was New York where I had moved back to and where I lived from 1958 to 1960. I brought my friend J.P. Miller in on the subject and we re-wrote the script. I think we improved it a great deal. I shot the film mainly to show people that I could make a movie, and while it was not completely successful, my point was proved. The story was based on an actual event. That's the way it is. And I brought my own Art Director from New York who had been doing television shows for me and we fought again to get the sets the way we wanted them. Most of the film was shot on location, though some of the interiors were shot in Hollywood. We built the boy's room—we took it right from a house we were in and re-built it. It was a question of economics. The film was made on a relatively cheap budget and shooting on location in New York for a Hollywood company is very expensive. Those were the days before Mayor Lindsay and that's when you had to pay off every other cop on the beat, and also you had to have a full New York crew covering the Hollywood crew so you were paying two crews. It was also a matter of scheduling. It was just impossible to do it all on location."

HAROLD HECHT PRESENTS
BURT LANCASTER BIRD MAN OF ALCATRAZ
KARL MALDEN / THELMA RITTER / NEVILLE BRAND / EDMOND O'BRIEN
A NORMA PRODUCTION UNITED ARTISTS

THE BIRDMAN OF ALCATRAZ 1962

Director John Frankenheimer • *Screenplay* Guy Trosper *based on the book by* Thomas E. Gaddis • *Photography* Burnett Guffey • *Art Director* Ferdie Carrere • *Editor* Edward Mann • *Sound* George Cooper • *Assistant Director* Dave Silver • *Music* Elmer Bernstein • *Executive Producer* Harold Hecht • *Producers* Stuart Millar, Guy Trosper • *Production/release* United Artists, June 8, 1962 (*note* although filmed in 1961, *Birdman of Alcatraz* was not released until after the director's fourth film, *All Fall Down*) • *Running Time* 147 minutes • *Location* Filmed at the Samuel Goldwyn Studio • *Available* on VHS and LD Soundtrack available on Boa Records

CAST

Robert Stroud •	Burt Lancaster
Warden Shoemaker •	Karl Malden
Elizabeth Stroud •	Thelma Ritter
Bull Ransom •	Neville Brand
Stella Johnson •	Betty Field
Feto Gomez •	Telly Savalas
Tom Gaddis •	Edmund O'Brien
Roy Comstock •	Hugh Marlow
Dr. Ellis •	Whit Bissell
Kramer •	Graham Denton
Kess Younger •	James Westerfield
Eddie Kassellis •	Leo Penn
Chaplain Wentzel •	Lewis Charles
Mrs. Woodrow Wilson •	Adrienne Marden

SYNOPSIS

In 1909, Robert Stroud is sentenced to twelve years imprisonment for killing a man, and, after forfeiting his chance of parole by attacking another prisoner, is treated as an unregenerate criminal by the warden, Shoemaker. When his mother, who has travelled halfway across the country, is refused permission to see him because it does not happen to be a visiting day, there is a struggle in which Stroud kills a warder. He is sentenced to death, but his mother persuades the President to commute the sentence to life imprisonment in solitary confinement.

One day he finds a fledgling sparrow in the exercise yard, rescues and cares for it, eventually teaching it tricks. When a new warden takes over after Shoemaker's hard *régime*, Stroud is allowed more privileges, acquires a canary, and finally a whole aviary. At the same time he becomes friendly with his warder, Bull Ransom. Through constant study, and practical care of his birds, he becomes an authority on rare bird diseases, and writes a classic text-book on the subject. After winning a prize in a magazine competition, he is visited by Stella Johnson, widow and bird-fancier, who proposes to go into business with him, marketing his bird medicines. The business prospers, but technical troubles arise with the prison authorities, which result in the birds being taken away.

By marrying the widow while still in solitary confinement, he manages to make his case headline news, and embarrasses the authorities to such an extent that he is allowed to keep the birds. Eventually, however, the publicity dies down, and he is transferred to Alcatraz. Here he turns his attention from the study of birds to the study of man, writing a book on penology which is confiscated. He also helps to quell a riot among his fellow convicts. In 1959, he is transferred to a Federal prison hospital, not a free man, but no longer in solitary confinement.

COMMENT

This film is almost pure documentary. It opens under an overcast sky, with a view of Alcatraz prison from the San Francisco waterfront. Edmund O'Brien, speaking as Thomas Gaddis, introduces this film of his book about the life of Robert Stroud, a man he had never met. As the film closes, we see that Gaddis is here to meet Stroud briefly, for the first and last time, as he is transferred from Alcatraz to a prison hospital.

In between is a remarkable, compact and fascinating narrative of the way in which a hardened criminal becomes so fully absorbed in a subject forced upon him by boredom and loneliness that his character changes completely. Seeing Lancaster in this role almost immediately after playing the assistant district attorney in *The Young Savages* is to realise what an excellent actor he is and how well he essays Stroud. After his initial sullenness and violence, he becomes a slow, quiet, thoughtful man, portrayed in an intelligently muted performance. Although, as Frankenheimer has said, the prison does look too clean and somewhat artificial (six years later he is to use actual locations in another drama of a man in prison, *The Fixer*) it is still highly realistic, particularly so in the laundry sequences, shot in darkness and steam with the prisoners in striped uniforms, and in the huge dining room where a band plays during meals. Frankenheimer's direction is so good that while one is always aware of Stroud's confined quarters, the film itself never seems constricted. The narrative would seem simple enough, but, in fact, the film uses a massive screenplay which shows crucial developments in Stroud's relationship with the Governor; who is played with great skill by Karl Malden; with his warder, Bull Ransom, a sympathetic and understanding performance by Neville Brand; and his attachment to his mother, a real American mama of the most possessive kind played with horrifying affection by Thelma Ritter.

The birds are handled and shown with scientific precision, with a long, stop-motion sequence showing the birth of a canary chick; and the almost wordless sequence of shots in which Stroud reluctantly rescues a bird during a storm, and is gradually drawn out from his own animal-like solitude to become a human being again, is nothing less than pure cinema—expressive, imaginative and emotionally honest. Almost ashamed of his concern over the bird, and then almost unwillingly taking responsibility for it, he is forced by this new interest to make contact again with human beings in order to get the articles he requires to pursue his studies. Here the film makes a telling contrast between prisoner and jailer, in which the prisoner discovers that his unfriendly attitude towards his keeper in some ways resembles that of the prison to him. The entire film is a small masterpiece of artistry and sensitivity, with memorable acting by Lancaster that stands out from his other roles. Telly Savalas is carried over from Frankenheimer's previous film and here portrays the rough prisoner in the next cell, who takes one of Stroud's birds purely to relieve his own loneliness.

The film is a poignant and profound depiction of a man, his mental, spiritual and physical conditions, his determination, his suffering and his astonishing achievements under the most oppressive environment—and of his refusal to let the system break him and to force him to live according to its dictates. The film glosses over Stroud's homosexuality, which could not be mentioned at that time due to the requirements of the Production Code. While the film, like the book, aroused public indignation, Stroud was soon forgotten, and while the film did not bring about his release, it did make things easier for him until his death in prison. That Stroud, a man in solitary confinement, was permitted to breed and study his birds, speaks of some charity to be found in the harsh world of prison life.

•••

JF "*The Young Savages* was my first encounter with Burt Lancaster. I think that he is one of the hardest-working individuals I've ever met. He's a true professional and he cares deeply about what he does. He's very considerate of other actors. I think he's one of the few men, one of the few actors I've met who really knows something about production. He directed his own film once, *The Kentuckian*, and that is why I think he respects directors. I find it very easy to work with him, and when he's correctly cast, there is nobody better. He told me that he never wanted to direct again.

"I directed his next film, *Birdman of Alcatraz*, because he owned the script, and it was up to him to approve the director. For him to play the leading role was really not ideal casting, but he was very, very good and I don't know who could have played it as effectively as Burt did. At one time, I owned the story to play on live television. The Bureau of Prisons came to CBS and said that if they did this show, they would never get any co-operation from them again. So CBS had no choice but to drop it and I'm glad they did because I don't know what possessed me to think that I could ever have realised it on live television with the birds, because birds are very, very difficult. It took days and weeks and months even to get these birds to react. There is no such thing as a trained bird. We had to wait until the bird was hungry enough to do one particular thing. Thank God the film was in black-and-white because for the one sparrow in the story I think we had to use twenty-seven different ones, each of which would do something different—they all came out looking like one bird but had it been in colour, we would have had to paint all the birds. No, it was a very difficult film to make.

"It is true that I wanted to use a real prison. But I did come in on the film a bit late after they had decided exactly how they were going to make it and they never even thought in terms of using a real prison. I did not have the power then that I have now to insist on my wishes. Quite frankly, I was very grateful to have the opportunity to direct the film because it was a story I'd always wanted to do. Also, at that time, I was really not so adamant about shooting on location as I am now because I hadn't done that much cinema work.

"I was beginning to like movies a lot more now.

In television you are terribly concerned with the editing process because you are editing the show live on the air. It was important to me in editing because I really did learn how to use close-ups, long shots, and so on. I think we had a tendency to use too many close-ups, but nevertheless we really were editing. Editing film then was a treat because we had a chance to do it over again. I was not completely happy in the environment of film during *Birdman*. I thought there was much too interference from various people. I didn't feel I had the control that I had in television, which, after all, is total. I felt the producer, the writer, and Burt were all trying to interfere. I didn't really feel free—I would just have to take time to relax and do it my way, because I wasn't interested in what the producer had to say or in what anybody else had to say. And that was my breakthrough in film because I did it the way I wanted to do it.

"There were many battles to fight which had nothing to do with shooting the film, and it took an ungodly long time to make because the first script was much too long. I had told the producer and writer it was much too long, but they said, 'This is the way we want to do it,' and 'After all, we developed the script and you didn't,' and that type of thing. In other words, I was a hired director and that settled the issue. So, of course, the first rough cut was something like four hours and twenty-five minutes long and the producer in panic said that I had to cut it. But I knew, and I said, that the film could not be cut—it was a film called *Birdman of Alcatraz* and it was an hour and twenty minutes long before a bird is seen—the only thing to be done was to rewrite it, which I did from the beginning. And Burt Lancaster was in complete agreement. So he went to do *Judgement at Nuremberg* for Kramer while we rewrote the opening of the film, and then we went back and re-shot it. So, instead of an hour and twenty minutes before you saw a bird, it was twenty minutes. If you want to do quick cutting between scenes showing a character as he develops into the person you hope to be telling the main story about, or if you want to tell the background about a character, then you have to construct a film in a completely different way. You must have a concept. You just can't take an hour and twenty minutes of film and cut it down to twenty minutes, not when you try to tell the plot ."

"By now I had moved from New York City and was living in Los Angeles. A previously published interview said it was Selznick who brought me to Hollywood. That's not true. I don't know where the writer got that from. My interest in Fitzgerald led to my meeting with Selznick. As I told you earlier, Fitzgerald meant a great deal to me in my life, and I always wanted to film Tender is the Night. I had arranged to meet Mr. Selznick, I was still very young, I'd only been directing for two years when I met him. He liked me very much and we became good friends. It was almost a father-son relationship. He would look at all my television shows and criticize them; he would tell me what he thought was good and bad. I learned an awful lot from Selznick. He did want me to direct Tender is the Night, we did begin it at 20th Century-Fox. But Fox didn't want me to direct it, being a television director, and they placed ridiculous restrictions on us. The film had to be made in thirty-five days, it could not be shot in Europe, and it all had to be shot on their back lot. I couldn't do that, and I wanted an unknown actor to play Dick Diver named Peter O'Toole and Fox said, 'We've never heard of him.' I wanted Jane Fonda as Rosemary. They'd never heard of her either. On and on it went. So I said, 'To hell with it.' David didn't really want to make it into a film if I didn't direct it so he just gave Fox the film and tried to be the Executive Producer but it didn't work. I heard of Peter O'Toole through some friends of mine and Selznick had heard of him too, and we tried to convince Twentieth Century-Fox that this was the man to play the part. We ran Sink the Bismark! in which he had a very small part, and The Day They Robbed the Bank of England—he had a very small part in that. Then I saw O'Toole on the stage and I tell you, he was superb. I regret never having the opportunity of making a film with him."

from left: *Karl Malden, Angela Lansbury, Brandon de Wilde, William Inge, Frankenheimer, Warren Beatty, and Eva Marie Saint at script readthrough for* All Fall Down.

ALL FALL DOWN 1962

Director John Frankenheimer • *Screenplay* William Inge *Based on the novel by* James Leo Herlihy • *Photography* Lionel Lindon • *Art Directors* George W. Davis, Preston Ames • *Visual Effects* Robert R. Hoag • *Set Decorators* Henry Grace, George R. Nelson • *Editor* Frederick Steinkamp • *Sound* Franklin Milton • *Assistant Director* Hal Polaire • *Music* Alex North • *Producer* John Houseman • *Production/release* Metro-Goldwyn-Mayer, March 14, 1962, Chicago (*note* although made after *Birdman of Alcatraz*, this film was released first) • *Running Time* 111 minutes • *Location* Key West, Florida; interiors shot at the MGM Studio • *Availability* VHS (*note* beware of computer-colored version).

CAST

Echo O'Brien	•	Eva Marie Saint
Berry-Berry Willart	•	Warren Beatty
Ralph Willart	•	Karl Malden
Annabel Willart	•	Angela Lansbury
Clinton Willart	•	Brandon de Wilde
Mrs. Mandel	•	Constance Ford
Schoolteacher	•	Barbara Baxley
Hedy	•	Evans Evans
Myra	•	Jennifer Howard
Bouncer	•	Madame Spivy
Captain Ramirez	•	Albert Paulson

SYNOPSIS

Berry-Berry Willart is a hopelessly unhappy drifter, living on women, always in and out of trouble with the police, and savagely resentful of any attempt to tie him down. But to his younger brother, Clinton, he is a romantic hero and an idol. Clinton goes down to Florida from their home in Cleveland, intending to lend Berry-Berry his savings for a fishing boat purchase, but the money goes on bailing Berry-Berry out of the local gaol. Clinton returns home disconsolately, to his mother's possessive love and his depressed father's solitary drinking. The house is brightened by the visits of Echo O'Brien, a thirtyish, unmarried woman, and the driver of an old-fashioned car, and on whom Clinton develops an adolescent crush. Berry-Berry makes a cautious homecoming, Echo's presence keeps him there and they fall in love. Clinton is torn between hero-worship and resentment at Berry-Berry's appropriation of Echo. Echo becomes pregnant, and Berry-Berry's reaction to the prospect of marriage and domestic entanglement sends her out, heart-broken, on a car drive which ends in her death. Clinton, who had overheard their argument, goes to Berry-Berry's room with the intention of shooting him. When it comes to it, however, he is unable to do shoot; he can feel only a kind of pity for his brother's inability to come to terms with life. In escaping from his brother's domination, Clinton also finds his way to a more stable relationship with his parents.

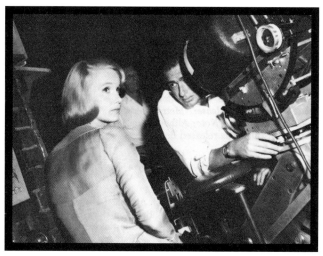

Eva Marie Saint with Frankenheimer.

COMMENT

Once again, as in *The Young Stranger*, Frankenheimer takes a subject that is overly-familiar, in this case, American family life, yet, with originality, perception and understanding he makes the familiar seem fresh. Between Herlihy and Inge, Frankenheimer is calmness and commonsense. Working again with Lionel Lindon, the impressive opening scene features the camera looking down on a Greyhound bus speeding across the Florida Keys, cutting to an interior view of the bus pulling into the seedy bus stop. Once again, we are back in the United States we know so well from films; a hot, dilapidated and ugly small town. An attractive theme opens Alex North's score, expressing the youth and idealism of Clinton, who sees everything with new and eager eyes. The shabbiness of the buildings, the sordid atmosphere, are not yet repellent to him. Once again we are struck by Frankenheimer's extraordinary visual sense, and his imaginative use of location: the strange-looking hotel, the filthy bar and brothel, the hot, dirty police-station and the corrupt policemen (in every film so far, Frankenheimer has been involved with the police, although here they are not an integral part of the narrative). As Berry-Berry, Warren Beatty has never been better before or since; he is what the lost son in *The Young Stranger* might well have become if the father's attempt to understand him in the fade-out scene had failed. This is true, even though Berry-Berry's family exists in a different social milieu.

The film moves to Cleveland, where we meet

the middle-class father and mother living in an old, large house, an incredibly fine set with all the atmosphere, shadows and sameness of year after year existence, where life has become empty, meaningless and loveless; where the father drinks in the basement and does jigsaw puzzles, and where the mother talks endlessly on the telephone and insists on decorating the house at Christmas although no one wants to celebrate it. The two of them, however, are determined never to be dull, and the father's loud attempts at humour and the mother's dashing around are vain efforts to try and impart life where none exists. This suffocating atmosphere has forced Berry-Berry to leave, but emotionally he is ruined. To come back to his agonisingly possessive mother, who loves him more than her own husband, cripples him still more. The younger brother is not yet affected. He brushes it aside and records it all in his notebooks. The performances of Karl Malden and Angela Lansbury as the parents are beyond praise, so perfectly do they create these all too painfully real people. Again, this is the fourth consecutive film in which Frankenheimer has been involved with mother figures: the quiet pretty, middle-aged mother in *The Young Stranger*, the accusing, cold and aging mother in *The Young Savages*, and the Possessive Mother in *Birdman*. (The best is yet to come in *The Manchurian Candidate*.) Angela Lansbury's monster of a mother; who isn't really as silly as she seems and does temper her possessive hell with her mute despair at the uselessness of life, is unforgettable, particularly in the scene where Malden throws the framed picture of Berry-Berry to the floor, cursing him, and she picks up the smashed remains sobbing "I love him, I love him!" This is one of the most violent displays of mother love in the cinema. Again, one marvels at Frankenheimer's skill in the use of the camera in confined interiors: in the scene where Clinton is in his bedroom, in the foreground, the mother is on the lower landing talking on the telephone, and the father is in the background sitting at the kitchen table, an exciting shot which conveys at once the thoughts and feelings of all three in that given moment and situation.

As he did in *The Young Savages* and to a lesser extent in *Birdman*, Frankenheimer manipulates an astonishing number of variations, incidents and sub-plots within the overall narrative, never losing any of them, never breaking the film down into episodic scenes. Another memorable moment is the father's ridiculous and defiant gesture in bringing home three beggars for Christmas (a nice Bunuelian touch this) and the mother's calculating victory over him. Malden, carried over from *Birdman*, proves his versatility by giving a totally different performance from that of the prison Governor. The style of the film is particularly beautiful, with its soft tones and lingering fades. Here, for the first time, Frankenheimer attempts to show a love scene; Berry-Berry and Echo, a girl who has suffered as a result of love and now hopes desperately that she has found it again (a role affectingly played by Eva Marie Saint), are walking along by a lake in the park. It is night time and a symphony concert is in progress. The orchestra is not shown, but we know there is a concert as the camera passes people sitting in chairs listening as it follows Berry-Berry and Echo. The two embrace and fall to the ground and swans appear on the water behind them. It is poetically filmed, and the actual love scene is restrained. Towards the end of the film, Frankenheimer is forced to exercise all the control he is capable of to prevent what has been a finely observed and depicted drama from sliding into Inge-Kazan hysteria as Echo drives away to be killed in a car accident and Clinton lies in wait for his brother planning to shoot him. These plot developments are to be regretted: broken-hearted girls do not die convenient deaths in car accidents and Clinton would have seen his brother in his true light, simply as a result of Berry-Berry's rejection of the girl. It is a tribute to the director that he does not allow these incidents to ruin the film for us, but persuades us that they are likely and acceptable.

Other scenes worth remembering are Berry-Berry's meeting with the bored, wealthy yachtswoman (Constance Ford) looking for sex; his encounter with the frustrated school teacher (Barbara Baxley); the scene with Evans Evans in the brothel; the skilful use of the camera in every scene where Berry-Berry kisses Echo at home but just as he is about to do so the camera moves away from the kiss to the faces of the parents and to Clinton, who has fallen in love with Echo. The dialogue is crisp, witty and to the point. Frankenheimer's assured control of actors is apparent throughout the film.

JF "*All Fall Down*, at MGM, was the beginning for me of real joy in making films. That was really a whole new turning point. One of the best relationships I ever had with a human being was with John Houseman, who is an utterly delightful, marvellous man. I had worked with him once on television. I'd done *Face of a Hero*, the Pierre Boulle story, which we talked about earlier, when he was producing *Playhouse 90*. We got along very well. In fact I lived in Malibu Beach because John Houseman lived there. I recall going down to see him one day—he had invited me to lunch when I was in California, which I hated, and I was feeling miserable. I drove down to the beach and went into John's house, which was always pleasant to visit because there were always people there you wanted to meet, the food was always great, and his wife is a marvellous woman. I looked around on that beautiful day on the ocean and I said, 'God, John, you're lucky to live here' and he said, 'Luck, dear boy, has nothing to do with it,' which is a line I used a great deal in *Grand Prix*, 'All you have to do is just move down here.' I asked him if he knew of any available houses and he said that he did know of one. He took me there and later my wife and I moved in for two and a half years. Then we bought a house in Malibu.

"Anyway, John used to be at MGM some years ago. He produced *Executive Suite*, *Julius Caesar*, *They Live by Night*, and others. He had just started a three-picture contract with MGM and he told me that one of the properties was a novel by James Leo Herlihy called *All Fall Down*, which, incidentally, I had read and loved, and another was Irving Shaw's *Two Weeks in Another Town*. He offered me the choice of filming one of them. I said, 'John, I love Herlihy's novel. I read it, I even tried to buy it,' which I had, 'and it was sold but I didn't know who had bought it.' When he told me that Bill Inge wanted to write it, I couldn't have been more pleased and excited. That was the beginning of all that was important because in the meantime George Axelrod and I had bought *The Manchurian Candidate* and we were working on that and the future seemed to be highly promising.

"The only thing I didn't like was MGM's insistence that we do the interiors and the mid-Western part of it at the studio, using their back lot. As John Houseman had agreed to this, there was really nothing I could do because we did need four seasons and they could do this change in the seasons artificially in the studio. I think the film would have been better if we had shot it in the mid-West. If I'd known then what I know now we would have shot it on location. The best part was filming on location in Key West. I had a fight with MGM who wanted to shoot the inside of the bus in process and I said, 'There's no way.' You can tell the difference—and how. In the end, there was a whole scene that took place inside the bus that we had to cut out. It just didn't play.

"The police had closed the brothel down and we had to open it up again. It smelled so badly that, to be able to shoot, we had to get incense from the Catholic church to burn—we never could bring ourselves to tell the church what we were using the incense for. As for the hotel, it wasn't a hotel, but a building I found and was so taken with that I put a desk in there and made it into a hotel. I thought the inside of the family house was good. It took a long time to work out the camera movements. You have an idea of how you want to do it, and then design the set the way you want it. It doesn't always succeed, but this time it did.

"Angela Lansbury is an exceptionally fine actress. We simply had to do that scene where she picks up the picture and says she loves Berry-Berry. Otherwise, the film would not have been valid. Berry-Berry, of course, is lost, there is little hope for him. But the younger brother no longer idealises his older brother. He's going out to face life, he's not going to despair, or give up. You know of course, that most audiences saw *All Fall Down* before *Birdman*, although *Birdman* was made first. We were still dubbing and working on *Birdman* while I was filming *All Fall Down*, which was a much easier film to make. The beginning of the film in Key West, especially the scene with my wife Evans at the bar with Brandon de Wilde, I thought was terribly good."

Frank Sinatra Laurence Harvey Janet Leigh
The Manchurian Candidate

An M·C PRODUCTION
RELEASED THRU
UNITED ARTISTS

THE MANCHURIAN CANDIDATE 1962

Director John Frankenheimer • *Screenplay* George Axelrod *based on the novel by* Richard Condon • *Photography* Lionel Lindon • *Production Designer* Richard Sylbert • *Editor* Ferris Webster • *Sound* Joe Edmondson • *Assistant Director* Joseph Behm • *Music* David Amram • *Executive Producer* Howard W. Koch • *Producers* George Axelrod, John Frankenheimer • *Production* M.C.Productions • *Release* United Artists, September 27, 1962; opened in New York, October 1962; taken out of distribution and re-released in 1987 • *Running Time* 126 minutes • *Location* Filmed at the Samuel Goldwyn Studios, Hollywood, and on location in Los Angeles and New York • *Availability* VHS and LD. Added in 1994 to the Library of Congress National Film Registry.

CAST

Bennett Marco	•	Frank Sinatra
Raymond Shaw	•	Laurence Harvey
Rosie	•	Janet Leigh
Raymond's Mother	•	Angela Lansbury
Chunjin	•	Henry Silva
Senator John Iselin	•	James Gregory
Jocie Jordan	•	Leslie Parrish
Yen Lo	•	Khigh Dhiegh
Corporal Melvin	•	James Edwards
Colonel	•	Douglas Henderson
Zilkov	•	Albert Paulsen
Secretary of Defence	•	Barry Kelley
Holborn Gaines	•	Lloyd Corrigan
Berezovo	•	Madame Spivy

SYNOPSIS

Sergeant Raymond Shaw comes back from the Korean war with a Congressional Medal of Honor. The action which earned Shaw his medal, however, exists only in the minds of the Sergeant and his platoon, all of whom had been captured by the Communists, brainwashed, and then returned to the American lines, but with a ticking bomb in their midst. The bomb is Shaw, now conditioned to kill, once a certain set of responses has been triggered, without memory of his action and consequently without any guilt. Shaking off his mother and stepfather, a puppet McCarthy dancing to his wife's orders, Shaw sets himself up as a journalist—and, under orders, murders his columnist employer. In the case of Major Marco, however, the brainwashing has been only partially successful, and when he and a Black corporal suffer nightmare memories of what really happened to the platoon, an army investigation gets under way. Meanwhile, Shaw is handed over by the Russians to his 'American operator'—none other, as it turns out, than his own mother, who plans to elevate her husband to the White House. Under her control, Shaw shoots down his own wife and her father, a crusading liberal senator. But Marco has now pieced together the whole extravagant plot, which involves Shaw's assassination of the Presidential nominee at a Madison Square Garden rally. Marco unlocks Shaw's captive mind, and the killer, acting consciously for the first time, turns the gun on his mother and stepfather, and then on himself.

COMMENT

The impact of this film was enormous. With it, John Frankenheimer became a force to be reckoned with in contemporary cinema. It established him as the most important film-maker at work in America or elsewhere. It came out at a time when it was clearly dangerous to speak of politics in the outspoken, satirical anti-McCarthy vein that characterized this picture. *The Manchurian Candidate*, based on Condon's book which Axelrod follows faithfully in his screenplay, provoked its expected share of criticism and cries for censorship. Fortunately, the film was too great an achievement, both commercially and artistically, to go down before it. Swept along by good reviews, Frank Sinatra's popularity, and the still strong tide of liberalism in the United States, it dealt a crushing blow to the extreme Right and spoke for sanity, commonsense, and freedom from fear in its most overt, psychological sense.

Within the framework of a thriller, the solid intelligence of the writing and Frankenheimer's cool, contained yet determined treatment result in a film of provocative and lively ideas, confirming many of the qualities which Frankenheimer had revealed in previous work—his continual visual inventiveness (the script contains no directions for filming the masterly brainwashing sequence, an extremely complicated piece of filming which he devised); his skill at choosing the right players and getting a telling sense of character from them (Angela Lansbury is carried over from *All Fall Down*, again a splendidly possessive mother, but entirely different from Berry-Berry's mother; James Gregory, Whit Bissell and James Edwards were all in *The Young Stranger*; Albert Paulson, the corrupt police officer in *All Fall Down* appears in the opposite role of the Russian, Zilkov; and both Frank Sinatra and Laurence Harvey give superlative, restrained performances); and again, Frankenheimer's acute sense of realism in his backgrounds and decors, neither of which are described in detail in the script. His settings for Miss Gertrude's 'bar' in the Korean prelude to the titles, like his street scenes in *The Young Savages* and in *The Fixer*, are filled with details, alive with people who appear to be living the scene, and composed in a manner suggesting the expressionism of early German cinema.

To come back to the brainwashing sequence, it was filmed three times in its entirety (from the viewpoint of the Garden Club ladies, the Russians, and the Black soldier) against three different sets so constructed that the camera could turn completely around them, the parts then being edited together to convey the various points of view. Another difficult sequence was the press conference of the Secretary of Defence (furiously played by Barry Kelley) in which Frankenheimer used television screens with great visual and dramatic skill. For example, in one shot we see Angela Lansbury, the mastermind, in the foreground, her Senator husband, the puppet, in the background, and the Secretary, the object of the Senator's accusation of Communism in the defense department, angrily reacting on the TV screen—everything combined in one frame reflecting the whole shot, yet filled with conflict and movement.

Just as the film itself is concerned with conditioning the minds of a group of soldiers, one of whom will become the key to the Communist take-over of the Government, so must Frankenheimer condition himself to make such a far-fetched subject real and convincing enough to persuade—and thus condition—an audience to accept what it is seeing as entirely credible. This he does in a series of finely timed, explosive and revealing situations laced with devastating black comedy, all of which use their fantastic backgrounds to comment on the political and social climate of the time. Audiences recognize that what is happening is extravagant, but what is being said and how the characters behave are uncomfortably real. Yet Frankenheimer never lectures, and his laconic humor is ever present as, for example, in John McGiver's remark to Iselin, at the fancy-dress party, that he is "at this Fascist rally because my daughter has assured me that it was important to her happiness that I come. There is no other reason." There is a beautiful sequence of fades, dissolves and superimpositions which begins in Raymond's apartment when he is telling Marco how lovable he once was, and the narrative flashbacks to the day when he met Jocie and was bitten by a snake. This is a moody, evocative and affecting revelation of Raymond's past character, and his relationship with his "terrible" mother. For the first time, the audience sees Raymond in a sympathetic light.

The entire assassination sequence is brilliantly directed, beginning with the clever establishing shots of Raymond at Madison Square Garden walking through the empty rows of tiered seats and finally arriving in a small room high above the arena. (These shots of Raymond were made for a deliberate "after effect": when the director later moved into the smaller stadium in Los Angeles with only small crowds of extras, the audience, when looking at tight close shots of crowds which actually extended no further than camera range, was still under the impression that the vastness of Madison Square Garden was "around them.") One scene that does not ring quite true is the one between Frank Sinatra and Janet Leigh which takes place in the taxi after she has been to the police station. Although they have only met that day on the train, and exchanged Condon's quirkishly amusing dialogue, audiences are surprised to find that within a few hours she is telling him, in the cab, "but if the policemen were the tiniest bit puzzled about you, they could have asked me. Oh yes, indeed, my darling Ben, they could have asked me and I would have told them." But neither this nor Raymond's first meeting with Jocie flaw a masterly creation, which closes with a chilling and deeply moving climax as Raymond, now no longer influenced by the playing cards, shoots his mother, his stepfather, and then turns the gun on himself. The sound of the gun turns immediately into a roll of thunder which effectively dramatizes and concludes the horror of the moment. There are very few camera directions in the script, and neither this idea nor the many other imaginative shots and sequences (like the use of screens at the press conference) are in the original script. They were all devised by the director, although Frankenheimer acknowledges some substantial assistance from Axelrod. As an example of what a director does to bring a scene to life, consider these script directions for the assassination scene: "The nominee is still on his feet, but Johnny and Raymond's mother have crumbled to the floor. The entire place is in pandemonium." Then study the filming of the sequence.

JF "The first film I really instigated and had complete control over was *The Manchurian Candidate*. This is the film I did exactly as I wanted; we had a lot of difficulties, George Axelrod and I, as it was not a subject that most studios wanted to make. But it meant a great deal to me, and this is the basis on which I decide what stories and subjects I want to film. You have to feel terribly involved, and it has to be something that means a great deal to you, that you feel very deeply about; and it has to be a statement that you want to make as a human being and as an artist. Anybody who becomes involved in a film for other reasons is doing it all wrong. Fortunately, all our difficulties disappeared because George was friendly with Frank Sinatra. He'd known him through the years and I think he'd seen him socially and told him he owned *The Manchurian Candidate* and Sinatra said, 'God, I always wanted to do that.' As soon as Sinatra said he wanted to do it, we could have shot it at any studio in town. After that, there were no problems.

"Frank was delightful to work with. All the stories I've heard about him I cannot believe. He's one of the most charming human beings I've ever met. He really worked terribly hard on this film. Without trying to economize or compromise in any way, we shot the entire film in thirty-nine days. We had actors who came in and knew their lines, and I must say I had a very clear concept of the entire movie due partially to George Axelrod whom I admire a great deal. We got along very well, and we talked out the whole film. I was also fortunate to have, as an Art Director, Richard Sylbert, who has done most of Kazan's films as well as *The Graduate*, and *Rosemary's Baby*, and he did *Grand Prix* for me. He's an imaginative Art Director and he built most of the sets for *The Manchurian Candidate* in the studio. Everybody thinks it was done on location. We did the Madison Square Garden scenes in just four days in Madison Square Garden and the rest of them in a local California stadium called the Olympic Auditorium and on the stage. But Sylbert is so clever you are never really aware of it.

"If you look at some of the plays like *The Comedian*, which I did on television, you'll see the same kind of style that I used in *The Manchurian Candidate*. It was the first time I'd had the courage, the assurance and self-confidence to go back to what I really had been good at in television. But it had taken so many years to do it—perhaps not that many when you start to think about it because *The Manchurian Candidate* was made in 1962, so in fact it had taken two years. I had complete control. I did not have this contractually on *All Fall Down*, but I assumed it because of my friendship with Houseman. I edited it right through to the finished print. I was able to do this on *Birdman* too, but only after many fights and arguments.

"Technically there were several challenges in *The Manchurian Candidate*. In what I call 'the lovable sequence' where Laurence Harvey is telling Frank Sinatra about his love affair and we go into flashbacks, there's a scene where his face is superimposed in the top left-hand corner and you see him with the girl as he describes what happened. You have to indicate that you want these things done at the laboratory, and usually they have to do it about five or six times. In this particular case I sent that sequence back fifteen times. First they didn't superimpose it. It went too quickly. I wanted a twenty-foot dissolve, which is long, but then they brought it in too fully. I sent it back because I wanted the face less strong. You have to play around with these effects before you get what you want. You have to know that this effect is going to happen when you're shooting the film and make allowances for it. The scenes must be framed in a certain way. I wanted to put Harvey's face up on the left side of the screen so I had to off-frame it and leave a lot of space on the right. You have to be very careful what the background is like so that you don't have pictures and shadows coming through on superimposition, unless you wanted to paint them out. What you require is a neutral background. And in the scene that's being superimposed, like the scene with the girl, I wanted to frame that on the right side of the screen because his face was going to be on the left side of the screen. That had to be all thought out beforehand. You must consider how sound effects will add drama to your film. Again, in *The Manchurian Candidate*, at the end, when Laurence Harvey turned the rifle on himself, the shot of the gun mixes with the thunder. It is frightening and tragic. It had started to rain earlier so it seemed quite logical that it would happen, rather than just bringing in the clap of thunder. That would have been melodramatic.

Angela Lansbury with Frankenheimer.

"It seems to me that to know how to use a camera you must have a visual sense. It is that something which makes the difference between a good film-maker and a poor film-maker. I don't think it's anything you can learn. You have to be born with it. Again in *The Manchurian Candidate*, in the sequence where Sinatra meets Janet Leigh in the train and they go and stand at the end of the coach, this was one of the longest shots I've held of two people talking where the camera didn't move except when the porter came through and she moved over to the side. It was intercut with quite a few close-ups though, and the back projection of the countryside flying past conveyed a feeling of motion within the frame. I just didn't see any need to move the camera and if you don't see any need to move it, you shouldn't move it. I am not out to prove that a camera has wheels. Lots of people have done that.

"Again, you must get characters to move quite naturally without giving audiences the feeling that you are moving people from here to there because we have a bit of movement. They should move but not in a forced way. It's something I usually work on during rehearsal. And if there is no reason to move, I don't move. Here are you and I sitting down at a table and we're not walking all around the room. That's something you have to think about.

"Now consider the scene in the Senate Hearing Room with the television cameras. If I hadn't directed live television, I could not have directed that sequence. The flashbacks pleased me. Until then, scenes showing television sets faked the picture you saw on the screen. They said you couldn't photograph pictures on a screen. They just didn't know how to do it. We had technicians in from CBS where I used to work and they showed them how to do it, to pulse their movie camera so that it would pick up the TV images. In *Seven Days in May* the use of screens was even more complex.

"I thought that Condon's *The Manchurian Candidate* was one of the best books I had ever read. I just couldn't put it down and after I had read it, I knew that I just had to make a film of it. It had great social and political significance for me at the time, and it has certainly been—unfortunately—a horribly prophetic film. It's frightening what has happened in our country since that film was made. It's amazing how often the picture is referred to in terms of techniques that are going on in North Vietnam at this point and in Korea and elsewhere—they come right out of *The Manchurian Candidate*. George Axelrod, who has a marvelously fertile mind, used to say to me, 'This could really very easily happen.'

"A lot of the things we just hinted at in the film. I

spent a great deal of time looking at newsreels of political conventions, going through all the books on brain-washing and the Korean War. Then we started to get absorbed in the story and realized that what we had was something that could very well be a lot closer to the truth than many people imagined. We consulted every book written about brainwashing, and I remember reading one called *In Every War But One*, about American prisoners of war in Korea, and not one prisoner ever attempted to escape. It was the story about how the Chinese brainwashed these men, what they did to them, and things like that; and while it wasn't quite as total as the brainwashing in *The Manchurian Candidate* it was nevertheless a very distinct type of brainwashing that they'd known.

"On another level we believed that we lived in a society that was brainwashed. And I wanted to do something about it. I think that our society is brainwashed by television commercials, by advertising, by politicians, by a censored press (which exists in this country whether you want to admit it or not) with its biased reporting. More and more I think that our society is becoming manipulated and controlled. Here was an individual trying to fight the inner conflicts which tormented him—a subject I've always been drawn to. I think everyone would agree that George Axelrod's screenplay of *The Manchurian Candidate* is probably one of the best adaptations from a novel to the screen with which I have been associated. I think people tend to forget George's contribution to the film. They always talk about it as a great film of mine, but George was very much responsible too. Also, the most important aspect is that this country was just recovering from the McCarthy era and nothing had ever been filmed about it. I wanted to do a picture that showed both how ludicrous McCarthy-style far-right politics are and how dangerous the far-left is also, how they were really exactly the same thing, and the idiocy of it all. I wanted to show that and I think we did."

Frank Sinatra Laurence Harvey Janet Leigh
The Manchurian Candidate

137   THE PLATFORM THROUGH THE TELESCOPIC SIGHT

Raymond moves the rifle so that the crossed hairs of the
sight meet in the center of the Nominee's forehead. They
hold there for a second. Then he swings the rifle ever so
slightly to the left, till Johnny's shoulder is spotted in
the crossed hairs.

138   INT. LIGHT BOOTH

Raymond lowers the rifle and waits. The Nominee's speech,
of course, continues through the loudspeakers.

139   TOP BALCONY

Marco is now racing toward the ladder to the light booth.

140   PLATFORM

                        NOMINEE
              '...Nor would I ask of any fellow
              American, that which...'

141   INT. LIGHT BOOTH

Raymond picks up the rifle.

142   PLATFORM - THROUGH THE TELESCOPIC SIGHT

The crossed hairs reach the Nominee's head. They hold there
for a moment. Then move on. Until they are centered on
Johnny's forehead.

143   THE LADDER TO THE BOX

Marco is climbing the ladder. The SOUND, from the box, of
two SHOTS, one after another in rapid succession, stops
him. He looks toward the platform.

144   PLATFORM - MARCO'S POV

The Nominee is still on his feet, but Johnny and Raymond's
Mother have crumbled to the floor. The entire place is in
pandemonium.

145   THE LADDER

Marco turns away and continues toward the box.

146   INT. LIGHT BOOTH

Raymond puts down the gun. He reaches into his pocket and
takes out a small metal object on a ribbon. It is the
Congressional Medal. He places it around his neck. Then he
picks up the gun. The CAMERA IS NOW SHOOTING over his
shoulder as the door to the box is torn open and Marco
appears. They stare at each other for a moment, oblivious
of the pandemonium below.

                        RAYMOND
                    (almost inaudibly)
              Hi, Ben...you couldn't have stopped
              them...the Army couldn't have...so..
              I had to...That's why I didn't call...
              Oh, God, Ben...

He raises the rifle. It is held in his hands as if his eyes
were the CAMERA. The rifle swings around until it is
pointing directly at the CAMERA. Then it goes off a third
time.

SEVEN DAYS IN MAY 1964

Director John Frankenheimer • *Screenplay* Rod Serling *based on the novel by* Fletcher Knebel and Charles W Bailey • *Photography* Ellsworth Fredericks • *Art Director* Cary Odell • *Set Decorator* Edward Boyle • *Editor* Ferris Webster • *Sound* Joe Edmondson • *Assistant Director* Hal Polaire • *Music* Jerry Goldsmith • *Producer* Edward Lewis • *Production* Seven Arts-Joel • *Release* Paramount, January 1964; première in Washington, February 1964 • *Running Time* 120 minutes • *Location* Paramount Studios, and on location in Washington DC and Arizona • *Cost* $M2.2 • *Availability* VHS and LD • Remade in 1994 by HBO Films as *The Enemy Within*—the Colonel is played by Forest Whitaker.

CAST

Gen. James M Scott	•	Burt Lancaster
Col. Martin Casey	•	Kirk Douglas
President Jordan Lyman	•	Fredric March
Eleanor Holbrook	•	Ava Gardner
Sen Raymond Clark	•	Edmond O'Brien
Paul Girard	•	Martin Balsam
Christopher Todd	•	George Macready
Sen Prentice	•	Whit Bissell
Harold McPherson	•	Hugh Marlowe
Arthur Corwin	•	Bart Burns
Col. Murdock	•	Richard Anderson
Lt. Hough	•	Jack Mullaney
Col. "Mutt" Henderson	•	Andrew Duggan
Col. Broderick	•	John Larkin
White House Physician	•	Malcolm Atterbury
Esther Townsend	•	Helen Kleeb
Admiral Barnswell	•	John Houseman
Bar Girl	•	Colette Jackson

SYNOPSIS

Acting against all the wishes and recommendations of the American military establishment, President Jordan Lyman has just successfully concluded a nuclear treaty with the Soviet Union. His Chief of Staff, General Scott, regards the President's policy as little short of treasonable, sending America unarmed into a future war. During a few days in May, Scott's aide, Colonel 'Jiggs' Casey, stumbles across several curious happenings—he learns of the existence of a top secret base somewhere in the Texas desert, whose location and purpose are unknown to military officialdom, and he hears of cryptic messages passing between Scott and other officers. Hesitantly, he deduces that Scott is planning a military coup, to take place on the following Sunday when the President will be isolated from his civilian staff during a military alert. Casey takes his story to the President, who sends out his most trusted colleagues to investigate. Southern Senator Raymond Clark is sent to locate the secret base, does so, but is held there incommunicado until brought out at gunpoint by an officer friend of Casey's. Presidential aide Paul Girard flies to Gibraltar to force a statement out of the foxy Admiral Barnswell, who has stayed on the sidelines of the plot, but Girard dies in an air crash during the homeward flight. Casey himself obtains from Eleanor Holbrook, Scott's former mistress, some highly incriminating letters. The President confronts Scott, but at the last moment cannot bring himself to use the letters. Scott remains convinced that in a showdown public opinion will be strongly on his side, and that his military allies will hold fast. When Lyman calls publicly for the resignation of the guilty officers, however, Scott's colleagues desert him. The news that the Barnswell statement has been found in the plane wreckage, and brought by courier to Washington, brings about Scott's final defeat, and the military rebellion is over.

Frankenheimer and Burt Lancaster take a break on the set of Seven Days in May.

COMMENT

Seven Days in May is the only film Frankenheimer has made which bears marked similarities to the one which precedes it. But, even so, such similarities are only in the nature of the subject, not in the treatment of it. Like *The Manchurian Candidate*, we are plunged into a world which, beneath its surface of peaceful normality, contains schemes and plots and ominous fantasies involving the struggle for political power in the United States. It seems entirely right that the director who brought *The Manchurian Candidate* to the screen so imaginatively should be the one to make Fletcher Knebel's and Charles W. Bailey's *Seven Days in May*. Once again, Frankenheimer, this time with screenplay writer, Rod Serling, remains faithful to the novel while creating a superb film. Both the book and the film are vivid and gripping accounts. The ominous notes of Goldsmith's score set the mood, and the low-key photography, the expert cross-cutting, the movements within the Pentagon, the car rides through dark and rainy streets, the encounter in the hot, white desert, the realistic sets, the rhythm and tempo, all create a compulsively ominous mystery amid a cold, Orwellian world of TV screens and electronic devices. Frankenheimer's great skill is his ability to hold an audience, to the extent that, even though most of the audience was probably already familiar with the book and its plot, the film in effect presents a new and unfamiliar world with which the audience becomes totally involved.

There are splendid performances from the entire cast. Burt Lancaster, far more deadly in his calm, almost silent manner, than he would have been as a bullish military man lusting after power; Kirk Douglas, from whose point of view the story unravels, takes the difficult part of a sincere man who must play the obnoxious role of "telling tales" to the President about a friend at the risk of looking foolish; Frederic March, an admirable President, ailing and losing the confidence of the nation, calling forth his last reserves of strength to fight out the crisis; and Edmond O'Brien (last seen briefly in *Birdman of Alcatraz*) giving his own likable version of a Laughton-type Senator from the South. Ava Gardner's Eleanor Holbrook is not really necessary to the plot—it does not seem likely that the few letters she had received from Lancaster's character during the time she was his mistress would be sufficient cause for the President to remove him from his position. And the sequence where Kirk Douglas visits her, and manipulates the conversation in such a way that she brings out the letters and, deciding to be rid of the past, drops them in the waste-paper basket, is not convincing. Frankenheimer himself regrets some of the dialogue in this scene. However, in spite of its lack of credibility, the sequence is never dull or boring. It is interesting to consider that Frankenheimer could not make a small scene like this seem credible, yet the entire plot of the film, a fantasy of disaster, is made totally believable, due to his calm and assured control, and his hypnotic involvement of audiences. Another aspect to admire is his use of the speeches given by the President. Scoffed at by some as "respectable, liberal lines," they are delivered by March with complete naturalism at times when they are logically called for and with great honesty and conviction. They re-state familiar principles perhaps, but they need to be said again. Frankenheimer handles them pointedly but never as clumsy propaganda, a trait which has marred previous movies involved with politics. The narrative may seem far-fetched now, but it nevertheless plausibly and intelligently projects a warning that this could happen in the future. The war-like pronouncements of many American military men place this film right on the line between fantasy and fact and it would take only the slightest push to move it over into truth. Who can tell what the effect of both the book and film has been. They might well have alerted the public so effectively that the generals have had second thoughts about continuing their war-like plans to seize power from the people. We shall never know, but it is entirely possible.

● ● ●

JF "In many ways, *Seven Days in May* was an appropriate film to follow *The Manchurian Candidate*, yet it was an accident that it happened that way. As a matter of fact, *Seven Days in May* led to the most important relationship I've ever had—my association with Eddie Lewis. Believe it or not, I was out of work after *The Manchurian Candidate*. This was the film which really marked what I wanted to do in films and how I wanted to make movies. In other words, I wanted to initiate the project, I wanted to have full control, I never wanted to go back to being hired as a director again. The agent I had at the time didn't really agree with me, believing that it was too early in my career to do things like that, and that the way it was done was for movie directors to go to a studio and make films for a studio. I didn't want to do it that way. You've probably read that I was offered the Edith Piaf story. This was true, but it would have been ludicrous for me to have accepted as I don't know that much about music. As I said to them, 'That's just fine, who's going to play it?' And they said, 'Well, Natalie Wood.' I replied, 'She's a very able actress but her French isn't very good.' They said, 'What are you talking about?' And I said, 'How the hell are you going to do Piaf's songs? They're the main things, and they have to be done in French.' And they said, 'We never thought of that. Well, it's really not too difficult, we'll just do them in English.' Finally, I said, 'No, you can't possibly do that. In the first place I love France and I could never get back into the country if I ever did this. They'd stone me at the border if I'd ever made the Edith Piaf story with an American actress singing all her songs in English.' Her life was made into a film some years later by a French director with a French actress.

"So I remained out of work. I was offered a number of scripts which were already complete with cast and that kind of thing and I just didn't want to do them. Then I became quite active in the American Civil Liberties Union, and they asked me to do a television programme reflecting their view of society today. They wanted me to direct it, George Axelrod to write it, and a man I'd never met, named Edward Lewis, to produce it. And so we went, George and I, to Eddie's office for a meeting. We sat down and discussed what we would like to do and we all realized simultaneously that this show was impossible to do for the simple reason it would cost too much money for television. And we decided we shouldn't do it, but in the course of it Eddie and I got along very well.

"He was Kirk Douglas' partner at that time (they had made *Lonely are the Brave*). When he called me, he said, 'I've always wanted to work with you. I have just read the galleys of a book called *Seven Days in May* and I'd like to send it to you to see what you think.' I read it and thought it was gripping, timely and well told. I called him back and told him so, and he said that the only way to really make a film was to buy the property, write the script, cast it, go in and make a deal. I had no money, I had to borrow it, but we did buy the book, and commissioned Rod Serling to write the screenplay. Then we cast it. We had Kirk Douglas, of course, because he was Lewis' partner. Then it just kept going. Everything worked out very well.

"*Seven Days in May* was as important to me as *The Manchurian Candidate*. I felt that the voice of the military was much too strong. Fred Cook wrote an extremely revealing book about it. We'd just finished eight years with President Eisenhower, which were in my opinion a very discouraging eight years for this country. All kinds of factions were trying to take power. This film was the opportunity to illustrate what a tremendous force the military-industrial complex is. Between them they control the national pride, they can either make or break a town or a city. If defense contracts are not renewed, or bases are closed, the whole economy of a city collapses. Los Angeles is a good example. Los Angeles is really built up around a military-industrial complex. God knows what would happen in Los Angeles if suddenly there were complete disarmament.

"There was not much resistance to our making the picture because we were financially sound with Kirk Douglas, Ava Gardner and Fredric March. We had the picture budgeted at a very realistic price of just $2,200,000. And we weren't asking anyone for co-operation. We did not ask the Pentagon for co-operation because we knew we wouldn't get it. But there was no active resistance to it. I'm sure the Pentagon weren't happy when they heard we were going to make it but at the same time they didn't try to censor us. I heard indirectly (I never had the pleasure of meeting him personally) that President Kennedy, said he very much wanted the film made. Pierre Salinger, who was his Press Secretary, was very helpful to us and when we shot the White House scenes he arranged for the President to go to Hyannisport. Now if the White House had not wanted the film made I can assure you that we could not have obtained permission to shoot a small riot in front of it. Pierre Salinger was also very gracious, taking us through the President's office and other rooms so that we could copy them accurately in the studio. The climate was very good.

"Everyone thinks there were some exterior shots of the Pentagon but there were none. Actually, what happened was we did shoot some stuff there. We had the camera in the back of a station wagon with a black cloth over it. We put Kirk Douglas in a car, and brought him to a motel right near the Pentagon where he changed into his Marine Colonel's outfit. We drove up in front of him and parked the station wagon. He drove up and parked his car, got out and walked into the Pentagon. Three men saluted him. Three other officers saluted him. They really thought he was a Colonel. He walked into the Pentagon. We had two cameras, each with a different lens. He turned right around, walked out, and got back into his car and drove off. This gave us entrance and exit shots. We were gone in about five minutes. We never asked permission or anything like that. Then we cut the scene out of the movie. We didn't need it. However, I would like to say that it gave me a sense of satisfaction to make a film about the place where I started to work as a mail boy.

"Earlier I mentioned the television scenes in *The Manchurian Candidate*, the ones in *Seven Days* were even more complicated. We used them in the Pentagon, where the guard could see who was coming up and down the corridor; in the General's office where Kirk Douglas could see Burt Lancaster coming down the corridor, in the telephone conversation between Fredric March and Burt Lancaster—each one had a television to see the other—and of course, during the President's speech. That was quite intricate because we had four monitors there, one for each Network. We had it all going from the tape truck, right on those monitors. I could do it only because of my live television training. The riot was well staged and I liked the confrontation between Freddie March and Burt Lancaster at the end of the film."

Frankenheimer makes a suggestion to Fredric March.

THE TRAIN 1964

Director John Frankenheimer • *Screenplay* Franklin Coen, Frank Davis, Walter Bernstein (*French version* Albert Husson) *based on the novel* Le Front de l'Art *by* Rose Valland • *Photography* Jean Tournier, Walter Wottitz • *Production Designer* Willy Holt • *Special Effects* Lee Zavitz • *Editors* David Bretherton, Gabriel Rongier • *Sound* Joseph de Bretagne • *Music* Maurice Jarre • *Producer* Jules Bricken • *Associate Producer* Bernard Farrel • *Production/ Release* United Artists-Ariane-Dear Films, September 1964 • *Running Time* 140 minutes • *Availability* VHS and LD • *Soundtrack* on United Artists Records • *Location* Made in Paris, Normandy and other locations in France over 186 days from August 1963 to May 1964. First two weeks of shooting were directed by Arthur Penn, who left after a disagreement with Burt Lancaster and Jules Bricken. Bernard Farrel directed some scenes until John Frankenheimer agreed to take over. Frankenheimer had their script rewritten with Ned Young and Howard Infell (who went uncredited) • *Release* New York and Paris, September 1964.

CAST

Labiche •	Burt Lancaster	*Lieut. of retreating convoy* •	Jean-Jacques Lecomte
Col. von Waldheim •	Paul Scofield	*Gen. von Lubitz* •	Richard Munch
Christine •	Jeanne Moreau	*Bernard* •	Bernard Lajarrige
Papa Boule •	Michel Simon	*Capt. Schmidt* •	Jean Bouchard
Mlle. Villard •	Suzanne Flon	*Sgt. Schwartz* •	Donald O'Brien
Pesquet •	Charles Millot	*Lt. Pilzer* •	Art Brauss
Didont •	Albert Rémy	*Sgt. Grote* •	Richard Baily
Stationmaster •	Jacques Marin	*Robert* •	Christian Fuin
Spinet •	Paul Bonifas	*Priest* •	Daniel Lecourtois
Major Herren •	Wolfgang Preiss	*General's Aide* •	Elmo Kindermann
Capt. Dietrich •	Howard Vernon	*Hubert* •	Jacques Blot
Major of retreating convoy •	Jean-Claude Bercq		

SYNOPSIS

Occupied France, 1944. As the Allies approach Paris, Colonel von Waldheim fanatically presses forward a plan to load a train with priceless art treasures from the Jeu de Paume museum and dispatch it to Germany. Madame Villard, the museum curator, informs the Resistance and tries to persuade Labiche, a railway inspector, to intercept it. Labiche refuses on the grounds that it may cost lives, and, in any case, he is mainly concerned with sabotaging an important armaments train. Papa Boule, an old railway man also in the Resistance, who is convinced of the value of this cargo, sabotages the train and is shot by the Germans. Allied air raids severely damage the marshalling yards but eventually the train carrying the works of art is made ready with Labiche as engineer. Owing to the clever strategems of the station staff, the Germans are led to believe that the train has passed into Germany whereas, in reality, it has returned to the original French station where an elaborately planned accident temporarily puts it out of action. Labiche, who is wounded while escaping from the Germans, is aided by Christine, a hotel keeper; when the train is started again, Labiche begins a one-man harassing campaign. Waldheim, now almost deranged by his obsessions, places hostages in the train and drives slowly forward until Labiche causes it to be permanently derailed. Panic breaks out as the retreating army passes by; the hostages are shot and the Germans abandon their leaders, leaving Waldheim and Labiche to face each other alone. Labiche shoots the German and wanders away leaving the paintings scattered over the deserted tracks.

COMMENT

As the film fictionalizes the truth somewhat (in actual fact, the train carrying the looted paintings never got farther than a few stations outside Paris), *The Train* is probably best described as an adventure made in a documentary tradition. It is too well-made and thoughtful a film, however, to be described merely as an "action adventure film." It is grim, gray and tragic, and nothing takes place which is not possible—even the seemingly impossible task of painting the roofs of the first three trucks white. It is a film to be seen time and time again, without any loss of excitement or involvement. Almost every film made today about the Second World War lacks a sense of period. They look as if they might be taking place today. While it is true that styles have not radically changed since the mid-forties, the majority of war stories we see convey the impression that the war is still on, that we are still fighting "somewhere over there." While this may be an advantage in that people are not allowed to forget the horror of war, it does destroy our sense of history. *The Train* is one of the few war films that conveys a true sense of period.

As with all of Frankenheimer's films, we are immediately involved in a sense of conflict, which then becomes a very real struggle. In the beginning, the obsessed German officer is in conflict with his own superiors over obtaining permission to commandeer a train to take away the paintings. Once he has succeeded, the conflict is between him and the railway workers who try and thwart him. The director's expert sense of narrative carries the events along with ever-mounting drama and excitement, and, at times, overwhelming tragedy as men are shot and killed. Most films such as this have a spectacular climax and then decline into anti-climactic dialogue or events. Frankenheimer can wreck trains and stage air raids, and still sustain interest in his characters and in the interim events. The atmosphere of the marshaling yards, the darkness of the huge repair shops, the tension in the signal box, the drab reality of the railway hotel, the encounter with Jeanne Moreau (again, no concession to an easy romance), the magnificent footplate photography (there were no models or process shots used, such as those that marred *Von Ryan's Express*), the clank of iron and the hiss of steam, and, most importantly, the agony of the ever-present violence and death are never needlessly exploited or sensationalized by the director.

Frankenheimer's insistence on using natural backgrounds gives the film a great feeling of actuality. The stark, dramatic outlines of the camouflaged armored locomotive emerging from the sheds is worthy of Eisenstein. The chase into the tunnel, with the shot from outside the far end showing the locomotive stopping inches from the opening, and the engineer pulling on the whistle chain to relieve his pent-up emotions, is masterly. The editing of the sequence leading up to the climactic smash-up is superb. The photography in the hotel, with the view through the window as Labiche goes over the wall, or returns and goes upstairs, conveys all the cramped, damp dinginess of the place. And the final scenes where Labiche again derails the train causing the audience to wait with baited breath for the suppressed yet furious reaction of Scofield as the German commander, is a reminder that we have never lost sight of or forgotten the actual story, the clash of wills between Waldheim and Labiche, in this very long film.

Frankenheimer's use of locations illustrates once again his eye for telling, pictorial details, his creation of atmosphere, his use of the weather, and of cameras which seem to breathe place, time and period. His set-ups are never less than original—he always goes one step further than we expect, as in the early sequence when the bombing raid is to take place at ten o'clock, and the camera finishes its shot by moving up to Lancaster's wrist watch, a "ten to one" zoom.

The director has been criticized, of course, for his ironic comments about the relative values of art and human life—whether paintings, no matter how artistic, are worth the price of human lives, particularly as the chances of recovering them after such a war are favorable, or whether it is worth sacrificing a few people in order to preserve masterpieces that will out-live them. Furthermore, is it acceptable to shoot German soldiers trying to steal these works, but unacceptable for Frenchmen to die trying to protect them? Where should the line be drawn between those things worth dying for and those which are not?

Note: In *Night of the Generals*, Peter O'Toole, playing a German officer, visits the Jeu de Paume to look at the paintings later to be stolen by a German officer von Waldheim, in *The Train*.)

JF "*The Train* was a film that I had no intention of ever doing. There was another director on the film but he left after about two weeks. I don't really know to this day exactly what happened. There was a conflict of personalities, a conflict over the type of film being made. I think the director, Arthur Penn, wanted to do one film, while the producer and Lancaster wanted to do another. Penn has since proved that he can make the type of film he wants to do with *Bonnie and Clyde*, so I think it was a difference in concept rather than anything else. Burt called me and asked if I would come over to France and direct it. I'd just finished *Seven Days in May* and I was quite tired. I didn't want to do it, yet he asked me to do it as a favour to him. And also, I wanted to go to Europe. On the way I read through the script. It was delivered to me just as I got on the plane. I thought it was pretty much appalling. It was neither fish nor fowl. The damned train didn't leave the station until page 140. When I arrived in Paris we shut down the production and we rewrote the script. I'd brought over Ned Young (he's dead now) and Howard Infell, and we re-wrote it. I wanted to include a point of view I felt strongly about which was that no work of art is worth a human life. But to say that the film is a statement of a theme like that is really being unfair to the film because in my opinion it is also a significant action movie. I don't think it's a film that you have to read a great deal of social significance into, but it *is* true to people and their environment. The point that so many people overlook is that what people do and how they think, feel and behave, is important in itself. It is important to recognize the validity of their lives, and you can show this in a film which is on the surface an action story. Honesty and reality are reflected in people's attitudes—there need not be great deeds or heroes or villains proclaiming great messages about life. It's just that you can recognize life. *The Train* is this kind of movie.

"It was done completely on location, and our problems were enormous, because nobody knew what they were getting into. Nobody knew what kind of film they were going to make. And by the time we really got the script rewritten (of course, it was never completely finished because as we were shooting we kept re-writing) and went to the locations that had been chosen in Normandy, the weather proved to be impossible. The weather is notoriously bad in Normandy (the Allies couldn't invade until June) and I was trying to shoot a film there, which, by the nature of the material, had to take place during the last three days of August. Well, we just ran out of weather. We'd get maybe one or two shots and then the fog would come in, and then the leaves just kept falling off the trees, the ice kept forming. So we had to shut down, and start again the following spring. This was a very important period for me because I had time at last to see Europe. I cut my film together, what I had, and I knew then what I had to shoot. Then I had about two or three months free and I just drove around Europe with my wife. I loved this time. It was most revealing and enjoyable.

"Smashing up the trains was easy to do. It's every boy's childhood fantasy. There isn't a child who ever owned an electric train who didn't want to do a wreck with it, putting a car across the track and sending the engine into it. Well, of course, we did just that. We put one engine across the track and sent the other one full speed into it. There were all kinds of complications. We had a very good special effects man named Lee Zavitz, who 'submarined' the track so that when the engine hit the other engine it would go down, not up as the French demolition men said it would. We had eight cameras set up. We sent the train full throttle into the other engine and shot it. It worked beautifully. But strangely, the little train wreck that preceded this one, with the engine supposedly derailed on purpose, really *was* dangerous. It was only supposed to be going seven miles an hour. This is shot differently from a train going seventy miles an hour. Then you prepare for what should happen and have everything secured. You have, like the accidents in *Grand Prix*, scenes done with remote cameras and scenes done with regular cameras, which is what I started doing with this little train. I had everything beautifully timed and planned. If a train is just going off the track at seven miles an hour you're very casual about it. You have your cameras right there to shoot it because it's not going very far. I had six cameras, but there were men on them. In fact, I was on one of them next to the track. And I had one camera I had completely forgotten about. The cameraman asked me what I wanted him to do with it, so I told them to dig a hole and bury it there right by the track. They did so and made it a remote camera. The French engineer on the train grew nervous and pulled the throttle back too far. The locomotive started off from a standing start and began to pick up speed. I was looking through the viewfinder of the camera (it had an 18mm lens on it which makes things go faster anyway) and the damned thing was coming at me. I looked over the viewfinder of the camera and I realized that he was going much too fast. By this time it was up to about fifteen miles an hour and thundering down right at us. It got up to around twenty-five, and as quickly as possible I hauled the cameramen out—three of them, I physically hauled them out. The train went flying off the track, ran over every camera we had, demolishing six of them, including two Arriflexes, two Mitchells—it was just awful. And the only camera that recorded the accident was that little camera that was buried. It was a fantastic shot because the wheels kept revolving right over the camera.

The bombing of the railway yard at the beginning of the film was done at a station called Jardin Ville. The French wanted to rip it up to lay new tracks. I said, 'I'll do it for you,' and we blew up the whole bloody place. It took us six weeks just to lay the dynamite. And I refused to use shots, re-staged or newsreel, of planes dropping their bombs. I'm so tired of shots of planes dropping bombs, so I did the entire air raid without showing a single aircraft. The aerial views of the armored train leaving the station were complicated too. We had to take down every television aerial. We did all our shots from rooftops, and as we could only have one run with the train we had to keep leaping ahead of it. Another difficult sequence was the one showing the locomotive racing for the tunnel to escape the strafing airplane. The close-up of the wheels braking was hard to get. I put a camera right on it and it just went flying off—another camera ruined. Then we put oil on the tracks to get the wheels to slide.

One thing I deeply regret now is that we did not use French-speaking actors when we dubbed the French into English. The old man, who was a leader of sorts, dubbed himself and he sounded very authentic. Jeanne Moreau spoke her own English too. If Burt Lancaster and I had that film to do over again, we would both do it differently. As I said, I came into the film after it started shooting, but once Burt became involved he began to live the film so intently that he said to me, 'My God, if

only we had started this together, I would have played it with a French accent. Then we wouldn't have to dub the other actors into that hoarse American-English, and the entire film would have been more convincing.' And it's true. We all make mistakes. Ideally, it should all have been spoken in French with English sub-titles, but you cannot do this with an expensive film made for the mass market. But I do think we caught the French flavor and got the period right. Someone criticized me for the suit Burt wears at the opening of the film as he walks across the railway yard. They said it was too modern. In fact, it was a 1941 suit that we had found to fit him.

"From the acting point of view, everything went very well. I loved working with Michel Simon, Paul Scofield was simply masterly, Jeanne Moreau was a delight, and Burt of course was in his element falling from trains, sliding down ladders, climbing walls, yet all the time *living* his part. I think that considering what we started out with, we ended up with a pretty good movie."

Frankenheimer with James Wong Howe

SECONDS 1966

Director John Frankenheimer • *Screenplay* Lewis John Carlino *based on the novel by* David Ely • *Photography* James Wong Howe • *Art Director* Ted Haworth • *Set Decorator* John Austin • *Editors* Ferris Webster, David Webster • *Sound* Joe Edmondson • *Assistant Directors* Francisco Day, Michael Glick • *Music* Jerry Goldsmith • *Paintings* John Hunter • *Titles* Saul Bass • *Producer* Edward Lewis • *Production* Paramount-Joel-Gibraltar • *Release* first shown at the Cannes Festival, May 1966; released in New York, September 1966 • *Running Time* 108 minutes • *Location* various locations in Los Angeles, Malibu, and New York • *Availability* released on VHS in January 1995 with the original wine-stomping scene.

CAST

Tony Wilson • Rock Hudson	*Mayberry* • Robert Brubaker
Norma Marcus • Salome Jens	*Mrs. Filter* • Dorothy Morris
Arthur Hamilton • John Randolph	*Secretary* • Barbara Werle
Old Man • Will Geer	*Man in Station* • Frank Campanella
Mr. Ruby • Jeff Corey	*Tailor Shop Presser* • Edgar Stehli
Dr. Innes • Richard Anderson	*Meat Man* • Aaron Magidow
Charlie • Murray Hamilton	*Nurse* • De De Young
Dr. Morris • Karl Swenson	*Girl in Boudoir* • Françoise Ruggieri
Davalo • Khigh Dheigh	
Emily Hamilton • Frances Reid	*Dayroom Attendant* • Thom Conroy
John • Wesley Addy	*Henry Bushman* • Ned Young
Texan • John Lawrence	*Mr. Filter* • Kirk Duncan
Plump Blonde • Elizabeth Fraser	*Doctor in Operating Room* • William Richard Wintersole
Sue Bushman • Dody Heath	

SYNOPSIS

Financially independent, but tired, dissatisfied and middle-aged, Arthur Hamilton is jolted out of his routine life by an extraordinary telephone call from an old friend, Charlie, whom he had thought dead. Charlie's message leads him, circuitously, to the headquarters of a monster corporation, headed by a wizened and studiously benign Southerner, which sells a special service to the jaded rich. Dependents are provided for, suitably disfigured corpses supplied, and, with the past cleared away, a surgically remodelled new man can step out into the world, his career chosen by the 'guidance adviser' after analysis under hypnosis. With trepidation, Hamilton becomes a client.

He emerges as Tony Wilson, painter, with a house in California, a lugubrious man-servant called John who is supplied by the organisation, and a ready-made collection of canvases. At first Tony cowers at home, afraid to face the world in his new identity. But a meeting on the beach with unconventional Norma, and an outing with her to the wine-making celebrations of a Californian grape-festival, releases the extrovert. He gives a party, all the guests being hand-picked by John. As the evening progresses, and under the influence of drink, he reverts to the Hamilton *persona*—to the horror of his guests, most of whom turn out to be clients of the organisation. When he learns that Norma, as well as John, are its employees, Tony revolts against a new life no more satisfying than the old. He visits his wife, claiming to be an old friend of her husband's, to find her content in her widowhood.

Then he goes back to the organisation, begging for a third chance. But he won't meet the condition laid down—that he, like his friend Charlie, should recommend another client. The organisation admits no wastage: his destiny is to provide the corpse for the next customer, and he goes struggling to his death.

COMMENT

The French and European critics at Cannes gave *Seconds* such a hostile reception and denounced it so bitterly for being "cruel and inhuman" that Frankenheimer refused to leave Monte Carlo (where he was filming *Grand Prix*) to attend his press conference at the Festival. Rock Hudson went alone and found it difficult to answer the many criticisms hurled at him, the director and the picture. Only the British and Americans responded positively to it, with one critic making the astute observation that in ten years' time, the Cinémathèque in Paris would hold a retrospective of Frankenheimer's work and then *Seconds* would be described as a masterpiece—a fact they failed to recognise then.

Seconds is a cold, grey, frightening picture of a dehumanised world, a skilful, controlled and intense amalgam of mystery, horror and science fiction based on the age-old theme of the search for eternal youth and the premise of a second chance. Arthur Hamilton gets his second chance because our calculating and efficient business methods (which have ruled out the human touch in both administration and deed) have conceived a foolproof system which makes it possible. Hamilton is a bored, over-weight banker with a dull marriage. Life is simply a monotonous round of driving to the commuter train, going to the office, suffering indigestion, and returning home to nothing.

What happens to Hamilton in his second life—how he comes to realise too late that he ruined his first one, that the promise and joys of youth were wasted in the frantic race for self-advancement and materialistic well-being; how, in the horrifying climax, he is taken away to become the cadaver for another second—is brilliantly told by Frankenheimer in an uncompromising yet moving and persuasive essay in science fiction set in contemporary life. Faithfully adapted by Lewis John Carlino from David Ely's engrossing novel, and photographed in a stark, distorted and mobile style by James Wong Howe, *Seconds* is not only Hamilton's story, but that of the old man, the company president, who started the "second life enterprise" as an idealistic venture, became the servant of high finance and found that his own existence, like that of the seconds he produced, was based on a fallacy—that what he was doing in life was right. But when he discovered the truth, he lacked the courage to change it.

In actual fact, the weakness of *Seconds* does not lie so much in the failure of the second act to show why Hamilton-Wilson didn't succeed in his second life, as in its attempt to convince audiences that the actor playing Hamilton could emerge, after plastic surgery, as Wilson played by Rock Hudson. This is where the star system worked against Frankenheimer. Had it been possible for him to use a fairly unknown actor, such as the actor playing Hamilton, the director could probably have overcome the difference in weight and height. In the early scenes showing Hudson emerging from the operation with scars on his face and unkempt hair, it does seem credible that the transformation has taken place. But when Wilson begins to look more like Rock Hudson, and Hudson, once out of bed, takes on his normal screen personality, the deception is not so easy to believe. Yet Frankenheimer is clever enough in everything he does in this film that one soon forgets Hamilton, and Wilson becomes a plausible figure in his own right, Hamilton becoming as much a lost person in the physical sense to the audience as he does to Wilson. Observant audiences may notice the photograph on the wall of Hamilton's study which he contemplates while talking to the mysterious caller on the phone who claims to be Charlie, his dead friend. The photograph is of Hamilton and Charlie, but Hamilton looks tall and not unlike Hudson, as indeed he will look when he becomes Wilson.

Everything about Seconds is enthralling in both content and technique. Its sense of cinema is overpowering, and Frankenheimer's imagination is constantly at work with memorable results—the opening title and credits sequence at Grand Central Station, with an anonymous man tracking Hamilton across the busy concourse and slipping something into his hand as he boards the train, the audience's immediate awareness of the boredom in Hamilton's life as his wife meets him at the train and they drive home; the tense atmosphere before the telephone call. As every scene unfolds, the air of mystery grows, veiled menace alternating with business-like efficiency and matter-of-fact developments. There is an oddly tender and sad sequence in which Frankenheimer, who seldom depicts the act of love between men and women, does something unusual—he shows the elderly Hamilton attempting, and failing, to make love to his wife. It is beautifully shot, without being overly explicit or distasteful.

James Wong Howe's photography has never been better than in this picture. His use of light and shade, the strong dramatic overtones and notes of near horror, the way he makes every exterior and handles interiors such as the pressing shop, the meat packing place, and the beach (not far from Frankenheimer's home, incidentally). A great many people disliked Seconds because it was too real in every respect: they could accept any amount of blood and gore in Frankenstein, where bodies were cut up and sewn together, no matter how real it all looked, because they knew it was still a fantasy world peopled by madmen and freaks. But Seconds is so believable that it becomes too terrifying for audiences to accept, including the horrific ending in which Wilson is pushed, kicking and screaming, along the corridors of headquarters back into the operating room, this time never to re-emerge.

F "When I returned from Europe, I had changed a great deal. I didn't realise it then but I had. I knew then that making films on location was really the only thing to do, and I was more than ever convinced that the subject matter had to be something that I deeply cared about because, after all, whether I wished to admit it or not, I did spend over a year of my life on The Train and it's not a subject that I cared that much about. I just swore to myself that this would never happen again. Now, I saw my own country from a different perspective, from a very tragic perspective because we were in Europe during the assassination of the President, and we were able to judge foreign reaction to us and to our behaviour. And I saw myself from a different perspective too. I was convinced by that time that films were my life and I should have always been making them. It's difficult to say what a year in Europe does to somebody, but it does change you. It was during The Train that I became confident that I could do a film like Grand Prix. I learned an awful lot during The Train, I think I really learned how to shoot action sequences, how to shoot them with a personal approach. It's funny, thinking back to the days of 1960 when people in Hollywood thought that anybody directing on a seventeen inch screen could not direct on a forty foot screen; then, having done *The Train*, I find myself being offered every action picture that was going to be made. Of course, I didn't want to do them but here I was. Suddenly I was an action director. The studios had quickly forgotten the past.

"*Seconds* was actually supposed to start right after *Seven Days in May*, but I had postponed it to do *The Train* which took longer than I had expected. Again, this was a story that Eddie Lewis and I had found. I had never met the author, David Ely, but we had been looking at the work of a young playwright in New York, Lewis John Carlino, and we wanted to work with him. We followed the same procedure as with *Seven Days in May*. We bought the book with our own money, hired the writer, chose the cast, and that was our second Paramount picture—we'd made a two-picture deal at Paramount. Then we showed it to Carlino, who wanted to write it for the screen. Essentially, its message was that an individual is what he is, that he has to live with his life. He cannot change anything, and all of today's literature and films about escapism are just rubbish because you cannot and should not ever try to escape from what you are. Your experience is what makes you the person you are. If you don't want to live with it, it's just too bad. Someone once said to Thomas Carlyle, 'I accept the world,' and his reply was 'You damned well better'—that's really what this film is about. It's also about all this nonsense in society that we must be forever young, this accent on youth in advertising and thinking which I'm very much opposed to. I wanted to make a matter-of-fact yet horrifying portrait of big business that will do anything for anybody providing you are willing to pay for it—an extension of the insurance company. It's a film that's very much against 'The Dream,' the belief that all you need to do in life is to be financially successful. Many people really believe that is the key. The film attempted to show that many men who did finally reach this point in their lives then discovered that life meant nothing to them and were prepared to throw it away just for a chance to start again, which is impossible.

"We had a great deal of difficulty casting it. While the book read terribly well and the script read well on paper, there came that moment when I had to sit down and say 'How am I going to direct the scene where he confronts his wife.' And actually in the original script there is also a scene where he confronts his daughter. How am I going to do these scenes and not have them recognise him? Then I thought, obviously it has to be one actor playing both parts, but how am I going to shoot close-ups of this fellow at the beginning? No matter how good the make-up is, I don't think you can really photograph that tight. If you can, then I've never seen it properly done, or if I've seen it done, I haven't been aware of it unless it has involved extreme character make-up like Dr. Jekyll and Mr. Hyde. The way I saw the film, the first part of it was one gigantic close-up with this man showing his doubt about his life. Originally, Kirk Douglas was supposed to play it. But I didn't feel that was a good idea because I didn't think we could disguise Kirk so that you wouldn't know it was the same fellow. Anyway, his commitments didn't allow him to play the part. I had a dream—the man to play this role was Laurence Olivier because that was the kind of acting we needed. But this was a film which Paramount did not really want to make, although they had to, but they didn't want Olivier.

"We finally decided on Rock Hudson, partly because he was so keen to try it, but also, of course, because we knew he would be good. We knew we were going to have a terrible problem getting audiences to believe that the man who went into the operating room to have plastic surgery could emerge as Rock Hudson. In reality, it's very possible to do that with plastic surgery; but his height was a problem. We put lifts on John Randolph and everything else but he wasn't as tall as Rock. However, I don't think it was too noticeable. I think the problem with the film was that we had no second act. In other words, we didn't make it clear why he didn't enjoy his new life. And I think people confuse that with the idea of John Randolph becoming Rock Hudson. I think if we could have successfully dramatised the second act, nobody would ever have questioned that; but we didn't, so the film was obscure. We thought we had shown why he failed, but after the film was finished I realised we had not. The book never even went into it, never really faced the problem at all, it just forgot completely about it. And some people were confused over the ending. After he is given the cranial drill, we end with a shot showing a man carrying a small girl. Now this was shot from a scene (originally in the film) where he met a little girl on the beach and was talking to her. Her father called her and she ran to him saying, 'Daddy, Daddy,' and he picked her up and carried her off, and we cut to Rock Hudson walking alone. I removed the scene, but then, when I looked at the ending, I thought that it worked even without the scene because I think people could read into it that this was his dream, that's what his life should have been, but it never was. Oddly enough, the actor playing the father with the child looks, in that last shot, like Rock Hudson, which makes the idea of a dream on his part seem even more definite.

"I also experimented with a certain lens—a 9.5mm lens. I think you have to have a concept of how a film is going to look before you even start to make it. I never feel secure about a film until I know in my mind what the film is going to look like. And it isn't shot for shot, it's a basic image. For instance, *The Manchurian Candidate*—the key to the way it was going to look was the scene in the press conference room with James Gregory over there and his face on the television screen; and at the convention with the candidate's face on the hat and at the same time the candidate up there. In other words, it was a film about double images in a strange kind of way. The brainwashed versus the unbrainwashed. The whole concept came to me and then I was very happy. I knew what I wanted to do. *Seven Days in May* again was the whole electronic world. 'Boom boom boom,' that's the way it had to be. *The Train* was sheer fact and the key to it was that it had to look like a documentary. Now, in *Seconds*, distortion was terribly important. How society had distorted this man, what the company had then turned him into, and, finally, when he was going to his death, a complete distortion of reality—the fact that it was all just utter nonsense—not the film, but the irony of it. I designed the hallucination set because it had to be almost psychedelic.

"The whole idea of the film was to make the story look as if it could really happen. The scene with Hamilton and his wife, where he finds he cannot make love to her, was shot with four Arriflexes. I worked one, Jimmy worked one and two camera operators were on the others. The grape-stomping scene wasn't in the book, but I needed a scene that was supposed to be his catharsis, that 'just let him be free.' I filmed it in Santa Barbara. The Legion of Decency, as it was then, made me cut the scene completely differently to how I had originally intended. I have the unexpur-gated version in the house somewhere. It didn't look like an orgy at all and it isn't, but the way the studio wanted it cut to get the film released, it did look like an orgy and that was not what I wanted. Some people have told me that *Seconds* works more effectively when they see it a second time. I think you should see a film twice, because, don't forget, a man who makes a worthwhile film has worked on it for a year of his life, and I don't think it is fair to sit through it only once. After all, many people read books twice, they go back to see famous paintings many times and see more in them. I think it has to be this way with films. I think the scene in *Seconds* between John Randolph and Will Geer, all done in one shot with John Randolph in the foreground and Will Geer in the background, moving into a two-shot and then into a close-up with Geer, is among the best scenes I've directed.

"I had splendid co-operation from Jimmy Wong Howe, who's a marvellous cameraman. We all know the film was a failure, but I think it makes an excellent case for not showing at film festivals. I brought the film to New York to show it to Paramount. The president of the company, George Weltner, saw it with his sales department, and wrote me a letter stating that in his opinion it was the strongest, most powerful film that he had ever seen, that the entire company was behind it, that if this film didn't make money it was certainly not the fault of the creators.

"I wanted to enter it at Cannes, so they pulled a lot of strings to do what I wanted, to make it the American entry. And it was a disaster. Most of the critics hated it. Paramount lost all faith in the film after that and they put no effort into selling it. They panicked and dumped the film. Some said it would not have done much better if it hadn't gone to Cannes, but maybe it would. We couldn't have done worse, because the reviews were certainly not very good for the most part. I think many critics were very unfair to Rock Hudson. I thought he was very good. But again, I can't complain because the critics have been very good to me in most cases; they were lying in wait for old Rock. I was sorry to see it because he really gave so much of himself. This was again a case of being only as good as your last film. It was fortunate that *Grand Prix* came out two months after *Seconds*. In other words, I didn't have to work with the failure of *Seconds* for very long. It's not pleasant to live with a commercial failure."

From left to right: *Phil Hill, Framkenheimer, Yves Montand, and James Garner, setting up another racing scene.*

GRAND PRIX 1966

Director John Frankenheimer • *Screenplay* Robert Alan Arthur • *Photography* (Eastmancolor, print by Metrocolor, Single Screen Cinerama System in Super Panavision 70) Lionel Lindon • *Production Designer* Richard Sylbert • *Special Effects* Milton Rice • *Supervising Editor* Frederic Steinkamp • *Editors* Henry Berman, Stewart Linder, Frank Santillo • *Sound* Gordon Daniels • *Sound Recording* Franklin Milton, Roy Charman • *Assistant Director* Enrico Isaaco • *Music* Maurice Jarre • *Visual Consultant/Montage/Titles* Saul Bass • *Second Unit Photography* John M. Stephens, Jean-Georges Fonteneille, Yann Le Masson • *Costumes* Sydney Guilaroff • *Racing Advisors* Phil Hill, Joachim Bonnier, Richie Gunter • *Technical Consultant* Carroll Shelby • *Producer* Edward Lewis • *Production Manager* William Kaplan • *Location Production Managers* Sacha Kamenka, Sam Gorodisky, Peter Crowhurst • *Production* Joel-JFP-Cherokee Film/A Douglas and Lewis Production • *Release* Metro-Goldwyn-Mayer, December 21, 1966 • *Running time* 179 minutes • *Formats* Available on VHS and LD • *Soundtrack* on MGM Records • *Location* locations in Monte Carlo, Monaco; Spa, Belgium; Brands Hatch, England; Clermont-Ferrand, France; Monza, Italy, over five months beginning in May 1966 • Originally presented with an intermission.

CAST

Peter Aron •	James Garner	*Monique Delvaux Sarti* •	Genevieve Page
Louise Frederickson •	Eva Marie Saint		
Jean-Pierre Sarti •	Yves Montand	*Wallace Bennett* •	Donald O'Brien
Izo Yamura •	Toshiro Mifune	*Children's Father* •	Jean Michaud
Scott Stoddard •	Brian Bedford	*Surgeon* •	Albert Rémy
Pat •	Jessica Walter	*Mrs Stoddard* •	Rachel Kempson
Nino Barlini •	Antonio Sabato	*Mr Stoddard* •	Ralph Michael
Lisa •	Francoise Hardy	*Sportscasters* •	Alan Fordney,
Agostini Manetta •	Adolfo Celi		Anthony Marsh,
Hugo Simon •	Claude Dauphin		Tommy Franklin
Guido •	Enzo Fiermonte	*Tim Randolph* •	Phil Hill
Jeff Jordan •	Jack Watson	*Journalist* •	Bernard Cahier

ON LOCATION

Monte Carlo, May 1966. It is uncomfortably hot. What breeze floats in over the harbor is lost in the noise and the burning stench of racing cars hurtling along past the stands packed with spectators. Frankenheimer, wearing a large desert hat, is walking along the roadside. He is bronzed from the sun, worried about the races; his actors in their cars, waiting for cues, are nervous. Chaos appears to be in charge, and the director, disappointed with the reception of *Seconds* at the Cannes Film Festival two days earlier, is trying to pull the day's shooting schedule together. This is an expensive, complicated and risky venture. There is a lull in the proceedings. It doesn't look like a regular film set because all the equipment is dispersed around the course and the cars are carrying small cameras taking the driver's point of view and shots of other cars tussling for positions. Brian Bedford and James Garner, in helmets and driving costumes, appear as from nowhere seeking advice from the director. Excusing himself, they disappear into the crowds. Frankenheimer has little time for breaks or meals. Once again he is consumed by the task of putting his story on film.

SYNOPSIS

In the Monaco Grand Prix, the first of the international season, American driver, Pete Aron, under contract to the British Jordan-B.R.M. team, causes a crash in which his British colleague, Scott Stoddard, is seriously injured. Aron is dismissed by his boss, Jeff Jordan, who is furious at the loss of his talented young driver. Aron finds some consolation in the person of Stoddard's wife, Pat, an ex-model who is bored with being the wife of a man who lives in the shadow of his dead brother, a former world champion. Meanwhile Jean-Pierre Sarti, twice world champion and determined to be so again before he retires, finds himself involved with fashion magazine editor Louise Frederickson, who is touring the circuits looking for a story.

Aron appeals in vain for a job with the Italian Manetta-Ferrari team, watches from the side-lines at the next race, eventually lands himself a contract with the Japanese team owned by industrialist Izo Yamura, and goes on to win the next two races. By this time Stoddard is racing again, and although still in great pain from his injuries, he is soon making a challenge for the world championship. After the British Grand Prix, four drivers—Aron, Stoddard, Sarti and the reckless young Italian Nino Barlini—are poised to take the championship. In the deciding race at Monza, Sarti is left at the starting grid, recovers, and seems set to win when he is killed in a crash. His team-mate, Barlini, is called into the pits, and the race is left open. In a tight finish Aron just beats Stoddard, who is now reunited with Pat, and takes the championship.

COMMENT

This is Frankenheimer's first film in colour and in 70mm, his first original screenplay since *The Young Stranger*, and his most expensive production in what is termed "the big picture" category (meaning a 70mm film for reserved seat performances). It is a superlative piece of film-making, visually exciting, and inventive in its use of the wide screen. Above all, it communicates the director's enthusiasm for the subject. Neither is he seduced by the glamour of the track, and throughout the film runs a strong undercurrent of criticism of a somewhat foolish endeavor, of empty lives, hollow victories, and of self-destruction. The dialogue is sharp and often witty, and the acting is strong and realistic—Garner, Montand, Bedford and others doing their own driving. The film reeks of the smell of oil, petrol, and burning tires. The atmosphere of the tracks, in smoggy sun or pouring rain, is finely captured, with Frankenheimer's use of colour alternating between the soft poetic tones of silent motion and the bright colors of frantic on-the-track activity. The use of actual interiors in hotels and homes further enhances the realism of the whole.

From its very beginning, the film promises to portray the realities of life behind-the-track. The manner in which Garner, who has never been better, is fired and the hard realities of being employed by the car manufacturers, offer a new and real insight into racing. The lives of the drivers seem familiar—waiting women, affairs, broken marriages, the stiff upper lip of the Englishman living in the shadow of his dead brother—but, in view of Frankenheimer's statement that all these things are based on actual happenings, we can only assume that this is one more case where what we think of as movie stereotypes are, in fact, real-life happenings and people. The director depicts the romantic relationship between Garner and Jessica Walter with sensitivity and restraint, and this is also true of the love affair between Yves Montand and Eva Marie Saint and its tragic outcome.

The film reunites Frankenheimer with Lionel Lindon, who photographed *The Young Savages*, *All Fall Down* and *The Manchurian Candidate*. Using specially constructed cameras mounted on the racing cars, the director and photographer bring the film to life with close-ups of drivers actually on the track, with zooms into cars, and the riveting helicopter shots of cars gliding silently like toys along the treacherous, winding roads and tracks. The recording of the sound of the engines is superb, and there are two frightening crashes, when one car leaps over the edge of a high track and another plunges into the sea.

Inevitably, one race looks much the same as the other, and monotony is bound to be a danger for a film which extends over the entire season of racing. Frankenheimer avoids this by using special effects in the wide screen with ingenious results, by creating interesting characters, and by making the audience feel involved in the world of motor racing, going from track to track and participating in all the fears, set-backs, disillusionments, and triumphs of the drivers and their teams. By the time the film ends, with Garner walking alone across the deserted, dusty track, the effect is not sentimental but bitter and ironic—the audience feels that it has lived through this season and there is very little that it has not learned about the world of motor car racing.

Eva Marie Saint and Frankenheimer on location in Monaco.

JF "MGM had seen *Seconds* when they agreed to finance *Grand Prix*, as they were pleased with it. They were not too happy about it after it opened, but consoled themselves knowing that it was not their film. I had thought of the idea of *Grand Prix*, while I was in France filming *The Train*. I have always been interested in automobile racing. I used to do it as an amateur—I loved it and still do. I wanted to try and show what racing was really like and every single incident in the film is based on truth. In some reviews, critics said that the story was not as good as the racing sequences. I think that is false criticism. While the racing sequences were done well, the story *was* good and if you look at what has happened in racing since that film was made you will see how true and tragic it was. Lorenzo Bandini was killed at exactly the same place that our accident happened in Monte Carlo. And Bandini, who was a Ferrari driver, helped me stage the accident. Jackie Stewart won the Dutch Grand Prix this year with a broken arm in plaster. Our man won the Dutch Grand Prix with a bad leg. Every incident in the film is based on something that really happened in racing.

"I don't particularly want to say who the actual people were, but I think it's no secret that the American driver played by James Garner was certainly based on Phil Hill. The English driver was certainly based on Stirling Moss. The Yves Montand character was a composite of three drivers—Fangio, Wolfgang von Tripps and Jean Behra, the French driver. Eva Marie Saint's character was based on an actual woman named Louise King who was married to Peter Collins, a Ferrari driver who was killed. She later became involved with Mike Hawthorne, Peter Collins' best friend, the world champion and also a Ferrari driver, and he was killed in a road accident. I can go through each character in that film and tell you who they were in real life, which I don't think you can do in many films.

"Robert Alan Arthur got credit for the screenplay. I had worked with Bob Arthur both as a writer and as a producer in television. He produced two shows that I did, one was called *People Kill People Sometimes*, on *NBC Sunday Showcase*, the other was called *The American* with Lee Marvin (about Ira Hayes who raised the flag at Iwo Jima), another good television show that they messed up in a subsequent film version. He wrote two television shows for me on *Playhouse 90*, *The Sound of Different Drummers* with Sterling Hayden, an original, and another original called *The Thundering Wave*, which we did with James Mason. I liked Bob very much and I thought he would be good with *Grand Prix*, so I sat down with him and worked out the story for the film. Well, Bob's dialogue was not quite what I wanted, so we brought in Bill Hanley, who has since written the script of *The Gypsy Moths*, to re-write the dialogue. It was an almost European way of making a film, the original story was mine, and the screenplay was Arthur's and the dialogue was by Hanley—and really quite good too. Of course, he got no credit from the Writers' Guild, which I think was too bad.

"Physically this was the most difficult film I have ever made. We had tremendous problems as we were working with so many things that were out of our control, such as actual races. What we did was to try to film against the background of the races and to shoot scenes during practice days and during race days, which was the only way we could ever get the crowds.

"I'm not saying it's my best film. But it was certainly one of the most satisfying films I've made because I've had a Walter Mitty idea all my life about what would have happened if I'd really been a Ferrari driver, and to be able to indulge your fantasies with ten-and-a-half million dollars is, I think, marvelous, and that's what I was able to do. I got the idea for the split screen and the multiple images from Francis Thompson and his film *To Be Alive* at the New York World Fair. It impressed me a great deal as did Charles Eames's film for IBM. I spent some time with Eames afterwards discussing split screen because *Grand Prix* was really ideally suited to it. I also got it, strangely enough, from the World Series on television. I watched and saw the technique they used. Naturally, it was not split screen but they would have, say, the batter at the plate, and they would show the pitcher winding up against tremendous tension and throwing the ball as hard as he could to him. The stands would be filled, you could feel the tension in the scene, but they had recorded an interview with either the pitcher or batter beforehand and they played this against the image of the immediate event. In other words, well before the game began, they would record, an interview with Harmon

Killibrew or Roger Maris or whoever it was, then during the game, during an exciting moment, you would hear a very calm voice saying, 'This is a very difficult ball park and to hit a home run here is almost impossible, especially against a right-hand pitcher,' then he would throw the ball at 115 miles an hour or whatever it is, and you would see the other man swing and hit it or he didn't—I thought it was a good technique, and I incorporated it in *Grand Prix*. I introduced the drivers this way with 'an interview' which had taken place before the race. Combining this with the possibilities of the split screen all led to the method and style I used.

"It made it possible for me to cut out the engine noise too at times. Having driven a racing car and driven one fairly well, I can only tell you that when you are driving you have little sensation of speed, and I tried to create that in the French Grand Prix which we shot completely on long lenses—on 1000mm lenses and others like that—where you got an almost slow motion effect. As a matter of fact, most people think that entire thing was done in slow motion, but it was not. It was done on long lenses and this stops the action. Many of my friends are leading race drivers, and they all loved the film. Whenever you use these techniques it has to be for a special effect. I don't think that split screens will ever be used dramatically to tell, for example, a suspense story, which, more than any type of film, requires one scene after the other. I do think it can be done for something like *Grand Prix* when you're dealing with past and present, doing a kind of minuscule examination of an entire season of racing, trying to portray five characters on the screen without enough time to get into each one of them as deeply as you would like to; but I could never see Bergman using it, let's put it that way. It's difficult for the audience to concentrate on more than one picture at a time, and if you are looking at one, you really aren't observing the other. With *Grand Prix*, what we did was to make one panel very easy to look at and then it wasn't necessary to look at the other. You had to look at either the one on the left or the right. A film-maker cannot be telling three plots at the same time because the audience won't follow them. What we were trying to do in *Grand Prix* was to show the other events taking place during a race, but if you wanted to you could keep on looking at the race. You could wander, which I think people do.

"I learned a lot about lenses and cameras. Panavision is a 35mm anamorphic process. Super-Panavision is a 65mm spherical process. Ultra Panavision is an anamorphic 65mm process. Panavision 70 is 35mm Panavision blown to 70mm. But there's a big difference between the anamorphic and the spherical. I filmed *Grand Prix* in spherical for the simple reason there's a greater choice of lenses and he equipment is much lighter. Kubrick did the same thing in *2001*. On the other hand, George Stevens in *The Greatest Story Ever Told* used the Ultra Panavision which was the anamorphic. Now on a Cinerama screen, which can look a very clumsy arrangement at best, the anamorphic, the Ultra Panavision, makes people appear thinner than they ordinarily are. People in the center of the screen are thinner, and on the edges they're about normal. With spherical Panavision, with Super-Panavision, they appear normal in the center of the screen but on the sides they do look a bit distorted. I wanted the distortion in my racing cars anyway.

Incidentally, there was not a single process shot in the entire film. Even the scene in which Garner drove the wife back to town down the mountainside was filmed as he was driving. We actually had the 70mm camera on the car. Bill Frick, who designed the camera mounts, did it. It added so much weight to the car, we had to jack up the suspension on the other side. And Garner was driving very fast. He drove very well. When I look back, I don't know how the hell we ever did that film. We were always shooting, usually when we weren't wanted and usually with everything out of our control. But we just *had* to get those crowds. I started filming early in May and finished it the first week in October. It was in the theatres by December 21, which is amazingly fast. MGM gave me six editors. I would work on the footage race by race, then I worked on the book part of it. At first, the Ferrari company wouldn't give us any co-operation at all, but then Eddie Lewis brought the rough cut of Monte Carlo to Ferrari who looked at it and was amazed. He said we could have everything— he gave us his factory, cars, everything. He loved the idea of the film and was really co-operative. When we asked him how much it would all cost, he said, 'Nothing. Either I give you co-operation or I don't. Nobody can ever buy me.'

"Although I had not originally wanted James

Garner for the role of the American driver—I thought it was a mistake—he was, I think, quite good. A nice change from the inane parts they give him. If I had got the actor I wanted, Steve McQueen, *Grand Prix* would have been an unqualified success. It's quite a successful film, but people do find fault with Garner's performance, and I do too. That was a compromise we had to make to get the film financed. We couldn't get McQueen, and the man I wanted to play the part after McQueen was Robert Redford, who turned it down. Metro always wanted what they called a good $400,000 actor, who was James Garner, because he'd make money for them. All my cards were on the table with Redford, and after he turned the film down I had nowhere to go. Metro were happy with Garner, so I agreed to go with him. It was an error, but we were stuck with it and we tried to make the most of it. I changed the script to go with Yves Montand, but the way the script was originally written, the Garner part was the central part. The whole point is you didn't give a damn about that character and you should have. It's really the only compromise we've ever made, Edward Lewis and I. And we knew we were making it when we did. Hitchcock once told me that his whole life in films has been compromise. I don't think it has been.

"I had seen Garner in *The Americanization of Emily* and I hoped he would be as good as he was in that. For the most part he was. Toshiro Mifune is a painstaking actor too. He learned all his English phonetically, but I had to dub him afterwards. It was an excellent dubbing job, in speech and recording. Most people think it was Mifune. Actually, when the film opened in New York he did speak his first scene. That was his voice. But then I changed it and put in the dubbed voice in the first part too, to make it consistent. Certain scenes between Eva Marie Saint and Yves Montand did I think come off very well.

"The special effects, the accidents, were very difficult to do. I had an excellent special effects man, Milton Rice, who devised a hydrogen cannon which worked on the principle of a pea shooter. The car was attached to a shaft and when the hydrogen exploded the car was literally propelled through the air like a projectile at about 125 to 135 miles an hour and you could aim it where you wanted it to go. All the wrecks were done that way. They were real cars, no models at all. That's why it was good. The same way as the train wrecks in *The Train*—they were real. Looking back, I found directing the racing sequences was a thrilling experience.

"I was also terrified of colour before *Grand Prix*, and I didn't want to make it in colour. The main reason I did was to tell the cars apart, the red car from the green car. Also, a film of this size and budget demanded colour. After I broke the sound barrier with colour, in more ways than one (I didn't mean that to be a pun), I stopped being afraid of it and got to like it. I find it twice as difficult to work in colour as black-and-white because in colour it comes out the way it really is. In black-and-white it only comes out black, white and gray, so that you have to work much more closely with the set designer and decorator and cameraman and costume designer than you used to do in black-and-white. Everyone talks about the artistic reasons for this great change to colour, but there's a commercial reason too, namely television sales being much higher in colour than in black-and-white. I think that's a tragedy and I only hope the situation will correct itself. It has to. We cannot abandon black-and-white films."

THE EXTRAORDINARY SEAMAN 1967

Director John Frankenheimer • *Screenplay* Phillip Rock, Hal Dresner *based on a story by* Phillip Rock • *Photography* (35mm Panavision Eastmancolor, print by Metrocolor) Lionel Lindon • *Art Directors* George W. Davis, Edward Carfagno • *Set Decorators* Henry Grace, Hugh Hunt • *Special Visual Effects* J. McMillan Johnson, Milton Rice • *Editor* Frederic Steinkamp • *Recording Supervisor* Franklin Milton • *Assistant Directors* Enrico Isaaco, Michael Glick • *Music* Maurice Jarre • *Make-Up* William Tuttle • *Hair Styles* Sydney Guilaroff • *Producer* Edward Lewis • *Associate Producer* Hal Dresner • *Co-Producer* John Cushingham • *Unit Production Manager* Russell Saunders • *Production* Edward Lewis and John Frankenheimer (co-production) • *Release* through Metro-Goldwyn-Mayer, December 1967 • *Running Time* 79 minutes • *Location* filmed in Mexico, Baha, and Santa Barbara, California.

CAST

Lt. Commander Finchhaven, R. N. •	David Niven
Jennifer Winslow •	Faye Dunaway
Lt. J/G Morton Krim •	Alan Alda
Cook 3/C W.W.J. Oglethorpe •	Mickey Rooney
Gunner's Mate Orville Toole •	Jack Carter
Ali Shar •	Juano Hernandez
Seaman 1/C Lightfoot Star •	Manu Tupou
Admiral Barnwell •	Barry Kelley
Dyak •	Leonard O. Smith
Dyak •	Richard Guizon
Dyak •	John Cochran
Admiral Shimagoshi •	Jerry Fujikawa

SYNOPSIS

Lt. Commander Finchhaven is a ghost, a 'Flying Englishman,' condemned by his ancestors to life aboard his First World War ship, H.M.S. *Curmudgeon*, until he vindicates his family honor by sinking an enemy cruiser. Finchhaven's proud family have a long history of gallantry and honor, of service to King and Country, dating back to the sixteenth century. But the records, paintings, tributes and titles are a sham—the Finchhavens have blundered their way through history, going from one disaster to another in peace and war, in and out of uniform. The final indignity comes during the First World War when the young Lt. Commander Finchhaven, in command of *Curmudgeon* in the Pacific, and more interested in ladies and liquor than military honors, falls overboard and is drowned at the very moment he could have sunk a German battleship. In fury and exasperation, his grandfather thunders down from the heavens and decrees that Finchhaven will live again.

Ten years later he is restored to life and given a second chance to redeem his blunder. But the war has ended and the luckless commander is condemned to sail the seas in *Curmudgeon* until another war provides him with the opportunity for gallantry. During this period, his ship has fallen on undignified times, being forced to sail around the islands as a lowly passenger vessel, among other degrading functions.

Then comes the Second World War, but without a crew Finchhaven is powerless to act. His ship is chartered by a local businessman, who eventually runs it aground after a party and leaves it to rot on the river bank. Out of the blue, so to speak, appears a small party of American sailors led by a young lieutenant who have lost their ship in a fog. Grandfather thunders down from the clouds to Finchhaven to take advantage of this last opportunity and make good his past mistake. The Americans, cheerful, helpful and mainly ineffectual, come upon a nearby garage-cum-repair shop where they obtain batteries and supplies needed to get the ship moving. Lacking money to pay for them, they agree to give free passage to the young lady in charge, who has been left there by her brother (the man who chartered *Curmudgeon* and abandoned her) to fend for herself in the face of the Japanese advance.

Curmudgeon is floated and Finchhaven sets out for Australia. On the way they encounter hazards and misadventures. Many of these are commented on wittily by the inclusion of excerpts from MGM's *News of the Day* newsreels and other films of the time concerning the progress of the war and the 'pursuit of victory.' The narrative is divided into chapters satirically titled after Churchill: Part I – Grand Alliance'; Part II – 'The Gathering Storm'; Part III – 'Closing the Ring'; Part IV – 'Their Finest Hour'; Part V – 'The Hinge of Fate'; Part VI – 'Triumph and Tragedy'. Vivien Leigh and Robert Taylor, Errol Flynn with Ann Sheridan, and Van Johnson appear in the 'newsreels' along with politicians of the day.

The Americans discover that Finchhaven never leaves the bridge, never sleeps or eats, keeps his uniform immaculate at all times, and drinks Scotch from a bottle that never runs dry. Eventually he tells them his story, and of his mission to sink a Japanese ship. The sailors, deciding that he is mad, hastily leave on a raft made by some island fishermen they had picked up, leaving behind only the young lieutenant and the girl. Finchhaven, coming upon the Japanese battleship, sees his moment of glory and release at hand, and rams it full speed. Unfortunately, it is the ship on which the Allies have accepted Japan's surrender. The war is over, Finchhaven has blundered again. The young American and the girl are saved and poor Finchhaven, with his inexhaustible supply of Scotch, realizes that the pursuit of glory is a foolish thing, and goes back to sail the Pacific again to await the next war. This time, *Curmudgeon* has become a sight-seeing ship for that terrible post-war tribe, the tourists.

COMMENT

After the success of *Grand Prix*, Frankenheimer might easily have been lost to the world of 'big pictures.' It is understandable, seeing that size and cost are all too frequently equated with achievement, that some directors are hesitant to give up this type of film for fear of being thought 'retrogressive,' or unable to keep up with the 'major league.' None of these attitudes bothered Frankenheimer, who, with his customary courage and independence, went on to make a comedy, a simple tale that appealed to him, that he believed would made a trenchant criticism of war simply by spoofing war. The result is a comedy with a difference, an elegant, beautifully made, non-violent movie, which is short, stylish, and to the point, yet one that manages to embrace the two World Wars. With a technique reminiscent of Carl Foreman's use of newsreels in *The Victors*, Frankenheimer makes a number of simple and amusing, telling and satirical, but never cruel, comments about individuals, their beliefs and behavior during wartime. The number of Hollywood service comedies that portray American soldiers, sailors and airmen as crude, vulgar and uneducated, are legion. Frankenheimer's motley crew, with Alan Alda (an extremely likeable young man, here making his first screen appearance), Mickey Rooney, Jack Carter, and Manu Tupou, could easily have been depicted as louts, particularly Rooney. While they are not exactly endearing, they are treated with sympathy and dignity. Faye Dunaway is little more than a passenger, but her presence alone is part of the film's air of quality and common-sense. Again, Frankenheimer does not drag in a 'romance' simply because she is there when none is needed in the narrative. It is indicated that in all probability, a relationship has been established between her and the young lieutenant, yet they might well part and never see each other again.

David Niven, after a succession of dreary roles, here excels himself as the ghost from a long-established British sea-faring family, condemned to sail the sea until he redeems a former blunder by a victory. Bearded and immaculate, Niven plays with mannered skill, witty nonchalance and emotional restraint, and yet with the empty despair of a man who knows that while on the outside he maintains the visage and posture of greatness, honor and tradition, he is, inside, a small, empty man who is aware these qualities are meaningless, misused, and have never brought him happiness.

The film is in its own quiet way the epitaph of an era—the crumbling of a cherished, centuries-old Western military ideal (a myth further destroyed by the *Pueblo* incident which came after) that sought to dignify war with such (old-fashioned) virtues as honor, decency and integrity. The cry, 'Don't give up the ship' is as dead as the age of innocence where war is concerned. *The Extraordinary Seaman* would not seem to have anything in common, at first sight, with *The Manchurian Candidate*, but in the light of contemporary events regarding Vietnam there is a strong thematic relationship reflecting the director's continuing preoccupation with our times. When Frankenheimer, as an 'inside joke,' shows a close-up of the Queen of Diamonds in *Seaman* he was not to know how prophetic this was to be in proving a link between this film and the Korean brainwashing in *The Manchurian Candidate* with what was to happen a few months later to Commander Bucher, in his own way an 'extraordinary seaman,' at the hands of the Korean communists. On a lighter note there is once again, as in many American service films, an interesting depiction of Anglo-American relations—an amusing contrast is made between British service and class formality and American free-and-easy attitudes.

For a first comedy, Frankenheimer has succeeded admirably in being visually as well as verbally funny. The very ship looks funny, the shape of it, the way it wallows along. The characters look comical, and behave in a constantly amusing way. The dialogue is pointed and witty, and cleverly cues the entry of the newsreel inserts. Even the offscreen commentary, written and delivered in newsreel tones and *clichés*, is lightly handled and never crushing in its straight delivery of unintentionally hilarious lines. Frankenheimer has not gone into slapstick, exaggeration, elaborate routines, or any of the accepted comedy forms. He is succinct, subtle, almost incidental at times, with moments of poetry and pathos, and, like all good comedy makers, short in running time. If the human race is tragic in the blunders it commits, the victories it wins, the efforts it makes to get anything done, then tragedy is indeed only another aspect of comedy for its endeavors are comic, and no grim chronicle of death and destruction could possibly be more revealing of the idiocy of human nature than this extraordinary portrait. It shows only too clearly that it is not so much the monsters of the world we need to fear. It is the fools who are many and make us laugh with their actions who ultimately cause us the deepest woes.

JF "*The Extraordinary Seaman*, the film which came after *Grand Prix*, was the only time I've used 35mm Panavision. I hated using it and I'll never use it again. But we did achieve some beautiful color effects and Lionel's shots of Niven on the bridge, the depth of focus and the use of light and shade were excellent. This was the fifth film I had done with Lionel Lindon. We have one scene of the boat being pulled along under the sun hanging low in the sky and reflected in the water. That's another thing—I break down every scene, every script, for the weather conditions I want. I use rain a lot. It's very effective, especially for drama. Too many film-makers fail to make use of the elements, and shoot everything under a hard, blue sky.

"*The Extraordinary Seaman* is an anti-war film. I'm not trying to describe it as a great film, or *the* anti-war film of our time. It's a comedy. I had never made a comedy before, and I think it's very funny. We shot it in Mexico because it was too expensive to shoot in California, and we also had three important factors to keep in mind. Number one was a boat, and it had to be a very special kind of boat. It had to be a boat that looked as though it could have been a British gun boat during the First World War, completely derelict at this point; number two, we had to have a navigable river, by that I mean a river that you could sail down to the sea; and number three, we had to have a jungle. Now we could find the jungle and the river in Hawaii but not a boat because the navy had taken all the boats that drew less than six feet of water and sent them to Vietnam. Finally we found a boat in Vera Cruz, Mexico, and about 150 miles south of Vera Cruz we found the exact location that we wanted. So we shot the film there.

"Although Phillip Rock wrote it as a film, it was originally published as a book. It had a rather interesting premise, but that's all it had. Phillip Rock's screenplay was brought to us by a friend of mine, Jack Cushingham. When I looked at it, I thought that the premise would work but we would have to change all the circumstances leading up to it and after, which we did. A young fellow named Hal Dresner wrote the screenplay. He's done quite a few films. He did the entire script for *Cool Hand Luke* and never received credit for it. And he wrote an original screenplay for Jack Lemmon, called *The April Fools*. He's very bright and was very much against the war in Vietnam (which I was too) and we decided we could really use this premise to make an anti-war statement. I think we did, and it terrified MGM. I believed we could more effectively protest against the Vietnam war by making a film like this than by making a film about the war itself because every evening people got the war in their living room in living color. Vietnam was the first *color* war, which is one of many reasons why so many people were against it. World War Two was a black and white war. Also you had to go to the movie theater to see the newsreels, a completely different thing. I don't think you can make an anti-war film by killing a lot of people and by showing 'how horrible war is' in the last five minutes after you've had two hours of fun with machine guns and bombs and all that kind of thing. I mean, one of the most atrocious war films ever made is *The Green Berets*. I'm against violence like this, I think it is unacceptable in movies and should not be tolerated. People use violence for violence's sake, and I think it's totally wrong that at the end they try and justify it by some pretentious statement.

"In *The Extraordinary Seaman*, no one is killed. I have one scene which is a newsreel of a naval battle between the United States Navy and the Japanese Navy where all you see is a close-up of huge guns going off and we play a Glenn Miller record over it. Then Dorothy Lamour comes on with a bond pitch, you know, 'Buy U.S. Bonds.' It's kind of a far-out film. Unfortunately we had a timing problem on the picture. Our script clerk was Mexican and unbeknown to us their method of timing is different from ours. So when he came and told me we were running long I didn't shoot all the scenes I had planned to use. Back at the studio the cutter doing the first assembly thought we had lost some of our film because we only came up with sixty-five minutes. running time. That was a truly horrible moment. Fortunately we had planned to use newsreels, so we used more of them. With one thing and another we brought the time up to the ninety minutes. we had been contracted to provide.

"Actually, it was the use of newsreel clips which gave us so much trouble with MGM and delayed the release of the film. We had legal problems and MGM insisted that we get clearance from the personalities we'd used, like Mrs. Truman, Loretta Young, and former President Eisenhower. But it was almost impossible to get clearances and I felt it was unnecessary. I took out Eisenhower, but I refused to cut any more newsreel footage. Although newsreels are public domain, if used in the newsreel context, I'm told it's a different matter if you use them to satirize the people involved. And we do satirize them. General Eisenhower, I think, was a very comic character. And every time I've had a chance to do it, I've taken off on Eisenhower, because to me he represents everything that is mediocre and bad about this country. And we make fun of General MacArthur too. And a lady who was never destined in life to be a President's wife, Bess Truman. There is that amusing footage of her trying to launch a ship, and the bottle will not break. We used that when we were trying to get the boat off the sand dunes. To me it's symbolically funny, and the film would not be the same without it. I wanted to include Nixon and his dog in the film, but I couldn't quite find a place to put them. We finally won the battle and the film was released the way we wanted it."

Mickey Rooney with Frankenheimer on location in Mexico.

Frankenheimer and Alan Bates prepare to film in Budapest.

THE FIXER 1968

Director John Frankenheimer • *Screenplay* Dalton Trumbo *based on the novel by* Bernard Malamud • *Photography* (Eastmancolor, print by Metrocolor) Marcel Grignon • *Art Director* Bela Zeichan • *Editor* Henry Berman • *Sound* Tommy Overton • *First Assistant Director* Gyula Kormos • *Music* Maurice Jarre • *Unit Managers* Eugene Nase, Jozsef Pasztor • *Camera Operator* Andre Domage • *Camera Assistant* Ivan Lakatos • *Chief Electrician* Bela Bolykovasky • *Continuity* Luch Lichtig • *Costume Supervisor* Gladys de Segonzac • *Property Man* Frank Agnone • *Choreographer* Agnes Roboz • *Secretary to Director* Nanette Siegert • *Production Secretary* Beatrix Varga • *Producer* Enrico Isaaco • *Production Manager* Dezso Jutasi • *Production* John Frankenheimer-Edward Lewis Productions • *Release* Metro-Goldwyn-Mayer, September 17, 1968 • *Running Time* 130 minutes (original running time was 150 minutes) • *Certificate* PG • *Formats* Available on VHS • *Location* filmed entirely on location in Budapest, Hungary.

CAST

Yakov Bok •	Alan Bates	*Akimytch* •	Roy Sone
Bibikov •	Dirk Bogarde	*Ostrovsky* •	Sydney Tafler
Marfa •	Georgia Brown	*Potseikin* •	Alfie Bass
Lebedev •	Hugh Griffith	*Boatman* •	Michael Balfour
Zinaida •	Elizabeth Hartman	*The Giggler* •	Danny Green
Grubeshov •	Ian Holm	*Negro Page* •	Helen Dowling
Count Odoevsky •	David Warner	*Berezhinsky* •	Peter Jeffrey
Raisl •	Carol White	*Gronfein* •	Stanley Meadows
Proshko •	Thomas Heathcote	*Latke* •	David Opatoshu
Father Anastasy •	Mike Pratt	*Tsar* •	William Hutt
Warden •	Francis De Wolff	*Priest* •	Murray Melvin
Deputy Warden •	George Murcell	*Zhenia* •	Norbert Viszlay
Zhitnyak •	David Lodge		

ON LOCATION

Budapest, January 1968. Darkness has fallen over a sad city. Snow lies on the ground, the air is cold and damp and a thick fog attempts to cloak the battle-scarred buildings and hide their pitted surfaces. The street lighting is feeble, tired trams clank over their rails as they turn at intersections and the few people on the street are hurrying home or going into one of the few cafes still open. In one window, streaming with condensation, a sign barely discernible in imperfect but enthusiastic English, reads: 'LONG HOT DOGS'— perhaps in recognition of MGM's presence here, as this is the first American film to be made behind the Iron Curtain since the outbreak of the Cold War.

Down among the maze of narrow streets twisting away from Lenin Boulevard comes the clatter of horses' hooves on cobblestones. Rounding a curve, we walk into the clutter and paraphernalia of a film, *The Fixer*, in the making. This is a story with enormous appeal and deep significance for John Frankenheimer. It is set in Kiev in the time of the Czar, but, as filming in Russia is not possible, Budapest makes a convincing stand-in. Around the camera are the director, Dalton Trumbo, Alan Bates, Dirk Bogarde, cinematographer Marcel Grignon, the lighting and recording technicians, all bundled up against the night air and an expected snowfall. They are about to film the charge of the mounted police into a group of demonstrators. This continues until dawn breaks, when the mainly Hungarian crew is free to leave and catch a few hours sleep. Frankenheimer, who always keeps up a punishing pace because he knows exactly what he is doing from one scene to the next, will discuss and set up the next sequences to be filmed and then take a few hours sleep himself.

SYNOPSIS

'Suffering I can gladly do without, I hate the taste of it, but if I must suffer, let it be for something'
Yakov Bok, The Fixer

Kiev 1911. Jewish life in Czarist Russia at the turn of the century revolved around the ghetto and the ever-present threat of a pogrom. This existence, restricted to the narrow attitudes and opportunities of the *shtetl* (village), was not for Yakov Bok, an intelligent but uneducated peasant who barely subsisted on scraps of food or a few kopeks earned from an occasional odd job. Yakov, bitter and alone after his wife, Raisl, has run off with another man, decides to leave the *shtetl* for the city of Kiev. Here, scratching out a precarious existence as a Gentile without identification papers, he falls in with an elderly gentleman, Lebedev. Though he fears that Lebedev, a member of the dreaded militant Black Hundreds (a group of fanatics dedicated to the persecution of all Jews) will discover his background, he accepts his offer of a job as a repairman. Zinaida, crippled daughter of Lebedev, fancies herself in love with Yakov and comes daily to watch him work. Yakov makes his first enemy and begins a chain of near-fatal events when he rebuffs her attempt to seduce him. But he performs his job well and Lebedev, who senses his native intelligence, offers the fixer a position as an overseer-accountant at his brick factory. When Yakov, completely dedicated to his job, halts the thievery of the factory's foreman, Proshko, he makes another enemy. Nevertheless, life goes much better than Yakov ever anticipated when he left the *shtetl*. Although lonely and without friends, his new job provides him with money for food and—more important—books. With the exception of young boys in the neighborhood, who plague him with their practical jokes, and the growing enmity of Proshko, he has few worries.

Then one of the boys, Zhenia Golov, is brutally murdered—stabbed to death with little sign of blood. Immediately a cry goes up among the superstitious Russians, certain that the crime was perpetrated by the Jews to acquire Christian blood for their mysterious Passover rituals. Yakov is arrested. While not specifically charged with the crime of ritual murder, he is interrogated by the prosecuting attorney, Grubeshov, as though he were the killer of the child. Grubeshov uses every form of mental and physical punishment to make Yakov confess that not only did he commit the murder, but that he was the tool of an international Jewish political organization dedicated to revolution. He is treated as a convicted murderer, even though no formal charges have been brought against him. Every fact, every suspicion, regardless of how remote and unbelievable, is translated into damaging evidence against him. By now the Government is dedicated to his conviction. Despite the almost total prejudice against him, Yakov finds an ally in Bibikov, a Government lawyer who realizes that the state is insistent upon a conviction of ritual murder because this will be an indictment against the entire Jewish race. Bibikov strongly suspects that Zhenia's mother, Marfa, a woman with criminal connections, murdered her son when he began babbling to his friends about her activities. When it becomes clear that Bibikov's knowledge and honesty are a serious threat to the case of the Government, his 'suicide' is arranged.

Yakov is by now the object of international attention and concern. Efforts are intensified to make him confess, for a confession is necessary to save the face of the Czar who has sanctioned the conspiracy against Yakov. Months become years and Yakov slowly realizes that his innocence is infinitely more precious to him than relief from constant torture and humiliation. Often delirious and at times near death, he will not sacrifice what he believes to be right, and demands the right to a trial. He gets his wish. Yakov Bok, the humble fixer, is at last taken to his trial.

'The figure of a handcuffed man emerges from the van, somewhat off balance, draws himself as tall as he can, steadies his uncertain footage, and summons all that remains in his small reservoir of human dignity he pauses for the briefest instant, calculating the black void beyond the doors of the courthouse.'
'So now it begins.
So let it.'

COMMENT

One of the most difficult subjects to write about and to film today is the story of Yakov Bok, a man who, without thoughts of being a hero of any kind, wanted nothing to do with honor and who learnt that life itself is a commitment. We live in a time when people are so hardened by cynicism, selfishness and a lack of faith in others that the thought of suffering for an ideal is almost laughable. Ours is an age of deals, barters, arrangements and compromises, where beliefs are changed to suit the mood of the moment, where few take a stand unless it is popular. In an age when Bonnie and Clyde are considered to be exciting and colorful, a man like Yakov Bok is seen as an embarrassment, an uncomfortable reminder of unpleasant facts, of responsibilities and decisions. Furthermore, his setting is a drab, loveless life, found at a dreary moment of history, in a faraway place of little interest or excitement to audiences saturated with crime, sex and violence.

Considering this climate, and the fact that audiences at large feel they have heard all there is to know about the persecution of the Jews in past times, the filming of Malamud's *The Assistant* was a courageous act on the part of Frankenheimer,

Lewis and MGM. It is a remarkable work of irresistible moral force—an awesome and meaningful revelation of suffering and injustice, depicted with skill and power, and devoid of sentimentality. It is a forceful, continuing chapter in Frankenheimer's single-minded preoccupation with human drama.

From the quiet, opening title sequence, accompanied by solo violin, in which the camera moves in close-ups over a bench of handyman's tools to the hands of the fixer at work, the quiet taps of his hammer introducing a new line of credits, to the deeply-moving climax when Bok steps out of the prison wagon into the crowd outside the courthouse (a surge of music here, emotionally and dramatically right, yet not overdone), this is a perfectly-realized film. It cannot be faulted in any respect; there is never a false scene, or one that does not come out as it should for reasons of color variance or technical difficulties. Filmed entirely in Budapest on location and at the Mafilm Studios (the first American film to be made in a Communist country), every moment of this picture is evidence of Frankenheimer's great skill and sensitivity as a film-maker, his ever-present sense of

Frankenheimer discusses the script with the writer Dalton Trumbo

cinema. The screenplay by Dalton Trumbo is a brilliant adaptation of the book, faithful to it in all respects, yet a highly imaginative piece of cinema, creating visual images out of pages of dialogue and description. Unlike *Doctor Zhivago*, where the viewer was always aware that Moscow was a set in Madrid, Frankenheimer makes us forget that he is in Budapest, and comes closer than any other Western film-maker to creating an authentic Russian background, mood and atmosphere, and, more importantly, Russian characters. He has followed Lean's practice in using British players to suggest a parallel Russian society, but with less accent and far more success. Alan Bates, in the title role, plays an exhausting part memorably, conveying Bok's stubborn humanity, and capacity for suffering, without making him seem any more than what we know he is: a simple peasant, with a gloomy sense of humor, an unpolitical man who was insignificant in the great scheme of things, gradually changed by suffering into a politically committed representative of his race. At times, Bates looks like a Christ-like figure but Frankenheimer makes no attempt to labor this point and there is no Christ-like ambiguity to the fixer's motives.

Among the impressive, Dostoievskian-looking cast, Dirk Bogarde is also magnificent as the court's defender, a haughty-looking man, wearing an aristocratic mask of melancholy detachment, who is nevertheless concerned about the corruption and degradation around him. The other players, apart from Ian Holm's ruthless, bigoted public prosecutor, have cameo appearances, but all of them are strong, vivid, compelling performances.

David Warner, almost unrecognisable as the Minister of Justice; Hugh Griffith, the drunken anti-Semite; Elizabeth Hartman, his love-starved, crippled daughter; Carol White as the fixer's barren wife; Georgia Brown as the murderously Dickensian-looking mother. Frankenheimer directs them all with great skill, and fashions and moves his narrative along with a deceptively simple yet clever technique.

Events are seen only as Yakov Bok sees them, or as they happen to him. For those who wondered how Frankenheimer would convey the years of imprisonment during which Yakov was painfully ill-used, and came to realise that he had a conscience to follow, the treatment here is masterly, and makes a fascinating comparison with *Birdman of Alcatraz*. The use of color makes us regret less that we have lost a great black-and-white film-maker. Here, in Marcel Grignon's photography, color is used so subtly that most of the time the audience is seldom aware of it, particularly in the pale illumination of the prison scenes, in the cramped quarters of Yakov's dark and agonising isolation. Once again, in his use of camera, settings, actors, music, writing, sound and editing, Frankenheimer maintains the high standards he sets for himself. With his vigorous and imaginative style, his uncanny ability to make film live with raw realism and unvarnished truths, he continues to assert the creative energies, his intelligence and sensibility, which have made him one of the few great directors at work today. *The Fixer* is a film of quiet moral force, a rejection of indifference to humanity, a call to integrity. It could not be more timely with its ironies and tragedy.

JF "*The Fixer* came about during that year when I was out of work. A fellow named Paul Sylbert, who is the twin brother of Dick Sylbert, my art director, whom I'd worked with in television, had been trying to write a script of Malamud's book, *The Assistant*. He and I wanted to do the film and we worked quite a bit on the script. Malamud knew about it, and his agent sent Eddie Lewis and myself the galleys of *The Fixer*, before it was published. We both read it and knew immediately we had to film it, because it really expresses more of what I feel about life than anything I've ever read. We had to ask ourselves, who was the best screenwriter in America? There's really only one and he's Dalton Trumbo. He wanted to do the script, there was no choice to be made, it was all very simple. We started out to try and get the best and we did.

"I feel better about *The Fixer* than anything I've ever done in my life. I think I profited a great deal by the mistakes I made in *Birdman of Alcatraz*, by using a set rather than a location, and by not really working that hard on the script, which I tried to do on *Birdman* but I couldn't, as I told you. I think

Dalton Trumbo's screenplay is a masterpiece. If I had messed up that screenplay, I should have been shot, it is such a beautiful work. Edward Lewis set up the production in Budapest and we made the picture for a very low figure. I think we got the finest English actors possible. It's difficult for me to talk about it. I can only tell you that I was deeply affected by the courage of this man.

"The first thing I do with all my films is to work intensively and for long periods of time with the writer. Then I read all the related material. In the case of *The Fixer,* there was another book published about the actual Mendel Beiles trial called *Blood Accusation* by a man named Samuels. We had to buy this book because we didn't want somebody going ahead and trying to make the Beiles case. We bought it for very little money, but the main thing is, I studied it. I went back through all the newspaper accounts of Beiles and did extensive research on what Russia looked like in that period, methods of transportation, costumes, insides of houses, everything. I try and do as much research as possible on every project, to immerse myself in it, the period and in the milieu. I'm most concerned with the visual aspect of the film, the way it is going to look. And, of course, casting. I'm very methodical about that. In *The Fixer* I interviewed over three thousand actors. I think that casting is extremely important, and I pride myself on the fact that my films are well cast. Of course, deciding who is going to play the leading role is always difficult. You just hope you do well. I listen to what everybody says and then I make up my own mind. We remained faithful to the book even to the ending, because the verdict had nothing to do with the theme of the story. The last line of the book was 'And some even shouted his name,' which is a very positive ending. We don't go into what the verdict was either. We all know it was based on the Mendel Beiles case, and he was found innocent. He died as an insurance salesman in New York in 1934.

"We tried to investigate the fact that the victory the man won was in being brought to trial. It took me about five readings of the book to find it, but Yakov Bok was offered complete amnesty—he was offered a pardon. Malamud, I think, presents it confusingly in the book. He had some obscure official we've never heard of come in and offer him a pardon, and Yakov says 'no.' But we have a char-

acter, whom we got from the book, the Minister of Justice, Count Odoevsky, come in and offer him a pardon. And he says 'no,' but he says it much more eloquently than just plain 'no,' I think that scene is probably the best scene in the film. Our film is about the dignity of the human being, about what a man really is capable of, about the growth of a simple human being who suddenly finds a strength he never knew he had. I think this is a very good story to tell. Bok is not a literate man—he's a peasant, and you see this great strength develop within him. And I think it's very important to show people what they are capable of. That's what the film is all about. Although Bok was a Jew, he could be any man, any time, anywhere.

"I thought the natural colours in *The Fixer* were splendid. The jail sequence was almost black-and-white. We over-exposed all the film, then instructed the lab to develop it normally so that we had an extremely thin negative, giving muted colours. I really wanted to use color like black-and-white. I was very careful with every prop, every costume, every set.

"In *The Fixer* there is hardly a single scene that does not please me. We added the yapping dog to Hugh Griffith's scenes to provide some humor, particularly when he throws the dog out. The Hungarian actress who was playing the maid never came in on cue because she couldn't understand the dialogue. She was supposed to come in and get the dog, and she spoiled about five takes. I said to Hugh, 'You know, it would be a much better idea if you took care of that dog,' and he looked at me and said, 'That's the smartest thing you've ever said!' So I rolled the camera, and you see what happened in the screen. Another small thing—when we saw Yakov working in the room after Griffith had given him work, he was mounting pictures, a painting (in the book he was painting the walls). We changed the painting to show the raising of Lazarus to provide another moment of humor. I wanted him to misplace the hand, to add to the feeling of familiarity between him and the daughter.

"One of the failings of the book is that the readers do not get the impression that concern was being expressed in the outside world. We had to rectify that because the world did care. That was true in the Beiles case, which came out of the research we did. When you read some critics and they talk about the narrative, the screenplay, and what's happened in the screenplay, they sometimes talk as if screenplays adapted from novels exist entirely by themselves, with no reference to the novel. In other words, they criticise a director for something that happens in the story development, completely overlooking that this is the way it was in the novel. I think this is invalid. In the first place if you choose to film a novel it is because you like it, and, in most cases, you want to be faithful to it. I'm not saying that you must film a novel exactly the way it is written. That's impossible. But you must remain true to its form and development if it has any worth. Sometimes, small scenes must be changed in detail, if not in content, such as the menstruation scene in *The Fixer*. In the book it was unconvincing to see blood in the first place. In the film, you cannot stand in a doorway and see blood on the girl's leg—it would be clumsy and distasteful.

"I've never made a film in which the dialogue did not have to be changed in some scenes because it didn't sound or play right. I like to have the writer there, but if he isn't there I'll change it if it doesn't play and if we have the time. Among the best films I've done are *The Manchurian Candidate* and *The Fixer* and the writer was there at all times.

"I have tried to avoid unnecessary violence in my films even though some of them have been about violent events. It hasn't been a conscious avoidance of violence altogether, however. There was a fair amount of violence in *The Manchurian Candidate* when you consider the murders. It was necessary there, after all, it really was. I don't believe in violence for the sake of exploitation. There is some violence in *The Fixer* and it has to be there because you have to show what this man went through in five years of prison, and what his captors did to him. The executives of Metro were worried about this one scene. They said, 'With the climate of today (!) it is dangerous to show this.' I said 'It has to be in there.' This is the scene where the Russians come and beat him for refusing to be converted to Christianity. They were looking for an excuse to beat him, and they do. I feel, and I hope audiences feel this when they see the scene, that it is not a scene of violence just put there for its own sake.

"*The Fixer* is among the few films which I have never compromised on because when something wasn't right we *did* do it again, including going back to Budapest after the shooting was over and re-shooting the ending because we didn't think the ending we had shot was right."

Producer Edward Lewis, Dirk Bogarde, and Frankenheimer in Budapest.

THE GYPSY MOTHS 1969

Director John Frankenheimer • *Screenplay* William Hanley *based on the novel by* James Drought • *Photography* (Eastmancolor, print by Metrocolor) Philip Lathrop • *Art Directors* George W. Davis, Cary Odell • *Set Decorators* Henry Grace, Jack Mills • *Special Visual Effects* J. McMillan Johnson, Carroll L. Shepphird • *Editor* Henry Berman • *Assistant Editor* Alex Beaton • *Sound Engineer* Tom Overton • *Recording Supervisor* Franklin Milton • *Assistant Director* Al Jennings • *Music* Elmer Bernstein • *Aerial Photographer* Carl Boenisch • *Property Master* Frank Agnone • *Wardrobe Designer* Bill Thomas *Make-up* William Tuttle *Hair Styles* Sydney Guilaroff *Producer* Edward Lewis • *Produced by* Hal Landers, Bobby Roberts • *Unit Production Manager* Jim Henderling • *Production* John Frankenheimer-Edward Lewis Productions • *Release* Metro-Goldwyn-Mayer, June 1969 • *Running Time* 110 minutes • *Classification* R • *Availability* VHS • *Soundtrack* available on Cinema Records • *Location* made at MGM Culver City Studios and on location in Wichita, El Dorado and Abilene, Kansas.

CAST

Mike Rettig	•	Burt Lancaster
Elizabeth Brandon	•	Deborah Kerr
Joe Browdy	•	Gene Hackman
Malcolm Webster	•	Scott Wilson
Allen Brandon	•	William Windon
Annie Burke	•	Bonnie Bedelia
Waitress	•	Sheree North
Pilot	•	Carl Reindel
Stand Owner	•	Ford Rainey
Announcer	•	Dick Donforth

ON LOCATION

Wichita, Kansas, Spring 1969. We are in a small city, like most others in the mid-Western states, with its shady, tree-lined residential streets, the equally unlovely blocks of shops, signs, gas stations and automobiles. Why should the visitor be surprised at this? Perhaps because, having spent his life watching films, he still somehow subconsciously expects to find an early mid-Western town, complete with saloon and hitching rail, horses and wagons, Randolph Scott or Joel McCrae.

It is summer and unbearably hot. An air-conditioned car takes us several miles into the countryside to an air-strip used by the owners of small, private planes. The grass is parched, a hot wind stirs the few trees standing by some simple huts built for club members and aviation officials. Normally the place is alive only at weekends but today there is unusual activity, the kind created by a film company at work. They are filming *The Gypsy Moths*. Oddly enough, there is no camera to be seen anywhere, although all the unit men usually to be found behind one are sitting around waiting.

There is a guard at the broken gate, hundreds of parked cars baking in the sun, groups of men who could only be unit workers, a mobile canteen, a large shed where parachutes are prepared, and a rickety-looking, although safely made, open stand; the tiered seats packed with townspeople shading themselves and waiting for something to happen. The children run in all directions and a truck dispensing soft drinks, hot dogs and ice cream is doing good business. Three small old biplanes are parked on the strip and one modern jet helicopter stands nearby.

A collection of electronic equipment, shaded from the sun, and used more for communications than cinematography, emits a succession of voices providing information about wind velocity, flying conditions, other planes in the vicinity and similar miscellaneous news. There is a period of quiet.

A screen door bangs shut and the lull is broken. The unit men, the extras and the people in the stands look to Frankenheimer who has emerged from the main hut wearing a large hat to protect himself from the sun, boots to ward off dust, casual shirt and trousers. In spite of the conventional dress, he remains a figure of authority. (In truth, he is shy and somewhat conscious of his height, to the extent that he stoops slightly.) His

greeting and handshake are cordial enough, but he wastes no time in conversation and passes on accompanied by Philip Lathrop, his cameraman for this picture. He conveys the impression that we might never have met before, or that it was perhaps only yesterday.

He looks no different now than on that first day. His manner is unchanged. It is not that he is unfriendly, but he is reserved and hesitant, at first, to express himself until he knows who he is talking to. He will not suffer fools easily and if confronted by them is quick to show impatience. Even if nothing seems to be happening, his involvement in what he is going to do commands all his thought and energies. He will allow nothing and nobody, except those working with him at that moment on the shot, to come between him and his work. And this sometimes cruel intensity is often com-pounded by the extra pressures and demands brought on by budgetary responsibilities, adverse weather conditions and the numerous other problems that make film-making so difficult.

The reason why we see no camera is because it is mounted in the helicopter, and small, portable cameras are mounted in the helmets of the parachute jumpers. The small planes take off, and then the helicopter. The assistant director tells the crowds by megaphone how they are to act as the jumpers come down in front of the stand.

There is a long wait until the planes have climbed to their planned altitude. The jumpers fall, the cameras are activated, and as the men float down, the colorful stripes of their parachutes bright against the hard blue sky, the helicopter flies in to photograph individual jumpers coming down to land. This is repeated throughout the day, with long periods of waiting as the planes land and take off, as the parachutes are re-folded and the cameras re-loaded. It is during these periods that the director returns to his office in the hut to devise and complete his sequence of shots.

The principal actors are not yet on location. What Frankenheimer is doing now would be second unit work in many other movies, but he avoids using a second unit whenever possible. What he is filming are not just parachute jumps for the sake of action—these scenes are integral parts of a drama, and if he himself has not directed them, they will not sufficiently convey his visual conception of the drama.

At night, in a hotel room turned into a small cinema, the rushes of yesterday's takes are projected. They impart an exhilarating feeling of dropping through the clouds, of floating through space. The colour is excellent, the photography alive and imaginative. There is already a feeling of drama here, although the drama is yet to be filmed. Frankenheimer consults several of his colleagues—his editor, production designer, cameraman, script-girl. He is satisfied to a degree, but worried over changing weather conditions and the amount of aerial photography still to be done. The last thing he wants to do is pack up and return to the studio. It is nine o'clock. The director began his day at seven.

(Note: four days later, John Philip Law, who was to be one of the jumpers, injures his hand so severely he has to leave the film. He is replaced by Scott Wilson.)

SYNOPSIS

From small town to small town, Rettig, Browdy and Malcolm tour the Midwest in a beat-up old car, towing behind them a dusty, canvas-covered trailer holding their equipment and worldly goods. They are sky-divers who live like gypsies, and flirt with death like moths flitting around a flame. Their business is giving 'thrill shows' to please the public. One hot, sultry July 2nd, the Gypsy Moths arrive in Bridgeville, Kansas, a small dreary town with an air-strip nearby ideal for a sky-diving show. They decide to put it on the next day, giving themselves twenty-four hours to promote the event.

Bridgeville is just another stop for Rettig—older, disillusioned and a bit bored with it all. To Browdy, bubbly and gregarious, it is a new playground. For Malcolm, younger and still groping for a meaning to life, the town is something special—the place where he had lived as a boy, before the death of his parents, and the town where his aunt, Elizabeth, and his uncle, Professor Brandon, still live. A telephone call from Malcolm brings an invitation for the three sky-divers to stay at the Brandon home while in Bridgeville, a welcome respite from third-rate motels and greasy-spoon restaurants. At the Brandon home, the sky-divers are treated to lemonade and shown the family album. Rettig, who with strong insight realises there is a coldness between his host and hostess, is attracted to the lovely woman, and accompanies her to a women's club, agreeing to lecture on sky-diving. Actually, his motive is to be near her.

That evening the three sky-divers go out on the town. Browdy picks up a topless dancer in a cheap beer joint. Malcolm wanders his own way, thinking of the attractive young college girl, Annie, who stays with the Brandons. Rettig returns to the Brandon house where Elizabeth is still up and about. He takes her for a walk through the neighbourhood park, unaware that her husband, Professor Brandon, is observing them from his bedroom window. They return to the house and become intimate in the living room. Brandon sees them, but neither speaks nor interferes.

There is a good-sized crowd at the air strip the next day for the sky-diving show, including Brandon and Annie, but Elizabeth has remained at home. It is an exciting event, building up to the climactic and highly dangerous cape stunt which Rettig will perform. Rettig, who has been taking needless risks in the last few weeks, much to the concern of his partners, seems in a world of his own as he crouches in the cabin of the plane, ready to make his death-taunting leap.

As he dives skyward, a look of serenity appears on his face. He is almost smiling as he plummets lower and lower, the earth looming ever nearer. The crowd is aghast. And almost unbelievably it happens. Rettig crashes into the earth, while the crowd screams in horror. Browdy and Malcolm rush to the crumpled figure that was Rettig. Malcolm examines the chute pack. There was no malfunction. Did Rettig take his own life, clinging to the belief that man has the right to choose his own time and means of dying?

The sorrowful group reassembles at the Brandon house that evening. Browdy has made the funeral arrangements, and suggests to Malcolm that they put on another show the next day, the Fourth of July, to raise funeral money. Malcolm agrees, provided it is just one jump, the cape jump that killed Rettig, and that he will do it rather than Browdy. Later that evening, Annie, sensing Malcolm's loneliness and despair, takes him into her bed.

The crowd is almost double in size the next day, anticipating that they may witness another death. This time, Elizabeth, too, is in the audience. Malcolm makes the leap successfully, but is almost trapped fatally by the hypnotising exhilaration of the moment. This, he tells Browdy, was his last jump. If man has the right to choose his way to die,

he reasons, man also has the right to choose his way to live.

Malcolm says farewell to the Brandons, Annie and Browdy. He takes the night train out of Bridgeville, presumably never to return. Browdy says he will drive the old car to Hollywood, hoping for a new career as a stunt-man in motion pictures. The Brandons return to their old way of life, although perhaps they understand each other better.

A script consultation with writer William Hanley.

COMMENT

The Gypsy Moths represents a further development of Frankenheimer's thoughts and feelings about society and the individual, and, once again, he moves in an entirely different direction from his previous films. This outwardly slight story is a study in existential pessimism, a look at characters who deliberately challenge and play with death in the air and at those who live out the drab years of a 'living death' on the ground. Taking the short, terse novel by James Drought as a basis, Frankenheimer and his writer followed the events and created the same characters as those in the book, but, in his realization of the screenplay in visual terms, the director has come closer than any other American film-maker to creating (without imitation) a Bergmanesque world of inner emotions and ambiguous means. It asks once more what we know about the inner struggles, feelings and frustrations of individuals who continually hide their true state of turmoil and self-doubt, who deny their inadequacies for fear of being seen as failures and who will not change their life—even when the choice is theirs to do so. There are five tormented characters in *The Gypsy Moths*, three wandering stuntmen and a man and wife. With little dialogue, scant explanations of background and motivation, and some subtle, delicately expressed symbolism, they come together as human moths in a slow dance with life and death.

The events take place over one weekend. Three travelling performers drive into the small, quiet town of Bridgeville. The youngest of the three, Malcolm, a youth not yet lost to the pointlessness and despair of life, has an aunt living here whom he has not seen for many years. For once they are invited to live in a home. Rettig is the quiet man of the three, silent, but possessing an intelligence that draws Malcolm's aunt to him. She thinks he is contemptuous of small-town people. They discuss their lives he is slowly possessed by her and they make love. Her husband, a supercilious and skeptical university professor, is in turn contemptuous of the three men and their activity. He sees his wife drawn to Rettig, and he knows she has been unfaithful. After leaving Rettig, she goes upstairs and gets into bed with her husband with neither saying a word. Has she done this before? Does he accept it as a punishment for his own lack of love? Is this the result of guilt they both feel over their lives, the fact that Malcolm is her son? Later, when Rettig is dead, she tells her husband that Rettig wanted her to go away with him, to change her life which he thought bored and loveless. 'The thought terrified me,' she says. Did it, or is this a defense for her cowardliness in not making a change in her life? Deborah Kerr and Burt Lancaster are beautifully cast as Rettig and the wife, and it is their sensitive and knowing performances that give these characters their inner significance. It is possible to look at them and know what they think and feel,

and recognize their anxieties and deceits, without explanation through dialogue.

The third jumper, a common and casual man, is portrayed with comic ease and pathetic ignorance by Gene Hackman. He goes to church every Sunday to prostrate himself and ask forgiveness and to be made worthy, and then spends the next week in forced hilarity, drinking and wenching, always talking of changing his way of life. The young man does not know what his future will be or what his present is all about. Scott Wilson, in a performance strikingly different to the one he gave in *In Cold Blood*, is a welcome change from the usual youth portrayals of the time, being intelligent, questioning and, at the time of Rettig's death, very moving. Why did Rettig choose to die? His death was not an accident. Was it to show that he made a choice, and in making it, forced the others to do likewise? The film is filled with questions, many of which cannot be answered.

Frankenheimer's technique, as expected, is superbly appropriate to his theme. He never coarsens his characters, no matter how low they fall in life. Sheree North, cheapened in countless Hollywood films, appears briefly as a topless dancer, yet in those few moments, the director depicts her with sympathy and understanding. These people are not repugnant characters, and Frankenheimer's restraint is everywhere apparent—in the performances, in the love scenes, in the moment of violence, in Rettig's death (vividly described in the book)—and his people are firmly rooted in their day-to-day existence, and not, as so often in Bergman, in places that seem to exist outside our known society. The location shooting around the town and at the air field, convey the very dust and smell of the place, and his interiors are, once again, masterly. The colors are somber inside, with the right touch of brightness outside. As in many of Frankenheimer's films, it rains, and the wind in the trees in the park and the sounds of traffic all contribute to the realism that makes his work so satisfying. His observations throughout, particularly those on the greed of people and their dishonesty, their fascination with death, are never sensationalized in the manner of some directors. Process shots are few, and barely discernable, and his flying sequences are brilliantly filmed and edited, exciting yet filled with that quality of humanity that makes them part of the drama.

J F "*The Gypsy Moths* was brought to us by Hal Landers and Bobby Roberts, who had never produced a film, and who had bought this book, a very obscure novel by a man named James Drought—he was so obscure he even published his own novels. But they had been fascinated by it and when Eddie Lewis and I announced we were producing films they came to us with it. We read it and we liked it. At the same time, Bill Hanley had read it independently of us, and saw an interesting film there. Since Bill had worked with us on *Grand Prix* and wanted to adapt it, we decided to film it. It also fitted in well with what I was trying to say at the time, the matter of choice.

"I think there is great dignity in being alive and I refuse to succumb to the popular belief that we're all victims. *The Gypsy Moths* is a story about choice, about the fact that we can make a choice about what we want to do in this life and that we really have no excuses. And I don't think we do. I don't think anyone really does anything they don't want to do. People tell you all about their problems, people say they have a terrible marriage, or they are in this kind of trouble, and that kind of trouble, and basically it's something that they really want. If somebody has an awful marriage, after all, he can get out of it. If somebody wants to smoke four packages of cigarettes a day and kill himself that way, he can do it. At the same time he can stop. If someone is making parachute jumps out of an airplane he can stop doing that. Our story in *The Gypsy Moths* concerns men who do jump out of airplanes, and everyone in the film makes a choice even though it takes place in only two days. The matter of choice and the study of self-destruction is important to me because I think so many people just go on wilfully destroying themselves. I did as much work on parachute jumping as I possibly could. I did everything short of jumping out of a plane, and it certainly wouldn't have helped me. But I watched the men who did. I talked to them, spent a lot of time with them. If anybody tells me this is a film about parachute jumping I'll be not a little annoyed and highly disappointed.

"The film was finished exactly the way I wanted the final cut to be. It was made under Robert O'Brien with Bob Weitman as head of production. Then management changed at MGM, and Bo Polk, with no film expertise, came in to head the studio. The first thing he did was to announce that he was going to re-cut the film, in other words, he was going to make it an 'M' rating instead of an 'R' rating. He cut out the entire love scene between Burt Lancaster and Deborah Kerr. I was in Afghanistan preparing *The Horsemen* when I heard about this. Theoretically they couldn't do that because my contract with Robert O'Brien said only the president of the company could make changes. It was only because I was a friend of O'Brien's that I put this in the contract because he had said 'It's better for me with the stockholders, you know I never will.' Which I did know. But he was out and I heard they had re-cut my movie. I *really* got furious. I sent a four-page telegram from Afghanistan, but there was very little I could do.

"They opened the film at the Radio City Music Hall with the 'M' rating. They had cut out other scenes. The film was poorly received in New York. It got some brilliant notices, but that was *my* cut those critics saw, you see? It was after they had seen it that the studio cut the film. So I had my lawyers threaten to sue them. They changed it back in general release to the 'R', but by that time it was too late. I liked the film very much the way I cut it, and I hated it the way Metro recut it.

"I think *The Gypsy Moths* was a good film, but it's almost impossible to make a film for a company whose management changes three times during the time you're making the film. There was a four hundred thousand dollar advertising budget allocated for Los Angeles. Then Polk was out and James Aubrey came in and just cut the budget drastically because, as you know, he stated publicly in *Time* magazine, that he hated the film. He made that ridiculous statement—'no-one wanted to go and see a love scene between Burt Lancaster and Deborah Kerr,' which I think got him into a lot of trouble. He would not spend money on the film at all, and when this happens they just don't perform. There's nothing you can do. You can have complete control over the film when you're making it, you can have final cut, you can have everything but you *cannot* control how the studios sell it if they want to cross you."

FRANKENHEIMER ON FILM-MAKING

Malibu Beach, December 1969. *This is how the world of film, his career in film-making, the nature of film and the manner of his devising of it, looked to John Frankenheimer, set against the political turmoil of the time in the United States. This conversation took place at his home in Malibu, where he had begun to make preparations to put* The Horsemen *into production in Afghanistan and* I Walk the Line *in Tennessee.*

"Months before I actually start filming, and after the screenplay is the way I want it, I send for my art director and we spend long periods of time imagining what the picture should look like, what should be the style. I used a lot of Andrew Wyeth's paintings in *Gypsy Moths*. When I say I used them, I mean as an example of what I wanted a scene to look like. Then my cameraman comes on and we discuss everything, thoroughly, and then, if we have locations to find, which we always do, then the art director, the cameraman and myself go off on location surveys and we find the place that really suits our needs.

"When I work, when I'm actually filming, I like to rehearse as much as possible before the film begins. While we're filming I like to have the actors over to the house to read the script, to talk about it. I cannot stand arguments on the set. I like to rehearse in private, I like to get all the problems sorted out before we really go before the cameras. I like to arrive on the set early, an hour before, and sit and think by myself. To get myself into the mood and atmosphere. When I'm setting up a scene I usually have the crew leave with the exception of the cameraman, the production designer, the propman and people like that, and I rehearse the entire scene on the set very thoroughly, then decide how to shoot it after that. Only in exceptional cases do I have a preconceived idea of how to shoot a scene unless it involves a very tricky use of a location or a very technical thing like the 360-degree shot in *The Manchurian Candidate*, which I certainly devised beforehand. It wasn't something I made up in the set because the entire set was constructed for that shot. But, in most cases, when it's just a scene in a room between two people, I try and rehearse it and see the best way to do it. If I'm on location, I know I have to show that I'm on location and not on a back lot, so I know when I'm setting up the scene that I have to set it up in such a way as to be able to make use of the location. After the film is finished, I usually take about four or five days off while we roughly assemble it, then I go in and just start taking it apart and spend a great deal of time on the editing

and recording. When I have finished what I call my cut of the film, I give it to my partner, Edward Lewis, and let him re-cut it if he wants to. Because I like to see what he thinks. He's very good at that. Then I'll look at it and we'll talk about it together and, in most cases, we'll agree on what parts of his were better than mine and vice versa. We'll then go back to a great deal of what I had and incorporate a lot of things that he had done. Then I work with the composer. In fact, I usually have him out during the shooting, talk to him about the kind of music and what we're going to do with it. Sometimes I think of scenes in terms of what we're going to do with them musically. I'm there all the time when the music is being done, and when the dubbing is being done too, as I'm naturally very conscious of sound effects. The fellows in the labs are very close to me, so when we do the answer print I sit with them and make sure it's done my way. Usually I run the first fifty prints that come out of the lab. After that I spot check them and if I find an inferior print I reject it. They know that. So they keep up their standards.

"No matter how much you visualise scenes you want to do in films, much is unpredictable and comes out in ways that are different from the concept, yet I hope this always happens. As I said previously, you cannot write out your methods on paper. Sometimes I would have no idea what I wanted to do with a scene and would go into it and be lucky, and sometimes not so lucky. At least, now I have a firm concept of what a film should look like. And a point of view. That's the main thing a director has to have—a point of view. While the scene may vary as to who sits down and who stands up and who goes where, what the scene is trying to say must be there. And that's important. After all, who sits down and who stands up and who crosses left and who crosses right is relatively unimportant as long as you get the effect of what you want in the scene and I know now what I want out of every scene. That's why I say I think I'm getting better. And I need hardly say how important editors are. I get along with them very well. They do what I tell them to do. And at the very beginning of the film I make sure they're making the same film as I am, because I don't want some 'genius' coming in and recutting all the material I had set out to do in a certain way. I have a very clear idea of how I want to edit my films. An editor I admire is Henry Berman. We work very closely together, we understand each other.

"I am frequently asked if I have an identifiable style. Some people think that if there are no exaggerated camera angles then a film is not particularly imaginative or it has no style. Well, I think that's wrong. I think two classic examples of filmmakers whose camerawork is superb in every film they do and yet does not call attention to itself are Wyler and Zinneman. When you look at *The Best Years of Our Lives* which Wyler did with Gregg Toland, there is that fantastic shot with Fredric March and Harold Russell, where Russell is playing the piano in the foreground and in the background Dana Andrews is making a call to Teresa Wright; March knows he's making it and never looks at him, and your eye goes right to him even though everything is sharp in the foreground. That to my mind is a great shot. And it doesn't call attention to itself unless you analyse it. One thing we got out of our system in television was what we call 'shooting through the wagon wheel.' Every director shooting his first Western decides to take that shot, and I had so many bad scripts in television that I did all that self-conscious nonsense of shooting under furniture, through martini glasses and through eye glasses. I don't believe in it unless the event calls for it. Now, in *Seconds*, the hallucinatory scene did call for a pyrotechnic type of camerawork, which we did. But I don't believe that camerawork for its own sake is artistically valid. I think one of the best examples of bad direction and bad camerawork is the work of Michael Winner, it's just atrocious, this awful kind of whirling camera. It isn't necessary. You become constricted by style if you say, 'I have this style, I cannot discard it, everything must conform to it.' You have set yourself artificial limitations, and the greatest example of it in literature is Hemingway. Hemingway set a style for himself that he would not go beyond. And his work suffers for it. Thomas Mann never did that. he let the style of his book be dictated by the subject matter. If you talk about film directors, Hitchcock has developed a style that people expect, and the subject matter has

suffered. Hitchcock did a film called *I Confess*, one of the best he's ever made, where he abandoned a lot of that style, and in *The Paradine Case*, where he really tried to deal with a serious subject. Then, when he really conforms to his style we get *Psycho*. I think Fred Zinneman has never let style bother him. And yet I would say that probably Fred Zinneman knows more about the camera than any other director around. David Lean has never let style bother him. If you take one of the greatest films ever made, *Brief Encounter*, it's certainly a different style from *Lawrence of Arabia*. Many critics, not directors, say you should be able to tell a director's film, almost as if he's signed it. I don't agree. Once you get trapped in that kind of thinking you've limited yourself, put yourself in a cubbyhole for the rest of your life, the rest of your career.

"Then we have the argument about whether form is more important than content. I can only say this—I don't think any director has ever made a great film with a bad script. But there have been many mediocre directors who have made very good films out of very good scripts. Take the case of Jean Negulesco who made *Johnny Belinda*. It was almost fool-proof. You have a bad scene, you can shoot it from any angle you want and it's not going to be any good. You can have Laurence Olivier playing the man, you can have Geraldine Page playing the woman, whoever you want, and it's not going to be any good.

"Take a film that has been really ignored like *Ride the High Country* [released as *Guns in the Afternoon* in Britain], Peckinpah's film where he had very mediocre actors like Randolph Scott. Yet he had good scenes in that—just imagine what the film would have been like if he'd had fine actors in it. I had a couple of dialogue scenes between Burt Lancaster and Paul Scofield in *The Train* that weren't good because it wasn't on the page. We knew these scenes were not what we wanted but we just didn't have time. It would have helped if we had the writer there.

"I believe in getting the best people you possibly can on your side when you're making a film and that means the best writer, the best actors, the best cameraman, the best propmen, the best sound man, and the best musician. It's difficult enough to make a film when everything is going well for you. When things are going badly it's almost impossible. Even when people all get along and they're all good at what they do, it's very difficult to make a good film. If people are fighting and you have weak people and lightweights on the crew, it's almost impossible. Those people who say film is a director's medium are not entirely right. I'd like to see what they'd do with the cameraman I had on *The Young Stranger* and some of the actors, writers and producers I've seen at work. Of course, films began with the directors having a great deal of power, and now many of us have regained it. But some of the people who say 'Oh well, sure it's a director's medium' completely forget about the contribution that other people make. I've always said that casting is sixty-five per cent of directing and it is. I think the actor's contribution is greatly overlooked in film, yet the actor is all-important because no matter how you photograph the film, you're still photographing the actor. You can photograph him from underneath a table, through garbage cans, through a chair or just take a straight shot of him but it's still the actor. And it's the actor who has to come across, the actor who has to do it. It's very simple for a director to hide behind the viewfinder of the camera and say 'Really, I was marvellous but the actors were no good.' That's unacceptable. After all, the director is responsible if he supposedly has all this power. He casts the actors. It's a lot less work, and the result is a lot better, to have Laurence Olivier in a film than Steve Reeves.

"One of my weaknesses has been the use of music and I think that's because I'm not musically oriented. I'm trying to improve in that area. I like working very much with Maurice Jarre. Before I met Maurice I found myself at sea with the composers. I didn't really know how to talk to them. But they were all good composers and they served me well. I communicated with Maurice and I think four of the best scores I've had have been *The Train, Grand Prix, The Extraordinary Seaman* and *The Fixer,* which Maurice has done. I feel the less music I use, the better. I try to devise my films so that natural sounds, not music, convey my intentions. Where the treatment calls for them, I like to use fades, and mixes, with scenes fading and mixing into another. Everything today is the abrupt, shock cut, or just sharp cutting. Some films call for that. We didn't have any fades or mixes in *The Fixer.* Everything was just straight cuts, but we had some voice dissolves, where I put the sound over another scene. In *All Fall Down* there are beautiful mixes and fades which give it the romantic, lyrical quality I wanted. Or they give you a definite sense of time changing. You don't have to wait until the next cut to realise you're in a different place.

"I believe that sets must be absolutely convincing. I start working on a set design with the production designer immediately, and I shoot everything I can on location. Even shooting outside, you also need an art director because sometimes you want to change the location. On *The Train* we had to knock down a wall in that hotel. Things like that. And I need an art director to help me choose locations. I'm very conscious of making sets authentic. That comes from television training, and, as I said before, research is invaluable. I shoot my locations first so that if we must have studio work, interiors or exteriors, I can match the weather in the studio. And that's very important, because if you shoot the studio first and then you get on a location that doesn't look at all like what's been done in the studio, if the weather is different, then the film suffers. I'm careful about the use of backings when I do use a set. They really have to be good. I try to get away from back projection in cars and so forth.

"Going to the last stage, we are now deeply involved in poster design and advertising campaigns. I've been unhappy with most of them. But I'm very pleased with *The Fixer.* This poster was designed in Budapest by a Hungarian artist. As for advertising campaigns, we can really influence the distributor a great deal if we put forward ideas and keep pushing them. But I leave most of that to Eddie Lewis.

"To a degree, I think the body of my work has given audiences an insight into what I am, what I think about life, people, society. The fight for the individual has been apparent in a lot of my work. I don't know whether there is such a thing as the conspiracy theory of society against the individual, yet society does tend to computerise the individual until it knocks him down. Many of my films are about the individual trying to find himself in society and trying to maintain his individuality in a mechanised world. I do feel that society wants everybody to be exactly the same. It's so much easier. I think the theme of the indomitability of the human spirit, the loneliness of the individual, and the fight against regimentation, are very much in evidence in my work. I have not filmed many stories showing my feelings about love and about relationships between men and women. I hope to change that in the near future. My films have been very masculine partly because it has only been lately in my life, that I think I've really had a good relationship with a woman [Evans Evans], and I understand much more now than I once did. Everything you do reflects your own personal life at one time or another. I think one must have gone through a great deal to really be able to tell someone else about human emotions. I don't think anyone ever sets out in life to 'go through a great deal.' I have been through some unpleasant experiences in my life involving people who I dearly loved being committed to mental institutions and so forth; the lady I was married to tried to kill herself, not, I might add, because she was married to me, but because she had suffered this pattern of grief all her life and I didn't know it. Divorce hurts no matter what one says about it. Everyone goes through their own personal struggle and everyone has problems. If you can use what's happened to you in your work, you're a very fortunate person. Most people can never use what has happened to them. If you work in a bank or in an office, you're not going to become a better accountant or a better typist because you've had awful things happen to you. In fact, it's probably going to affect your work negatively. People in my profession, unless they are defeated by problems, are in a position to channel and analyse what has happened to them, and not let them affect them too much personally. They are able to understand human difficulties more intimately.

"Ours is a profession of communication, and if you've lived in a cocoon all your life, if you've lived in a vacuum, you have nothing to communicate to anyone. So that while I'm not, as I've said before, a masochist, I don't regret anything that's ever happened to me. I think it's all valuable and some day it will be on the screen. I am very happily married to Evans Evans. It is rewarding to be finally happy with someone, to have a relationship that really works. It enables you to devote yourself without conflicts to what you do. Evans, having been an actress (she is no longer active because of

her relationship with me), understands what I'm up against. She has helped me a great deal by just being with me. When it comes to children I think it's difficult for someone in our profession to really be a father and to have a family. It is one long conflict. I have two children by my former marriage and I certainly will never be elected father of the year. You value your limited free time so much that when you have it, you don't want to share it with anyone else except the woman you are with—who in this case, happens to be my wife. It's just terribly difficult because I know what it entails to bring up children properly. You have to give them so much of yourself and so much time, and I don't have it. Maybe in a few years I will, but not right now. I don't want to fail at being a parent again. Once is enough, or twice is enough, because I have two children, and I don't feel I've been nearly as close to them as I would have liked to have been. I blame myself a lot for that. Until I can give them a father's care I don't want any more children.

"I have never felt in anything I have ever done that I've had enough time to do it. Everything I've ever done would be so much better if I could do it again, or if I had one more day or two more days to shoot it. I can look at films I've made and look at scenes which dismay me. I'll give you specific examples: take the film that people say is my best, *The Manchurian Candidate*. There is a scene in there that absolutely appals me, which I would give anything to do over again. It is the scene between Angela Lansbury and James Gregory when she is talking about giving a party for Jocelyn, the other Senator's daughter. She says to Jimmy Gregory, 'Shut up, you just keep going and I'll do the thinking.' This is done in front of the hairdresser and other people when it should have been a very private scene. I think it is a badly directed scene, and every time I see the film I cringe. And I would love to re-shoot that. In *Seven Days in May* in the scene where Kirk Douglas goes to visit Ava Gardner, I now ask myself would she so easily have thrown her letters out? Well, I was partly responsible for that screenplay, we had to think of a way to do it. I must have thought it was right at the time otherwise I wouldn't have shot it. There were some lines in that film which are embarrassing. I wish to hell I could cut them out at this point. Like—'I'll tell you the truth. I'll give you a steak medium rare and the truth which is very rare.' I hate that. In everything, everything could be better if I'd had more time. There's no answer to it, because you can keep on, keep on, keep on and you never reach perfection. When Hitchcock said his life had been compromise, maybe he was right. Because you are always working against a budget, against a schedule, against actors' commitment and things like that. You always discover these faults after the fact. You learn to settle and you have to fight against that. You say 'That's great' and you believe it is at the time. It is only after you look at it again and you say 'Maybe this could have been better.' By that time the actor is usually off doing another film.

"I do feel, going back to what I said earlier, that with two to three hundred people involved in making a film, with the crew and the actors, and having so many people in one enterprise, there has to be a certain degree of compromise. Three hundred people never operate together at 100% peak efficiency. You always think that perhaps if you'd replaced a particular person it would have been better. You are at the mercy of an awful lot of people in film. I think it's important to say that. You must have the smallest details right. My father once told me this about living, 'if the small things in your life are right, the big things will be right.'

"It is difficult to talk about the responsibilities of being a film-maker without sounding pompous. I can only tell you that I've been making films because it's something I've always wanted to do. Something that I have spent my life trying to find out how to do. If I look back on my life and the time I acted in school plays, when I was eight years old and trying to get out of a basic shyness, when I look back on it, though I didn't know it at the time, everything I ever did as a child involved a great deal of fantasy. I've always had that kind of mind. I think I am fortunate in finding my own place in life, which is making films. I trace it back and there was a lot of luck involved. Certainly there had to be a special ability too, otherwise you wouldn't continue the work, but I must say the element of luck was very great. Someone once said, I'd rather be lucky than smart, which is strange but true. I was lucky, but the fact that I was lucky has nothing to do with the fact that film-making is also what I should be doing in my life. I know that. I don't think I would ever have been happy doing anything else. There are lots of things I want to do, but they are all connected with making films. I'm not a smug, self-satisfied person saying 'This is really what I'm doing and it's great and I'm marvellous,' because I don't believe that. I believe that I'm really just beginning to make films. I'm just beginning to find out what it's all about.

"Without being pretentious, I think you have a special responsibility when making films. Above all, you have to be honest *to* yourself, honest *with* yourself, and do the things that you believe should be done. It's hard not to compromise yourself doing a film because, in spite of what most people say, it's not a director's medium. You're terribly dependent on so many people in making a film. This brings me to the question most frequently asked of me and other directors concerning topical issues. Some people say that American film-makers are ignoring the three most important issues in America today—the Vietnam war, racial problems and poverty. They are probably right when they say that. But it's difficult to make a film about something that isn't resolved yet. I am primarily a film director and not a social reformer. We have to start with that. I am not a politician, I don't have the answers to the racial problem. I cannot make a film about the question because I don't know what I want to say. I am certainly against people marching on my house and setting it on fire, for no reason. I'm against being shot at simply because I happen to be white and somebody else happens to be black. I think black people have a very valid point. I don't know what I would do if I were black. I think some day when I know more about it I would like to make a film about this. As far as the question of poverty is concerned I think it has been treated quite often in American films going back even before *The Grapes of Wrath*. I don't think I can make a better film than *The Grapes of Wrath*. I mean, what am I going to do, make a film about Appalachia? About Kentucky? It would be the same thing.

"In a strange way I like to think that through the films I make, if audiences go to see them, I provide people with hope. I'm certain *The Fixer* does. They say to themselves, maybe I can do that, maybe I could be that strong, maybe I could go out and make something of myself. But I don't want to make a film about poverty. Indications of poverty and attitudes toward it can be shown in stories which move against such a background, if only momentarily. You don't necessarily have to comment about the fact that we see some people living in dilapidated houses. The fact that they live like that is evidence that poverty exists. Some day I may make a film about poverty, about what it is. But right now I don't have a subject. I don't think you should deal with it as an abstract idea. You have to feel something very deeply, you have to know what you are talking about. I would not know how to end a film about it, unless it was a completely hopeless film: about a man who stays home all week because he can't get a job, who just gets a welfare cheque, who has no respect from his family, who ends up leaving them. This happens all the time, but I don't know what the answer is yet, and neither do governments. I don't think it's up to the dramatist, the director or the film-maker, or whatever you want to call him, to write the third act. It's up to society to do that.

"Those actors and film-makers who have gone out and supported civil rights have been very courageous men and women. It's said that artists in the public eye are not supposed to hold political beliefs. Well, I think as citizens they are entitled to express themselves about whatever it is they believe in. A very well-known actor, who has gone out and said what he believed in about civil rights, has jeopardised his own career to a certain extent. People who support Wallace and the Rightists certainly won't go and see his films, and I think this takes courage on their part and I admire them a great deal. They are entitled to their political beliefs. As we say in *The Fixer*—Spinoza said it originally—there is no such thing as an unpolitical man. You have to take a stand in life. I was very impressed with and devoted to Senator Robert Kennedy. I believed in what he stood for, he believed in what he stood for and I tried in my own way to do what I could to see him elected. I arranged, supervised and directed all his television film appearances. I dedicated myself to that in full. I believed in his platform. There's no sense in reiterating it, we've all read about it, and know it. He represented hope and pride, respect and harmony for America. His death was an irreplaceable loss.

"We are in terrible trouble in this country. We had an impossible choice last November between Hubert Humphrey and Richard Nixon. I've learned from Senator Kennedy that you have to vote. You have to make your voice felt, but I didn't know what to do personally. I had no interest in either of them. The deaths of the Kennedys were probably the most horrible events to happen in America since Lincoln's assassination; there was no doubt that Robert Kennedy was going to be President. When we played *The Manchurian Candidate*, when we played the game, we asked ourselves who would Mao Tse-tung like to see as President of the United States more than anyone else. And the answer was Richard Nixon, because he could destroy the country. I think most politicians are corrupt individuals. They have to be by the nature of the game. They have to play games, it's like being an agent, in motion pictures. I think agents are corrupt too, trying to appeal to everybody all the time. Robert Kennedy was not like that. I think he represented everything that was good in this country. And there's been a terrible void since he was killed.

"As a film-maker who has worked in Europe there are several observations I would like to make about working in Hollywood. In the beginning I had a difficult crew for my first film but, since then, I have been in a position to pick who I want. Compared with the position of European film-makers, I think Americans probably have more help than any other director in the world. Their technicians are the finest, there is no doubt about it. I think they are spoiled, but they're awfully good and there's a whole generation of new technicians coming along now in California, who are genuinely interested in the film they're doing. When the big studios were in control these people would be carried from film to film and they really didn't care what film they were making, but I find that my crew and those of my friends, like Norman Jewison, Mike Nichols, people like that, certainly do care about what they're doing. There's no group I'd rather work with than a really good American crew. I think that to elevate European film-makers above American film-makers is entirely wrong. I have very definite thoughts about this. I would like to know how many of the American critics who have idealised certain European film-makers speak the language of the film-maker. I'd like to know how much Swedish, French, Russian, Czechoslovakian or Italian, these critics speak. I say this because I do speak fluent French, and passable Italian and

German. The dialogue I understand in these films is appalling. I think Otto Preminger said it best when we were together on a panel with a critic who was a moderator. Someone asked Otto what he thought of his *Saint Joan* and he said, 'I loved it. Perhaps everybody loves their ugliest child best,' but he said, 'if I had shown you the French version of *Saint Joan* with sub-titles you would have praised it too.' I think there is a great deal to be said for that. When the Academy of Motion Picture Arts and Sciences give the best screenplay award of the year to *Divorce, Italian Style*, you really have to throw up your hands and ask what is going on. The simple reason is that they gave it to the sub-title writer. Because screenplay means words. And how many people in the Motion Picture Academy speak Italian? Very few.

"I think it is easier to idealise images on the screen when you don't understand what is being said. It is terribly in and terribly snobbish to do this. I don't go along with this at all. I think there are marvelous films being made in Europe. But there are also marvelous films being made here. Let's take last year: four superbly directed films that come to mind right away, *In Cold Blood, Bonnie and Clyde, In the Heat of the Night* and *The Graduate*. Far surpassing anything that came out of Europe during a similar time. I don't like to make lists because I always forget certain other things and people get offended, but I think this cultism among certain critics has to end. I think the most harmful of all cults has been the Godard cult. I think he is a very talented fellow, but I don't want to comment on his work. Cults grow up and they're fed by certain people, you are never going to stop that. I hope his doesn't destroy him.

"I think the less a critic knows a film-maker the better. I like to remain completely anonymous with critics. My work is there on the screen, it has nothing to do with whether I wear an open shirt, or a tie or wear my hair long or short, whether I'm kind or whether I shout. I can give you an example. I got favorable reviews in *The New York Times* from the television critic until I met him. We got along very well. We became close in about two meetings, but I never got a good review after that because he thought others might think he was playing favorites. The personal relationship between film-maker and critic is a dangerous thing. Critics should judge what is on the screen, but they should also do

their homework and know something about films. A Ph.D. or an M.A. in English literature from some university does not qualify a man to become a film critic. I think being a film critic is a difficult, responsible profession. You must do a tremendous amount of research to be a good film critic, to know life and to be knowledgeable. There are very few. Nobody likes to get a bad review, least of all from a bad critic. There are certain daily papers that you have no respect for at all. Bad reviews hurt. They do. I don't think I know anyone who deliberately wants to get a bad review. You have to have some kind of equilibrium of your own to know the merits of your work. Critics can write terrible reviews of a film like *Seconds*, but I know it was good, and that in ten years from now, people will be writing about that film. While they might have given *The Young Stranger* very good reviews, I know that was a poor film. When you stop to think, it is very strange now, people always talk to me about *The Manchurian Candidate*. It is considered one of 'the' American movies of the past thirty years. Yet when that film came out it did not get very good reviews. Many of the people who panned it have since called it one of the greatest films ever made. I don't go along with that either. I don't think it was one of the greatest films ever made. I think it was a *good* film. I certainly don't believe I've ever made a film that is the 'greatest' ever done. Someday I hope to make a film half as good as *Citizen Kane* or *Umberto D*, or *Wild Strawberries* or *The Grand Illusion*, just to mention a few. I certainly don't think I've done it up to this point. I have a chance with *The Fixer*. I happen to love *The Fixer*. I don't know how other people will react to it, but to me it is my best work. A great deal depends on the interpretation of 'greatness.' I think that Welles is a good example, often used. I think *The Magnificent Ambersons* was beautiful; there were certain things in *Touch of Evil* that were incredible, and in *The Lady from Shanghai*. He's an extremely gifted man. I think De Sica has made many memorable films—*The Bicycle Thief, Shoeshine*; and so have Fellini, Bergman, David Lean, George Stevens, William Wyler, Billy Wilder, John Ford, Fred Zinneman. It's always easy to praise the man who has done the least. Some have only made four or five films and died young, or stopped making films. But the man who keeps on making films tends over the years perhaps to get lost in his own creativity—not himself as a person, but in the eyes of others, in many cases critics. If a film-maker can go on continually making good films this in itself is an achievement.

"I think that talent finds its own level sooner or later. I don't believe there are undiscovered geniuses in the garrets of Greenwich Village, Paris or London—I think that when talented people express themselves, sooner or later what they do is appreciated. I've been treated very well in this profession and critics have been very good to me. However, I think that daily newspapers and some weekly magazines must be more discriminating when they hire a film critic. I'm very tired of critics who say, 'We really don't have to know anything about a film in order to review it. All we have to do is see what's on the screen.' Well, that's ludicrous. If you read the history of criticism and go back to Chesterton and writers like him, it's quite different. And many films as I said deserve to be seen twice. I also believe that the public and the critics should not know the difficulties and problems which arise during the making of a film. The less bad publicity you get during production the better you're likely to come off, because it does influence a critic and it does influence the public. They say it is not going to be any good because the script was changed, the cost is soaring, the stars are quarrelling, it was raining all the time or, in the case of snow, it's artificial snow they're using. Few can tell the difference between real snow and artificial snow, when the latter is properly used. I remember in one of the first television shows I directed, the second or third show on *Danger*, which was right after I started (I'd directed a total of about six shows), we had an interesting experience with snow. The script was based on a *New Yorker* story 'The True One' about a boy who came into the country illegally from Puerto Rico carrying smallpox. He thinks the police are trying to find him because he was in the country illegally. They were really trying to tell him he had smallpox. John Cassavetes, Miriam Colon, and several other good actors made up the cast. The dialogue was unbelievably bad, so we made the boy say everything in Spanish. I re-wrote the script so that the chase took place on the fire escape in some tenement houses outside Studio 61 in New York. We were really outside (remember this is live television—no film) and Johnny Cassavetes had to go up to the top of the roof, and threaten to jump off, which he supposedly did, onto a net under-neath. We had a double for him at one point (we shot on a long shot) just before he jumped, then we threw a dummy off the top of the roof, and, as soon as we got the double, Cassavetes had to run down six flights of steps and get into the net by the time the dummy fell. You're really taking your life in your hands directing like that, but it worked. Since it was a live show it went out at ten o'clock at night New York time. On this night a blizzard started, and we shot this sequence in a driving snow storm. It was fantastic, the way it looked. And what happened? We got about ten calls after the show, from people complaining—when are these guys going to stop using phoney snow? I've always believed there is no other nation in the world making films as provocative, self-critical, as socially revealing, as those of American directors. Russian critics give learned discussions on the 'lack of realism' in certain American films, yet their directors, and many in other countries, could never make films we do in the United States, because of their lack of freedom. In France it is impossible for them to deal with any political issue like *Seven Days in May*. The French told me, 'We could never make that film here.' And it's true of England. They are supposed to be noted for their freedom of speech and people say, look at the English, they're always being very critical of them-selves. They're not really. They make a lot of come-dies in which they say, 'Aren't we quaint and funny characters?' But I haven't seen any British films about their racial problems. Go through all the countries and you won't find one whose films are as self-critical and reveal such an awareness of what life is about as those in America. This is not to say that everything about American movies is satis-factory. The potential of being great is always there. And occasionally one is. Here we are exposed to every American film made. In France the French see every French film made, but in America only the best French films are represented here. The same is true of other countries. It's a very strange thing.

"There are good films being made all over the world, and I think that is a rewarding aspect about being a film director. You say, 'Do you feel a certain responsibility?' and the answer is, 'Yes.' I feel that what we do is going to be universally seen. It's not like doing television which is going to be broadcast only in the United States. I think you have a tremendous responsibility to your country. If you are going to criticise it, then you must criticise it fairly and justly. I want my films to reflect honestly what I feel about America and what goes on here. We are allowed more freedom, we are given more recognition for our work than artists in almost any other country. Fellini, and many others like him, can't get their films financed unless an American company finances it. If Fellini were an American and had the reputation as an American that he has in Italy as an Italian, there would be absolutely no question that he could make any film he chose. Antonioni's movies are now being financed by MGM. Not by Italian companies. British film-makers are financed by Americans. This is also true of Truffaut. He desperately wanted to make an English-language film. The fact that he failed has nothing to do with it. It is too easy to criticise American directors, and it is very difficult to praise them, and I think a lot of them should be highly praised.

"As for the description 'the new Hollywood', well, films are made today where they take place. It's not my wish to get away from 'Hollywood,' because I don't like it. My films seem to take place in places other than California, and I go there to make them. With the number of cinema schools that have come up, with the number of young people trying to get into movie making, I think film companies will realise they have to change certain existing rules for entrance to the unions. Keeping a closed door on unions is not the way to do it. But I don't know what the answer is. I know that a lot of the unions' demands are unfair. I think it is economically impossible to continue using enormous crews in making a film. We should be permitted to cut down when we want to. The unions are going to have to realise this.

"There is talk of a 'renaissance' in American films. There have always been good films made in Hollywood; now they are better as a result of more freedom. People say Hollywood is finished as a film centre, it is all television, and movies will be made where they should be made. It is where they are completed that matters. Most film are completed right here. What worries me is this distressing tendency for big business to take over film companies, companies that may have been big business themselves but at least they were run by film people. Now we have industrialists in control. It's like a car company taking managers into the automobile business who know nothing about automobiles. But this seems to be what the corporate set-up is these days, with conglomerates getting together, run by dull businessmen who have made a lot of money and have always secretly wanted to have something to do with movies. As long as they realise they don't know anything about films, and leave the making of the films to the film-makers, I can accept the situation. The independent film-maker has more control now than he ever had, because the new people who own the companies know absolutely nothing about making a film. They don't even pretend to know, like some did in the old days. As long as the money is available to make films, that's really all I care about. I don't give a damn who finances me as long as it isn't some munitions maker or something like that. All I want is the money to make a film and be left alone. If I'm being financed by a whisky corporation or a computer firm, it doesn't really make that much difference to me, as long as I can make my film. What I cannot do is attend long meetings with these people. When I was much younger I used to say, 'I never want to do this or that.' I've lived to regret it. I want to film all kinds of subjects and stories. I have no plans at the moment to make a Western, or a musical. At the moment I don't think I ever want to do this type of film, yet something may happen, something may come along that might change my mind about it completely. It almost did when I saw *Man of La Mancha*. If Carl Foreman handed me *High Noon*, I'd do it. I don't think that there are any rules. I don't have the same ideas at thirty-nine that I had at twenty-nine. If a subject interests me, I would like to film it.

"Other writers and observers talk about 'a new Hollywood.' So far as I'm concerned, I wish we could lose the term 'Hollywood' and 'Hollywood movies.' Why not—'American films' and 'American film-makers'? Most French films are made in Paris, but they are not called 'Parisian movies.' Although most British studios are just outside London they are not called 'London' or 'Pinewood' films, and Italian movies are not called 'Roman films.' I know Hollywood is an historic name going back to the early days when it was pre-eminent in film-making, when all production took place here. But now, with cinema being so international and with so many movies made

"The town and the countryside were absolutely authentic. You wouldn't get that atmosphere on a studio lot. That's the problem with shooting on a set, there's never a surprise, never! But locations will give them to you. For instance, when we found that courtroom with President Kennedy's picture, and the American flag like that, we rewrote the whole scene. The art director, the cameraman, David Walsh, and I really said that we couldn't have any bright, disturbing color, because this is supposed to be a very depressing place, and any bright color is going to make a picture postcard out of it. So we had to mute everything. We also decided we would have no red in the film whatsoever, except for the final blood on Peck. This presented problems in signs, like Coca-Cola signs, which we had to mute way down, and various things in the town we had to repaint. The boy's 'Uncle Sam' hat we had to mute down. We used a gauze to shoot every shot, except for the very long lens shots, and we did achieve a very muted color effect, I thought. I took the style for that picture from Wyeth. I made everybody look at Wyeth's paintings and composed shots in his style.

"The making of the film was highly technical under uncontrolled conditions, yet we were trying to control the conditions. We were very lucky to have the cloudy weather, mind you. I had an excellent assistant director on that picture named Phil Parslow. He moved that company around. He had all kinds 'ifs'— 'If it's cloudy weather, we go here. If it's sunny, we go here. If it's raining, we go here.' We were able to move by means of radios and things like that very quickly. That whole last scene I shot in one day, and the weather was just *black*. I mean, we didn't have any exposure in some of the stuff and we just shot it, and of course it came out—it's the best stuff in the film.

"I remember the role of Gregory Peck's father was very difficult to cast, and it suddenly occurred to me one night that my wife's grandfather was the prototype I was looking for. At the time he was ninety-two. The idea came to me—why not use him in the movie? His name was J. C. Evans, and everyone used to call him Daddy Beau. In reality, in the movie, he should have been about eighty years old, I remember calling him up and asking him if he wanted to be in my film, and sent him the script. He called Evans back and said 'If they want me to play the part of that older man, then they have to put me in make-up because I don't look nearly that old!' We cast him and he was perfect. He had an element of reality that was just stunning.

"The car became a character in the picture and, of course, with the car chase we put Johnny Cash's 'Flesh and Blood' song over it, because that was a perfect place to do it. I've done car chases around circuits and the last thing I wanted to do was just another car chase. This picture was definitely directed around the songs. When the Sheriff was looking for the still, the song 'On This Side of the Law' was already written but was recorded to fill the time of the sequence. I remember one marvelous scene with Estelle Parsons and Peck when he was leaving and she said 'Oh God, Henry, what am I gonna do, Henry? What are we gonna do?' As expressive an actress as she it, it was just *too much*. I didn't want to see it. The 'Oh God, Henry' on its own did it much better, so that's all she said. She did have a long speech, and I have to say that Estelle is one of the great actresses we have in America, and the speech was *too* moving, *too* hard to take. In fact, it was going to take away from the scenes to follow.

"I tried to make the McCain family much more sympathetic than Jones had done in the book. I really sympathized with them, because they had so little. They said 'We lose this out there. That's all we got; we'll be like niggers, that's it.' In the book the Gregory Peck character might have drowned, he just fades away. Our ending leaves him alone. We arrived at it by a process of elimination. We thought first of all, that he should commit suicide, but that didn't work. It was much better to have him there at the end of the road and know what's going to happen to him—which is, becoming part of this life, one of those faces just looking out seeing nothing. Johnny Cash and I worked on the song I mentioned earlier, called 'Face of Despair'. We wanted to use that as the title for the film, but Columbia was quite opposed to it, they thought it was going to be a completely uncommercial title, but nevertheless, 'Face of Despair' is really what it is about. Much of what you are not told about the character played by Gregory Peck, because he didn't say anything, you learn from the lyrics of the song. Johnny Cash *is* the sound of Nashville, Tennessee. Anyone from that region is somehow or other indebted to Johnny Cash, because he is certainly the best known and, I think, the best country singer. He worked very hard with me on the film and, I think he did some compelling work. We tried to use Johnny as the voice or the conscience, if you will, of the Gregory Peck character. We tried to show through the songs those things that Peck could never really say. I think Gregory Peck did a marvelous job on the film. I loved working with him, he's very professional, an excellent actor.

"Originally, I was not going to direct *I Walk the Line* for our company. I was going to do *The Horsemen*. But Omar Sharif became unavailable because of a prior commitment he had to James Clavell, and I was off for ten months with nothing to do, which didn't bother me, except that I was being paid by Columbia and the studio asked me as a favor if I would direct the film, rather than someone else if there would be the ten-month hiatus. I reluctantly agreed to do it. They had three films invested in Gregory Peck at that time, *The Chairman*, *MacKenna's Gold*, and *Marooned*. They were very high on Greg, and strongly suggested he be in the film—this was before I was going to direct it. So to keep them quite happy, because it was a new relationship, we agreed. They said 'OK, we'll do *The Horsemen* for you, but you do *An Exile* for us.' I honestly didn't want Greg. Both Columbia and Eddie Lewis persuaded me to go and speak with him which I did, and he impressed me a great deal, and said to me how anxious he was to do a picture like this, to change

his 'image'—I quote. Well, I was very, very moved by him as a man, and as an actor; I thought, 'If I were in his position and I had been playing all these safe roles and I found a story I wanted to do, I wonder how I would handle myself with a director who I wanted to work with, and this actor's handing himself over.' Anyway, I agreed to him being on the film. But when the film was completed, and the other two pictures Peck had made with Columbia had opened and had been disasters, they looked at my film, and said, 'Yeah, well we think it's a marvelous film, the only problem is that Gregory Peck is in it,' forgetting completely that it was *they* who insisted that Greg be in the film. We said, 'Well, wait a minute, you were the ones who insisted that Gregory Peck be in the film,' because, quite honestly, my choice for the part was Gene Hackman, but they would not finance the picture with him. Finally somebody spoke up, 'Oh, if only we had an actor like Gene Hackman . . . .' That's when I hit the ceiling. Well, the long and short of it is that they did not sell the picture well at all and it lost money. They blamed this on Greg's being in it, and said I lost four million dollars for them. They also paid Greg three-quarters of a million dollars, which is what he was getting at the time. It's a great lesson to me, because never again will I ever do a favor for anybody. I've done two now, one for Burt Lancaster with *The Train*, which worked out pretty well, and this one for Columbia, in spite of my better judgement."

THE HORSEMEN 1971

Director John Frankenheimer • *Producer* Edward Lewis • *Associate Producer* Enrico Isasco • *Production Company* John Frankenheimer Productions/Edward Lewis Productions Inc., with the co-operation of Afghan Films • *Screenplay* Dalton Trumbo *based on the novel by* Joseph Kessel • *Camera* Claude Renoir (Super Panavision in color) • *Editor* Harold F. Kress • *Sound* Tom Overton • *Costume Designer* Jacqueline Moreau • *Art Director* Pierre Louis Thevenet • *Music* Georges Delerue • *Distribution* Columbia Pictures • *Classification* MPPA GP • *Release* June 1971 • *Running Time* 109 mins (20 minutes were cut from the film before release, completely removing actress Despo's part, although she remains credited) • *Location* made on location in Afghanistan in the summer of 1969, with additional shooting from April to July 1970 at Sevilla Films Studio and locations in Spain • *Soundtrack* on Sunflower Records • *Availability* VHS • *Cost* $M6.

CAST

Uraz •	Omar Sharif	Scribe •	John Ruddock
Tursen •	Jack Palance	Rahim •	Mark Colleano
Zereh •	Leigh Taylor-Young	Quadir •	Sy Temple
Mukhi •	David De	Bacha to Ghulam •	Aziz Resh
Hayatal •	Peter Jeffrey	Gypsy Woman •	Vida St. Romaine
Osman Bey •	Mohammad Shamsi	Chaikana Proprietor •	Leon Lissek
		Aqqual •	Milton Reid
Mizrar •	George Murcell	Salih •	Salman Peer
Merchant of Kandahar •	Eric Pohlmann	Ghulam •	Ricardo Palacios
		Little Governor •	Jesus Tordesilla
Uljan •	Despo	Head Syce •	J. L. Chinchilla
Zam Haiji •	Vernon Dobtcheff	King •	P. De Quevedo
Amjad Khan •	Ishaq Bux	Messenger •	Carlos Casaravilla
District Chief •	Saeed Jaffrey	Nurse •	Barbara Wain

ON LOCATION

Spain, June 1970. We drive out of Madrid for what seems a long distance up into the mountains. We swing around the dusty road, and there, under the white clouds high in the blue sky is a village in Afghanistan, with brightly decorated buses, unfamiliar–looking buildings, and a hundred or more extras dressed up in peasant clothing with beards, dark hair, a variety of hats and ribbons—the tapestry of life re-created from its natural setting so far away. Frankenheimer is some distance from the crowd, talking quietly to Jack Palance and Omar Sharif, giving them instructions, suggestions, ways of moving within the scene. Everything must link up to dovetail with scenes previously shot in Kabul.

This is the director's way with his cast, from film to film. What he actually says to them during these moments of intense discussion, he will never say—these are private moments and are part of the bond he creates with his actors. His Rolls Royce, brought from London, is standing by, and he drives some distance down the road to the tent serving as the canteen. We sit in a far corner to take lunch and talk, although he is continually interrupted by assistant directors and others with questions about the following scenes to be shot. The meal finished, Frankenheimer gets up to leave. "This film has been a struggle, shooting in two different countries, and as you know only too well because I've said it before, it is not just one individual's effort in making a film. You have to surround yourself with the very best people you can—it's so easy to mess it up, it's so easy to compromise and I would say that the most important thing is to really strive not to compromise. But you are put under tremendous pressure, any director would be. There are the pressures of budget, and the pressures of time if you're shooting a picture on location. You've seen the problems we've had with the weather, and now Columbia wants to shorten the film."

We return to the location where the next scene has been set up ready for shooting. Frankenheimer goes over to Claude Renoir and talks animatedly with him for over fifteen minutes. Renoir nods in agreement and the director walks back down the grassy slope and settles into his director's chair.

"I was talking to Claude about the color effect, the concept we are aiming for. It's so much more difficult to do a color film than a black and white film because with black and white, you were really only concerned with shades of gray. With color, you have to work much closer than you ever did with your set designer, costume designer, the photographer. You have to be more selective with the way you shoot certain scenes in terms of light. I find it about three times as difficult and also three times as rewarding, to work in color as in black and white, I really do. It's a really difficult thing to convey color the way you really see it. You have to wait for the light to be just right and then you shoot very quickly. You rehearse, rehearse, rehearse, then you wait till the sky and the clouds are right. With black and white, there was so little difference between shooting in sunlight or when it was overcast. Learning how to control and use color is an entire education it itself."

Working in Kabul

SYNOPSIS

Uraz, son of Tursen, is driven by a fierce ambition to rival his father, now old and crippled, but still renowned as the bravest horseman in Afghanistan. Selecting Uraz to represent his province in the Royal Buzkashi, Tursen promises that if he wins, the magnificent horse he is to ride—fifth generation of its bloodline and trained by Tursen himself—will be his. Though the horse is indeed magnificent, Uraz falls and breaks his leg.

Ashamed and angry, he escapes from hospital, tears the cast from his leg, and sets off with the horse, which he claims (since it won, though with another rider from the team). Reluctantly attended by the groom, Mukhi, who fears for the horse and agrees to go only when Uraz promises him the horse in the event of his death, Uraz deliberately picks the most hazardous road home. On the way, feverish from his infected leg, he is nursed devotedly by a nomad girl, Zereh, but on recovering,

Uraz spurns her as untouchable and gives her to Mukhi.

As they continue through storm and avalanche, the vengeful Zereh eventually persuades Mukhi to try to kill his master and claim the horse. Uraz ropes the pair and brings them home as prisoners—neither of them aware that one night Uraz had his gangrenous leg amputated by a peasant. Tursen then humiliates Uraz by making him pronounce Mukhi innocent since temptation was unfairly placed in his way, and awards the horse to the groom.

However, Tursen relents sufficiently to lend Uraz the money to buy the horse back, and after practicing secretly, Uraz gives a dazzling display of acrobatic horsemanship at a banquet attended by his father. He then removes his boot to reveal that he has only one leg, and sets out on the road, 'on a journey from nowhere to nowhere.'

COMMENT

Unlike many directors of note Frankenheimer never fails to reveal in the opening shots the background against which his story is set. From the first sequences with their awe-inspiring vistas of the vast ranges of Afghanistan's mountains, *The Horsemen* is a marvelously impressive film surging with excitement, conflict and passion. A continuously moving, sweeping Panavision panorama in muted colors, this beginning is compellingly silent as befits the empty landscape. A lone horseman on the edge of a sheer cliff sounds a long-stemmed horn across the valley. This atmospheric prelude then erupts into movement with the audience being drawn into an astonishing display of horsemanship known as the Buzkashi in which the fierce riders, polo fashion, fight for the possession of a dead goat. The pace is fast, the struggle furious, and the skill of the riders almost unbelievable. There is no music, only the thunder of hooves, the clash of bodies, and the sound of whips and shouts as the riders slash at each other in the pursuit of victory. The remarkable camera movement, the editing of sound and image, are cinema at its most enthralling taking us into the very heart of the sport from a point of view no spectator could ever hope to have.

With his customary eye for detail, Franken-heimer brings to life the backstreets of Kabul. The camera moves fluidly between craftsmen and tradesmen, the restless mobs betting on fighting animals, from rams to camels, birds even, and musicians and dancers. There are meticulously detailed and vivid scenes of the crowd following its daily patterns of work and pleasure. The characters of Omar Sharif, Jack Palance, Leigh Taylor-Young and David De emerge from this pulsating background with complete naturalness, Sharif in particular giving an entirely convincing performance as the somewhat vain, arrogant son who is jealous of his father.

As the story unfolds, in a perceptive screenplay by Dalton Trumbo based on Joseph Kessel's novel, the superstitions, traditions, rituals, religious beliefs and family values of this alien culture are cleverly brought out in the relationships between the various characters. All are marked by outwardly simple yet complex beliefs and behaviors. Uraz's long and painful journey with a broken leg over difficult mountain trails in the snow and freezing cold is a compelling part of the film—as the audience, we believe in his determination to survive the elements and emerge strong and valiant; although we also know that his belief in faith rather than in the science of medicine to restore his leg is not going to be sustained. Throughout, scenes of great natural beauty composed with imagination and feeling contrast with the life of man and beast. Movement and emotion are everywhere apparent and scenes—such as the cut to the horse neighing as the axe falls on Uraz's diseased leg—are dramatically effective. The second race, the Royal Buzkashi, is not a matter of repeating the first match; it looks different and is filmed as skillfully as the opening game, this time with Georges Delerue's apt and always appropriate score adding a further dimen-

sion to the drama. Although Uraz wins he feels that he has lost; he bids his father goodbye to start on another journey to discover perhaps a new sense of completeness, this one spiritual rather than physical. The ending is sad yet strangely beautiful as the silhouetted figures begin their journey. The association of many diverse elements in this always honest and realistic character study set within a harsh and physical milieu permitted Frankenheimer to bring a concentration of visual and lyrical poetry to bear on an extremely difficult undertaking.

JF "I think *The Horsemen* has tremendous meaning for today, because it's a story of a man trying to find out who he is. The fact that it takes place in Afghanistan is only interesting from an audience standpoint. This movie is about a man trying to find his own identity, the same theme as *All Fall Down*, as *Midnight Cowboy*. It's a quest also, about a man taking a voyage to find it's like *Easy Rider*, only instead of riding a motorcycle, he's on horseback. And I think it's a very modern film because it's about finding one's identity. That's why I made it.

"Was this an accurate picture of what life is like in Afghanistan? Yes! Life is like this in Afghanistan, exactly the way I depicted it. I spent a lot of time there, I saw a lot there, but this was a story that I loved reading because I identified completely with that character who was trying to search for what life for him meant. Walter Cronkie once said to me when I was working for CBS, 'The day will come when you're going to leave the company that gave you your break, and go on to other places, other projects. You might come back and they'll pay you three times as much.' Well, of course, it was true. I left CBS, went to NBC, did four shows and came back and CBS tripled my salary. In other words, what has to happen to every individual in life, is that somewhere along the line the umbilical cord must be cut. In this film the son realizes he cannot live in the same place where his father lives. It's that simple. The conflict between them will never end. I think most men find this out sooner or later. I found this out in my own life with my father. It still affects me, and you can see it in my films. I'm

sure you did. You have to break away, and this is what he does at the end of the film. He's man enough to prove himself, but for what? He finds that out.

"I'm glad I made this film after *The Fixer*. With *The Fixer*, in retrospect, what I think happened was that I played the violence too much. I think I made it almost *impossible* for an audience to sit there. I deliberately played the pain. With *The Horsemen*, I had a choice. The man's got a broken leg that must be amputated. You could show insert after insert of his leg, with the blood seeping out of it and the pus gathering, and drive the audience right out of the theatre. Or you could simply play the value of the scene, because you know he's got a broken leg. If I hadn't made *The Fixer*, I would have been inclined to show the insert of the leg being chopped off. I learned a lesson from that. I covered myself—I took a shot with the leg exposed. At the same time I covered the scene in a different way, so that if I decided that it was too much for an audience, I could always cut it out. It's a rare thing for me because my threshold for pain is very high—I can suffer a lot of pain, I can look at gruesome sights, and it doesn't affect me. I've been in hospitals, watched an operation on a woman who had cancer. Her insides were out on the table, and the surgeon was putting them back saying 'Well, she's got about six weeks, and that's it.' It saddens me, but the sight of this didn't turn my stomach. As a filmmaker, I have to be very careful how I depict painful and violent scenes. I have to watch myself, because I know this about myself. I know also that I'm capable of tremendous violence, which is why

I'm not a violent man. The effect of the violence in *The Fixer* was almost intolerable but more from the fact that it took place under very real circumstances. Unfortunately, with *The Fixer* it frequently looked so much like a documentary that the violence affected audiences far more than the gratuitous violence of the average television show showing heads being blown off and all sorts of brutality.

"I'm also glad I did *The Horsemen* after *Grand Prix*, because if I had shot *Grand Prix* in a similar way to this film, I would have saved an awful lot of time and money. What I would have done to change it would have been to shoot the races the year before, cut the races together, know exactly where I needed the close-ups of the actors and go out and shoot them. And this is what we did with *The Horsemen*. We shot Buzkashi the year before in Kabul, so that I knew exactly where I needed the close-ups of Omar Sharif and Jack Palance and the other characters, and I didn't have to spend *months* out on the field, having Sharif going to the right and left and back again, with a blue guy, a red guy, or a white guy next to him. During *Grand Prix*, I had Yves Montand and the other drivers doing lap after lap after lap of every circuit with different combinations of cars behind them. One camera was mounted on a race car. I had a crew of two hundred people standing around and I had to get them out of the shot, as the car came by. It would have been ludicrous to have all these people on salary there. At least in *Grand Prix* they were on the road, and we knew when they were going to be passing by. With the tribesmen on those goddamned horses, you didn't know where the hell they were going. You have riders going this way, that way, every way, and it would have been impossible to shoot the way we did *Grand Prix*. We had cameras all over the field. It was a lucky break that we did it this way, because if we'd had to do it the other way I would have had to close down the picture, cut the races in and bring Sharif back. As it was, he was only available for a week-and-a-half in Kabul, and that was the time I needed him in Afghanistan.

"In the meantime, I went over there to shoot the second unit, because nobody could shoot the second unit like I could, *and* I'd be pleased with my own work and not with anybody else's work. Also, the studio would not have given a second unit director the money they would have given me to shoot a second unit. So, when I went over there to shoot the second unit, they gave me everything I wanted. I've always hated second units—I've always managed to cut out every shot a second unit ever made in a film of mine, and I would go out on Sundays and re-shoot it myself. So I just decided to shoot the whole damned second unit myself.

"We were in Afghanistan—when I'm talking about 'we', that's my wife and myself, and a whole French camera unit—for about three and a half months. Jimmy Wong Howe was supposed to do that also, but again his illness prevented him from working with us. I went over there without a chief cameraman. I just took three operators whom I knew very well from having worked in France. We had three camera crews and we shot these endless Buzkashi games and a lot of landscapes. We shot everything that we needed in Afghanistan and the rest of it was shot in Spain where Claude Renoir joined us as our cinematographer—like his father, he is a true artist. This film was based on a novel by Kessel and the screenplay was by Dalton Trumbo. Joseph Kessel, to the French, is what Ernest Hemingway is to the Americans. This was a very important novel in France and the film won the French *Prix de Triomphe*—their equivalent of an Academy Award. In both *I Walk the Line* and *The Horsemen*, we followed the storyline of the novels quite carefully.

"A terrible thing happened during the making of *The Horsemen*. We set out to make a roadshow picture to run three hours. Midway through the shooting in Spain the Columbia management changed again. They came over to see me and I was told they no longer wanted to make a road-show picture, that they now wanted to make a movie that ran the normal length of time—two hours and ten minutes, no more. Well, I was shocked.

"I remember I was in the middle of filming a very intricate sequence of a caravan of trucks, and those Afghan trucks were painted in a special way with beautiful colours. We had painted Spanish trucks, and the costumes were those we had brought back from Afghanistan. I think we had about fifteen hundred extras out that day, and they told me this during lunch, saying to me 'Does this change anything for you, does it change too much for you?' I said, 'Well, the first thing that happens is that we could send everybody home today, because obviously if you want a two-hour-and-ten-minute movie, what we are filming right now won't be in the movie. This is a big scene of tremendous scope, we can give you a passage of time and you are not going to have time for it. So, we'll just cancel it.' It was a horrible experience, because we had to re-edit the film and the script. It was a terrible blow, it really was. It altered everything about the movie, the look of it, the balance of the narrative. What we had planned, what we visualized, we weren't allowed to do. As it is, I think *The Horsemen* came out very well in spite of all the obstacles. Afghanistan was an extraordinary place and I don't think anyone will see it like that again. We were lucky to be there. You could see why nobody could ever conquer such a fiercely proud people, and I believe we conveyed this in the film.

"Fortunately, the actors were a pleasure to work with. Leigh Taylor Young was a lovely woman, Jack Palance was marvelous—I had worked with him often in television—and Omar Sharif was a courteous and brilliant actor. When you look at this movie, you have to be aware that most of the actors are speaking English with their own or assumed dialect as opposed to them simply being Americans playing foreign characters. A good example of this was Bergman's *Sonata*. I saw it in Swedish, with English sub-titles, with Liv Ullman and Ingrid Bergman. I was deeply impressed by it. Later it was on the Z Channel, our movie channel on TV, and it was dubbed into English by these two actresses, both of whom were bilingual, and the English text was really representative of what was originally said and it still sounded very Swedish. I think *The Horsemen* sounds authentic in the same way.

"Sadly however, this film marked the end of my association with Edward Lewis—we didn't know at the time, but it did. We had planned to make many more movies together. I still feel that it was perhaps the definitive relationship of my career.

The Horsemen played an important part in the continued success of John Frankenheimer's career. It marked a crucial turning point for him, bringing about a time a great change in relationships and working conditions, and a coming to terms with a new reality. Uncertainty and anxiety weighed heavily upon him.

"We are having this conversation just before *The Horsemen* opens commercially, and I must tell you that the success of *The Horsemen* is terribly important to me, perhaps more than any film has ever been. For the simple reason that the last two films, *The Gypsy Moths* and *I Walk the Line*, have not worked—commercially or critically, for the most part. And now, the damned *Extraordinary Seaman*, which Metro never released properly, is being thrown back at me. Aside from *The Fixer* it's been a disappointing period. I badly need *The Horsemen* to be a success. It affects our future more than any other film we've ever done—when I say 'we,' I'm talking about Edward Lewis and myself. Yet, in France, both *The Gypsy Moths* and *I Walk the Line* are considered two of the finest American films made in the last ten years. The reviews have been extraordinary. I can't believe that *I Walk the Line* could have been stepped upon by the American critics the way it was. I'm bitter about it, if you want to know the truth. I don't understand it, because there is no doubt about the fact that a film like *I Walk the Line* needed critical acclaim to succeed. It's not a standard formula film. The point is that the distributing companies, if they don't believe in a film, will not spend the money on advertising, they will not book them into the good houses, and so forth. They just lose confidence in the film and feel it's almost cheaper just to dump it than to spend money on bringing it before the public. I don't like the advertising for *The Horsemen*. I don't like those pictures—cheap stuff done in Italy—and I've got the good material coming from New York. Did you know that on some of the color pictures we had, the title was *The Horseman*, by the way, and not *The Horsemen*, which didn't surprise me. I will say that Columbia has got behind *The Horsemen*. Well, of course, they have to, they have told everybody it cost four and a half million dollars. We might as well tell them the truth—that it cost six million dollars! With that much money invested in it, they've got to spend money to try and make it work! Of course, that makes it harder for us to break even. Put it this way,

if we do *Grand Prix* business we're at home. This was the last film to pay Omar Sharif his exorbitant salary—they gave him seven hundred thousand dollars, plus twenty per cent overhead, so there's a million right there. So now we're down to five million dollars. The rest of it was overheads, travelling, and the fact that it was a *very* difficult film to make. I mean, after all, we had to go to Afghanistan, where no film industry exists.

"However, considering what happened since our original screenplay, it's better than I ever hoped for. There were many sequences in the script that were expository from a character called the 'wise man'—the old wise man who spent page after page explaining to us what this movie is about, explaining to us that the father hated the son and the son was trying to help him which we shot with Alan Webb. But they are not in the film, because we don't need them. Alan Webb is a superb actor, and it certainly had nothing to do with Alan's performance, but we just didn't need the scenes. Palance is very good in this film, I think, and it's the best thing Omar's ever done. Jack Palance was *not* my first choice for the part. I wanted Laurence Olivier for it. Paramount wouldn't let me have him for *Seconds*, but Columbia didn't object. But he was not available because of his recent operation, and he was afraid he would have to be involved in physical action which he didn't want to do, and also he could not give us the time we required. Jack couldn't ride horses as well as the others, and, if the truth were known, there isn't one shot of Jack Palance on a horse in this picture. All the shots of Palance on a horse I had to cut out, because he didn't ride as well as others. When he was riding the horse to jump we put him on a sawhorse on the camera car and he's going up and down. Olivier could have done the part without ever being on a horse. I'd worked with Jack in television, as you know, and I recalled his great kind of mongol-looking face, his strength, his ability with languages—Jack speaks six languages, all of them well—and his devotion to a role. I sent the script to him, and luckily he liked it. He was ready to take a chance on playing a much older part. I think the makeup job on Jack is really quite extraordinary. He came over there and he *really* worked. He and Omar worked well together. I was afraid they would not because I had heard a strong rumor that they did not get along because of a squabble during the filming of that disaster they did called *Che!* So I went to Omar first and I said, 'Listen Omar, Jack Palance is playing the part. Does that bother you?' He said, 'No, I like Jack very much, I don't think Jack likes me.' I went to Jack and said, 'Is there a problem with Omar?' He said, 'Not at all.' We discussed the matter, and it turns out that there had been a complete misunderstanding on *Che!* and they were both very thankful for a chance to straighten it out.

"I have to put Sharif into my 'favorite actor' category, along with Alan Bates and Gene Hackman. I'd love to find a screenplay to accommodate those three actors. Sharif is a professional, he's good, he works hard, he's an inspiration to the rest of the cast. All the things I have said about Alan Bates, I would say about Sharif. He was dedicated to this film—he did all kinds of difficult things on his horse, but he's not out to prove to the world that this is something he can do. He loves to play bridge, he likes his son, he likes his life in Paris. He is not by nature an athlete. He just really went ahead and did it. He rides well, but he rode above and beyond what we thought he could do. That stunt, let me tell you, being on the side of the horse and coming up over it, is one of the most difficult things you can do, because you're pulling yourself up by your leg and one arm, and you're galloping along at full speed. You can't see where the horse is going. He did it. If people don't accept one of my films it's because they don't like my work. The actors did what I wanted them to do—and more.

"Now, listen carefully to the score. I had heard quite a bit of Georges Delerue's music, I like him very much and I think we worked well together. He understood the film very well, right from the very beginning. There was no need to explain to him what the story was about. I have worked with Maurice Jarre a great deal, and I now find that I'm turning toward Georges Delerue. I certainly want to work with him again. I like Maurice Jarre very much but he lives in California now and Georges is in Paris, so I see him quite a bit socially. One of the pitfalls we had to avoid in this film was that we had to continually work to keep it from being a western. The music in this respect was really important. I mean, we couldn't just give it the old western 'they went thataway' sound. I think Georges succeeded well on this.

"One must also mention Claude Renoir's work. James Wong Howe started the movie—he worked for a week but there's nothing of Howe left in the film, it's Renoir. And, as I've said, I did all the Afghanistan stuff myself. I just did not have a director of photography—I didn't need one, because I can read a light meter as well as anybody else—and I'm a very good photographer, but I needed good operators, and that's what I had out there. I had an operator who was functioning as a lighting cameraman when we needed lights. It was fantastically difficult shooting the races because I was scared to death of horses. You know I love cars, but I don't like horses and I will never intentionally get on another one as long as I live.

"This picture appealed to me for a lot of reasons. I loved the theme, which is again the search for identity and the father-son relationship, which was the theme of my very first picture, *The Young Stranger*. My own life has been very close to it. My struggle in life was breaking away from the influence of my father. It's a subject which is very personal to me. That's why it's done with such a *lack* of sentimentality. That last scene when they look at each other and *don't* touch—I like that scene. You might expect them to throw their arms around each other. There's a moment when they each *want* to, but neither one will because they're both very proud men.

"Outside of France almost everybody has, or at least they say they have, read the book. It is to the French what *For Whom the Bell Tolls* is to us. But here, *nobody* seems to have read the book though the translation was pretty good. Trumbo and I tried to figure out how to write it for an audience unfamiliar with it. Trumbo came up with about five versions of the book's narration, one of which was six pages long. What we did was put a very short narration over it, and I think that's all the audience has to know about what the object of the game is. I think some people don't believe the savagery of that game, but I have been in it and it's much wilder than that—I've seen them ride over fallen riders.

"The book opens with a procession of trucks going over the Hindu-Kush pass through this great vista of mountains. I had to use the opening titles of this film to show the audience what the country was like—quickly and dramatically. So I did the sweeping helicopter shot to get into the country right away—to show its beauty, its inaccessibility, to show exactly what we're dealing with here. Now at the beginning of this film, audiences don't know this country is Afghanistan because the name doesn't arise until later. Immediately after the film opens, all the reviews will tell them it's Afghanistan."

INTERVIEW WITH FRANKENHEIMER, ONTARIO 1971

John Frankenheimer at the Ontario Film Theatre, Toronto, 10 June 1971, on the occasion of the Canadian première of The Horsemen.

Gerald Pratley The first question is about the opening scenes of the film, with the camera going over the pass into Afghanistan—how were these scenes made?

John Frankenheimer We did these scenes with a helicopter. We brought the helicopter with us to Afghanistan. We flew everything in because there was absolutely no equipment there except for one Arriflex. We flew an Alouette 3 in and assembled it there. We flew over those mountains and photographed all that stuff from the helicopter and with the Tyler helicopter mount, which we brought in also. That was all done in Afghanistan with the specific purpose of using it for the titles.

Question How many Afghan actors were used and, secondly, how did Mr. Frankenheimer shoot the scenes with Omar Sharif riding with only half his leg? [*audience laughs*]

JF To answer your first question, there were a lot of Afghans in the film. You saw them in the Buzkashi sequences, there were at least eighty thousand of them in it. The way we did that was really very simple. The real Buzkashi is played in October but we got to Kabul in May. We said to our Afghan liaison people, 'We're going to need a crowd out there.' They said, 'Well, how many do you need?' We told them maybe five or six thousand, and they said we would never get them. But we had an idea. I work with the same technicians most of the time, and when we did *Grand Prix* and we needed a crowd at Monza, in Italy, we had a lottery where we gave away two cars for several days—it was a lot cheaper than paying forty thousand extras. We had forty thousand Italians out there, just roaring away for whoever we wanted them to roar for. It was terrific. So we thought we might pull off the same thing in Afghanistan. And they said, 'Well, it *can't* work; it just *can't* work.' This was before we started shooting, and we said, 'Well, we're going to try. What we want you to do is advertise over the radio that we're giving away a Volkswagen the first day, and then on each succeeding day prizes like motorcycles and so forth.' They said, 'Well, we'll advertise it, but you won't get anybody.' Because of the heat, we had to start shooting around about six o'clock in the morning, which meant we had to leave for the location about four-thirty. My driver

spoke about three or four words of English, and that was it—and he couldn't drive either. Anyway, he came running into the house at four-thirty, and he said '*Everybody!*' I said, 'What do you mean, 'Everybody'?' Well, we arrived and when I tried to get to the field, I couldn't get there. The dirt road was just *packed* with people. The Afghans had five thousand tickets that they were going to give out, and there was a hundred thousand people there. It was a riot—I mean, it really was a riot. We had to evacuate the whole crew out of there, until the mess was sorted out. It wasn't until the afternoon that they called us and said it was safe to come back. We shot every day with about eighty thousand people watching the game. They came out to watch the game and to win a motorcycle or whatever it was, but they cared more about coming out and watching the game. It's their national sport and it was amazing. I just never expected anything like that, you've never seen anything until you've seen a hundred thousand people trying to get into space for five and, after all, I'm not that well *known* in Afghanistan. It was a very frightening day because I really thought we were out of business. The Afghans are marvelous people and we used them continually throughout the film. We only encountered one problem—they did not want their women to be photographed, even wearing their veils. Most of the women that you see in the picture with those veils on, are really members of my crew. As far as shooting Omar Sharif's leg is concerned, I figured that if I could get the audience to believe it with one shot, which is the first time you see it, that you would believe it for the rest of the picture. The problem, then, was how to do that. You think his leg is tied behind him, but it isn't. What he did was put his right leg behind him so it was hidden from the camera. It was that simple. I tried to be tricky with it—I had him sitting on a bale of hay so that all the wise ones in the audience would say that the leg is buried in the hay so when he stands, they think that the film will have to cut before he stands up. Of course, we didn't, and then everybody believes it. Then they say, 'Well, how the devil did they do that?' The answer is that it was strictly a camera angle. If you put the camera anywhere but there, you would have seen the leg. As a matter of fact, for those of you who go back and see the picture a second time, you'll see the shadow of his real leg on the wall, unfortunately.

Question What about your treatment of the animals?

JF In the first place, we did not film anything that did not occur. If you're talking about the camel fights or the ram fights, they happened. We did not stage them. The dead horse in the game was a stock shot taken some time before. We did not do anything at all to cause an animal to be injured while we were filming. There is one shot in the ram fight where the ram runs out and that ram was drugged. Within five minutes he was okay. All the sounds, naturally, were put in later.

Question In the beginning of the film, you make comparisons—the leaders, the jet plane going over, and then later on we have trucks and the Volkswagen ambulance. Was this a conscious theme in the film, or was it something that just happened?

JF The comparisons were very conscious. The object of all that was to tell you that this was Afghanistan today. Everything was carefully planned, as were all the shots showing modern conveyances, including the tow truck which we happened to pick up, with the horse. That was the only way I had of showing you that it was not a thousand years ago, because aside from those few things of modern society, Afghanistan itself has not changed in over a thousand years.

Question Why did you think the novel would make a good movie, and why did you choose it?

JF I chose the story for many reasons. I think it has a modern theme to it about a man who's looking for his own identity, if you will. It's an adventure story between the father and the son that is very touching. I read it first when it was published in French by Joseph Kessel and, I bought it right away because it was a story that appealed to me. If a story appeals to me, if I really love it, then will spend two years of my life filming it. Otherwise I'm not interested.

Question Do you have a good working relationship with your producers? Did they support you during your difficulties in the making of this film?

JF The most important and meaningful development in my career has been my relationship with Edward Lewis. In Eddie, I found a partner who is not only tremendously and creatively gifted, I also found my *alter ego*. We get along so well that I never question what he does, and he never questions what I do. Eddie Lewis is able to work well with writers, he's able to, in a sense, edit me which is very good in that I can go way out and Eddie will say, 'I don't think that's good.' But not in a way that destroys me. He has been able to negotiate incredible financial arrangements for us, and also incredible freedom. I don't think a man can produce and direct, I really don't think it's possible because the producer's function fights the director's function, and I just don't think the two are compatible. I'm perhaps one of the luckiest men alive to have arrived at a partnership with a gifted man who is in my opinion the finest producer there is, and if my work is better now than it was before, and if it continues to get better, I think Eddie Lewis is tremendously responsible because he lets me make the movie that I want to make—or rather the movie *we* want to make, because we do agree and if we don't agree then we won't make the film. There may be a story he likes very much that I don't like, and *vice versa*. Once we decide that we're going to make a film, we believe it is the film we should make. And his function is so diverse that it's almost impossible to describe. He's the man really responsible for getting the film made. He is able to talk to these people who finance films in a way that I never could. I always feel that if I have to talk about what I'm going to do then I can't do it. I don't know why I want to take certain shots the way I did. I just know they have to be there. And if I could explain to you beforehand every reason I have for doing something, I don't think I could ever do it. I am in many ways a non-articulate man. I can't always make the point I want to make. It's not because of my lack of vocabulary, it's just because I find that, by doing it, that's the way I express myself. I can't always talk about it and I have a terrible fear that if I talk it out too much I won't be able to do it. Eddie Lewis can put into words many things that I cannot. I think his contribution to every film that we've worked on together has been immense. We plan to be making films together for a long time. My pressures are not always those of other directors. Anything I want to do, as long as Eddie and I agree that it should be done, can be done. We certainly have never come upon a screenplay that we could not have made had we wanted to, and we have no excuses for any film of ours because I have been able, as a director, to do anything on these films that I wanted to do, with the possible exception of the casting of James Garner in *Grand Prix*.

Question Has *The Horsemen* been screened at any other place?

JF I have previewed the film twice in America, once in March and once in April. This is the first time an audience has come into a theatre knowing the title of the film it was going to see. I changed the film after the first preview. I cut fifteen minutes out of it. Has anybody here read the book? In France it is as well known as, for instance, *For Whom the Bell Tolls* is in English-speaking countries. You asked me what the response was. The first time I had the feeling of over-length in two expository scenes that are no longer in the film, the imaginary voice of Kessel telling us what was happening. We really didn't need it, and it's too bad, because they were really good scenes. I took a few lines out where we got some bad laughs. For instance, in the love scene between Sharif and the girl at the end, she says, 'Wait, you'll tear my dress.' He looks at her and he says, 'You really are a whore, aren't you?' I just felt like falling through the floor at that moment. So I took that out. In all, I took about fifteen minutes out. At first, the sound had been mixed and recorded in a studio in Paris where it sounded great in the dubbing room, but when we got into the theatre, it was very difficult to understand. The problem was that we had not used Westrex equipment, which is the best. We had to re-dub the whole picture—when I say re-dub it I mean re-mix it—which took a long time. The reaction the second time was really very good. That's when I said, 'That's it.' And that's the last time I'd seen the picture with an audience.

GP This prompts me to ask you, John, a question about language and dubbing. Is the use of English by the characters an accurate representation of the way they would speak English if they did? There have been so many films made in Hollywood in the past set in the Far East and the characters all talk with this peculiar kind of pseudo-poetic, semi-biblical English which became a joke. To do what you have done requires a certain amount of courage, I think, to bring it off.

JF It is a dramatic convention whereby the audience must believe the characters are speaking their own language. This always becomes a problem, so I took Omar Sharif's accent as the mean. In other words, I took the way Omar Sharif speaks English normally and made recordings of his voice and gave them to all the actors telling them, 'This is the accent I want.' Now, more or less, we have it. With Peter Jeffrey, he's very English, but he's such a good actor I didn't want to change him. The laughable 'thee' and 'thou' style which, as you say, was done in so many bad Hollywood movies, came out of the direct translation from the French and it was terrible. We changed it, and we just took for granted that this was a convention we were going to use.

Question Are you satisfied with the film as it stands now. If not, what would you change?

JF I think that any director who says he's perfectly satisfied with the film that he's made is not perhaps telling the truth. I guess I'm satisfied with this one at the moment because I haven't been away from it that long. I've been about three years on this film, so I'm pretty objective about it. I mean, I've cut out some of the best stuff because I didn't think it played. That's a very difficult thing to do, sitting there in the editing room and having to cut away some of the stuff you spent days and hours and even weeks on. I have to get away from the film, to see what the public and critical reaction is. All these things weigh on my value judgement, I think. I've done all I can do with the film. Let's put it this way: I honestly believe that there's no way, right now, that I can take this film and go back and re-edit it and make it any better than it is. What you're seeing is the best I know how to do with it at this moment. [*audience applauds*] And I feel that for the first time I have tried—I don't know if it's been successful or not—but I've tried to combine adventure with the psychological aspects of *The Manchurian Candidate*. I don't think one can say that this is just an adventure film. I think you have to say that it has a very intimate story to it. As a matter of fact, I'm afraid that people who are just going to see an adventure film may be disappointed. I don't think I can really classify my films that way. I must tell you that it's the theme of something that interests me. It's not really the story, because there are only about five or six basic stories—they've all been told time and time again. What appeals to me, more than anything else, are what it says, and, almost equally as important, the characters. People say why don't you take an original, why don't you do that? Well, an original is one of the hardest things to do. It's easy to write the plot line, but the characters are difficult to create. Sometimes one takes a novel because the characters are so rich, the characters are *there*. Now in my opinion, these characters are there in *The Horsemen*. And these are characters that we developed—the way Kessel did—we didn't change them. I have several projects with characters who interest me in the future—one of them is a rather simple, adventure picture, if you will, and another is a very complicated, psychological picture, the life story of Sir Richard Burton, the translator of *The Arabian Nights*, among others. We call it *The Devil Drives*. I hope we do it in the next couple of years. I can't really tell you what I prefer doing, I haven't been able to think much about anything else except this film during the last couple of years. I really don't know what I'm going to do next.

Question I'm a cinematographer. Do you like using Panavision?

JF The reason I'm using Panavision, and why I probably think I will continue to, is that number one, I think that I was frightened of Panavision. I think I was frightened by the aspect ratio, having been used to the postage-stamp ratio of television. I really didn't know how to frame for it at first. I was frightened of the lack of depth of focus, but I've solved that and I can go into quite some detail getting the person in the foreground and the person in the background perfectly in focus. It's almost like using two different lenses—there's a line, obviously, on the screen, but what you have to do is try and find a place in your exterior where you can put that line, like a crack in a wall, or avoid holding on too long, so the audience doesn't go, 'Wait a minute; what's that?' The advantage with Panavision is that your film cannot be destroyed by a projectionist. With Panavision you're using all your negative. Panavision has also come up with some tools for the director that are marvelous, like Panafocal lens, which goes from a forty-five millimeter to a hundred and ten in the principle of the zoom. You don't use it as a zoom you just change the lens by pushing back a lever on the lens to get exactly what you want without constantly unscrewing things. The Panaflex camera is marvelous—you look into it and see exactly what you're framing without having to worry about the whole question of parallax which, you do with standard cameras. The standard Panaflex camera has all kinds of things that one does not have in others. You go to Panavision with a problem and they'll try and solve it for you. They are on the side of the movie-maker. I had an eight hundred millimeter lens last year in Afghanistan and I loved that lens. I had the serial number and I said, 'I want that same lens back again.' And I have it. They really try and help you, and I try and support them. I've learned to use it. I've learned to frame for it. I'm still learning, but I think I've picked up a lot on this film. And talking of cameras, I often slate a scene at the end of the take. I find that the 'bing-bang' by the clapper board in front of the actor's face is very distracting. I had a guy once on *The Fixer* in Hungary who screamed, he'd clamp that thing down in front of an actor's face and the actor couldn't act. There was one time I filmed in a small hut and it was an end slate. I threw everybody out including this guy—I couldn't have him in there, there wasn't room. It was incredibly hot, and we did this long scene and I'd completely forgotten about him when suddenly, the door burst open, and he came through there with his clapper board knocking down everybody in his path. We ended up with a crane shot of Ian Holm with his back to the board. It was the funniest thing and we've got it all on camera.

Question I thought *Seconds* was an excellent film, I was wondering how you managed to cast Rock Hudson?

JF This was one of those stories that was very difficult because it read a lot better than what you finally were faced with having to do. In the book, by David Ely, in the scene where he had to face his wife, you can read that scene, and say, 'I'll believe that,' but when you're faced with the fact of having to film it, you realize that you can't have the same actor play the part from the beginning, and then have him go through plastic surgery and do a makeup job on him, and have it come out so that his wife won't recognize him. In spite of the fact that I bought that story for Laurence Olivier, I couldn't use him because Paramount wouldn't finance the picture with Olivier. If I had, probably Olivier would have played it from beginning to end. But you need an actor of that caliber to be able to pull that off. So then I decided I wanted two actors. A friend of mine, without my knowledge had given the script to Rock Hudson, and Rock called me and asked if we could meet. He wanted more than anything else to play that part. I was very taken with what he said, and I thought, 'Why not? I think it could work.' Then, the hard problem was to find an unknown actor in his late forties who could play the first part, because that's the problem. You could find an unknown YOUNG actor, but to find an unknown actor in his forties, it's pretty hard because by that time, you've either made it or you haven't. I knew this one actor in New York who had been blacklisted through all the McCarthy period and had never really been able to work, and that was John Randolph. I'd always wanted to work with him, and, as a matter of fact, I found out later that when CBS told me he wasn't available for a show, it was because they'd never asked him. Now we did a lot of work; we built up Randolph two inches, we put a toupee on him, we had him use his left hand, and so on, all to make that transition to Rock Hudson believable. We knew we had a problem with it, which is why we did the whole scene with the bandages and surgical procedures. For some people it worked, and for some people it didn't. I think the movie was a failure, because audiences didn't know what kind of a movie they were going to see. Those who went to see a Rock Hudson movie were very disappointed because Doris Day didn't appear and those who would have gone to see that kind of movie didn't go because Rock Hudson was in it. I have to say that I think Rock was really marvelous in that film and I think he's a very underrated actor. It's unfortunate that an actor who put so much effort into his work—which he did—came off really unrecognized. It was partially my fault. There were a lot of reasons why that film went wrong, but one of them was my insistence that Paramount put it into the Cannes Festival and it didn't work.

Question Because of the makeup involved, why did you choose Jack Palance to be in *The Horsemen*?

JF Well, it's very simple. Because you had to have an actor who could play the young part, and then because of the flashback, you had to have a massive actor, much bigger than Sharif. Also it had to be an actor who could be believable as an Afghan, and Jack, with those marvelous high cheekbones, really was just perfect for it. Also, I had worked with Jack a great deal on television, and I knew him and I think—aside from *Shane*, and *Panic in the Streets*—that Jack really was never correctly used in films. He did *The Last Tycoon* for me on American television in 1957, and was simply fantastic. He also did the worst television show ever done, for me, *The Death of Manolete*, and it practically killed both of us—I figured I owed Jack something after that. When this part came up he was really the first one I thought of. You couldn't put an old man in that part and have him play young, you had to have a young man and have him play old. Jack is a consummate actor, for instance, to get the feeling of age, we put weights around his waist and on his arms so that he wouldn't have to think that it was difficult to lift them up. I mean, God, it's a miracle he ever got off the bed! [*laughter*]

Gerald Pratley Thank you, ladies and gentlemen. On behalf of the Ontario Film Theatre and the Science Center, we thank Mr. Frankenheimer for coming here with his film.

JF I want to thank you for listening to me, I appreciate being here. These talks are always touch-and-go, the questions have been very good, you've been marvelous, and thank you very much. [*applause*]

LIFE IN PARIS, 1972

June 1972. After The Horsemen *opened to relatively good reviews and a successful run in the cinemas, John Frankenheimer and Evans Evans returned to Paris.*

"I go out a great deal in Paris, now I have learned to speak French almost fluently. I don't read as well in French as I do in English. I have some difficulties giving long lectures in French, but I've done these question-and-answer sessions in French, at the Cinemathèque and other places like that, and I've done them rather well. I've appeared on French television. We have many French friends. I have learned to cook well—I've gone to the Cordon Bleu, between editing and recording. I now have a diploma from the Cordon Bleu—not the full Master's diploma, but I'm just *beginning*—I have the three-month certificate and I've gone through another three-month course. I'm a rather good French cook at this point and I enjoy it very much. *And* I go to a lot of films. I find that life in Paris is very pleasant. It reminds me of what New York was about twenty years ago. You're not afraid to walk down the street, for instance. We go to other people's houses, we go away for weekends, I go away to London quite often. It's only an hour away and I have friends there and I go to the theatre as often as possible. The nice thing about Paris and London is that you have one city for government, theatre and film, unlike America where there are three cities for that. So I find that we have a great many more friends outside the film business than I did in Los Angeles, there are so many more opportunities to meet different kinds of people. They all know something about what you do—it's not like it's a total mystery to them. There's less invasion of privacy in that society, people don't want to know all the intimate secrets of your life the first time they meet you. This is not to say I dislike California. In fact, we'll probably end up back in America pretty soon. I don't want you to think that this is a permanent move because it's not. It's just that we shot *The Horsemen* in Afghanistan and in Spain, and we had to edit it in Europe. I much prefer cutting in Paris to Madrid. I've just stayed on here.

I think that the next picture I do will probably be in Paris. After that I really don't know. I've stopped any kind of competitive driving. I just feel that too many of my best friends have been killed driving. Certainly, it's terrible to look at the credits of *Grand Prix* now. Look at the number of drivers who are dead, and the number who have been seriously hurt, very badly hurt, such as Mike Parks, Graham Hill—the statistics are appalling. It makes me think that it's not something I should be doing. I do drive a lot, but I drive out in the country and obey the speed limit. Meanwhile I know what my next film will be. It's called *Impossible Object* and I expect to start in a few months time."

Frankenheimer and Evans Evans.

IMPOSSIBLE OBJECT (Story of a Love Story) 1973

Director John Frankenheimer • *Production Company* Franco-Italian Film/Robert Bradford Productions/Euro-International Films • *Executive Producer* Robert Bradford • *Producer* Jud Kinberg • *Screenplay from his novel* Nicolas Mosley • *Camera* Claude Renoir (Eastmancolor/wide-screen) • *Editor* Albert Jurgenson • *Sound* Antoine Petitjean • *Art Direction* Alexandre Trauner • *Music* Michel Legrand • *Classification* MPAA:NR • *Release* May 1973 • *Distribution* Valoria Films • *Running time* 110 mins • *Location* Filmed on location in Paris, and Azila in Morocco • Originally to be directed by Joseph Losey with Dirk Bogarde and Catherine Deneuve • Screened at Cannes (out-of-competition) in May 1973, The Teheran International Film Festival, June 1975 and the Stratford (Ontario) International Film Festival, September 1975 • *Cost* $2.5M • *Soundtrack* on Bell Records • *Formats* available on VHS.

CAST

Harry	•	Alan Bates
Nathalie	•	Dominique Sanda
Elizabeth	•	Evans Evans
Woman	•	Lea Massari
Georges	•	Michel Auclair
Cleo	•	Laurence De Monaghan

SYNOPSIS

Harry is writing a novel in his home in the country in the South of France where he lives with his American wife, Elizabeth, and three young sons. Visiting a local museum one day he meets Nathalie, who is married. This is the beginning of a passionate affair. Her husband, Georges, learns of this and sends thugs to warn Harry away. Harry goes on holiday to Africa with Elizabeth. On their return Harry goes to Paris to continue writing his novel. In a small cluttered apartment he is both-ered by plumbers and involved in other incidents. He and Nathalie then go to Africa to have a child after Elizabeth and Georges apparently agree. A boating accident leads to the death of the child and this brings about the return of Harry to Elizabeth and Nathalie to Georges. Years later Harry and Nathalie meet again in Rome and it all begins once again. Or does it? Has his imagination intruded into reality during the writing of his novel?

COMMENT

Having edited *The Horsemen* in Paris, Frankenheimer fell in love with the way of life there, and, in particular, with Nicolas Mosley's novel *Impossible Object*. In filming this story, seemingly impossible to bring to the screen, he succeeded beyond all expectation. Frankenheimer had done nothing like it previously and has done nothing like it since. Noted for his dramatic masculine subjects, it is easy to forget that in his own quiet way the director has always been a romantic at heart but shy in nature. *Impossible Object* was years ahead of its time and in its manipulation of thoughts and imagination he proved himself to be as adept as Antonioni, Godard and Fellini in allowing the narrative to flow freely in time and place. It is hard to know most of the time what is actually real in the life of the writer and what events, coming about as the result of meeting the sensual Nathalie in the local museum, are actually imagined by him. Yet so engagingly and cleverly are scenes juxtaposed, blended together and intercut between the real and the imaginary that the sequences never become frustrating to watch. Mosley's screenplay is genuinely romantic, lightly spun, yet never frivolous nor superficial. The story, one of the oldest in literature, on stage and screen, is about the eternal triangle, telling of the happily married family man who falls deeply in love to the point of obsession with another married woman. Their contented family life is told naturally without cloying sentiments or painful dullness. The dialogue for the most part is sharp and double-edged. "Yes, everybody's happy" says Elizabeth, the wife, beautifully played by Evans Evans, yet knowing this is illusory. Alan Bates, rascally appealing as the writer-husband who prefers not to be outwardly demonstrative, cloaks his feelings in outrageous remarks and witty comments and goes from one extreme to the other dwelling on the torments of a writer in love, believing that to make love last it is best to be together and apart.

Nothing is quite what it seems. Questions and answers are often ambiguous, yet the editing is clear within its complicated patterns, with scenes being poetically mixed and superimposed on each other. Instead of seeing him writing, we see what he is visualizing, then we hear the typewriter and realize that invention and real life may not always be extricable. Light-hearted love scenes abound, delicately filmed with more nudity than was usual at this time, and always depicted in good taste, with grace and beauty, from the serious to the comic, from fantasy to tragedy. The whole is a sensitive exploration of individuals who love too much, never knowing what they truly want out of life. This is exquisitely played out under Claude Renoir's luminous lighting of the warm Riviera region and Alexander Trauner's beautiful settings, accompanied by Michel Legrand's unobtrusively romantic score.

Being cinema in its purest form, this film resists translation into words. The boating scene, as an example, with its huge waves, is dramatically arresting—a feeling of dread achieved with only the sound of sea and wind. The closing scene with its avenue of trees, so obviously a symbol of France, yielding up doors opening to memories of the past is a wickedly surreal touch. In contemplating the meaning of life, love and fidelity, of passionate relationships with their consuming emotional and physical pleasures and torments, this is a frequently moving and sad examination of happiness, guilt and eventual despair, and, surprisingly perhaps for its time, the agony of being a wife in an uncertain relationship without apparent boundaries. As a portrait of British and American eccentrics abroad, *Impossible Object* has few equals on the screen.

F"I suppose I could call *Impossible Object* my first independent picture. I loved the novel by Nicolas Mosley and he wrote a splendid screenplay from it. The film came to me through a man named Jud Kinberg and was set up with a London company run by man named Robert Bradford who was German but a naturalized American. He married an Englishwoman who turned out to be Barbara Taylor Bradford, but we didn't know that at the time, nobody did. So Bradford put up the money to make the picture, around $2½ million. This was before the Arab oil crisis when films were not all that expensive to do.

"It represents a completely different kind of movie for me. I was going through a phase in my life when I thought I wanted to live permanently in Europe. I had been deeply affected by the death of Bobby Kennedy. Evans and I loved France, we thought we wanted to stay there, and I wanted to see if I could work within their system. It turned out to be terribly disappointing for me because the French producers are worse than the American studio system. At least in the American studio system at that time you had certain individuals who were intelligent, who could read scripts and give you some kind of artistic opinion. With French producers, they are only interested in how much it is going to cost, and who's in it.

"We had difficult financing problems with the picture. I asked Alan Bates to join us. Nicolas Mosley wrote the script, we got Dominique Sanda, Lea Massari and Evans. We had the great Alexandre Trauner design it, and Claude Renoir, again, to shoot it. The picture looked and played, I think, really well, but never got a chance in North America because it was mishandled. I remember when Michel Legrand was scoring the picture, Bradford came on the stage and said, 'It's the best picture that I've ever seen and we're going to get a tremendous price for it in America.' I said, 'Well, Bob, thanks for the compliment but it's not the *best* picture. I think it's a *good* movie, but what you said about price you can't say about any movie because that's not up to us. I think the movie works but it must be marketed very carefully. I think it really has to be handled with great care.' So he started off asking for so much money for it that nobody would pay it. Then, when you come down in price, the distributors think there's something wrong. We never did get the American distribution we wanted. Bradford was inexperienced in the ways of American distribution. I don't blame him. It was very, very disappointing, but these things happen. We took a print of it and entered it in the Atlanta Festival. We won, Fox almost bought it, but it became the picture that was never really seen!

"It's a story about the creative process, using a great deal of oneself and a great deal of one's own sense, if you will, and own experience of what you do as an artist. Some of it was fantasy, and some of it was real, and we used the images of Greek and Roman sculpture that were part of the setting. Mosley's script was difficult to film. I'm not sure I totally succeeded with it, but it's one I really enjoyed doing. I liked Mosley and worked with him very well. He writes for an audience far above the average movie-goer. I never thought or intended this to be a movie for a broad audience— rather it was a question of making the script work for those who were attracted to it, and Kinberg did this with me. We shot it in Paris and in a little town called Azila in Morocco, near Tangiers. I felt confident when we began that I had a very good grasp of the material. I felt an empathy with it and I think I knew what I was doing.

"There's some extraordinary stuff in there. We made the shot of Dominique Sanda pregnant when she actually was pregnant with the child she had by Christian Marker before we started the film. In fact, we held up the film waiting for her and so, when she was really pregnant, she allowed herself to be photographed. I think some of the dream sequences worked very well and there's a good blending of the unreal with the real. I'm never really satisfied with anything I do, so if you ask me how I feel about it, I could have done it better. We shot the picture in ten weeks. All the editing and scoring was done in Paris. Michel Legrand did the music—a nice man and a good musician, better then than now."

FRANKENHEIMER AT STRATFORD, ONTARIO, 1975

Two years later John Frankenheimer and Evans Evans, with John Russell Taylor and the author discuss Impossible Object *following its showing at the Stratford International Film Festival, Ontario, Canada, September 20, 1975.*

JF Our main difficulty with this film was that the company went bankrupt before we released it and it's now held by banks in France and Switzerland, and no one really knows who owns it. Trying to find out has been very frustrating. Someone tells us Alexander Salkind owns it. He says that he bought the rights—certain rights, anyway. But nonetheless, all the negatives, the tracks, the prints, are locked in the LTC Labs to prevent Salkind getting to them, because the Lab hasn't been paid. One tries to convince the manager that the only way he can get paid is to release the film to make money to pay him. I had almost given up on the picture because in life there comes a time when you must put things behind you and forget them. Last night was the first time that either Evans or I have seen our movie in front of an English-speaking audience. We've seen it with a French-speaking audience, some of whom claimed to speak English, and we've also seen it with an Iranian audience at the Teheran Film Festival last June. Your response to it has been revealing for us. The film was a joy to make because of the people involved in it. I not only speak of Evans but also of Alan Bates. We did *The Fixer* together, and working with him and Dominique Sanda was a rewarding experience. We made it in France, because that's where we were living for quite a few years. What the film meant to me was, in a sense, going *back* to the intimate story I had done for years in television. I just wanted to get away from my growing reputation as an action picture director, which started with *The Train*. Up until then, being an ex-television director, the only action they would ever give me to direct was somebody walking across a room, because they didn't think we knew how to do anything else. The subject interested me—'what is commitment?,' the story of a man who finds it impossible to commit himself. I also wanted to experiment with the tantalizing theme of what is real, and what isn't, and I wanted to search around in time past, in time fantasy and in time present. That about answers that question. The producer who got royally taken with this enterprise was Jud Kinberg, who brought it to me in the first place.

He's an American, a very nice fellow, who was living in Europe—I think he probably still is—and he was one of the co-producers of the William Wyler picture *The Collector*. He brought it to me, and through him I met Nicolas Mosley.

Question How would you like to change the picture?

JF I'd certainly like to try and get rid of the fantasy sequence where he goes to Rome. I haven't seen it, as I told you, for two years, but looking at it last night bears out a conviction I had that the picture would be better if we removed some of the flashes, to show it more as a straightforward story. But it is too late now, even though this is my print, which I stole—that's the only way I could get it out of France, I just borrowed the print and never gave it back.

Question I'd like to ask you about *French Connection II* in terms of having to follow through from the original.

JF I found myself with both limitations and advantages—the advantages being that Gene Hackman had given such a realistic performance in the first film we could write the whole story about him giving him a great deal more to do than if we didn't know what kind of character we had. The disadvantage came with this being the first time I had ever directed an actor who had already played the role before. I suddenly realized what these television directors go through trying to direct somebody like Jim Arness who doesn't want to know. He's played the role in *Gunsmoke* for ten years. Hackman was not like that. He could have been, but he wasn't. The other drawback when starting a film like that is, 'My God! The first one was so good.' You can be overawed by the first picture, and I couldn't let that happen to me. For a while, before I ever started filming I thought, 'My God, why did I ever say I'd do it?' Then after I decided what I wanted to do with the movie, that worry disappeared. After all, my reason for doing the film was centered on the sequence dealing with the withdrawal, and I tried to make everything else work around it. I also tried to continually change the rhythm and the pace so the audience could never really anticipate what was going to happen next. I didn't want to go in a straight line the way I think Billy Friedkin's film did—which I admired incidentally, I thought it was a superb motion picture. But it went from the beginning and never stopped and I decided I wanted some highs and lows in my film; that was the only way that I could make it work for me. Those are conscious decisions you make before you ever start to film. At least I do.

Question Do you approach the filming of a play like *The Icemen Cometh* in a manner different from your other kinds of film.

JF I would say that it was very similar to when I used to do 'Playhouse 90.' I was able to film from beginning to end. Evans was in it and she can tell you the rehearsals were marvelous because we were working in continuity.

Evans Evans I think it was certainly different for all the actors, because it was one of the few films that any of us had been in that was really like being in a play. We were all together, everybody had to be there every day. We were a closely-knit group, we rehearsed together, the set was Harry's Bar—we all began to feel drunk. We would walk out of the studio in a kind of stagger! And we, the actors, all of us, talked about the play constantly, including Freddie March. Even for him—who'd done so many plays and films—it was unique, and Robert Ryan agreed.

JF The only film I had previously made like this—where we did it in continuity—was *Birdman of Alcatraz*. This we did from beginning to end, making filming much easier, but obviously this can't be done with most movies because if a script calls for a location, say, here in Stratford with three scenes, one taking place in the middle, one at the end and one at the beginning of the movie, obviously this can't be filmed in continuity. All three scenes must be filmed here, and then go on to the next location. In films like *Grand Prix*, it was impossible to work in continuity. But it's by far the best possible way to work. A director knows what he's got, and doesn't have to carry the whole movie around in his head all the time. Also with O'Neill there was one other difference from other films, which was that we were very sure of the text. We knew that the text [*some laughter from the audience*]—well, you laugh but we knew the scenes would work. A film that's original, *The Fixer* for instance, is different—I wasn't sure if some of its scenes as written would work within the whole, and what I would do is cover them—in other words take many takes so that if I wanted to drop lines, if I wanted to change dialogue in the cutting afterwards, I had several takes to play with. With *The Iceman Cometh*, an established play, we knew that wouldn't be necessary. What I would do in many scenes was to take long, flowing shots with two cameras, sometimes three cameras. All the scenes between Robert Ryan and Jeff Bridges were shot at the same time with the reverses shot at the same time, and the cameramen would have cues: when to zoom in, when not to zoom in and so forth. Now that's fine with a continuous scene; if it's not, it can't be done because the action isn't a perfect match and it's very difficult to cut into a scene like that because there is very little protection.

Question I want to ask you about the script of *Impossible Object*. Is it seen on the screen pretty much as it was written, and how much did Mosley actually structure, and how much of it is yours? Could you describe how that developed?

JF Primarily it's the same story, but told from about seven different points of view becoming, finally, the one point of view. What you saw last night is pretty much what we wrote, but is certainly nothing like what we started out with. We worked on the script for, oh, easily three months, before we considered it finished, but we never could solve the pool sequence to our satisfaction. It just didn't work. We kidded ourselves that it worked—I don't think it ever really did. For some people it works, for me it didn't; that's why I tell you I'd like to change it.

Question It's a very opposite approach to the same problem that Joseph Losey and Harold Pinter faced in bringing Nicolas Mosley's other novel *Accident* to the screen. It's highly-wrought in a stream of consciousness, and they crystallize it into a very literal story. I think *Accident* works on its own terms, but whether it's a popular representation of Mosley's original is another matter. I think you've obviously gone much further in trying to find a film equivalent of Mosley's literary style.

JF I admired *Accident*. I thought it was a superb movie. Our production lacked one element that *Accident* had, and that was Harold Pinter. I don't think the two novels are really comparable—

Impossible Object is a much more complicated structure.

Question Yes, the styles are rather similar in the two novels, but the structures are different. In the direction of the main characters, did you develop the shape of the characters or did it develop simply because you were following the sequence?

JF We didn't film in sequence at all. No, not obviously, but very definitely, Alan Bates and I did work on arriving at that. I'm glad it happened for you, because that was deliberate.

Question What bothered me was the meaning of the nursing scene where she gets angry with Alan Bates for babysitting. I felt as though this were some kind of watery abortion. Was that what you had in mind, or am I alone in feeling this way?

JF I don't know if you are alone. The death of the baby is absolutely essential to make the film work. It would *not* have worked without it, because in a sense what you get is the entire situation starting again at the very end of it, which is absolutely essential to the material. There was no way we could *not* kill the baby. It was his indecision, his lack of being able to make a decision or a commitment, that brought about the death of that baby.

Question Isn't it part of the problem there, though, the result of so much flash-backing and forwarding and fantasy stuff that the issue becomes a little obscure?

JF I don't think the film is easy on an audience—it's really not meant to be *French Connection II*. I don't want to use the word 'indulge' myself, because I don't think it is an indulgence. I was trying to find a whole other way to tell a story—either successfully or not. It was not a conventional use of time, place and events. I found it interesting to experiment

From left to right: Gerald Pratley, Frankenheimer, Evans Evans, and John Russell Taylor meet the festival audience at Stratford.

this way, it's not interesting when the film isn't released and no one sees it! I've made some errors in it, but let me remark on why the film wasn't released. When we finished, as I said, the company went bankrupt, but the man who put up the money for it was a naturalized German-American who was living in Paris. He looked at the film and said, quite, 'This is the greatest film ever made.' I said, 'No, it's not. It's really not,' I said, 'This is a film with problems.' He said, 'Don't be silly, there are no problems. I'm going to ask two million dollars for the North American rights, and beside that anybody from there must come to Paris to see it.' Well, he was out of his mind! You can't ask two million for the North American rights—they didn't ask that for *Borsalino*. What he should have done is take a distribution deal with a percentage of the gross. Anyway, one thing led to another and, needless to say, the heads of Warner Bros., Fox and so forth, did not get on a plane to run over to see it—they sent their representatives from Europe to see it. They always say 'No' for the simple reason that if they buy a film, it takes money away from their own budget to make films. Also, there is no such thing as a film that's too expensive. There's only a film that isn't commercial. By the time the studio heads in Hollywood had had a chance to see the movie, they'd already been given reports that it was not, quite, 'commercial.' In spite of that we had three offers to distribute the film, one by Roger Corman, who distributed Bergman's film *Cries and Whispers*, and did a successful job of it in the United States. The other two were United Artists and Columbia—no great guarantees, but a terrific percentage of the gross. It was turned down because by that time, the banks called in their money. It's being used as a tax write-off, and we have a feeling that, like *The Producers*, they've sold about 180 per cent of this movie so that if it ever came out and made any money, there'd be a lot of people who'd go to jail. That is the feeling we get because we did have a very definite chance to have Roger release it. Roger had meetings with them and told me that it was all set, and then at the last minute, they dropped it. I can't see why they would do that because Roger offered them a seven-city opening, Toronto was one of them, a guaranteed amount that he would spend on publicity, and they found excuses not to accept that. I can't really understand why. Now, quite honestly, it's probably too late for the movie, unless it becomes a collector's item. I made *Impossible Object* for a world that, two or three years ago, was not worrying about a recession, that was not having the economic problems of today. It doesn't deal with those problems, but in today's society, where there are such pressing problems, people are liable to say, 'Well, so *what*, the guy can't make a commitment between Evans Evans and Dominique Sanda—he's got a horrific problem, you know . . .'

Question I don't think that's true. A story like this, whatever its faults, always has an audience. It's a story that has no particular time.

JF Speaking aesthetically, yes, but I feel that it has a very special time. I find the film has dated in many ways because of the subject matter. I'm talking on a commercial basis, you understand—how do you *sell* this movie now? I don't know. I certainly knew how to sell it them.

Question About the film and the gentleman's concern about the 'watery abortion'—how important to the story is it for that little baby to be a real person? That little baby never became real to me.

JF I don't know how to answer that. The baby was very definitely real to me. Maybe it was something that Sanda didn't do to make it more real for her. You see, for Harry, the very fact that children, babies, his wife, were never real, meant that he found it really difficult to relate to them. Dominique has such an otherworldly quality, that perhaps she didn't make caring about it as a mother real enough. It was about the relationship between the two of them—the fact that they were fighting and the baby, instead of becoming a living object drawing them together, drew them apart. The baby, then, was really no answer.

John Russell Taylor Does it seem ironic to you that, as a result of the non-release of the film, most Americans know about it from the *Playboy* story about it, which seems to raise a problem. We seem to be selling images of films, rather than the films themselves. Obviously this is a film which is very important to you, but the image projected as a result of this feature was, I think, that of a sex film, that it was outrageous, that it appeared to be a sort of orgy. Do you think that this image, this treatment in advance of the film's expected opening would, in fact, have damaged it by conveying a false impression of what it is truly all about?

JF No. [A*udience laughs.*] If the film had opened

around the time when it was planned, around the *Playboy* break, I think it would have definitely helped it. Perhaps audiences might have expected something different, but I gather they would have come in to see it. There is a certain eroticism and sensuality in it, at least I certainly hope so, it was meant to be there. At the time we made it audiences had not become quite so inured to what they see on the screen today, as in *Last Tango in Paris*. If everything had gone according to plan, it would have been shown about four months after *Last Tango*. I don't think *Playboy* hurt at all. What did hurt was the idiot demanding two million dollars. There were so many things that were just so *badly* done. He had to get some money out of it, so he decided he was going to show it at Cannes, out of competition, which was silly, because I had arranged to go to Berlin with it. 'Unless something extraordinary comes along,' I was told several times, 'this is going to win Berlin.' That would have been nice—to win Berlin. As it was, it was shown at five-thirty in the afternoon on a very hot day at Cannes, which—those of you who have been to the festival know—is a terrible time to show any film, because it's between the afternoon and the evening performance, everybody's trying to get ready for the evening, and they're tired and they're hot and they want a drink, and the audience is packed into the Grand Palais. It was very interesting to see the reaction, however, for the simple reason that the critics I knew in Paris and for whom I had arranged special screenings, gave it really quite marvelous notices, but those who saw it at the Grand Palais were very mixed in their opinions.

Question I think the difficulty with the baby for us, if not for you, is that the scenes showing the mother with the baby in the basket at the market, then nursing the baby in the field are unconvincing, and, then, in the boat sequence—the baby simply becomes a parcel that gets lost. And it was unclear to me how the museum and restaurant scenes related to Alan Bates.

JF Well, I don't agree with you about the baby. As for the meeting in the museum and the restaurant, this was the beginning of the relationship and the boat sequence was to be the end of it, until they re-met—or did they meet again?—in the café in Rome. I feel that they did. But the sequence in the museum was supposed to be the first time they met. Perhaps some of this could be re-edited but I don't think I'm ever going to be able to get the material that I need to re-edit the film from behind lock and key in Paris. What you say is interesting because I think that, like anything else, if certain things disturb you and take away from your concentration on the forward progress of the story then this takes away from your attention span of the movie and from your identifying with the character. If certain things really annoy you, you say, 'I don't like that. I don't want it.' I feel it's more important to please an audience in its identification of the character. That's the only way I can answer that. But remember, the structure of *Impossible Object* was not intended to be linear.

Question The day of the party—was that a flashback?

JF It was a flash-forward, an advance in time—is it in his imagination or isn't it? As I said, I was playing around with what's real and what isn't. Nevertheless, he had a premonition of what was going to happen. I think it's confusing. You're right to mention it, and I think that's a scene I might re-edit.

Question The relationship really seemed to last a long time. Was the meeting in the museum after the boat scene?

JF I'll tell you why you might think that. It was partly a directorial mistake. In order to get the change of seasons, we shot the exit from the museum long before we started the movie. In fact we shot it the same day we took the pregnant shot of Dominique Sanda, and we started the movie after that. We shot with a double for Dominique coming out of the museum with Alan Bates, for real. If you noticed, we go across the bare trees and end up on the island, but they come out of the museum holding hands. I had all the time in the world and why I didn't shoot another version, where they didn't come out holding hands, I don't know, because it would have been much clearer if they were not holding hands and it was the first time they met. I find it, each time I look at the film, very disturbing. But quite honestly we didn't know what we were doing at that particular time, it was the first shot of the movie. I've learned—but you know, you don't learn if you don't make mistakes, and then you think you might just as well stop, because you drive yourself crazy. It becomes harder and harder to do each movie instead of becoming easier, because you say, 'God, I don't want to repeat myself,' you know, 'I've done this scene this way before.' But just because you do it differently doesn't mean it's better. I can understand how you could arrive at your impressions.

Question It seemed it would be a very interesting way to have the relationship work, to have it last for a long time and then hear the husband say, 'You told me before it was over.'

JF I meant to give the feeling after the museum that it had been going on for a while. They meet at the museum, and you have a feeling that they see each other, they don't and so forth and so on, because he did say, in the scene in his office, 'You said it was over before.' As I said before, it's not an easy film. It wasn't an easy film to figure out when we were making it; we really wanted the audience to know, and to feel. I think it's a *flawed* film—I'm not trying to sit here and defend it as being the perfect realization of what I had in mind. I can tell you what I set out to do, but whether I did or not, that's for you to decide—after all, you are the final judge, not me.

Question Do you control the advertising of your films? I can see how it can be terribly frustrating for a director, who's put such an awful lot of himself into his work, to see the studios pull out scenes to sensationalize the film.

JF I'll tell you how that usually happens. If the director has any standing at all—and the producer—they are given consultation rights in the advertising campaign of the movie. Usually, the first ads to appear for a film are pretty much what the director and the producer wanted. If the film doesn't do business, that's when the fellas up there really take over, and they pull out *anything* that they think will get people into the theatres. That's when you lose total control. There are usually two or three advertising campaigns prepared for a film. There is the sedate one, then there is the exploitative one. They use different campaigns in different parts of the hemisphere, strangely. For big cities, they will use the more sophisticated campaign; for the small towns they will use the sensational campaign. Then if the film doesn't do business, they'll either do one of two

things: they'll change the advertising campaign, which is to use the methods that you are talking, about which have nothing to do with what the movie's about, or they'll just pull all the advertising and take out the picture.

John Russell Taylor This was rather the point I was trying to get at when I asked you how you felt about the publicity for the film being the feature in *Playboy*, because the sex element of it is an important part of the film, obviously, but is pointing to an element of sensationalism not present in the film. Again I had a feeling that had the film come out at that time, perhaps, a number of people would go to it, or *not* go to it, because they thought it was somehow going to be primarily a sex film, an erotic film.

JF The type of people who wouldn't go to it because it was a sex film, wouldn't be reading *Playboy* in the first place. [audience laughs] It's not exactly *Time* magazine.

John Russell Taylor But on the other hand, the people who might go to it thinking it was a sex film because they read about it in *Playboy* might then be rather disturbed by how little sex there is in there for them.

JF Dominique Sanda is not that bad, John. [*Audience laughs.*] No, I don't think so; I won't let you get away with that.

GP: I would like to thank very much Evans Evans and John Frankenheimer for coming to Stratford today from Los Angeles. We look forward to your next film, John, what, a year from now?

JF: Well, I've just time for a commercial break. [*audience laughs and applauds*]

Note: During the two-year period which elapsed between Frankenheimer completing Impossible Object *(1973) and its showing at the Stratford Film Festival in 1975, he had made* The Iceman Cometh, 99 and 44/100% Dead *and* French Connection II.

RETURN FROM FRANCE, 1973

"The years in France were very important to me. I didn't realize it but filming *The Train* was going to change my life because it exposed Evans and myself to France and we both fell in love with it. Not just the country, but a way of life completely different from California. It was wonderful not to be totally consumed by this business and to be able to lead a life with individuals who were outside of it all. I had time to seriously study history, art, and cooking. As I said to you in Paris, I went and worked at the Cordon Bleu and in several very fine restaurants as a cook. I learned to enjoy my life in a way I had never done before. I worked with Michel Guéraid at the Pot au Feau at Ille Ansiers just outside of Paris and at the Tour d'Argent for a while. I'd had a very unhappy marriage in the first few years of my directing career and I rarely had time, until now, to sit back and breathe and enjoy my life.

"Remember, we never intended to stay in France for long, but the opportunity presented itself when I edited *The Horsemen* in Paris and we stayed on for the opening. Little by little we both realized that we loved it there and we fitted in very well. We both started to concentrate on learning French. We had a coach from the Comedie Française who came to our apartment for two hours every day—an hour with Evans, an hour with me— over a period of about two years. As time passed we found excuses not to leave. Just before I came back to film *Iceman*, we actually looked at an apartment to buy on the rue de Barque right by the Université, and were about to make a bid on it but we held off because of the filming commitment.

"We came back, and a friend of ours—who later became my assistant, Max Whitehouse—rented a house for us in Malibu because our home was still rented out. Within three weeks we purchased it. We knew from the first night that's where we wanted to be—a strange feeling. I have lived in Malibu since being with Evans. Evans and I have been together since January of '61 and, excepting the years in Paris, we spent all our time there until four years ago, when we moved into this house in Beverly Hills. When Evans and I married that changed my life too. It was a very happy time for us in France, a period in our lives I've always felt that no matter what, nobody can ever take away. We had it when we were fairly young, and we enjoyed doing many things I don't think I would do now. It was a very important and healing time, and I came back feeling very optimistic.

"We were friendly with Bertrand Tavernier, when he was still a critic, I knew Truffaut, but I didn't know Louis Malle—I still don't, and never met Godard. I did get to know David Lean, and this was a great privilege. I greatly admire his films and they have strongly influenced my own work. I first met him with William Wyler in California and then later in England. Wyler had invited me to dinner. When I entered, this very tall man stood up and Wyler introduced us. I couldn't believe I was meeting David Lean. We all spent until five in the morning talking about films.

It was a beautiful time in Paris, and it was responsible for *Impossible Object* which I do think was an important step in my career. Then a call from Edward Lewis brought us home for *The Iceman Cometh*. This was to be produced by the American Film Theatre group run by Ely Landau."

Hickey (Lee Marvin) holds forth at the 'Last Chance' Saloon.

THE ICEMAN COMETH 1973

Director John Frankenheimer • *Executive Producer* Edward Lewis • *Producer* Ely A. Landau • *Production Company* Henry T. Weinstein and The American Film Theatre • *Screenplay* from the play by Eugene O'Neill, text edited by Thomas Quinn Curtiss • *Camera* Ralph Woolsey (wide-screen-color) • *Editing* Harold Kress • *Costume Designer* Dorothy Jeakins • *Art Direction* Jack Martin Smith • *Distribution* AFT Distributing Corporation • *Classification* PG • *Release* October 1973 • *Running Time* 239 mins • *Soundtrack* on Caedmon Records (dialogue) • Presented by The Ely Landau Organization, Inc., and American Express Films, Inc., in association with Cinevision, Ltée. One of eight plays on film produced by The American Film Theatre in 1973.

CAST

Hickey	•	Lee Marvin
Harry Hope	•	Fredric March
Larry Slade	•	Robert Ryan
Don Parritt	•	Jeff Bridges
Willie Oban	•	Bradford Dillman
Hugo Kalmar	•	Sorrell Booke
Margie	•	Hildy Brooks
Pearl	•	Nancy Juno Dawson
Cora	•	Evans Evans
The Captain	•	Martyn Green
Joe Mott	•	Moses Gunn
Pat McGloin	•	Clifton James
Jimmy Tomorow	•	John McLiam
Chuck Morello	•	Stephen Pearlman
Rocky Pioggi	•	Tom Pedi
The General	•	George Voskoven
Moran	•	Bart Burns
Lieb	•	Don McGovern

SYNOPSIS

Seated at their tables in the back room of seedy Harry Hope's 'Last Chance' Saloon in New York's Greenwich Village are the regular patrons—a collection of has-beens who live on drinks and pipe dreams. They have begun this summer day in 1912 just as they have all others in recent memory, in varying degrees of intoxication.

But there is anticipation in the air this morning. As each patron rouses briefly, he speaks of the impending arrival of Hickey (Lee Marvin), an amiable hardware 'drummer' who buys drinks for everyone and has a line of humorous patter including jokes about his wife and the iceman. Hickey never misses Harry Hope's birthday party, which is scheduled for that night.

The only patron fully awake is Larry Slade (Robert Ryan), a former anarchist who has lost faith in everything, and now wants only to drink and wait for death. Larry shows little interest when he is joined by young Don Parritt (Jeff Bridges), newly arrived from the West Coast. Don seeks Larry's help. His mother, an old friend of Larry's from movement days, has been betrayed to the police. Larry, however, is not inclined to get involved in anybody's problems and changes the subject of conversation.

Gradually the other patrons begin to stir, complaining and carrying on in monologues. The chief grumbler is Harry Hope (Fredric March), owner of the bar. He hasn't been out of the saloon since his wife's death 20 years ago. The rest of the group at the bar includes Hugo Kalmer (played by Sorrell Booke), a former anarchist editor who is no longer of any use to the movement; a British Captain from the Boer War (Martyn Green), who drinks and talks of returning to England, and his constant companion, 'General' Wetgjoen (George Voskovec), a former Boer Commando who talks of returning to South Africa; Jimmy Tomorrow (John McLiam), a journalist always planning to go back to work 'tomorrow'; former police lieutenant McGloin (Clifton James), who dreams of being reinstated; Joe Mott (Moses Gunn), once the owner of a black gambling house, always envisioning a

Harry Hope (Fredric March) and Larry Slade (Robert Ryan).

new stake; and Willie (Bradford Dillman), a Harvard Law School graduate who drinks rather than face the life that once had so much promise for him. Rocky (Tom Pedi) tends bar.

A little later, streetwalkers Pearl (Hildy Brooks), Margie (Nancy Juno Dawson), Cora (Evans Evans) and Cora's boyfriend, Chuck (Stephen Pearlman), the day bartender, enter and sit down to wait for Hickey and the party.

Finally, Hickey arrives. However, this is a new Hickey. He orders drinks for everyone but refuses to drink himself claiming that he does not need it anymore. Hickey insists he is going to help each of them find peace in the same way he has, by ridding them of their foolish dreams. At first, the others think Hickey is having them on, but they soon realize that he is serious.

Last minute preparations are made for Harry Hope's birthday party. Everyone is on edge because of Hickey. He is employing all his best salesman tactics—sincerity, sweet talk, cajoling, even ridicule—to get each of his old friends to see the truth about themselves.

Hickey is devoting special attention to Larry, telling him that he's weak, unable to face any kind of trouble in life, but afraid to die. Protesting vigorously, Larry says he's eager for death, that it's his only goal. While Larry seems relatively unaffected, young Parritt is strangely troubled by the proceedings. He confesses to Larry that he betrayed his mother out of patriotism and loss of faith in the anarchist movement.

At midnight Harry Hope enters to the shouts of 'Happy Birthday.' But instead of being his usual likeable self, Harry has a chip on his shoulder. Hickey has also been working hard on the saloon owner. With everyone so upset that they are turning against each other, the party is a dismal failure. Angered and frustrated by Hickey's actions, the guests tease him about his wife and the iceman. In reply, Hickey explains that his wife is dead, but tells them not to grieve because she is at peace. He offers no further explanations.

Working through the night, Hickey is such a irresible salesman that he convinces each of the has-beens to try to fulfill his dream by going out into the world and facing reality. Reluctantly each one sets out, except Larry who has been unaffected by Hickey. Meanwhile Parritt again corners Larry. He explains that it was not patrio-

tism that motivated his betrayal of his mother, but the fact that he was infatuated with a whore and needed money. Harry Hope is the last to leave. He goes out to take a walk around the neighborhood—a trip he has been postponing for twenty years. He returns in a matter of minutes in a state of panic and vows never to go out again.

By evening all the patrons have returned. Like Harry, none has begun to accomplish his dreams. Common sense told each one in his moment of truth that his dream was impossible But contrary to what Hickey predicted, none is happier. In fact, they all find now that even whiskey fails to ease their desperation. As Harry says, Hickey has taken the kick away.

As the evening wears on, Hickey becomes increasingly concerned that his friends have not found peace and freedom from guilt. If his method did not work for his friends, maybe he doesn't have all the answers for himself either. He addresses his friends with a passionate plea for understanding as he begins a narrative about his life with his wife. Two policemen enter and hear his speech. Hickey has called them himself. Hickey relates how his wife loved him and kept forgiving him for his drinking, for his whores and for his lies. It was her dream that Hickey would reform. When he realized that he couldn't, he killed her to preserve her dream. As Hickey confesses, Parritt admits to Larry that he betrayed his mother, not for money, but because he hated her.

At the end of the speech, Hickey blurts out his own unconscious hatred of his wife. In frantic denial, he pleads insanity. All his friends are quick to seize on this explanation. If Hickey is insane, then all his preaching was crazy, Their own actions were not those of desperate men unable to realize their dreams, but those of rational men dealing with sudden insanity—humoring Hickey by pretending to go along with him.

Only Larry and Parritt are changed. Parritt now knows what he must do and commits suicide with nobody but Larry even noticing. Larry realizes that he has been clinging tenaciously to life, despite all his protestations about wishing to die. He is too weak to commit suicide, but now will wait with real eagerness for death. For the others, the kick is now restored to their 'booze', and they resume their normal existence, having had their illusions and dreams of tomorrow returned to them.

COMMENT

In 1972, Ely A. Landau devised a series of plays on film called *The American Film Theatre* directed by distinguished film-makers. There were two series between 1973 and 1974, each consisting of twelve films. These were shown one night only in cities throughout North America to audiences who had paid for them in advance on a subscription policy similar to stage performances. This was but one of the many methods of presenting specialized films tried out at that time in an attempt to bring audiences back into the cinemas and away from their television sets. Landau thought that if the stage origin of these films was emphasized by presenting them as plays, an entirely new audience would be attracted to the cinema. It worked for the first series, which opened with *The Iceman Cometh*, but the subscription did not sell out for the second group leaving many empty seats available to be purchased at the time of the performance.

As Frankenheimer has said, this is a straightforward, intimate, closely-shot play on film, yet requiring a different approach when considering where to place the camera, when to move it, how to move and control the players, where to cut in reaction shots, how to give the feel of film to an entirely closed and confined set. The emphasis falls entirely on the actors, and, in this respect, the cast never fails the director in their truthful portrayal of O'Neill's desperate people. The excellence of the cast and the fame of the play make this four-hour work (with one intermission) a rewarding experience. The principal characters, are superbly played—Fredric March, in his last film, depicts Harry with a fragile majesty; Lee Marvin as Hickey, cleverly walks the tightrope between exhortation and nimble wit, tending to emphasize the former quality, but is effective none-the-less; Robert Ryan, as the doomed Larry, brings a noble and heroic perspective to the glib cynic who, like O'Neill, is always close to death and likes to reason, in the darkness of decline, with a purpose both forceful and final. Among the lesser roles, Bradford Dillman's Willie Oban, who likes to come up with a joke, is played with dignity and confidence; Jeff Bridges, as Don Parritt, is an effective symbol of innocence keeping hope alive with quiet resignation; Sorrell

Booke's Hugo Kalmar, the anarchist, mixes fear and humor convincingly. The remainder of this thoughtfully directed cast is suitably bleak. While some of the director's interpretations here of O'Neill's outcasts are not always what followers of the play have come to expect, there is no denying the force and truth of their portrayals.

Frankenheimer, without extensive experience in the theatre since his early days, has mounted the play handsomely and brought it to the screen with understanding, certainty and control. To complain about it being stagebound (as some reviewers did) and failing to 'open up the screen' as most plays on film frequently do, is to deny the purpose of the series: to present plays as they are staged in the theatre but with the benefit of close-ups and the intimacy that film can bring. This was not a filmed stage performance, however, but one acted and set in a space devised to provide room for unobtrusive camera movement. Considered by most theatregoers to be O'Neill's finest play, its despairing yet absorbing view of the human condition comes to us with the poignant light of truth.

JF "When I studied O'Neill's *The Iceman Cometh* in college, my English professor dogmatically stated that this was a play about the necessity of guarding illusion in life— that O'Neill's message was: life without illusion is unlivable. To this day, as evidenced by the numerous critical opinions of the film version of *Iceman*, this is an opinion still held by many. However, it is not mine and this is the main reason I chose to do the film. In my opinion, *Iceman* is far more complex. It is not a work about having to live with illusion but rather one that explores the necessity and the horrible pain of living without it. Larry Slade, the character portrayed by Robert Ryan in the film, is O'Neill speaking to us—at the end of the play, he is the character stripped of illusion yet having to continue with life. It is for this reason that the film ends with a close-up of Larry.

"To make this concept of *Iceman* work, it must be perfectly clear to an audience that Hickey is *sane*. It has been argued that Hickey is a madman—that when he admits his insanity near the end of the film that this is to be taken literally. I believe that Hickey was sane when he killed his wife and is sane when he comes to the bar.

"With this concept in mind, I was determined to get Lee Marvin for Hickey. Lee is not only a superb actor, but we have a marvelous work relationship that goes back to the days of *Climax* on CBS. We did our first show together in 1955. Lee had the strength, the presence, and the humor that the role demanded and, most of all, he shared my point of view about the character.

"More or less the same was true in the choice of Fredric March for Harry. Freddie was in retirement but we had such a fine relationship during *Seven Days in May* that I could not think of doing *Iceman* without him. This was also the case with Bob Ryan with whom I had worked in the 1960 television version of *The Snows of Kilimanjaro*. Choosing the rest of the cast was not so easy. I feel very lucky that Jeff Bridges was available to play Parritt for it is, next to Hickey, the most difficult role in the film. Fortunately for everyone concerned, Bradford Dillman wanted to do Willie Oban—I think his performance turned out to be the most surprising to me, for I never thought it possible that an actor could bring me so much. Brad's performance is largely his own. I like to think I had the good sense to just let him alone.

"I had stipulated as a condition of my directing the film that I be allowed three weeks of rehearsal and that we shoot in continuity. Rehearsal was invaluable, for if the film were to succeed the acting would not only have to be excellent, it would have to be all in the same style—that is, real ensemble acting. I wanted a feeling that these actors had worked together for years. As it turned out, every member of the cast and crew, myself included, found ourselves in a unique atmosphere—we all felt exceptionally close to one another—everyone was trying to help in his or her best fashion. There was never an unpleasant moment during practically a three-month period. Here I think a word of thanks is in order to Ely Landau, who not only made the whole project possible, but left us completely alone and never interfered in any way.

"I was very aware from the outset what the problems were. First of all, there is the extraordinary length of O'Neill's original—over 4fl hours. Second, the entire action takes place in one set. And third, the impact of the play comes from the cumulative effect of the ensemble playing. Thomas Quinn Curtiss, film critic of the Paris *Herald Tribune*, who personally knew O'Neill and who is regarded as an expert on his work agreed to edit, or cut, the text. Since I was living in Paris at the time, Tom and I worked very closely together. In all, I think we cut well over 1/ hours—eliminating the brother-in-law Ed Mosher, giving his best lines to McGloin, and generally shortening a great many scenes—among them Hickey's monologue. It is a tribute to O'Neill that we were unable to keep most of the cuts we made. During rehearsal we replaced at least half of the lines we had taken out and for a very simple reason—they were needed to make the scenes work.

"A critic once said to O'Neill, 'Do you realize that Parritt repeats himself twenty-one times?' 'Wrong,' said O'Neill, 'he repeats himself twenty-three times and I mean every one of them. Each one is there for a reason.' He was right. For the most part we found that the line we eliminated four pages earlier made another line unplayable. This was the case in many scenes between Bob Ryan and Jeff Bridges, but particularly true of Hickey's soliloquy. This is the scene that must explode almost in a sexual sense. O'Neill himself often referred to this joke—the husband sitting downstairs calls up to his wife,

'Has the Iceman come yet?' 'No,' replies his wife, 'but he's breathin' hard.' In other words, Hickey has to reach a point of catharsis. He has to reach an unbelievable emotional climax during this scene. Lee Marvin and I found that rehearsal did not help here. We both knew what had to be done, but it was not until we were faced with really having to do it, that the speech began to come alive. It was staged in segments of four to eight minutes, with very few camera cuts and no additional coverage. So no protection shots were taken, and this, incidentally, was true throughout the filming. We were so sure of the material that a lot of extra coverage was unnecessary. In essence, we elected to make the film as long as it had to be. It turned out to be a little under four hours. Of course, if it had not been for the American Film Theatre, the film would never have been made, for what major studio could or would finance such a venture?

"Four hours in one set—that was another problem. I must confess now that, at the beginning, we almost fell victim to the old trap of 'opening it up'. In our first draft Tom and I began the film in the street outside the bar, went out with Harry Hope, saw the boy on the fire escape and ended with a long dolly shot away from the bar. Once we started rehearsal, we began to realize how impossible it would be to do that, because in spite of the fact that *Iceman* claims to be a very realistic play, it is not at all—rather, to quote Stanley Kauffman, it is a 'symbolic play'. Thus it had to be kept within the romantic or idealized setting of the four walls.

"The problem was how to vary camera angles without making the camera obtrusive—to keep the audience orientated, and never to lose the actors. Above all, I did not want to forget about an actor for ten or fifteen minutes and then arbitrarily cut to him for his line, like shooting skeet. To avoid this, Ralph Woolsey, the cinematographer, and I planned the entire film as a montage of shots, utilizing maximum depth of focus. The most common composition was a large head in the foreground with two or three other characters sharp in the background. We shot the film in 185.1 using Panavision equipment. For many sequences we shot with two cameras—in the case of the banquet scene, three. The lens most often used was the 20 to 120 zoom. Occasionally, to hold focus, we had to use a split diopter, but not often. We forced the film two stops to give us extra depth without increasing the light level to a point where working conditions would have been unbearable.

"I must add that, contrary to what many thought, Robert Ryan had no idea he was suffering from the cancer that was to kill him three months later. True, he had had the disease but both he and his doctors thought he was cured. Bob was very proud of the work he did in the film and felt that he had waited all his artistic life to play the role of Larry. Of course, he never saw it.

"I can say without any reservation that the *Iceman* was the finest experience of my professional life and I'm very glad it did not come too early."

Note: this the text of a talk given by John Frankenheimer to the Directors' Guild of America following the première of The Iceman Cometh.

99 AND 44/100% DEAD 1974

Director John Frankenheimer • *Producer* Joe Wizan • *Associate Producer* Mickey Borofsky • *Production Company* Joe Wizan/Vashon Productions • *Distribution* 20th Century Fox Film Corporation • *Screenplay* Robert Dillon • *Camera* Ralph Woolsey (Anamorphic—wide screen/DeLuxe color) • *Editor* Harold F. Kress • *Sound* Theodore Soderberg • *Costume Designer* Ronald Talsky • *Art Director* Herman Blumenthal • *Special Effects* Ira Anderson Jr., Paul Pollard Sr. • *Music* Henry Mancini • *Classification* PG • *Release* June 1974 • *Running time* 98 mins • *British title* Call Harry Crown • *Location* made at 20th Century-Fox Studios and on location in Seattle and Los Angeles from August to September 1973 • Novel from Ace Books • *Soundtrack* on RCA Records • *Formats* VHS

CAST

Harry Crown	•	Richard Harris
Uncle Frank	•	Edmond O'Brien
Big Eddie	•	Bradford Dillman
Buffy	•	Ann Turkel
Dolly	•	Constance Ford
Tony	•	David Hall
Baby	•	Kathrine Baumann
Clara	•	Janice Heiden
Zuckerman	•	Chuck Connors
North	•	Max Kleven
Guard	•	Karl Lucas
Burt	•	Anthony Brubaker
Shoes	•	Jerry Summers
Jake	•	Roy Jenson
Driver	•	Bennie Dobbins
Gunman	•	Chuck Roberson

ON LOCATION

Seattle, August 1973. We are in a run-down deserted part of the city, close to the waterfront. Trucks with equipment line the streets together with the trailers accommodating the leading players. The sea glistens with a dull and sullen resentfulness, as though disapproving of the antics being carried out by strangely garbed characters firing guns at each other, but then like all good films, the reality comes to life not so much in front of the cameras but when these short takes are put together in the editing and tried out in different sequences, until the whole life of them shines forth from the screen. John Frankenheimer is somewhat puzzled and dismayed. It is a familiar form of frustration for the director: in spite of rehearsals the parts do not seem to be working, but it's difficult to say or know why. He cannot see them coming together as he envisioned them before shooting began. Richard Harris will try again, and again, with the other players in the scene. Frankenheimer walks over to them after each take to make suggestions. Suddenly it seems right. The next take has caught the essence, the spirit of the moment. Another take and Frankenheimer is satisfied. Over lunch in his trailer he muses over the morning's filming:

"My principal concern with this picture is in bringing out the comic aspects of what is actually a true to life gangster melodrama. I want to make these characters absurd, as well as being deadly, yet to show that somewhere inside them even they have a strange sense of honor. I hope it comes through to audiences.

"I have tremendous confidence in the management of Fox, from Gordon Stulberg, president of the company, to Jere Henshaw, the vice-president, to Alan Ladd Jr., down. I think they are honest men, and so far they have left me alone. The relationship between me and Fox could not be better. I would never do a film for Jim Aubrey at MGM after what he did to *The Gypsy Moths*, unless I had an iron-clad contract and a million dollars extra were put in the bank in escrow, just to pay for infringements of contract. You know that *Ryan's Daughter* was not going to get a PG rating because of that one scene with Sarah Miles. Aubrey protested the rating and it was changed to PG without cuts being made. But if it had to have been cut, Aubrey would have done so without David Lean's permission even though Lean had final cut stipulated in his contract. 'Let Lean sue me,' would have been Aubrey's retort. There just no way of trusting Aubrey and Metro-Goldwyn-Mayer. Look at what he did to Peckinpah's film in Pat Garrett. Just ask Sam about it. Peckinpah's a terrifically good director, and a very strong man, but he couldn't stop Aubrey cutting his film.

"I wanted Richard Harris for this part because I did not want an American to play it. I thought to go a little off-key with an Irishman would be fun. He has tremendous strength; and he's a very untapped actor—he's an extraordinary person and a great actor and I hope I'm able to get from him what I think he can give to this role. It's an exaggeration of what's happening to people and events in a style more like *The Manchurian Candidate* rather than *Seconds*, if you will—well, we shall see, we still have several weeks' work in front of us before returning to LA."

SYNOPSIS

With his mob decimated when rival gang boss, Big Eddie, declares war in an attempt to become king of the underworld, Uncle Frank hires his old friend, Harry Crown. An ace trouble-shooter, Harry has his doubts about Tony, the inexperienced young hoodlum assigned as his aide. Harry looks up schoolteacher Buffy; an old girlfriend, and he renews acquaintance with 'Claw' Zuckerman, a dementedly sadistic killer with a metal claw replacing one hand (the result of an earlier encounter when Harry caught him mistreating a girl) who has been hired by Big Eddie.

Claw is furious when Harry rescues a call girl, Baby, from his clutches, and also when, despite information received from an informer in Uncle Frank's camp, he fails to prevent Harry from destroying a shipment of Big Eddie's contraband liquor. Evading pursuit, Harry takes refuge with Uncle Frank's predatory mistress, Clara. Next morning, though jealously refusing to believe he

has not succumbed to Clara, Buffy runs Big Eddie's blockade in her school bus to help Harry get away.

Meanwhile Baby, to Tony's distress, vanishes. While looking for her, Harry receives an offer of employment from Big Eddie, and, when he refuses, is sent scurrying to the schoolhouse to find that Buffy has disappeared and that Baby, tortured and drugged, is wired to a bomb. He manages to rescue Baby and clear the schoolhouse before the bomb explodes. He and Tony then trace Big Eddie to a laundry, and dispose of his gang before Tony is wounded. Harry then kills Claw, but with Big Eddie holding Buffy hostage, he is forced to disarm. But Uncle Frank arrives to dispose of Big Eddie, who reveals before dying that Clara was the informer. While Uncle Frank deals with her, Harry and Buffy bid a fond farewell to Tony and Baby, and set off on a cruise after foiling one last assassination attempt.

COMMENT

Ever in quest of unusual material, Frankenheimer turned from the darkness of O'Neill to the brightness of pop art cartoons and the lightness of a satirical swipe at the screen's thick-headed gangsters. The title comes from Procter and Gamble's claim that their Ivory bath soap is "99 and 44/100%" pure. Comedy being so subjective, it was not surprising that certain critics found this film somewhat deadening while others enjoyed the humor and social criticism that the director intended. Had it been made today, the broad humor enjoyed by the present younger generation would no doubt have proved it a wild success. (It took some time for *The Rocky Horror Picture Show* coming a year later to find a cult following.)

Frankenheimer, in a sequence of his customarily well-thought out camera movements, opens with the US flag flying forlornly over the Seattle docks. An air of menace pervades the scene. A car draws up. A man with a huge cigar drops a body in the ocean. The camera goes dreamily under water with it to reveal a forest of bodies standing up with feet encased in concrete blocks. A catchy tune by Mancini at first makes light of the macabre scene, then turns into a jazz motif as we enter the war

between Uncle Frank and Big Eddie, the two rival gangsters, and the arrival of Harry Crown.

With three such superlative players as Richard Harris, Bradford Dillman and Edmond O'Brien taking the roles of Harry, Eddie and Uncle Frank, the complicated double-crossing chain of events which follow are easily sustained in a series of comically conventional, dumb-gangster screen accidents and encounters. Broadly and enjoyably depicted, they are often witty, and endowed with Frankenheimer's stylistic sense of the absurd, they also remind the viewer of characters in James Bond and "superhero" films. The "molls" are attractive and likeable, with an underlying (and genuine) romanticism—as in the scene where Harry pulls a feather out of Buffy's bra, embraces her, picks her up and carries her away. Everyone smokes long cigars, a deadly bomb is detonated by a troublesome fly, Chuck Norris's metal claw is filled with numerous accessories, Uncle Frank wears a long black coat, and his assistant, Tony, wears a white suit at all times. Big Eddie's men, the villains, wear identical black suits and hats. There is a beautiful shot of Clara through the bathroom shutters, a hilarious school bus chase, but no blood bursts and no heavy-handed violence. Richard Harris and the bomb is surely a take-off of his similar scene in Lester's *Juggernaut*. In this film, Harris parodies the strong man throughout—he's the comical hero who, while being one of the gangsters, uses their methods for a moral purpose to rise above them and save the day. (Harris, years later, brings another version of this character to the screen in Clint Eastwood's *Unforgiven*.)

JF "Every film is a beginning over again, seeking the means to create the link that binds the director with his audience by what he puts on the strip of film in his camera and is then projected before them on the screen. I always find it difficult, if not impossible, to describe, to even know at times what it is all about. I love working with actors, I have never had any trouble with most of the actors who have been in my films, and I continue to get along very well with them. After all, they are the principal means by which I have to express myself—through them and, of course, the camera. Obviously I use the camera to see what I want to see as opposed to using it to do it from somebody's point of view other than mine—the script. I use it to put on the screen what I want the audience to see. I don't suppose that's different from other directors but I believe in moving the camera, I tend to do long shots, long takes in one. I use wide-angle lenses and compose shots in depth and, having said that, each scene dictates what I do with the camera. I try and use it to conform to the demands of the script rather than the other way round. I don't try and make the script conform to my camera. I try and use the camera as a character in the story rather than just recording what is going on. Knowing where to put the camera is not something that can be taught. You can learn a great deal about composition by looking at paintings and photographs and films you admire. I've seen filmmakers try to copy what I do but I don't think they've done it successfully; but imitation is the sincerest form of flattery, as they say!

"In many ways I still prefer black and white, I often achieve black and white effects while using color. You have to be very careful with the costumes, the production design and the props. I will not allow anybody to wear anything red in a

The camerawork is fluid and the follies are underlined by the imaginative use of sound and score. It may not always work, but the attempt is unusual and at times avant-garde. The title is also an ironic counterpoint to the comedy and the contents: Ivory soap may be pure but Procter and Gamble, noted for its repressive industrial tactics and mass pollution, is anything but a pure or model company.

movie of mine and I just don't want to see a red car or a bright blue car in the background. I don't want any bright colors. Today we are obligated to use color. I still think you can get better effects, moods and atmosphere on black and white, and I believe black and white is a hell of a lot better suited to the kind of movies I make, including this one."

• • •

"While I was doing *The Iceman*, Joe Wizan came to me and gave me this script for *99 and 44/100% Dead*. I had read this script three years before and didn't want to do it then. But I read it again and I suddenly realized what the writer was getting at— it's about deep relationships between people who *care* in the absolutely wild, wicked, violent society that we live in. Harry Crown is perfectly equipped to deal with such a society, and he's a deeply caring man; he won't show his feelings except for certain people, like the girl he meets. It's a Howard Hawks western rewritten for cynics. In other words, to me it's John Wayne coming in to clean up the town. It's got terrific style. In this picture people bite the dust—we don't have them killed in slow motion with their insides coming out, none that kind of violence. It's like the movies I used to love to see when I was younger. I remember Edward G. Robinson, James Cagney, the mobsters standing there with guns flaming—but I don't remember who they *shot*. That's what we wanted to do here. What I love about the characters is that they have no past and no future. It's strictly for *now*, that's what it is. I like that, but I'll tell you the truth, I wanted to make a picture that *worked* in America, that Americans could identify with and have fun with. *The Horsemen* didn't.

"*99 and 44/100% Dead* was not a script that was easy to read. You really have to see movie scripts, because they are just not made to be read. You know what movie scripts are? Guides for the director, and that's it. You describe scenes in a few words, yet look what it entails in actually filming them. Remember the classic line in *Ben Hur*? 'Scene 89, the Chariot Race', in two lines. How long did it take Andrew Marton to film? Four months, wasn't it?

"We created a comic-strip effect, and I tried to evoke the look of pop-art by Roy Lichtenstein. But it didn't succeed. I just don't think I did the right job on it because, looking back, it was not the right material for me. I'm a more serious type of semi-documentary, realistic director, and for me to try and parody my own style was wrong, even though I put as much of myself, even more, into doing it, into trying to make it a success. When something is going and desperation sets in and the script doesn't seem to be working, you say, 'My God, what can I do?' and you try everything you can.

"The studio rather let us down too—even as I let them down. The production personnel they advised me to hire were inferior and we got—as Sidney Pollack calls it—into a question of damage control rather early in the game. We had a totally inept production manager who had to be fired. By the time we brought in Melvin Dellar, a true expert, the ship was sinking. Dellar was fabulous and he almost saved it with me. I think I was the wrong director for it, and I realized that—I tried everything I knew and I just couldn't get it to work. I had the same cameraman as I did *Iceman*, Ralph Woolsey. Our collaboration there was excellent but on this picture it was terrible. I was just undone by ineptness at every level, which I just didn't realize.

"I argued with Richard Harris continually telling him to stop playing up the comedy and humor of the situation and trying to be bigger than life as Harry, to be cute as Harry. I wanted him to be real. I wanted him almost to be the character he was in Lindsay Anderson's *This Sporting Life*—one of the best movies I've seen, and Harris' performance in that was extraordinary—that was the way to do the movie. I couldn't persuade him to do this, the studio didn't help, and the more I tried to get him to play it my way the more he fell behind. He and I did not get along through the first two-thirds of the movie, and I think that hurt us, but we finally became friends for the last third. We worked well together from then on. If you look at what we shot in the last third, it's much better than the footage we shot in the first two-thirds. I'm not blaming

Richard and I'm not blaming myself. There was a difference of opinion as to how he should play his character. It should have been more of a Michael Caine take-off from his spy movies. Bradford Dillman gives a delightful, over-the-top performance. He almost made the movie single-handedly. There were three beautiful young actresses—Ann Turkel, Kathrine Baumann, and Janice Heiden. Turkel later married Richard Harris.

"When we started filming I was reported as saying that 'It's the same kind of movie as *The Manchurian Candidate*, but the style deals in the absurd.' That's what I said at the time but it certainly didn't turn out that way! There were elements in the movie that were larger than life, and while I successfully stylized those in *The Manchurian Candidate* with depth of focus shots and played it absolutely straight, I didn't benefit from my experience in this picture. Then I cast my friend Edmund O'Brien who had been great for me in television, and on the screen, in *Birdman of Alcatraz* and *Seven Days in May*. Eddie was down on his luck when I cast him. I thought he would be perfect as Uncle Frank, but the problem was that he could hardly see. His sight had almost gone, and he couldn't remember the lines. Because his eyes were so bad we couldn't put them on cue cards. I realize now that I should have put a hearing aid in his ear and had the lines read to him. George Roy Hill did it on television before me and that's what I should have done, but I didn't think of it at the time. We worked with great difficulty, in short takes, and again we fell horrendously behind.

"We lost the forest for the trees trying to get through every day, to finally get it done. It was a terrible experience all told. I stylized the attack on the factory without really knowing how to do it. I did it well in a later movie called *The Challenge*, when Scott Gordon and Toshiro Mifune attacked that big complex making their way through hundreds of people. I learned how to do it well probably from doing it badly in *99*.

"In spite of these failures I thought the film was different in many ways, with little touches like Chuck Connors unscrewing his claw. There were many good moments but to me the movie as a whole does not work. That doesn't mean I don't like certain elements: Mancini's music, the stunt work by Max Kleven. It's a pity the whole didn't come together in the way I had envisioned it."

INT. UNCLE FRANK'S TOWNHOUSE - ANGLE ON STAIRS -   349
NIGHT

Clara comes down them. Somebody is leaning on the buzzer.
She wears a caftan, looking just as good this late hour
as if the evening were starting. The CAMERA GOES with
her as she reaches the main floor and hits a call button,
the kind that unlocks doors. She moves swiftly toward the
kitchen, hearing the footsteps coming up the stairs that
lead below. She opens the door.

ANOTHER ANGLE   350

Harry stands there. In the brighter light, he looks
rotten. His face is cut in a couple of places, his hands
are grubby. He still drips in his filthy clothes. He
looks up and sees Clara. His eyes are filled with grit,
but you'd have to weld up a guy's lids before he couldn't
see Clara.

CLOSE ON CLARA   351

Her perfect mouth opens in shock.

                    CLARA
          Harry.

CLOSE ON HARRY   A-351

He's moving inside.

                    HARRY
          Yeah.

He closes the door behind him, the thin edge of the steel
plate inside the wood clicking closed sharply.

ANOTHER ANGLE   B-351

Harry starts into the house. Slow. Gravity is getting
to be an enemy. The CAMERA MOVES with him. Clara follows
behind, edging into the deep shadows in the room.

The house is empty. There are bars on the windows and most
are shuttered. The light is grey and dark.

CLOSE ON HARRY   C-351

He moves to a window and pulls back a curtain to look
outside.

HIS P.O.V. - STREET OUTSIDE   352

Two black cars are stationed across the street. Men in
them. They watch the house.

BACK TO SCENE   353

Clara's voice is soft and even.

                    CLARA
          They've been out there all night.

Harry moves slowly from window to window. He closes
shutters. He locks up tight.

                    HARRY
          Where's Frank?

She is still in shadows.

                    CLARA
          He was at the downtown office.
          He didn't come home.

ANOTHER ANGLE   A-353

Shutters click into place. Harry goes past her up the
stairs to Frank's study. Slowly, she follows behind.

ON DEPARTURE FOR PARIS

Malibu, Autumn, 1974.

"Take the time we spent in Paris with *Impossible Object* and the time I was doing *The Horsemen* in Spain, going backwards and forwards, returning to Los Angeles, to Hollywood, living here in Malibu, yes, I notice changes in places, people and in the business itself. The movie industry in America is a disaster area, people are out of work, there are hardly any films being made, and this confusing Supreme Court decision on 'community standards' makes the situation worse. We don't know where it's going to end, and I don't think we'll know for two years until our test case is put before the courts. It's truly horrendous, what Warren Burger, the Chief Justice, did—absolutely inexcusable. Censorship has always been hard on movies. Now we've got so many things going against us, we've got television, boating, even barbeques, everything you could possibly think of, and now with these obscenity charges, we have every vigilante and every madman in the country going after us. The quality of our films will suffer because studios are not going to take risks. One studio said, 'we want to make movies, not lawsuits'. We cannot make different prints for different places. It's not going to work that way. It's going to have an adverse effect on the range of subjects and stories we can film. It would be unthinkable to even try to start making *Last Tango in Paris* now, with the recent Supreme Court decision. I think I'm going to have problems distributing *Impossible Object* due to nudity, sex and so forth. Very definitely. This situation is politically motivated. I wish I had been wrong in what I said about Richard Nixon. It's not nice to be right in that context. I think I said during our conversation then that we should get out of Vietnam, and we did. But his second term doesn't look as though [*laughs*] it's going better than his first; at least he's been cut down to size now, and it's terrible, awful , what's happened. I wish I had not been prophetic. *Seven Days in May* comes close to being true when the military establishment is discussed. It seems to be running the political side of the government—bombing whoever they want to, going berserk in Cambodia. *Seven Days* is a cartoon now! But you ask me if I see changes in Hollywood? Yes, I've seen changes, many directors aren't making movies. I don't know what they're living on or what they're doing. There's a group of new young directors who are very good. I think George Lucas is going to be a giant of a director. *American Graffiti* is simply marvelous. Bogdanovich is superb, and my friend, Billy Friedkin, really has come into his own with *French Connection*, and Francis Ford Coppola is a director to watch. They're good—they're getting better. There are an awful lot of good new filmmakers. I find something interesting in my life today: I was a director when I was twenty-four years old, then directing CBS' *Playhouse 90* when I was twenty-six, and then directing feature films when I was thirty. It's funny now to be forty-three and having people think, 'He's been around a long time,' you know. I've been director for nineteen years, and I was always looked on as the young director, now I would like to get rid of that nonsense, I know that I continue to get better at what I do. Whatever I've done, I've done—that's who I am. I think there's a certain security in knowing that one has managed to make it through practically twenty years in filmmaking. What's important is to go on trying to find and film good projects. I have a new agent now, a young man named Jeff Berg from CMA. I have confidence in him; I like him and he's helped me considerably. I hadn't had an agent for years. And now that Evans and I have decided we no longer want to live in Europe but in America because we are Americans. No sooner do we make that decision than the next film I'm going to do is a sequel to *The French Connection* with Gene Hackman, in France, in Marseilles!"

FRENCH CONNECTION II 1975

Director John Frankenheimer • *Producer* Robert L. Rosen • *Production Company* 20th Century-Fox • *Screenplay* Robert & Laurie Dillon, Alexander Jacobs, *from a story by the Dillons* • *Camera* Claude Renoir (DeLuxe color/wide-screen) • *Editor* Tom Rolf • *Sound* Ted Soderberg, Bernard Bats • *Production Design* Jacques Saulnier • *Costume designer* Jacques Fonteray • *Art Direction* Gérard Viard, Georges Glon • *Special Effects* Lee Zavitz • *Music* Don Ellis • *Distribution* 20th Century-Fox • *Classification* R • *Release* April 1975 • *Running Time* 119 mins • *Other titles* French Connection No. 2, French Connection 2 • *Location* made at 20th Century-Fox Studios, Los Angeles, studios in Boulogne, Paris, and on location in Marseilles, over ten weeks beginning in August 1974 • In development since late 1972, originally to be produced by Phil D'Antoni and written by James Poe • *Formats* VHS and LD.

CAST

"Popeye" Doyle •	Gene Hackman
Alain Charnier •	Fernando Rey
Inspector Barthelemy •	Bernard Fresson
Raoul Diron •	Jean-Pierre Castaldi,
Miletto •	Charles Millot
Mère Charnier •	Cathleen Nesbitt
Old Pro •	Pierre Collet
Jacques •	Philippe Leotard
U.S. Colonel •	Ed Lauter
Immigration Officer •	Jacques Dynam
Dutch Captain •	Raoul Delfosse
Manfred •	Patrick Floersheim

SYNOPSIS

New York detective 'Popeye' Doyle arrives in Marseilles, assigned to help the local police break the heroin smuggling ring of Doyle's old enemy, Alain Charnier (unknowingly, in fact, Doyle has been sent as bait for Charnier), Meeting his opposite number on the local force, Barthelemy, Doyle finds that his violent reputation has preceded him and won him few friends. Chafing at the way he is excluded from police operations, Doyle attempts to take a hand during a drugs raid, and his action results in the death of an undercover officer.

Lonely, bored and speaking no French, Doyle wanders disconsolately about Marseilles. One night he eludes the two policemen assigned by Barthelemy to follow him and keep him out of trouble, only to find himself kidnapped by Charnier's men. In an attempt to find out what Doyle has learned, Charnier treats him with heroin for three weeks then returns him, near death, to the police. Doyle is saved but is forced to go through the painful process of 'cold turkey' once he is no longer being injected with heroin.

Later scouting through Marseilles, he finds the hotel where he was held prisoner, sets it on fire, and beats information about Charnier from one of its inhabitants. Racing to the harbor, the police find Charnier's men removing canisters of heroin from the hull of a ship in dry dock. Their attack is a failure, however; the thugs escape and the next day Doyle is ordered to leave Marseilles. He nevertheless persuades Barthelemy to watch the captain of the ship, who eventually leads them to one of Charnier's lieutenants and the factory where the heroin is processed.

Surprised by the police, most of the gang is rounded up. Charnier escapes, but Doyle, pursuing him relentlessly on foot, and chasing him exhaustedly around the harbor when Charnier attempts to leave by yacht, finally gets in his shot and brings Charnier down.

COMMENT

For many experienced and distinguished directors, the task of taking on a sequel to an important, highly praised and commercially successful film is usually considered to be somewhat insulting and demeaning. The screenplay will probably be inferior to the original and going over the previous director's ground leads to unfavorable comparisons with the original. But such was not the case with Frankenheimer and *French Connection II*.

Frankenheimer knew Friedkin as a friend, and, making sure he did have a good screenplay to work from, had the confidence to take it on, knowing that his film would be above any comparisons that might be leveled at him by the critics. Also, *French Connection II* was set in France where the director had lived, where he was familiar with the people, and also spoke their language. He was not then, working on alien ground and his resulting picture thoroughly understood its setting and the motives and behavior of the characters it deals with, mostly French. Nor did the director attempt to imitate either the style or the events of the original. His film exists as a work in its own right. What is consistent with its predecessor, however, is the outlook, mentality and behavior of the central figure, "Popeye" Doyle—angry, contemptuous of other races, but never corrupt or delinquent in his duty.

Opening with a suspenseful yet different sound in the title music, we are taken into the port of Marseilles through a series of well-planned camera movements conveying a quiet yet threatening air—Frankenheimer is, for the third time, working with Claude Renoir. Doyle arrives, ridiculous in his pork pie hat, as the intolerant, impatient American in action, coarse and rude in speech, but with the vulgarian's instinctive understanding of the criminal world and its inhabitants. Shunned by the detectives he must work with he wanders around, alone and with a deep dislike of everything French—including the food. The impact of these sequences comes from the well-observed low-key details of other people's daily existence as seen from the Café Florida, a natural draw for Doyle because of its American name, and where he indulges in his craving for whisky and

Hershey bars. Between the exciting police raid at the opening and the very long and gripping closing shot with Doyle running for a punishing distance along the waterfront following the boat taking Charnier to attempted freedom, Frankenheimer resists introducing any violence for its own sake but concentrates on making ordinary and drearily depressing days come quietly alive with menace and emotion.

Throughout the long and difficult sequence of Doyle's capture and drugging by Charnier, Gene Hackman's performance is full of pain and anger, incoherent in his explosions of rage, his swearing at the "Frogs", his feelings of guilt brought on by his Catholic upbringing. Breaking down and weeping uncontrollably, he brings a tragic depth to this sensitively played and unnerving portrayal, directed mostly in close-ups. Frankenheimer continues to show his interest in industrial processes with documentary scenes of drugs being refined and distributed. He fills the screen with conflicts and contrasts depicting crowds on the street, a cat running into the sewer, close-ups of trolley lines,

the wind blowing rubbish along wet alleyways. Using suspenseful tracking shots, and imaginative sound and editing techniques, he continually sustains audience interest.

Among many gems is the sequence where Doyle is visited by Charnier's mother, an old English lady movingly played by Cathleen Nesbit, who talks endlessly about "never being listened to" and while comforting him, quietly steals his watch. We see her arm is punctured by repeated drug injections. Charnier is played with cold perfection by Fernando Rey, while Bernard Fresson is the likeable and efficient French detective. Although Doyle emerges victorious from his trials, there is no joy in the achievement. When he fires the last shot killing Charnier escaping on his yacht, the final scenes suggest that life for him remains a void. He will never understand what motivates him. Yet this character, played in a rage of turmoil and frustration, has carried us into a vivid and gripping depiction of the world of drugs and despair and of those who inhabit it. This is a sequel surpassing in many ways the original.

Frankenheimer shows the pioneer American film director, King Vidor (left), one of the hand-held cameras used during the filming of French Connection II.

JF "We made the entire picture in France. It came about as a result of 99. In other words, I was there and the studio liked me, thank goodness! And this was before we started 99! I spoke French, I had long thought of doing a picture about being a stranger in France, and Bob Dillon, who wrote the script for 99, came up with the idea. They asked me if I wanted to direct *French Connection II*. They had made a deal with Gene Hackman, and decided to make the film in France. They remembered that I lived there. I said 'Yes, I'll do *French Connection II* provided you come up with a good story.' And we did. Dillon's 'Popeye' Doyle continues to chase Charnier, the criminal from the first film, and becomes hooked on narcotics. He suffers withdrawal, but finally catches Charnier. A very simple concept when you came right down to it, and, like all good plots it can be told in three sentences or less. Both Fox and Gene Hackman agreed more or less straight away. Laurie Dillon, who is credited as a writer, was Bob Dillon's wife. He had just tried to get her into the Writers' Guild, but she had absolutely nothing to do with the picture. We had two other writers who contributed greatly to the script—Alexander Jacobs and Pete Hamill. The latter should have been credited but wasn't.

"I was determined to produce and direct this picture because I had lived in France, I knew France and I knew exactly how I wanted to go about it. Fox wanted their own man, Robert Rosen. I didn't want anyone, but I met Bob Rosen, and actually it turned out to be the second most important relationship in my career—we've since done several movies together. He was a brilliant line producer. If Bob Rosen was combined with Eddie Lewis the film business would have the genius of all time. Eddie Lewis was the greatest above-the-line producer I've ever known the way he could put pictures together, make deals, and give people what they wanted. Bob Rosen is the best below-the-line producer I've ever worked with. He knows all the nuts and bolts of movie-making, he communicates clearly and directly with people, knows how to get things done, is creatively very good, and never sacrifices the movie to the budget, yet we still came in under budget.

"99 was a picture that was wrong for me, *French Connection II* was a picture that was ideally right for me. The semi-documentary style, the realism I like to bring to the screen, worked well in it. Also, Gene Hackman is probably among the two or three finest movie actors I have ever worked with. His performance in this picture was absolutely thrilling. The entire sequence where Hackman is going 'cold turkey' is thought by many to be improvised, but, in reality, every moment, every word of it, was written by Pete Hamill. Now, mind you, that was an idea in the Dillon script, he thought of it but his dialogue was not right. Then Alexander Jacobs came in and solved problems in structure. Jacobs was English, which meant we had to bring in Hamill, an American, to write the dialogue for 'Popeye' Doyle.

"I think another element you will find interesting is that there are no sub-titles. We used the French language as a weapon against 'Popeye' Doyle. We had actors talking French, nothing to do with the plot, but he couldn't understand them and it drove him crazy. The audience couldn't understand it either and they were just as vexed as 'Popeye' Doyle—the device worked. The picture was difficult to dub into French as you can imagine, because in the French version everybody spoke French, so it didn't have that element. We just had the Doyle character speak French with an American accent. Now Fernando Rey is a remarkable actor but, being Spanish, I would not have cast him. I got stuck with him because he was in the first picture. Billy Friedkin is a brilliant director, but he doesn't speak French, and unwittingly he cast this Spanish actor as Charnier. After he finished the movie, it was pointed out to him that Rey spoke French with a Spanish accent, so he had to be dubbed. I didn't realize Fernando Rey was dubbed in the first picture, as he didn't say very much, if you remember. In our picture he had more to say, with a very thick Spanish accent, and he had to be dubbed in English and French. But he was a wonderful actor, and very good in the role.

"The production designer, Jacques Saulnier, was very good. He built the police station and the jail in the studio. I've done two movies with prison backgrounds—*Birdman, The Fixer, and now French Connection II*. I prefer the real thing which we used in *The Fixer*. Unfortunately it was so cramped we had to restrict the camera positions and the lighting to such an extent that some audiences got the impression that it was a set. Jacques built the entire backdrop outside the window of the police station and it was extremely realistic. It was forced perspective and three dimensional. he also bult all the rooftops and the Marseilles skyline.

"Our stunt co-ordinator was none other than Hal Needham. He and Bob Rosen were very good friends. Needham as a stuntman is absolutely fearless, and he will do anything. We did not get along terribly well, but I respect him. Don Ellis wrote the music for the first *French Connection*. He was a jazz musician who died recently. Billy Friedkin chose him and I felt obliged to go with him in the second one. I was satisfied with what he did for the picture. many of the crew I had used on *The Horsemen* and *Impossible Object*. They could not have been better. Incidentally, being a Fox picture, Robert Rosen was the below- and above-the-line producer—the above-the-line producer deals with creative elements, financial offers, the studio, the actors, the business of getting the movie done, and the below-the-line producer deals with it from the financial standpoint and he can help a director a great deal. They are on the set throughout filming.

"This was my third picture with Claude Renoir, an artist on film who instinctively understands what a director needs. There are cinematographers who are no help at all. Seeing that he had made so many gentle and lovely French films I thought this picture would be hard on him. 'I'm not sure you can do this,' I told him, 'because the way the first film was shot we're going to film most of this one with handheld or with long lenses. It's got to look jagged and raw. You should look at the first picture.' He did, and came back saying, 'I don't anticipate any difficulties with this approach. A lighting cameraman is a lighting cameraman.' On one occasion a situation arose where he saved the day—or the night! The nightime dry dock sequence was very tough to shoot and to light. Renoir had to light up half of Marseilles in the background to show where we were. Otherwise we conveyed no sense of the city at all. We'd shoot in one direction and then turn around and shoot in the opposite direction, but to change all the lights for the second direction was an enormous job. What I tried to do was decide at the beginning of the night on one direction, and then not to have to change that same night.

"But one night there was nothing I could do. It was summer and the nights were fairly short. We had to change, and it had been a tense night with a great deal of action and a lot of rough stuff. It was about a two-hour job to change the lights. About three-quarters of an hour after I had given the order to change I realised in horror that I'd forgotten a key shot in the other direction. I went to Claude and told him what happened. 'How long will it take to relight it' I asked, fearing the worst. 'How long will it take to get the actors here' he replied. I asked him what he meant and he said that he wanted to protect us from something like this happening and kept the original lighting, adding more on the other side. 'Bring the actor in,' he said, 'and we'll shoot the scenes.' You can imagine my relief. He was a true collaborator.

"When the picture opened it received some of the finest reviews I've ever had, but the picture was not as successful as the first one financially, although it more than recovered its cost. I think audiences didn't realize it was a sequel. They thought it was a re-release of the first one, the way it was marketed. This was before sequels became popular. *Godfather II* came out right after it. Gordon Stulberg left Fox and in came a new management team headed by Alan Ladd Jr. They never understood this picture, they had had nothing to do with its inception and nothing to do with its being shot. They inherited the movie and I don't think they knew what to do with it.

"I must mention Catherine Nesbitt, an idol of mine. I had seen her in T. S. Eliot's *The Cocktail Party* on Broadway and I deeply admired her. I thought she was just so magnificent, and I so much wanted to work with her. We created this part for her, she came over from England, and was so pleased and anxious to play it. She suffered badly from arthritis in her hands. I thought she was one of the most beautiful women who had ever lived. I don't know if you have seen pictures of her when she was young, but for her to expose herself that way in the film was so brave and she was so good!

"I think it's among the best movies I ever made. Making this film was such a satisfying experience for me. I think of Claude Renoir, and of Lionel Linden, James Wong Howe, Gerry Fisher—in my opinion I've worked with four great cameramen in my time. Furthermore, *French Connection II* was for its period and even still for today, a disturbing portrait of our society in distress."

BLACK SUNDAY 1977

Director John Frankenheimer • *Producer* Robert Evans • *Executive Producer* Robert L. Rosen • *Production Company* Robert Evans Productions/Gelderse Maatschapij N.V. • *Screenplay* Ernest Lehman, Kenneth Ross, Ivan Moffat, *based on the novel by* Thomas Harris • *Camera* John A. Alonzo (Movielab color/Anamorphic wide-screen) • *Editor* Tom Rolf • *Sound* John K. Wilkinson, Gene Cantamessa • *Costume Design* Ray Summers • *Art Director* Walter Tyler • *Set Decoration* Jerry Wunderlich • *Music* John Williams • *Distribution* Paramount Pictures • *Classification* R • *Release* March 1977 • *Running Time* 143 mins • *Location* made in Los Angeles, Washington DC, Miami, and in the Middle East • *Running time* originally ran 143 mins but was re-edited slightly to reduce the original R rating to a PG rating • Novel from Bantam Books • *Soundtrack* available on GSF Records • *Formats* VHS and LD • *Cost* $M7.5

CAST

Major Kabakov • Robert Shaw	*Simmons* • Nick Nicolary
Michael Lander • Bruce Dern	*Jackson* • Michael Joseph Reynolds
Dahlia Iyad • Marthe Keller	
Corley • Fritz Weaver	*TV cameraman* • Hunter Von Leer
Robert Moshevsky • Steven Keats	*VA Receptionist* • Sarah Fankboner
Fasil • Bekim Fehmiu	*Head nurse* • Kathy Thornton
Muzi • Michael V. Gazzo	*Lansing* • Frank Logan
Pugh • William Daniels	*Miami desk clerk* • Frank Man
Colonel Riaf • Walter Gotell	*SWAT captain* • Kenneth I. Harms
Nageeb • Victor Campos	*Girl hostage* • Kim Nichols
Fowler • Walter Brooke	*Bellhop* • Bert Madrid
Watchman • James Jeter	*TV Controller* • John Frankenheimer
Freighter captain • Clyde Kusatsu	*Themselves* • Joseph Robbie, Robert Wussler, Pat Summerall, Tom Brookshier
Farley • Tom McFadden	
Vickers • Robert Patten	
Israeli ambassador • Than Wyenn	
Pearson • Jack Rader	

ON LOCATION

Orange Bowl, Miami, Florida, September 1976. A sweltering hot summer's day. The Orange Bowl looking immense from the middle of the field, is vast with tiers of empty seats on one side. The opposite is colorful and lively being filled with townspeople playing spectators pretending to watch a game which isn't being played at the moment. The field is littered with equipment of all kinds including cameras and cranes, ropes and wires, trucks and other vehicles, and seemingly hundreds of technicians and crew. This equipment and the people scampering or sitting around are dwarfed by the cone of a huge blimp sitting motionless in the center like a bloated monster missing a vital part. Its aluminum-colored sheeting flaps slightly in the hot breeze, as though it were taking its last breath. This is an immense mock-up of the nose of the Goodyear Blimp which has—or will appear to do so—landed in the field as a result of terrorist activity. Close-up shots and frontal shots, and others will be taken to be used to create the dramatic effects of this near-disaster; the trucks pull it and drag it into position. The scene appears to be one of mass confusion. How it works itself out and into the final cutting of the picture is one of the continuing marvels of filmmaking.

A row of director's chairs form an uneven line over to the side of the field not far from the barrier behind which the seats of spectators rise. The chairs have the usual names printed on the back rest: the director, producer, cinematographer, set designer, continuity, and the actors: Bruce Dern, Marthe Keller, Robert Shaw, Bekim Fehmiu. Bags of fruit and containers of coffee are plentiful. A Canadian student from Montreal writing her thesis on the films of Frankenheimer is engaged in an intense conversation with him. He is interrupted by the crackle of worried and impatient voices on the 'walkie-talkies', carried around by all unit members, asking for advice, permissions and explanations about the intricacies of the set-up. Robert Shaw talks firmly, spiritedly and knowledgeably to an attentive Bruce Dern - not about the film but the IRA. There has been another terrorist bombing in Belfast and London. Shaw, an Irishman himself, is outraged. It seems fitting that as the story of *Black Sunday* is about PLO terrorism he should be talking about the IRA. Shaw is no supporter of it; he speaks with authority and conviction - if Northern Island falls to the IRA it will want to rule all of Ireland and a bloody civil war would follow lasting many years. (Shaw never lived to see the outcome of this struggle. He died in 1978, aged 51, a year after the release of *Black Sunday*.) Frankenheimer, wearing a safari hat and jacket, rises looking taller than ever, and suggests we go to his trailer outside the stadium. It will be several hours yet before the scene will be ready for filming. Taking off his hat and pouring a Scotch, Frankenheimer, looking tired and sounding somewhat abstract, had looked at the morning rushes and was pleased with what he had seen. "It does look compelling both physically and dramatically. This is a picture that just had to be shot in 'Scope. The subject calls for it, and we have any number of marvelously composed shots of the blimp crossing the screen and coming in over the Bowl. Perhaps Joe Mankiewicz was right when he said, on the introduction to CinemaScope, that it was fit only to photograph snakes and letter-boxes, but it certainly is great for airships. I think we have a splendid screenplay, an intelligent adaptation of Thomas Harris' novel by Ernest Lehman, Kenneth Ross and Ivan Moffat. There is great depth to the characters and far more to the story than a raid by terrorists on the Superbowl. Robert Shaw, as the Israeli 'guerilla', for example, sees both sides of the PLO-Middle East conflict, while the motivations of Marthe Keller, as the Black September activist, and Bruce Dern, the mentally unbalanced pilot, have a dramatic and human depth essential to making this a true political thriller with frightening references to what has been happening in real life. They are all victims of circumstances. Shaw is a great actor, Keller is so understanding of her role, and Bruce Dern, well, he's as eccentric as he's made out to be, but one of the best actors to work with. He's constantly trying to help and always very funny, one of the funniest men I've ever met. But eccentric— he runs twelve miles a day! He's a real marathon runner, a triathlon athlete! He's also totally dedicated, but for him everything in life is just a little bit off. His perception of reality is different from yours and mine, but once accepted he becomes a good friend and he's a great person to have on your side. I wouldn't want Bruce as an enemy, I really wouldn't, it would scare me, but thank God he's not. I can't help liking him. No, I haven't seen this new picture of his, Michael Ritchie's *Diggstown*, but I hear Bruce is terrific in it.

The studio doesn't like it and won't spend the money to promote it; as a result nobody in this world has seen it yet. [*Note: it was not released until 1992.*] I think you'll find that in *Black Sunday*, we're giving Bruce the opportunity to realize his best and most fully developed screen characterization." Dern himself enters the trailer and with an uncanny sense of perception says, "Hey you guys, you talking about me?" "Of course," replied Frankenheimer, "you'll never be the same after you've finished here . . . " There follows much joking between the two as they both leave the trailer to return to the set, Dern professing astonishment over the indignities JF heaps upon him.

SYNOPSIS

A tape-recorded message from the Black September movement, due to be delivered after a forthcoming terrorist attack in the United States, is seized in Beirut during a surprise raid by Israeli commandos (although their leader, Major Kabakov, is unable to kill one of the plotters, Dahlia Iyad, when he comes upon her in the shower). While Kabakov and his assistant, Robert Moshevsky, join FBI agent, Corley, in trying to discover the target of the attack, Dahlia visits her American contact, Michael Lander, a navy pilot captured in Vietnam and deeply bitter about his country since being court-martialled for co-operating (after brain-washing) with his captors. Lander now pilots the Goodyear airship used in TV coverage of football games and is constructing, for the Palestinians, a device to explode thousands of steel darts over the national championship game to be held in Miami's Super Bowl.

While unloading plastic explosives from a Japanese freighter, Dahlia and Lander are spotted by the coast guard but escape. Kabakov is subsequently injured when a bomb explodes to silence the ship's captain. Dahlia fails to penetrate Kabakov's hospital room, but kills Moshevsky instead. Kabakov later blackmails a Middle East politician into telling him about Dahlia. The Black September leader, Fasil, consequently tries to persuade Dahlia to abandon the operation. But Fasil is spotted in Miami by the FBI and killed in a shoot-out.

Just before the game, Lander is replaced as the blimp pilot, but he and Dahlia kill the substitute and trick their way aboard the airship. Alerted to the danger threatening the Super Bowl game by a leaflet found in Fasil's hotel room, Kabakov and Corley realise what is happening when the dead pilot is found. They pursue the blimp by helicopter, kill Dahlia and Lander, and tow the craft out to sea where its darts explode harmlessly.

COMMENT

In bringing political subjects successfully to the screen Frankenheimer has few equals. Apart from the obviously outright portrayals of politicians at work—*The Manchurian Candidate*, *Seven Days in May*, *Dead Bang*—few of his films are without political undercurrents and references to particular current events of one kind or another. In *Black Sunday* he sweeps in with an intelligent, nerve-wracking drama about Arab-Israeli terrorism. Opening in Beirut, without title music, with a gripping sense of time and place, introducing the brilliant Robert Shaw in close-ups, the film unfolds unerringly without a wasted moment. Every scene, every sentence, carries us into the brutal, horrifying world of organized terrorism. These are modulated, however, by the almost as frightening realism of drab, everyday events. With his customary documentary style, we encounter, for example, a sad group of Vietnam veterans waiting for attention at a hospital with an unhelpful receptionist and a doctor who isn't prepared.

Conflicts arise from the beginning and the tension never flags. Americans in France, and Israelis in the US, are all mired in opposition, with the local police and the FBI adding to the confusion. The narrative, however, is never confused and the motivations of the characters with their opposing beliefs run deep with anger and frustration. Shaw, as the Israeli agent whose family was killed by the Arabs, is sick and weary of the struggle and its accompanying violence, and has come to see both sides of the dispute. The likelihood of expecting any settlement between Arabs and Jews has slipped away. Bruce Dern, at his unhinged best, is convincingly deadly as never before.

The scenes in the stadium, a clever and convincing combination of the actual game with staged sequences, are gripping in their excitement and feeling of danger. The director's power in maintaining rhythm and pacing and in foreseeing his method of editing is skillfully in evidence, while the sheer visual drama of the huge blimp coming down over the stadium is action cinema at its terrifying best. John Williams' score heightens the drama of the tense crowds, the impending danger, the burning fuse, the turning rotor blades, the startling scenes of the helicopter pursuing the blimp with Shaw transferring from one to the other, and the final climax showing the blimp being towed out over the ocean—these are all masterfully filmed and edited.

At the finale, there is a touching scene in black-

and-white of a coffin being taken on to an airplane with the camera looking up at Shaw's face. Shaw, as Kabakov, had hesitated in the opening scene to shoot Dahlia and she escaped. In the closing scene, she hesitates to shoot him and is herself destroyed. In a thoughtful moment, we are made aware of two individuals who, in normal times, could have been friends, even lovers. Fate, however, decrees otherwise: one dies for her

beliefs, the other goes on living for a cause without control in a life without meaning. In ending the film by sending Kabakov out over the vast and empty ocean, Frankenheimer symbolizes the futility of violence in this particular struggle: the attempt has failed, there will be another terrorist attack, and yet another. Some will be foiled, others will succeed. The pattern is continually repeated and innocent people keep losing their lives.

Producer Robert Evans with Frankenheimer.

F "Having finished *French Connection II*, I didn't have another movie in mind until talking with Irving Lazar, who wanted to represent me. He had a book he thought I could do and arranged for Paramount to see *French Connection II* and they agreed to let me do *Black Sunday*. Ernest Lehman was writing the script. It came in much too long, a hundred pages too long. I asked Paramount to sign on Robert Rosen to co-ordinate production. Bob Evans was the above-the-line producer, and he was instrumental in getting us Robert Shaw, Marthe Keller and Bruce Dern. And we were almost immediately strapped with certain production realities—which were that the Super Bowl was going to be played the last week in January and it was already December.

"One of the most difficult tasks facing us, of course, was getting permission to use the Goodyear blimp. Here was this friendly symbol of Goodyear going up to carry a bomb into a football stadium—you can imagine what that meeting was

like! The only reason we got it, I think, was that I had had an excellent relationship with Goodyear's Public Relations department when we made *Grand Prix*. I had done everything I promised to do for them then. Bob Rosen, meanwhile, had gone to Germany and found an alternative blimp, but it would have been extremely impracticable to bring the German blimp over. Today there are lots of blimps around, but in 1976 there was only the Goodyear one, so we asked them but they turned us down. So we said 'Well, if you don't, we're going to bring in the German blimp, and everybody will think it's the Goodyear blimp anyway, and we'll do anything we want with it. If you co-operate with us, you could advise us on what you want the blimp to do. It will also be publicity, in a strange kind of way, for Goodyear.' Then they agreed. Actually we used three Goodyear blimps in the picture—one in Miami, one in Huston, and one in Los Angeles.

"The other difficulty, of course, was getting the

rights to the Super Bowl. This was absolutely necessary, and luckily for us it was being played that year at the Orange Bowl in Miami—if it had been played in an enclosed stadium, we couldn't have made the movie, because an enclosed stadium cannot be attacked with a blimp. Joe Robbie, the President and owner of the Miami Dolphins, secured the co-operation of the National Football League and the right to actually film during the Super Bowl, a huge concession for us. We knew that we faced a situation full of unknown complexities, not unlike *Grand Prix*. Here we were going to base a movie on a real event. What, we had to ask ourselves, would happen if it pours with rain, what happens if we have a hell of a wind, because if the wind is over twenty miles an hour, the blimp can't take off. We would have been absolutely finished. What we did was to organize a very extensive second unit and begin filming before the picture ever started. We obtained permission to film a Miami Dolphins game during the regular season which was not being carried on national TV, and so started earlier in the day—and the blimp came too! We had cameras in the stands, we had all kinds of equipment, and we got that shot of the blimp coming right toward the stadium, that famous shot over the light tower. Then we had an extensive aerial second unit shooting doubles with the helicopter, the 'picture helicopter', and the blimp, with Robert Shaw and Fritz Weaver. We had a very brave stunt man, by the name of Howard Curtis, who actually came out of that helicopter on that cable doubling Robert Shaw, suspended in the air. Ironically and tragically, Howard Curtis was killed on his next movie in a parachute jump. But this man had more courage than anybody I've ever seen.

"The budget we came up with was $8 million—in 1976 money. I said that I could make the movie for no more than $7fi million. To do this, Bob Rosen came up with an idea to approach the charity National United Way, and in return for Robert Shaw narrating a film for them, and me directing it, see if they would give us enough extras to save us half a million dollars. They agreed, and we had over a thousand a day in the stands. That was really not enough, but for a concentrated section here or there, it worked.

"While we were in Miami, we looked at that section of Miami Beach, which we show in the movie, where elderly people sit, and we thought how exciting it would be to devise a chase sequence through there, with Robert Shaw chasing Bekim Fehmiu when he takes the little girl hostage. I think that was one of the best sequences in the movie, though it was never in the script: we put it in after looking at the location.

"The filming of the Super Bowl itself was our raw potential. We had to film our actors and not interfere with the game, because if we had interfered at all with the game, we would be thrown out. So now the question was, where are we going to put our cameras? Every place I found to put a camera, I was told that I couldn't put a camera there because television already had that position. So, to make a long story short, the CBS camera crew there turned out to be my old crew when I had worked in live TV, and of course I knew them all. I explained my problem to Johnny Lincoln, a cameraman for the CBS crew, and he said 'No problem at all, put your cameras right next to ours!' They gave me everything because of our past association.

"The most difficult shot we had to get was Robert Shaw running the length of that field into the television camera. Needless to say there were over five thousand photographers on the sidelines and a hundred thousand spectators in the stadium. If we had said that Robert Shaw is going to make a run in the middle of the third quarter, all those photographers would have turned around and shot him, ruining the scene. So we had to film this very secretly. We put four of our cameras at a certain moment on Robert Shaw, and waited and waited. Pete Roselle—the then President of the NFL—knew this was the big shot but at the same time, he did not want to disrupt the game. So he said 'You can shoot this when the ball's at the other end of the field, and I'll tell you when.' The game went on, and on, and on, and still Pete had not given us permission. I was getting very nervous. Bob suddenly said to me 'I'm ready on the set, I think you ought to just shoot it.' I called all my cameras, spoke with the assistant director standing with Robert Shaw and told him to stand by. We were given special passes to get into the Orange Bowl. If you lose your pass they just throw you out. These passes came with a thick, plastic-type string to go around your neck. It's impossible to break this string. The moment came for Robert Shaw to run. He'd been waiting, and he was a very athletic man, and the adrenalin was so strong in him that he took his pass and just ripped it right off his neck. He came over the protecting rail and out and nobody knew who he was. Two security officials tried to stop him from getting on the field. You can see him just go right through them and knock them aside! He came right down the sidelines and ran. Today we could never do this—in those days, terrorism was not as much a threat as it is today.

"But then came the day we had to create panic in the Orange Bowl in wide shots. To do that, we had to fill the Orange Bowl with people, which is not all that difficult, but awfully expensive. We devised a raffle as I'd done on *Grand Prix*. Miami television and radio stations and newspapers were immensely helpful, spreading the news that cash prizes and a part in the movie were to be given away, and that a big show with a stunt man would take place. The townspeople poured out to the Orange Bowl on a Sunday. We had three-man camera crews on triple time, twenty-two National Football League players from the Miami Dolphins, pick-up crews wearing the uniforms of the Pittsburg Steelers and the Dallas Cowboys, and we started at eight-thirty in the morning. By nine o'clock we had fifty thousand people in the stands and it was absolutely marvelous. Then, at 9:30, it

started to rain and the heavens opened up. I'd never seen it rain that way—and it kept raining. We were desperate. We didn't know what to do. We knew that we could never recreate this day and even if we could, it would cost us (at that time) a half-million dollars extra (about two million today), and disrupt our schedule for going back to California. There was nothing we could do. We sat in my trailer while it continued to rain. It was raining so hard—the Orange Bowl has eaves that come out over the stands—that people couldn't even get out of the stadium. Finally, we decided to pull the plug—an appropriate phrase in view of all the water around us—and I got my assistant director on the radio, his name was Gerry, to make an announcement using the loudspeaker system with a microphone installed in the center of the field where he could talk to the extras. But it was raining so hard he couldn't get to this microphone, so he turned around underneath the Stadium and walked toward the elevator to take him up to the press box where he could make the announcement. On his way there, he met the girl with whom he had spent the night before. They went up together, and he stopped the elevator between the first floor and the press box and they did what they had done the night before. Now I didn't know any of this until later. I'm still sitting in my trailer, I haven't heard any announcement, and suddenly I look out the window and there is blue sky. That girl had delayed the announcement and saved us half-a-million dollars. She got the cash prize and the part in the picture. And we filmed all that day and got everything!

"I think that, because *Black Sunday* as a novel was highly successful, Ernest Lehman tried to put too much in. We brought in Kenneth Ross, the English writer who had done *Day of the Jackal*. Working around the clock with three teams of secretaries, he restructured the script and got it down to shooting length. But we still felt we were missing an element in the picture—in the second act. We didn't know how Robert Shaw was going to identify the Marthe Keller character. In the book, Thomas Harris does it in a very long two hundred page section. There was no time for this in a movie. Years ago, I knew Ivan Moffat, who was George Stevens's associate producer on *Shane* and *A Place in the Sun*, who had written the script for *Tender is the Night*. I called Ivan, and he came in, started

work, and invented the character of the Egyptian ambassador, and that solved our difficulties. Ivan also rewrote some dramatic scenes including Bruce Dern's big breakdown. The three writers contributed greatly toward making this as near-perfect a script as I have ever had to work from, but a director has to see where and when certain points are not working and to make them right. All three received the screen credit they deserved.

"It has been remarked that from beginning to end, the film never loses the tension required for this particular plot. Much of this comes from the editing. Tom Rolf's work was excellent, but don't forget that sequences must be planned before you can edit them into the whole. Everything, almost, was pre-planned in *Black Sunday*, every cut, every transition, and we made a conscious decision not to try and be clever with transitional shots for shock effect or devices. We put out a good wide shot that told the story and put the title right on the screen—'Los Angeles, Tuesday, 5:30'—there could be no confusion on the part of the audience and it moved the story along too, as did John Williams' very appropriate score.

"I think *Black Sunday* ranks high among my movies, but what irked us most of all was that at about the same time Universal was filming *Two Minute Warning*. It killed us! We didn't know about it. *Two Minute Warning* was really nothing like *Black Sunday* but looked it—their setting was also a football stadium but with a sniper. It came out six months before our film because we just couldn't get our opticals done in time. So, where *Black Sunday* was favorably reviewed, and we were told it was going to be highly profitable, it turned out not to be so. The picture did all right, but it was not a champion at the box office. I think a lot of this had to do with *Two Minute Warning*, and the fact that we were the last in that train of disaster subjects.

"We shot most of the 'outside the stadium' scenes at Helm Hills. We were looking for a double for the Beirut scenes and I said, I know the exact place, in Tangiers, because I've shot there, and that's where we went. At Paramount Barry Diller, Charles Bludhorn and Bob Evans thought they had the biggest picture the studio had ever made. So did Michael Eisner. They were disappointed, but they gave me an exclusive contract for three years after that for a sizeable sum of money. But I wish more people had seen it."

```
39      INT. WAITING ROOM - V.A. BUILDING - DAY              39
&                                                            &
40      A number of men sit on wooden chairs reading maga-   40
        zines or staring at the floor.  Lander steps up to
        a desk where a listless RECEPTIONIST sits reading a
        paperback.  Behind her a door is nameplated "H. PUGH."

                        LANDER
                My name's Lander.  I've an
                appointment with Mister Pugh
                at ten-thirty.

                        RECEPTIONIST
                    (without looking)
                Disability?

                        LANDER
                No.

                        RECEPTIONIST
                Did you take a number?

                        LANDER
                No.

                        RECEPTIONIST
                    (reading)
                Then take a number.

        Lander takes a numbered disc from a tray.  It is
        number 52.

                        RECEPTIONIST
                    (continuing)
                Your number will be called.

        Lander sits down and looks at the men:  some battle-
        scarred, some off-balance.  A shabby young man leaves
        Pugh's office.  The Receptionist, without looking up,
        leans over to a desk mike.

                        RECEPTIONIST
                    (continuing)
                Twenty-four!

        Lander looks again at his disc, gets to his feet to
        protest.  Then stops.  Sits down again.  Sits abso-
        lutely still.


41      EXT. SHABBY DOWNTOWN PARKING LOT - LOS ANGELES - DAY  41

        Dahlia, wearing large dark glasses and a wide-brimmed
        hat, gets out of a car in the parking lot, gets her
        ticket.  Leaves.


42      INT. WAITING ROOM AT V.A. - DAY                      42

        Lander still sits.  A rough old veteran with whisky-
        red face comes out of Pugh's office.

                        RECEPTIONIST
                Twenty-seven!


43      INT. CORRIDOR OF OFFICE BUILDING - DAY               43

        She looks for names on glass doors.  Comes to:  S.
        MUZI -- IMPORTER-EXPORTER.  Tries door handle.  Locked.
        She knocks.  After a moment a large shadow appears on
        the other side of the glass.  A heavy man of no engag-
        ing countenance looks at her, unchains the door, lets
        her in.


44      INT. MUZI'S OFFICE - DAY                             44

        Dahlia enters.  It's the sort of situation she's not
        at ease with.  The man says nothing.  He goes behind
        his desk, looking at her.

                        DAHLIA
                I've come about the shipment of
                Madonna statues from Hong Kong.

                        MUZI
                Identification.

                        DAHLIA
                Gaza.

                        MUZI
                Yes, well I've some bad news for you.
```

PROPHECY 1979

Director John Frankenheimer • *Producer* Robert L. Rosen • *Production Company* Paramount Pictures Corporation • *Screenplay* David Seltzer • *Camera* Harry Stradling Jr. (Color Movielab/wide screen) • *Editing* Tom Rolf • *Sound* John K. Wilkinson, Gene Cantamesa • *Costume Designer* Ray Summers • *Art Direction* William Craig Smith • *Music* Leonard Rosenman • *Distribution* Paramount Pictures Corporation • *Classification* PG Release June 1979 • *Running time* 102 mins • *Working title* The Windsor Project • *Location* made at Paramount Studios and on location in British Columbia and Franklin Canyon, Los Angeles • *Novel* from Ballantine Books • *Formats* VHS.

CAST

Maggie Vern	•	Talia Shire
Rob Vern	•	Robert Foxworth
John Hawks	•	Armand Assante
Bethel Isely	•	Richard Dysart
Ramona	•	Victoria Racimo
M'Rai	•	George Clutesi
Pilot	•	Tom McFadden
Cellist	•	Evans Evans
Father	•	Burke Byrnes
Kirsten	•	Mia Bendixsen
Paulie	•	Johnny Timko
Kelso	•	Everett L. Creach
Sheriff	•	Charles H. Gray
Black woman	•	Livingston Holmes
Vic Shusette	•	Graham Jarvis
Rescuers	•	James H. Burk, Bob Terhune, Lon Katzman
Indians	•	Steve Shemayme, John A. Shemayme
Sheriff's deputy	•	Jaye Durkus
Tenement boy	•	Renato Moore
Tenement men	•	Mel Waters, Roosevelt Smith, Eric Mansker
Social worker	•	Cheri Bergen
Stage manager	•	Cliff Hutchison
Lumberjack	•	Thomas P. May

SYNOPSIS

The Environmental Protection Agency sends Rob Vern, a doctor with strong social convictions, to a rural area of Maine ostensibly to report on a lumber mill, actually to monitor growing ill will between its employees and the forest-dwelling Indians, who are believed responsible for the disappearance of several company personnel. Rob and his musician wife, Maggie (who, since Rob opposes their having children, has not revealed that she is pregnant), meet the mill manager Isely and witness a confrontation between lumber workers and the Indians led by John Hawks. Rob is puzzled by the unnatural ferociousness of the local wildlife and the size of fish in the lake, and is told by Hawks and his girlfriend, Ramona, of the Indians' worsening ill-health. In fact, mercury poisoning, which the mill has introduced to the local waters and which Rob eventually detects, has caused the changes and has even produced a huge mutant bear responsible for the recent mysterious deaths. The Indians are blamed, however, when a family of campers is savagely killed, and Hawks flees into the forest to escape arrest. Rob, Maggie and Ramona join him at the scene of the killings, and the group heads for the camp of Ramona's grandfather M'Rai, taking with them two hideously deformed infant creatures which Maggie finds.

The party, later joined by Isely and the sheriff's posse, are attacked by the bear, which kills the sheriff, and later Isely who attempts to get to a radio post. The others escape in an abandoned truck but are pursued and cornered by the creature, which kills M'Rai and Hawks before Rob destroys it in a final desperate struggle. As he and Maggie are flown back to the city (with Maggie uncertain whether the baby she is carrying will be deformed by mercury poisoning), another creature rears into view below.

COMMENT

Few critics had any kind words to say about *Prophecy*. The film, shot in British Columbia, followed a period of deep depression and private agony for Frankenheimer brought on by the commercial failure of *Black Sunday* and difficulties in setting up other projects. *Prophecy* did little to alleviate this. Two years after finishing *Black Sunday*, Frankenheimer left for Vancouver to make this unusual subject, one of serious purpose compromised at times for the sake of an excitement arrived at by unconvincing means. Frankenheimer, however, would be the last film-maker to make excuses for perceived shortcomings and accepts, as he always does, criticism without complaint. If it proves to be impossible, due to production weaknesses, to make sequences play as convincingly as they should, he accepts responsibility, and blames no one else, although indeed, many other factors could be called into question.

Prophecy is not a monster story, just as *King Kong*—to which *Prophecy* bears some relationship—was not an orthodox monster melodrama. The creature here is a mutant bear, pathetically deformed by mercury poisoning in the once pure waters of forest areas in North America, and also the cause of the deaths of several native people. While never preaching, Frankenheimer says a great deal about poverty, discrimination, and the dangers of pollution. Industrial and governmental complacency in the face of dangers to the environment is forcefully stated. Society as a whole is faulted for its lack of attention to the dangers of indiscriminate logging and for failing to understand how precarious our accepted notions of present-day civilization have become. In the carefully detailed narrative, ecological concerns are linked to the relationship between the doctor and his wife and the struggle of the native people against the loggers stripping their lands—a confrontation which erupted several years later in

British Columbia and Quebec and continues to this day. As for the deformed creatures, we feel sympathy for them as we did for *King Kong* at the hands of his tormentors.

This was not an easy film to make yet Frankenheimer never misses the inherent drama depicted in imaginatively staged sequences—helicopters in driving rain, the campers' death in a flurry of shredded sleeping bags, the documentary scenes of paper-making, the use of chemicals—with marvelously angled close-ups and camera movements. A thoughtful score by Leonard Rosenman merges well with the natural sounds of the forest. Contrasts between slum life in the city and concerts of classical music, each so far from the other, are bound together by quiet, convincing performances, particularly those of Robert Foxworth and Talia Shire. This is not a conventional horror film. There is anger and compassion, tragedy and turmoil, and as the principals fly out from the troubled land beneath them, so pristine from above, the film ends with a naturally realized warning as yet another mutant rises from the lakes. The many concerns in this picture may not always come together as a wholly compelling revelation of events distant from most of us, but the topicality of what it has to say about human carelessness and selfishness cannot be denied.

IF *"Black Sunday* came out in 1977 after filming it in 1976, *Prophecy* was filmed in 1978 and was shown in 1979. During the years between I was supposed to do *Brakes* for Dino de Laurentiis, but, after six months' work, that didn't work out. George B. Higgins wrote the screenplay and it then turned out that Dino wanted a different movie from the one I wanted to make. Dino was very honorable—I liked him—so we sold it and I went back to work at Paramount. Michael Eisner wanted me to do a 'monster movie', Bob Rosen, now under contract to Paramount as a result of *Black Sunday*, and Bob Evans wanted me to do *The Players*, a tennis picture. I worked for months on that with him and then I changed my mind—much as I play and love tennis. So we did the 'monster picture,' *Prophecy*. David Seltzer wrote it. We thought the story and the events was a valid premise; that out of pollution and contamination came a deformed animal, a monster, as if it were a precursor of a great tragedy about to happen in society. I thought the picture could be a more serious one than what came out on the screen. I think I made a mistake in the choice of who should do the monster, I think we showed the monster too much and the picture wasn't frightening. Michael Eisner wanted a PG rating and I wanted an R. The picture as an R was very disturbing, but it had to be re-cut to PG, and I think that really hurt us. We cut out pieces and sequences that were quite frightening, It was a decision made by Michael, I didn't agree with it, and it's the only time that a studio has forced me to re-cut one of my films. They got their PG and they made money.

"The script was pretty much what you saw. We shot the script—it read better than it played. I went to Vancouver to shoot because the forests and the environment were all there, with a paper mill, and because, economically, everything worked for that location. Some of the trick scenes were done on location, others in the studio, some of it was optical, or a stuntman in a suit.

"I was largely disappointed with the result. Bob Rosen came back from seeing the dailies, and, time after time, he said 'There are among the best I've ever seen' yet we had to compromise the picture in the editing, and so we lost the intent. We had a very good composer, though, in Leonard Rosenman. I last worked with him on *The Young Stranger*."

THE CHALLENGE 1982

Director John Frankenheimer • *Executive Producer* Lyle S. Poncher • *Producers* Robert L. Rosen, Ron Beckman • *Production Company* A Lyle Poncher, Robert L. Rosen, Ron Beckman production for CBS Theatrical Film Corporation • *Screenplay* Richard Maxwell, John Sayles, Ivan Moffat • *Camera* Kozo Okazaki (Eastmancolor /wide-screen) • *Editing* Jack Wheeler • *Sound* John T. Reitz, David E. Campbell, Joe D. Citarella • *Production Design* Yoshiyuki Ishida • *Set Decorator* Koichi Hamamura • *Music* Jerry Goldsmith; extracts from Symphony in G minor, no. 40, by Wolfgang Amadeus Mozart, Air from Overture in D by Johann Sebastian Bach • *Distribution* New World Mutual Pictures • *Classification* PG • *Release* October 8, 1982 • *Running Time* 112 mins • *Working title* The Equals • *Location* made on location in Kyoto, Japan, and in Los Angeles • Screened at Manila International Film Festival January 25, 1982 • *Availability* VHS.

CAST

Rick Murphy	• Scott Glenn	*Girl in gym*	• Pamela Bowman
Sensei Yoshida	• Toshiro Mifune	*Hanger-on*	• Roy Andrews
Akiko Yoshida	• Donna Kei Benz	*Jorge*	• Henry Celis
Hideo Yoshida	• Atsuo Nakamura	*Hashimoto*	• Kazunaga Tsuji
Ando	• Calvin Jung	*Thug*	• Kusuo Kita
Go	• Clyde Kusatsu	*Tanaka*	• Naoto Fujita
Toshio Yoshida	• Sab Shimono	*Oshima*	• Masao Hisanori
Kubo	• Kiyoaki Nagai	*Toshio as a child*	• Ryuji Yamashita
Jiro	• Kenta Fukasaku	*Customs officer*	• Toshio Chiba
Takeshi Yoshida	• Shog Shimada	*Porter*	• Minoru Sanada
Instructor	• Yoshio Inaba	*Van's driver*	• Shigehero Kino
Old Man	• Seiji Miyaguchi	*Taxi Driver*	• Katsutoshi Nakayama
Sensei's wife	• Miiko Taka		
Kuroko, boxer	• Akio Kameda	*Thug's driver*	• Masatoshi Ishikawa
Knifeman	• Hisashi Osaka	*1st con person*	• Eriko Sugita
1st TV monitor girl	• Yuko Okamoto	*2nd con person*	• Munehisa Fujita
2nd TV monitor girl	• Taw Matsuda	*Cashier*	• Sanaye Nakahara
Fight promoter	• Pat McNamara	*Waitress*	• Kanata Uyeno

SYNOPSIS

Kyoto 1945. An ancient family ceremony, in which two treasured swords known as 'the equals,' are passed from aged warrior Takeshi Yoshida to his eldest son Sensei, is disrupted by young brother Hideo, who steals the swords and in the process wounds Sensei's young son Toshio.

Los Angeles 1982. Down-on-his-luck pugilist Rick Murphy is approached by the wheelchair-bound Toshio, and his sister Akiko to help transport one of the swords back to Japan. But on their arrival, they are kidnapped and Toshio is killed by Hideo's henchman Ando, who finds that the sword Rick is carrying is a fake. Taken to Hideo, Rick learns that he had lost one of the swords during the war, that it had been traced to Los Angeles by Sensei, and that the two brothers are equally determined to unite 'the equals.' Rick is then helped to escape from Ando and his thugs by Akiko, who takes him to the community where, in contrast to Hideo's techno-logical empire, Sensei trains young disciples in the traditional martial arts. Rick takes his pay and leaves, but is bribed by Ando to return to the acad-emy, offer himself as a pupil, then steal the second sword (which has been recovered from its hiding place in Toshio's wheelchair).

At the last moment, Rick is unable to make off with the sword, and offers himself as a genuine disciple to Sensei, undergoing the grueling ritual of being buried alive to prove himself. His martial skills grow, as does his relationship with Akiko, who intimates that Sensei would like to pass the swords on to him. Rick saves Sensei from a trap by Hideo, then helps foil an attempt by Sensei's assis-tant to steal his sword. But the kidnapping of Akiko finally impels Sensei to confront his brother in his electronic bastion (followed covertly by Rick). They penetrate the building's security, but Sensei is wounded by Ando while dueling with Hideo for the swords. Rick takes over, emerging triumphant from a desperate and bloody struggle.

COMMENT

This time, Frankenheimer's fascination with far places and different societies takes him to Japan, a notoriously problematic place for foreign film-makers. Unless these stories set in other countries are concerned with individuals from their own country living or visiting abroad, with the events seen through their eyes and not from, in this case, the perspective of the Japanese characters, the result will probably be a distorted Western view of the country they are depicting. As with many other Asian societies, only the Japanese can truly portray their country and its people on film—although many of their own film-makers have done their part in misrepresenting themselves in the interests of commercial cinema.

To Frankenheimer's credit, in filming a story involving more Japanese characters than Ameri-can, he has taken great pains to present them truthfully in words, deeds and manners. By surrounding himself with a large cast of splendid Japanese actors—and meeting once again with Toshiro Mifune, whom he cast in *Grand Prix* (before he could speak English)—and an almost exclusive unit of Japanese technicians, he has made a film which comes to the screen looking and sounding convincingly Japanese—from the beautifully designed opening titles, leading us into the story, to the closing credits accompanied throughout by an authentic-sounding and dramatically-effective score by Jerry Goldsmith.

We are taken quickly and surely into the story with the introduction of Rick Murphy, the lost American, a boxer, rude and demanding, stupid when drunk, disillusioned with himself and his life, and by implication, the tarnished and tire-some American dream. Perfectly played by Scott Glenn, he is open to any financially attractive proposition. His shabby lifestyle is in sharp contrast to the Japanese way of life, epitomized by the family home with its garden, the simple furni-ture in clean and uncluttered interiors. As in all his films, the director establishes time and place with a sharp eye for detail. The Japanese are naturally gracious and polite, but their dark side begins to appear in the struggle over the two treasured family swords. In his meeting with the little boy, the boxer finds some relief from his own anger. These are gentle and charming moments, leading into the imaginative succession of shots showing him stealing the sword with only his shadow seen through the translucent door—a setting we know from so many classic Japanese films—and the affecting moments when he returns the sword, kneels and asks forgiveness. The detailed depiction of the martial arts training is one more example of the director's documentary interest in processes and methods and it seems altogether believable that this failed boxer would find a new purpose in perfecting himself in another society's defensive pastimes. There is a beautifully stylized love scene dissolving into the clouds with a wide-angle view of Kyoto—and another day begins with a typical local procession becoming part of the cat and mouse game being played out between the brothers with the American in- between—a symbol perhaps of Japanese-American relations today.

The story is complicated and at first seems not to have much substance—the brothers fighting over a set of family swords—until looked at from the point of view of tradition and family honor. One brother is traditional and honorable, the other is modern, a calculating industrialist with no time for traditions. They both meet and fight out their battle for control of the two swords in a Samurai encounter set in the wealthy brother's starkly modern headquarters. Violence is ignited by hatred, swords are crossed, blood is spilt and lives lost over what are symbols and a misplaced sense of honor. The underlying text of the entire story takes us from Huston's depiction of America meeting Japan in *The Barbarian and the Geisha* to the greater impact of the American way of life in Japan today, brought about a century later by the Second World War. The swords symbolize the two countries, once separate, but now among the leading players in the world's economy, both damaged by political corruption. Ando, the Japanese-American gangster, is the man between.

Although the story ends with triumph over adversity, of good vanquishing evil, with the American discovering a new meaning and morality to his life from his encounter with a people he knew almost nothing about, and who at times are no longer sure of themselves with their American connection, Frankenheimer never leaves us feeling complacent. There is always a sense of sadness, of not knowing what the future holds. Doyle, an American in France, no doubt went back to New York unchanged in attitude; but Rick Murphy, an American in Japan, has accepted a challenge to be different from what he once was. The film closes with a view of the city. We arrived, and now we depart. Frankenheimer, like David Lean, always brings us a compelling sense of place.

Toshiro Mifune with Frankenheimer.

"For an American director to go to Japan, to be involved in Japanese society, is like skating on thin ice. Although Japan is a very open country compared to what it was, there are still cultural traditions, organizations, methods, habits and procedures that are still fairly incomprehensible to us from the West. I went there to tell a story about an American, to work mostly with Japanese technicians—Japanese crews—and to make this film with Japanese actors. To be with Toshiro Mifune again was a pleasure. We hadn't seen each other since *Grand Prix*. Without Mifune we couldn't have made the movie—he treated us so well. He opened doors, we used his studio, he brought us together with actors and the technicians—he was much more than an actor, he was the conduit. He was a great example.

"The film came at a time when CBS had decided they were going to make films for theatres. The man in charge of CBS Films was named Donald March. He and Nancy Hardin had this project and asked me to do it—it was really that simple. I liked the idea and I got Robert Rosen involved. Scott Glenn was coming off *Urban Cowboy*, and we thought he would be the perfect actor for it. We went over to Tokyo and made the movie. Richard Maxwell wrote the first script—it was his idea—then John Sayles came over and completely re-wrote it. Then we brought Ivan Moffat in to re-write part of what Sayles did—but Sayles gave us an interesting interpretation.

"The Paramount contract was over and I had been involved with another movie that I didn't make, with Lorimar, called *Destinies*. And as a result I was looking for something to do. *The Challenge* came along, and it seemed like a rewarding idea to go over there and try to make a movie about two samurai swords which have great mythical and historical significance. The idea was to bring the two swords together—two swords owned by two different brothers. An American was the unwitting accomplice here. As a matter of fact, we found an American in Osaka who had a martial arts establishment. We used him as our technical advisor. His name is Steven Seagal!

"Working with the team was very difficult. The word 'no' doesn't exist in Japanese and they try so hard to please and by trying to please, create lots of problems. It was extremely difficult just trying to communicate what we wanted to do. There were moments of complete improvisation, for instance. We went from Kyoto to Tokyo to shoot the abduction on a street filled with electronic displays, like a big fair. I've never seen anything like it. We arrived in Tokyo in pouring rain and there was no one there. Everyone was attending a religious procession. I said to Kozo that we should shoot this religious procession and we did. The Japanese are such a structured group of people—everything in Japan has to be pre-planned. It's very orderly, but this was not an orderly movie because the script was constantly being changed. Unfortunately, the writers' strike was on around that time so we couldn't finish the script before the picture started. It was very difficult, but we got through it, and actually it was rather enjoyable.

"In human terms, this story was the rite of passage of a man who started life as a boxer and who ended up as a samurai. It was the samurai tradition that interested me, and I loved the transition this character made. His gradual acceptance of the Japanese ethic—I thought the only way to explain that to an audience would be to put them in his position. It has to be explained. He goes through hell and he becomes something very special. He's a totally different person at the end of the picture than he was at the beginning. I think that's fascinating. It was, if you will, in homage as well to all those Kung Fu movies. It had much more to do with Japanese culture, with the samurai, and with what that life was about; and honor—I suppose it's really a movie about honor. This is a man who is a thug, a person who has no morals, who grows into a man of great dignity—thus it becomes a film about dignity too.

"As I have said, I was looking at it through the eyes of someone from the country I was from—in this case, Scott Glenn. I wouldn't want to go and make an indigenous Japanese film about the life of a samurai. I think that would be presumptuous of me. And in the same way as *Year of the Gun*, which came almost ten years later, I did not want to go to Italy and do the definitive film about the Red Brigade, but to see it through the eyes of an American journalist who was trying to write a book.

"I had a lot of difficulty with translation—to the extent that I didn't realize our woman translator was really not saying what I was saying, because in Japan women have a different language to men. She was not allowed by tradition to say many of the things I was saying, so I was wondering why nothing was getting done. She was asking in a very plaintive way something I was asking for quite strongly. So, finally, I found a Chinese girl, who had been director Jerry London's interpreter on *Shogun*, Wey Hung. She was tri-lingual, had none of the inhibitions of Japanese women and translated literally what I said. From that moment on I had no translation problems at all.

"We had quite a lot of locations around the Kyoto area, except for the festival, the parade where the girl gets kidnapped, that happened in Tokyo. The huge scene at the end, where they storm this bastion of commerce, was a tremendous challenge for me. We used this great building in Kyoto and after much deliberation, we went ahead and did it. It went over a bit bigger than life taking a lot of dramatic license, and we just made it work. You just have to bend to the wind, and say we're going to make it happen, we're going to make it believable for an audience, and that's what we tried to do.

"When we finished the film there were difficulties, again, with distribution. CBS closed the film division and the producers were forced to go out and make distribution deals with outside companies. We ended up with a very small distribution company which didn't have the money or didn't choose to spend what was needed to publicize the movie. From the time we started the film until the time we finished there was a big management change, and that is the death knell for any creative person The new management comes in and discredits the old one. CBS didn't make a distribution deal with any of the majors because they thought they were going to have their own distribution company. Then that fell through and Mr Paley decided he really didn't want to be in the movie business after all. They made a quick distribution deal with a new company and that didn't work. So, as a result, the film was really never seen by a wide audience. Yet I loved the film—it's a shame. I think CBS made four or five films. These were uncertain times with the entire system hesitating between movies and television. CBS drew back. It was disappointing, and much to my dismay and sense of accomplishment, this situation returned with three of my yet to be made films."

THE RAINMAKER 1982

Director John Frankenheimer • *Executive Producer* Richard H. Frank • *Producer* Marica Govons • *Production Company* Paramount for HBO • *Screenplay* from a stage play in three acts by N. Richard Nash • *Camera* George Riesenberger (video tape) • *Editor* Danny White • *Set Designer* Rosaria Sinisi • *Art Director* Bill Bohnert • *Costume Designer* Dorothy Jeakins • *Music* Fred Hellerman • *Running time* 130 mins. plus two 2-minute intermissions • A Paramount video presentation • Filmed by Paramount, dir. Joseph Anthony, in 1956 with Katharine Hepburn and Burt Lancaster; staged as a musical on Broadway in 1960 under the title *110 In the Shade*.

CAST

Starbuck •	Tommy Lee Jones
Lizzie Curry •	Tuesday Weld
Jimmie Curry •	William Katt
Pa Curry •	Lonny Chapman
Noah Curry •	James Cromwell
Sheriff •	William Traylor
Deputy File •	Taylor Lacher

SYNOPSIS

Kansas, in 1913, is stricken by drought. The cattle are dying, and there is a ready audience for Starbuck, a confidence trickster and self-styled rainmaker. Calling at the farmhouse where H. C. Curry lives with his sons, Noah and Jimmy, and daughter Lizzie, Starbuck soon senses the family tensions. Curry has allowed his authority to pass to the mean-spirited Noah; Jimmy resents Noah's contempt for his girl friend Snookie; and Lizzie, desperately anxious to marry but convinced that she is plain and unattractive, is further saddened by her family's well-meant but clumsy efforts to find her a husband in File, the deputy sheriff.

Opposed by Lizzie and Noah, Curry decides to gamble on Starbuck's powers as a rainmaker. Starbuck helps Jimmy defy his brother, and his strength and confidence fascinate the reluctant Lizzie. He makes love to her, persuades her that she really has the beauty he sees in her, and asks her to go away with him. Arriving to arrest Starbuck, File is persuaded to let him go free. File now realises that he loves Lizzie, and she sees that her future lies with him rather than in Starbuck's dream-world. Driving away, Starbuck at last finds his own dream fulfilled—a sudden storm ends the drought.

COMMENT

The Rainmaker is another welcome detour by Frankenheimer from his better-known style of film-making into what might be called a restful visit to the stage. A distant cousin to *The Iceman Cometh*, Nash's play arrives almost ten years after Frankenheimer's filming of the O'Neill play. The dark intensity of O'Neill, however, is not to be found here. *The Rainmaker* is a lighter work, with life's frustrations resolved in an aura of romance and innocence. While Nash is as much concerned as O'Neill with personal relationships, he does not give up on his characters. Frankenheimer well understands this and it is interesting to compare his treatment of this play with the manner in which he filmed O'Neill. One gets the impression that this was staged for the summer circuit and given the full benefit of the director's skill in adapting stage-into-television-into film knowing exactly at every turn how to extract from the actors the right interpretation of their characters' behavior.

This play of the 1950s seems dated by the standards and attitudes of the nineties. The emotions it expresses, while honest enough, come to us now in a different language. Yet it is not difficult to believe in these characters. They are simple but not silly, possessed of emotions they come to understand and to live with. They are fundamentally decent, honest and caring, and played with understanding and sensitivity. Tuesday Weld is lovely and believable, a spirited facade masking the lost and uncertain aspects of her inner self with a Gish-like brightness and trust—a striking contrast to her Alma McCain in *I Walk the Line*. Tommy Lee Jones, in his early days, must compete with the memory of Burt Lancaster's lively portrayal twenty-six years earlier in Joseph Anthony's film version, and he does so convincingly and without bombast. William Traylor gives a restrained and intelligent performance as the likeable sheriff. Lonny Chapman as the father, and William Katt, as his son Jimmy, convey the look and feel of typical country characters. James Cromwell thoughtfully portrays Noah as the serious elder brother, somewhat out of things, who thinks he knows what is best for the others, never finding out what is best for himself.

Frankenheimer's staging and direction is clean and confident. The film opens with the camera at the back of the theatre moving up over the audience to the curtain, which raises, and then on to the stage. Four cameras are used, providing the film or the TV audience with alternate points of view. While the play seems to be taking place on the theatre stage, it was, like *Iceman*, actually filmed on a studio interior set, but a much less complicated one. (*Iceman*'s set appeared to be a real bar setting.) The framing of the characters "on stage" is always imaginatively done without looking contrived.

The play is in three acts with two two-minute intermissions for commercials. Act 1 is quietly portrayed as the family discusses ordinary events of the day and matters relating to themselves, ending with the flamboyant arrival of Starbuck. Act 2 rises in drama and movement, while Act 3 cleverly brings us even closer to the participants in close-ups and intimate shots, winding up the proceedings with a concluding sense of resolution. Scene changes within the three acts are smoothly devised—the camera pulls back from a close-up on a candle to reveal the table and the family sitting around it; a close-up of the hands of Starbuck and Lizzie dissolves into the hands of Noah nervously drumming on the table; a close-up of a telegraph machine tapping out a message pulls back to show us the sheriff in his office. These are pleasingly carried out, and, although it seems that we are on stage at all times, we are never stage-bound. Each act sees the curtain come down, and the shot from the rear of the audience to the curtain rising is repeated. At the end, the cast steps forward to take its curtain call, each actor being identified on the screen (as in the heyday of the cinema), and flowers are handed up to Miss Weld. Frankenheimer perfectly captures the essence of the play, and, although restricted to a stage of cardboard sets, it is transformed into a fluid stream of visual images. The editing, typical of the director's incisive style, is always in keeping with the movements and responses of the actors, making us feel closer to the events than the 'live' audience. One can hear every word and there are no added, overly-loud sound effects. The color is pastel-shaded, suggesting an appropriate country air. Like the American Film Theatre series, the presentation is reminiscent of Paul Czinner's series of opera and ballet on film made for the Rank Organization in the early fifties. Although its time has passed, it remains oddly affecting and pleasant to remember.

IF *"The Rainmaker* followed *The Challenge*, the film I did in Japan. Dick Pike from Paramount called me and asked if I'd like to direct this. He explained that they had contracted to do three or four plays for HBO, and that they wanted to mount a stage performance and film it. I said that didn't appeal to me at all. Then he told me that Tommy Lee Jones and Tuesday Weld were interested in being in it. I said, "The only way I will do this for you, Dick, is to rehearse it the way we used to rehearse *Playhouse 90*, then to film your theatre audience and a proscenium, and then show the audience leaving the theatre. Then we'll film the play exactly the way I used to do on television." In other words, have it look like the camera-involved, wide, close-cut work that I do. And they agreed to that. We rehearsed for three-and-a-half weeks in Hollywood and then we went to Provo, Utah, and shot the production on a sound stage there. The funny thing about it is that I blocked it and did everything on tape exactly the way I did my *Playhouse 90s*. I did one act at a time and I even camera cut it the way I used to do my *Playhouse 90s* right on the air, so that I didn't even have to edit it—that's the way it was. The principle was the same as *Iceman*, but it didn't take as long because I did it on video, on tape not on film. I took three and a half weeks rehearsal and taped the entire play in four days.

"We never used stage directions, it was completely different. It had nothing to do with the stage play whatsoever—it was staged for the camera and not for the proscenium, and acted for the camera, not for the stage. So, in a sense, I returned to my television technique. It only took up four weeks of my time. It was fun. Working with Tommy Lee and particularly with Tuesday Weld was a rewarding experience. I love that play, which is why I did it. Mind you, I thought the set was terrible! I never saw the set until I got to Provo—and it was a time in my life when I wasn't making certain decisions as well I should have. I should have changed the whole set. I didn't like the set, but I loved the actors."

from left Victoria Tennant, Frankenheimer, producer Edie Landau, and Michael Caine.

THE HOLCROFT COVENANT 1985

Director John Frankenheimer • *Executive Producer* Mort Abrahams • *Producers* Edie & Ely Landau • *Production Company* Thorn EMI Screen Entertainment Productions • *Screenplay* George Axelrod, Edward Anhalt, John Hopkins, *based on the novel by* Robert Ludlum • *Camera* Gerry Fisher (Technicolor/wide-screen) • *Editor* Ralph Sheldon • *Sound* Hugh Strain • *Production Design* Peter Mullins • *Costume Designer* Derek Hyde • *Music* Stanislas Syrewicz • *Classification* R/BBFC Rating 15 • *Release* September 1985 • *Running Time* 112 mins • *Distribution* Columbia-EMI-Warner(UK)/Universal Films (USA) • *Location* made at Twickenham Studios, England, and on location in London, Berlin, Munich and Geneva in the summer and fall of 1983, with post-production in London in early 1984 • Originally to star James Caan, who was replaced by Michael Caine at the last minute • *Release* in London, September 1985, and in New York, October 1985 • *Availability* VHS and LD.

CAST

Noel Holcroft •	Michael Caine	*General von Tiebolt* •	Hugo Bower
Johann Tennyson •	Anthony Andrews	*Hard Hat* •	Michael Balfour
Helden Tennyson •	Victoria Tennant	*Assassin* •	Tharita Olivera De Sera
Althene Holcroft •	Lilli Palmer		
Jurgen Maas •	Mario Adorf	*Fritzl* •	Guntbert Warns
Ernst Manfredi •	Michael Lonsdale	*Oberst's guard* •	Paul Humpoletz
Leighton •	Bernard Hepton	*Concièrge* •	Tom Deininger
Oberst •	Richard Munch	*Policeman* •	Keith Edwards
Anthony Beaumont •	Carl Rigg	*Switchboard operator* •	Andrea Browne
Frederick Leger •	André Penvern		
Hartman •	Andrew Bradford	*Executive secretary* •	Shelley Thompson
Lieutenant Miles •	Shane Rimmer	*Manfredi's secretary* •	Eve Adam
General Clausen •	Alexander Kerst	*Carnival director* •	Jorge Trees
General Kessler •	Michael Wolf	*Rescuer* •	Tim Condren

SYNOPSIS

Berlin 1945. Prior to committing suicide, three Nazi generals, Clausen, Kessler and von Tiebolt, consign a fortune to the safe custody of a neutral contact, Manfredi, covenanted to their offspring in forty years' time.

The present. New York architect Noel Holcroft (Clausen's son) is summoned to Geneva by Manfredi's son and told of the covenant, involving some four billion dollars, which is meant to foster a better world, and is due to be activated in a few days' time. Back in New York, Holcroft finds a stranger, Baldwin, dead in his apartment, and a previous phone message from the latter urging him to make contact in London with von Tiebolt's daughter, Helden Tennyson. She and Leighton, supposedly an MI5 functionary, escort Holcroft to the rural home of Oberst, a dedicated anti-Nazi, who accuses Holcroft of seeking to spearhead a neo-Nazi revival. Once he has disproved this, Holcroft is introduced to Helden's brother, Johann, an enigmatic journalist who sends Helden and Holcroft (now being shadowed by an assassin, Beaumont) to contact Kessler's son, the prominent musician Jurgen Maas, in Berlin. It transpires that an attempt in New York to murder Holcroft's anti-Nazi mother has been at Maas' behest; Helden is subsequently abducted in Berlin by Beaumont, but is rescued by Holcroft after a shoot-out in which Beaumont is killed.

En route to Geneva, Helden and Holcroft are waylaid by Leighton and taken to see Oberst, only to find that both he and Holcroft's mother have been murdered by Johann. Leighton (actually in Oberst's employ) now identifies Johann as the leader of a neo-Nazi scheme to promote world-wide anarchy by using the covenant to finance terrorism; but Holcroft subsequently realises from a stray remark of Helden's that she is also implicated (in fact, she and her brother are having an incestuous affair). The signing takes place, but Holcroft calls a press conference to expose the plot and, in the ensuing affray, he shoots the deranged Johann. Holcroft later confesses both his love for Helden and his awareness of her involvement. He gives her the opportunity to kill him, but she shoots herself instead.

COMMENT

The Holcroft Covenant might well be held up as an example of what happens to a director when he goes to help a friend. Asked at the last minute by Edie and Ely Landau (with whom he had made *The Iceman Cometh*) to direct this picture after the original director had (wisely perhaps) backed out, Frankenheimer then lost the leading actor, James Caan, who left London for the US suffering from drug addiction and was replaced, after a quick search, by Michael Caine. He then found himself working from a tedious, clumsy novel by Robert Ludlum, which three good screenwriters, Axelrod, Anhalt, Hopkins, could do little to improve.

The resulting film, concerning Nazis old and new, weaves a tangled tale of conspiracy and deceit straining credulity to breaking point. That this confused narrative does not break into pieces is due entirely to Frankenheimer's skill in holding it together and keeping it moving with stylish, lively settings, dramatic camerawork by Gerry Fisher, and a first rate group of actors led by the energetic and compelling Caine, who actually seem to believe in what they are doing. As might be expected, critics made unfavorable comparisons with *The Manchurian Candidate* and *Seven Days in May*. To the director's credit, however, he has not made here another cold war 'coming out' spy drama, but a fast-paced, tightly edited adventure—somewhat surreal and sensual. The film immediately establishes mood and character in the opening carnival sequences in Berlin. Moments of comedy, intentional and otherwise, abound, with the edgy Axelrod dialogue.

As in *The Challenge*, the story opens in black and white in 1945 at the end of the war and moves forward to the present. Foretelling future events once again, the director deals here with the neo-Nazi movement (to which he later returns in different circumstances in *Dead Bang*), and if some of it seems murky it could be said that no one was entirely certain of what the political situation was like in the two Germanys while the Berlin Wall was still in place. What did the West accomplish during forty years of communism? After three influential German generals commit suicide because fascism has lost, who is who and who is not what they seem is uppermost throughout as everyone searches for an identity to improve their life while questioning that of the others. The director steers a firm course and takes us on a colorful and fast-moving Cook's tour of European locations, never leaving us to wonder where we are, and making good use of his expert techniques with television screens at the closing press conference. The somewhat surprising revelation of incest emerging at the ending seems convincing by reason of its highly emotionally but controlled scenes of eroticism. The closing is powerful—alone in the room, the camera travels up to Holcroft's back, but Helden, instead of shooting him, shoots herself; not original perhaps, but the method of filming makes it seem so. The director employs a fine cast of familiar players (bringing back the wonderful Lili Palmer). Victoria Tennant is a refreshing addition.

F"I was in France as President of the Jury at the Alvoriz Film Festival when I got a call at the Ritz Hotel from my agent, Peter Warwick, to tell me that Ely Landau and his wife wanted me to direct *The Holcroft Covenant*. I particularly liked the book by Robert Ludlum and met with him when I returned to the United States to discuss the filming of it. James Caan was to play Noel Holcroft. There were script problems, with the first draft written by John Hopkins. I went over to London to prepare the picture, James Caan came over, and, in the meantime, I had George Axelrod rewriting the picture. This was the first time I had worked with him since *The Manchurian Candidate*. Caan had an addiction to cocaine. He got to Heathrow, but instead of getting on a plane to Munich, he went to Miami. So there we were, ready to shoot but without a leading player—it was June 30, 1984, and I didn't know what to do. By this time Ely Landau had had a stroke. His wife Edie was producing the movie with Mort Abrahams, with whom she worked in television. They were no help and were in the wrong profession. It was actually the completion bond company—Gertrude Soames, the film financer, and David Korda, who worked for them—who came to our rescue. There were all kinds of financial restrictions on this movie. As most of the money was coming from England, a certain amount had to be spent on British technicians and actors, so it would have been impossible to hire another American actor. I'd always wanted to work with Michael Caine. I contacted his agent, Dennis Selinger, convinced the producers that this was a good idea, called his lawyer, and within a couple of days we had Michael Caine. We had to rewrite the script from Caan to Caine—not an easy thing to do. We did it though, and we shot the movie mainly in Germany and in England.

"Otto Plaschkes was indispensable as our line producer. The two producers were neutralized, which is the best way you can describe it because it was chaos before. Abrahams was sent back to the United States, and Mrs. Landau stayed in New York, and we went and shot the movie. It was a very pleasant experience. I loved London and, as a matter of fact, I stayed over there a year and a half after the film was finished and, because it was an Eady Plan movie, I had to cut it in London. All the post-production was done there, which was very enjoyable, and it marked the first time I worked with Gerry Fisher—long associated with Joseph Losey.

"Ludlum thought it was really by far and away the best film made from any of his books. But difficulties over distribution rights arose. The financing company, EMI, had a deal with Universal calling for the studio to distribute EMI films in North America. We had a screening with Universal and they were pleased with the movie. They said, 'We can make money with this movie, but what we need are the videocassette, TV and cable rights to back us up on the money we are going to spend, in case we lose.' EMI refused to agree. So Universal said, 'In that case, we can't spend the money necessary to advertise it,' and they gave it a very limited release. As a result, the movie just wasn't seen.

"I had an interesting cast, Anthony Andrews and Victoria Tennant—and Lilli Palmer, a woman I was in love with when I was eighteen and she was acting on the Broadway stage. I never met her, I had always wanted to put her into one of my films and luckily, with this one, I did. She was truly divine. Michael Caine was a pleasure to work with, the consummate actor. I think I gave the characters depth and credibility and the situation was believable—it was, after all a continuation of the series of spy thrillers and espionage and intrigue plots the screen has made familiar to us."

RIVIERA 1986

Director "Alan Smithee" (John Frankenheimer) • *Producer* Robert L Rosen • *Executive Producer/Writer* Michael Sloan • *Camera* Bernard Lutic, Henri Decae (Eastmancolor) • *Editors* various • *Supplier* MTM Productions • *Running Time* 120 mins • *Broadcast* Sunday May 31, 1987, 9 p.m. ABC-TV as an ABC Sunday Night Movie.

CAST

Ben Masters
Elyssa Davalos
Patrick Bauchau
Richard Hamilton
Michael Lonsdale
Jon Finch
Shane Rimmer
Lalla Ward
Geoffrey Chater
Patrick Monckton
Jacques Marin
George Murcell
Tony Jay
Danil Torppe
Jason Nardone
Daniel Emilfork
Stefan Gryff
Neville Rofallu
Francis Terzian
Sergeo Rousakov
Fred Waugh
Paolo Harzman
Lisa Turner

SYNOPSIS

The 'Bureau,' an American organization, sends a singer-spy to the Riviera to seek out a former agent and to ascertain whether or not he is still loyal to his former employer. She finds him turning his dead father's chateau into a hotel, but still true to his calling. The Bureau dispatches the two of them, now romantically involved, on the trail of a mole in the Bureau's higher levels. Meanwhile, a friend has been having difficulties helping the daughter of an archeologist who has fallen among thieves. They all end up in the tomb of Ramses VI, where the mole is identified and the villains vanquished.

COMMENT

'Made as a two-hour pilot for ABC-TV's pilot group of last year, this feature is long on atmosphere and short on original plot material. Directed by John Frankenheimer (who had his name removed from the credits), *Riviera* strives to keep two basic story-lines afloat combining them for the finale.' (From *Variety*, June 10, 1987)

JF "After *Holcroft* I got involved with Frederick Forsyth and Michael Caine on the Forsyth novel *The Fourth Protocol* which I was going to do as part of a triumvirate—three partners. George Axelrod wrote the screenplay and Forsyth was going to raise financing through sources in London. I was paid for it and spent six months with Forsyth trying to get this movie made. We came back to this country and tried the major studios. We had a good script but got turned down because of 'budgetary problems' and the fact that it was to be an all-British movie. This was a lean time financially for me, I had to work. An agent called me and said 'MTM—Mary Tyler Moore—wants to do a television series based on two characters, a soldier of fortune and an ex-CIA operator who lives in the South of France. They are calling it *Riviera* and they want to shoot the whole thing in France. They asked me if you would direct the pilot. If you did the pilot, you would not only be well paid for it but you will then get a rather large percentage of every one of the episodes to follow, even though you will not be required to direct them—your royalty payments.' I didn't really want to, but I thought about it and agreed to read the script because I love living and working in the South of France—I was then living in London. The script needed work and, rather reluctantly, I agreed. I came back to California and met with the writer, a pleasant fellow named Michael Sloan, the MTM people and the executive producer, a man named Barry Whites. I asked for Bob Rosen as producer, they agreed, and we went to France to set it up and choose the locations. I came back here with the producers to cast the lead role, and we revised the script.

"I also wanted to see if I could adapt my techniques to television schedules, which are shorter than in feature productions. I'd never done filmed television. The television I did was either live or on tape. We went over there, we shot it and it was a challenging yet satisfying experience. I did it comfortably within the time period. It was a two-hour film and I think we had thirty-one or thirty-two days, more than most television films. It was an all-French crew. Ben Masters played the lead, Elyssa Davalos played the girl, and Patrick Bauchau played the soldier of fortune. It was shot in English. The actress became temperamental. Whether it's television or a feature, after about a week of shooting, the director becomes a hostage, because unprincipled actors can do anything they want and there's little he can do. It was a nightmare working with her, one horrible disagreement after another. Aside from that, I was confident I had met the demands of TV filming. We shot on 35mm with veteran Henri Decae.

"This picture was my kind of movie, I came back to LA and I edited with Bob Shugrue, with whom I had worked before. I liked him, I liked what we had, and showed it to the MTM executives. In a strange way, they were noncommittal. I sensed that they thought this film was above the intelligence level of the average television viewer. This was the script that had been approved and which we had shot, this is what I felt it should be. They showed it to ABC, and ABC agreed with them that it had to be shaped more for the masses. I tried to accommodate them by making some changes, but it was no use. They took it over (contractually they could), and re-cut it into something that didn't really resemble one bit what I had shot. The storyline changed, everything changed. The writer, Michael Sloan, re-cut it—he was also one of the executive producers. He re-wrote and I think re-directed scenes, they re-looped dialogue with other voices. They sent me over a tape. I looked at it, and went into the bathroom and threw up. Not only because it was terrible, but because I had agreed to it in the first place and then compromised what I had done, hoping to make it acceptable to them. I had no-one to blame but myself. Why I thought I was going to change the system, I don't know. If it had been the work of rank-and-file television directors it would have been different. I had used long, sweeping shots and a lot of stuff on one take, and this they couldn't re-cut. So, they chopped it up. It had been a very stylish piece when I had finished, but when I saw what they presented, it had absolutely nothing to it.

"For one last try I went back to them and tried to reason with them. I said 'What you've got here now is pulp, it doesn't make any sense. What I gave you I thought was a work with style, good taste, a good story, humor and action.' They didn't want to hear it. I said 'Is there nothing I can do to convince you that what I gave you is much better?' They wouldn't budge. I had no alternative then but to go to the Directors Guild. The only protection directors have if they feel their work has been totally violated, is to have their names removed from the credits. That is a terrific admission of defeat, I don't have to tell you. Here you spend all this time emotionally and physically making what you believe in, and you end up saying 'It's out of my hands, it's ruined!' The Directors Guild have a synonym, a name, a *nom-de-plume* if you will, for this situation. He's called 'Allan Smithee.' I then had to petition the Board of the Directors Guild to allow me to take my name off, because otherwise anyone can use this in a dispute. There must be a legitimate reason. The Board deemed that my reasons were valid, that indeed the film had been destroyed, and that my name should be removed. This was a deep disappointment and very traumatic. The film was eventually shown 'directed by Allan Smithee', it was a total disaster, and there never was a series. Mary Tyler Moore had nothing to do with this. She had sold the studio by the time I finished the film. So much for that!"

● ● ●

"I have gone through a difficult period lasting many years. I made decisions about my career which turned out not to be wise and these sent me in the wrong direction about what I thought was best for me. Much of this began after *Black Sunday*. At that time, I knew enough never to count on success being a certainty in the movies.

"Everyone at the studio predicted *Black Sunday* would be an enormous financial and critical success and I came to believe it too. It received good reviews, eventually recovered its cost, but didn't really make its mark. I became deeply depressed. It affected me badly, and I turned to drinking heavily. There had been alcoholism in the half-Irish side of my family, and my father was a practicing alcoholic. I've always enjoyed a good Scotch, but I never got drunk, and I never drank when I worked. After *Black Sunday* I just went over the edge. The drink began to affect my decisions, such as taking on *Prophecy*. Then *The Challenge* didn't help, listening and working with two languages, the dubbing and the looping, my mind couldn't sort out the confusion. The personal complications arising from this left me tormented for years and affected my career badly.

"I spent the '80s putting my life back together, but I don't want anyone to think that I thought of myself as a victim during that awful time, because I wasn't. Yul Brynner used to tell me that no matter what life was like at any given moment, good or bad, there's one thing of which you can always be sure: it would change. Evans stood by me, helped me, got me into to the Program and now my life is much improved. I pulled myself out of drinking and from that day on I haven't touched wine or spirits—only tea."

52 PICK-UP 1986

Director John Frankenheimer • *Executive Producer* Henry T. Weinstein • *Producers* Menahem Golan, Yorman Globus • *Production Company* Cannon Films, Inc. • *Screenplay* Elmore Leonard, John Steppling, *based on the novel by* Elmore Leonard • *Camera* Jost Vacano (TVC color/wide-screen) • *Editor* Robert F. Shugrue • *Sound* Richard Alexander, Michael Casper, Andy MacDonald • *Production Designer* Philip Harrison • *Art Director* Russell Christian • *Costume Designer* Ray Summers • *Music* composed and performed by Gary Chang • *Distribution* Cannon Releasing Corporation • *Classification* R • *Release* October 1986 • *Running Time* 114 mins • *Location* made on location in Los Angeles • *Soundtrack* on Varese Sarabande • *Formats* available on VHS and LD • *Cost* $M7.4 • The novel had been filmed previously by Cannon Films as *The Ambassador* (1984) directed by J. Lee Thompson.

CAST

Harry Mitchell • Roy Scheider			Christopher Cory,
Barbara Mitchell • Ann-Margret			Maurice Jenkins,
Doreen • Vanity			John Kahnen,
Alan Raimy • John Glover			Bobby Ponce, Ray
Leo Franks • Robert Trebor			Vela
Jim O'Boyle • Lonny Chapman	*Injured driver*	•	Robin Bronfman
Cini • Kelly Preston	*O'Boyle's wife*	•	Debra Burger
Bobby Shy • Clarence Williams III	*Janet*	•	Laisa Carrie
Mark Averson • Doug McClure	*Drug dealer*	•	Blackie Dammett
Dan Lowenthal • Alex Henteloff	*Lisa*	•	Barbara Ferris
Counter girl • Michelle Walker	*Policeman*	•	John Francis
Test site worker • Philip Bartko	*James Boyer*	•	Conroy Gedeon
Partygoers • Tom Byron, Harvey	*Ed Salvan*	•	Bill Gratton
Cowen, Ron Jeremy	*Patron*	•	Jai M Jefferson
Hyatt, Amber Lynn,	*Lady in hall*	•	Lenora Logan
Sharon Mitchell,	*Passer-by*	•	Mark M. Mayuga
Ines Ochoa, Ilyson	*Nude models*	•	Lorrie Lovett,
Palmeter, Katherine			Sandra Perron,
Poland, Debra Satell,			Barbara Summers
Shirley Thompson,	*Grady*	•	William J. Murphy
Amy White	*Tom*	•	Anthony Palmer
Factory workers • Charles Bowden,	*Vendor*	•	Frank Sivero
Marc Castenada,	*Celebrity voice*	•	Arlin Miller
Mike Caruso,	*impersonation*		
Steven Clawson,			

SYNOPSIS

Indulging in his only affair in twenty-three years of marriage, Harry Mitchell finds himself held at gunpoint by three masked men, forced to watch a video of his love-making with a young model called Cini, and faced with a $100,000 blackmail demand. An ex-army major who has built up his own successful business, Harry rejects the advice of his lawyer O'Boyle to call in the police since the publicity would ruin his wife Barbara's budding political career as a candidate in the council elections.

After first shamefacedly confessing to the shocked and hurt Barbara, he delivers an envelope containing strips of paper and a rude message instead of the first payment. The three men promptly stage a repeat performance, this time forcing Harry to watch a video recording of the murder of Cini, staged in such a way that he can be framed for the killing if he remains recalcitrant. Shaken but even more determined not to submit, Harry visits the porn shop where Cini had worked as a photographic model in order to question her friend Doreen. Tentatively identifying the nervous owner, Leo Franks, as one of the three blackmailers, Harry is pointed by Doreen in the direction of Alan Raimy, manager of a sex cinema. Bluffing Raimy into acknowledging that he is involved, Harry convinces him that all he can raise is $50,000 and suggests that he persuade his partners to settle for that. Having sown a little dissension by saying that Leo was his informant as to Alan's identity, Harry adds to it by telling hit man Bobby Shy, sent to kill him because the business has gone sour, that Alan evidently means to keep his $50,000 offer to himself. Alan soothes Bobby by explaining that he hadn't wanted to mention the money in front of the traitorous Leo. The terrified Leo meanwhile vainly offers to go with Harry to the police, revealing that the evidence implicating him in the killing is tenuous since Cini's body has been disposed of. Bobby kills Leo, while Alan kidnaps Barbara, sets up a meeting with Harry, and disposes of Bobby. Harry receives the drugged Barbara in exchange for the $52,000 and his new Jaguar. But Harry has rigged the car with a self-locking and auto-destruct device. It blows up with Alan inside. (The title *52 Pick-Up*, is a police term.)

COMMENT

This film, marking Frankenheimer's return to form, shows a potent imagination at work in a powerful and thoughtful film. It deals once again with his preoccupation with ethical dilemmas and the question of moral choice. In this fascinating and terrifying study of evil cleverly interwoven with a matter-of-fact black humor recalling the world of Huston's *Asphalt Jungle*, the director has "picked-up" Elmore Leonard's laconic novel with much of the dialogue intact and taken us into the underworld of pornographic cinema, sex shops and drug dealing. After a quiet opening shot of a swimming pool from above, establishing Harry's well-to-do life, we see the industrial practices at his factory. He telephones his wife to say that he will be late, as she puts down the phone, we see from her expression that she knows instinctively where he is going.

What follows is one of the most tightly plotted and constructed films one could wish for, and certainly ranks among the best of Frankenheimer's work. The use of light and shade, the shadows of blinds across faces, reflections from mirrors, imaginative transitions from scene to scene, the growing tension, the way the actors move, the claustrophobic camera movements, the night club scenes and sex parties, the hysteria, the murders, the nightmares, the rain-swept streets, all are conveyed with a startling realism, making these familiar methods seem original again—and without a trace of the sensationalism which marks other films about the underworld. The whole is cleverly balanced by the portrayal of the three evil blackmailers so ordinary and casual about life and death with their almost Dickensian comical dialogue, but who are truly loathsome cowards whom Harry, determined to prevent them get the better of him, knowingly plays against each other. The underworld has never seemed so plausible and the making of the snuff film never so cruel and ugly. The harsh music by Chang adds to the imaginative use of sound.

Without being superficial or sentimental, the blackness of the whole is lightened by the portrayals of Roy Scheider, as the quiet, sometimes desperate, unbreakable Harry, who seems genuinely to regret his infidelity, and Ann-Margret, who plays with a gentle, intelligent understanding and sensitivity as she becomes the pawn in the struggle between Harry and his tormentors. The three villains played by Robert Trebor, Clarence Williams and John Glover, work splendidly together and cleverly convey their characters' faults and failings, their weaknesses

and suspicions, eventually destroying themselves. Frankenheimer, who impressed everyone with his use of television screens in *The Manchurian Candidate* and in several films since, here uses video techniques with a vivid expertise nothing short of astounding in today's cinema, particularly in the opening pornographic sequences, with little that is explicit, all being conveyed by impressionistic shapes, shadows and suggestion. Harry's engineering background makes it seem entirely probable that he knew how to blow up his beloved Jaguar and destroy the last vestige of evil in his life. But as he and Barbara walk away across the gloomy bridge with the camera drawing back and away from their struggle, we know that it is not necessarily a conventional happy ending. The darkness of this time will never entirely be banished from their lives.

The cast of 52 Pick-Up *meets with Frankenheimer for a first script reading.* From left *Doug McClure, Lonny Chapman, John Glover, Ann-Margret, Vanity, Frankenheimer, Kelly Preston, Roy Scheider, Clarence Williams III and Robert Trbor.*

JF "After the *Riviera* fiasco, I was living in Europe, and one day, leaving Los Angeles for London, I picked up the novel *52 Pick-Up* by Elmore Leonard at the airport, and read it on the flight over. When I arrived in London, I called my agent, Peter Riley, and got him to find out who owned the book. It turned out to be Cannon, who, when we asked, were delighted to let me make a film of it. I've always liked Leonard's books, this one in particular, but it turned out that Cannon had already made it under the title, *The Ambassador* in 1983, with Robert Mitchum and Ellen Burstyn, and directed by J. Lee Thompson. This adaptation actually had little to with *52 Pick-Up*. It was Rock Hudson's last screen appearance. I knew that no-one was even going to remember that movie.

"Henry Weinstein, who had been a friend for many years, was working at Cannon as their Vice President in Charge of Production and he was very helpful. He wanted to work with me to get this picture made. We worked on the script with a young Los Angeles dramatist, John Steppling. Weinstein touted his talent and as I didn't have anybody else in mind whom I felt would be right for it, I agreed—but with some doubts. Steppling did an inadequate job. He contributed nothing and he took away a lot of Elmore Leonard. I was stuck with a script that wasn't what I wanted. Roy Scheider had contacted me about being in the picture. I always wanted to work with him. Menahem Golan said 'Fine, we'll hire him,' and after a week of negotiation, Roy was signed on. He had the same reaction to the script that I did, that it missed Leonard's book. I didn't know Elmore Leonard, but I called him and said, 'I read *52 Pick-Up*, I love your dialogue, and we have a script that doesn't work.' Leonard had tried writing screenplays in his time, and was disenchanted with the medium because he was constantly being re-written and changed by people he thought, quite honestly, were incompetent. I sent him the script, he read it, called me back saying 'I see what you mean.' I said 'Why don't you and I, with Roy Scheider who knows pictures well, write the dialogue?' That's what we did. I told him the elements of his book I liked, and we kept those in. He sent me pages, Roy and I went over them, changed them, always going back to the book. In about three weeks we had a good script based completely on his book. It was good, gritty material for me. Nobody does villains better than Elmore Leonard, and his dialogue is laconic with a mordant wit. He loves films and said it's the best ever made of one of his books. I'm glad he's pleased. Ludlum said the same about *Holcroft*.

"Henry Weinstein told me that Cannon wanted to shoot the movie in Pittsburgh rather than Detroit, where the book was based. I said 'Why Pittsburgh?' He said 'Well, we can get deals in Pittsburgh, great locations, and it's an interesting place to make a movie.' I called the art director and the production manager and we went to Pittsburgh. We certainly found suitable locations. When we came back the budget had been drawn up and Menaham Golan called me into his office. I'd heard all kinds of stories about Menahem and I went in with a feeling of dread. He said 'I've got the budget and I think it's a million dollars too high. I'm not going to spend a penny more than seven million four, and this budget is at eight million four. You're going to have to cut a million dollars out of this budget otherwise we're not going to make the movie.' I said 'Menahem, why do you insist on making this movie in Pittsburgh? If we could make the movie here in Los Angeles where every location exists, we would save airplane fares and living expenses, amounting to about a million dollars.' He said 'I don't want to make the movie in Pittsburgh.' I said 'But I was told you did.' He said 'No, I don't care where you make the movie!' I said 'Great, then we've just saved a million dollars. We'll make the picture here in Los Angeles on your budget.'

"Then came the business of casting. I looked forward to working with Ann-Margret, she seemed the perfect choice for the wife. In casting the three heavies, well, who could be better than John Glover as the leading thug, together with Robert Trebor and Clarence Williams III. With Vanity, Kelly Preston, Lonny Chapman and Doug McClure, we put together a superb cast, and rehearsed for two weeks. We were going to do the picture non-union in Los Angeles, meaning we couldn't use one of the better-known union cameramen here. I had seen the German picture directed by Wolfgang Petersen *Das Boot*, and the camerawork by Jost Vacano, and particularly the lighting, really impressed me. There were all kinds of immigration problems, but we got him. He had an Arriflex on gyroscopes that he used so well in the submarine, and he used it here. There was no studio work. We rented space on Santa Monica Boulevard. and built our sets there over a weekend. The Mafia came in and demanded protection money, but when they realized it was a film set and not a commercial enterprise they backed away. The picture came in on budget—among the best of my experiences—and then I cut the picture together with Bob Shugrue. I finished it and then came the time to show it to the powers-that-be, in this case Menahem and Yoram Globus. I'd hardly seen Menahem at all.

"I had only one problem on the whole picture—to show Roy Scheider's emotional breakdown when he drives away in his Jaguar after watching the execution of his girlfriend. I wanted it to rain. I wanted him stopped, I wanted to put a pattern of light across his face. I thought—We'll have him come to a train crossing, the gate comes down, train comes across, the lights are flashing through the windscreen. The production manager told me that a train was going to cost about $75,000 dollars and that I couldn't have it. I had to go to Menahem, who said I could have it, but if I could find a cheaper way, he would prefer it. When somebody treats you like that, you begin to think about what could be done instead. It occurred to me that if I staged an automobile accident with red police flashers and he was stopped as a result, I could achieve the same effect without spending the $75,000, and that's what I did. I promised Golan I would stay on budget, and by doing that, I never heard from him. I had complete creative control on the picture. I never had comments about any of the rushes, nobody at the office ever saw them except Golan, and he would occasionally say how much he liked them.

"The picture was almost two hours long—an hour and fifty-five minutes. I showed it to Menahem Golan on Sunday night, and he said 'The picture is absolutely wonderful, but it's long. If you meet me at eight-thirty tomorrow morning in the cutting room, I have some ideas I want to talk to you about on where to shorten it.' I agreed, but I didn't sleep that night! I arrived promptly at eight-thirty and he was already there with the cutter. I tried not to show it, but I was very uptight. Then, much to my surprise, he said 'Before we start this I want to say to you that this picture is *your* picture, you have final cut,' which I didn't have contractually, 'and anything I suggest you don't have to do at all. If you say I'm not going to do any of it, fine, we'll release the picture the way you want it.' He continued 'If you find anything I say valuable, good.' He had about ten points, five of which were good. I agreed to cut the five—moments here and there—and that's how we released the picture. Working with Menahem was unexpectedly pleasant and trouble-free!

"Now the problems really started because the other part of Cannon took over, which was Yoram, in charge of distribution. He was a likeable man and treated me very well, except that he just wouldn't spend the money necessary to open the picture. There wasn't enough advertising, so consequently the picture did not do what we hoped it would because the public didn't know about it. People who see this picture on a video say 'My God, what a fascinating movie!' They didn't know it had been in cinemas."

DEAD BANG 1989

Director John Frankenheimer • *Producer* Steve Roth • *Executive Producers* Robert L. Rosen, Robert Foster • *Production Company* A Lorimar Film Entertainment Company presentation of a Steve Roth production • *Screenplay* Robert Foster • *Camera* Gerry Fisher (Alpha Cine color, Metrocolor prints, wide-screen) • *Editor* Robert F. Shugrue • *Sound* Claude Hazanavicious, Charles Wilborn, Jay M. Harding, Bill W. Benton John J. Stephens • *Art Direction* Ken Adam • *Costume Designer* Jodie Tillen • *Music* Gary Chang, Michael Kamen • *Distribution* Warner Brothers • *Classification* R • *Release* March 1989 • *Running Time* 105 mins • Alternate pre-release title *In For the Kill* • *Location* on location in Calgary, Drumheller and High River, province of Alberta, and in Los Angeles, over three months beginning in April 1988 • Novel from Berkley Books • *Availability* VHS and LD • Based on the true story of LA Homicide Detective Jerry Beck, who, while investigating the murder of a fellow officer, uncovers a white-supremacy organization.

CAST

Jerry Beck •	Don Johnson	*Ponchito* •	Ricardo Ascencio
Linda •	Penelope Ann Miller	*Officer Franklin* •	William Taylor
Arthur Kressler •	William Forsythe	*Female officer* •	Trudy Forbes
Elliot Webly •	Bob Balaban	*Reverend Gebhardt* •	Michael Hibbins
Bobby Burns •	Frank Military	*Mrs. Geghardt* •	Evans Evans
John Burns •	Tate Donovan	*Bogan,* •	Stephen E. Miller
Chief Dixon •	Tim Reid	*Oklahoma officer*	
Agent Gilroy •	James B. Douglas	*Daughter* •	Dawn Mortensen
Chief Hillard •	Brad Sullivan	*Cottonwood officer* •	Frank C. Turner
Louisa •	Phyllis Guerrini	*Juancho* •	Lennard Camarillo
Bikers •	Darwyn Swalve,	*Detective John* •	Jerome Beck
	David H. "Hutch"	*Helpful person* •	Valerie Pearson
	Van Dalsem,	*Man in car* •	Dominick Louis
	Ron Jeremy Hyatt		Clark
Detective Bilson •	Sam Scarber	*Priest* •	Billy Boyle
Sergeant Kimble •	Mic Rodgers	*Mark Beck* •	Justin Stillwell
Edwin Gates •	Tiger Haynes	*Karen Beck* •	Christine Cable
Officers •	Garwin Sanford,	*Teacher* •	Maureen Thomas
	Lon Katzman	*Dixon's men* •	Ron Carothers,
James "Hard Rock" •	Daniel Quinn		Ernie Jackson
Ellis		*Dixon's wife* •	Juliana Carter
LAPD officer •	Jarion Monroe		

SYNOPSIS

Los Angeles homicide detective Jerry Beck, in the middle of a divorce, returns to his cheap apartment beneath the Burbank airport flight paths to find a court injunction forbidding him from seeing his children. That night, a convenience store owner and a patrolman are cold-bloodedly gunned down, and Beck comes up with a likely suspect in the recently paroled Bobby Burns. Insisting that Burns' parole offlcer, Elliot Webly, meet him the next day, Christmas Day, Beck attends a police party and spends the night with a woman, Linda, who leaves hurriedly the next morning. With Webly, Beck bursts into the Hell's Angels hangout where he expects to catch Burns, but finds only his younger brother John. Beck is further frustrated by a phone call to his wife, and angered to realise that Linda was the dead patrolman's ex-wife, who now asks Beck to kill his killer. A murderous raid by Burns and his henchmen on a bar in Cottonwood, Arizona, leads Beck and the local sheriff's men to a ranch from which the killers escape, leaving behind a storehouse of white supremacist literature.

FBI agent Arthur Kressler arrives on the scene, and although dismissing the likelihood of any significance racist organization, joins Beck in following its trail to Oklahoma and the Aryan National Church run by Reverend Gebhardt. The two law offlcers argue over tactics, and the uptight Kressler protests at Beck's belligerent attitude. When Beck is then nearly kidnapped by Burns, and involved in a messy shoot-out from which the killer escapes, his superior officer insists he has behavioral problems and should see a psychiatrist. Beck offends the latter, Dr. Krantz, by finding his attempts at bonhomie comical, and threatens him when Krantz intimates that he will not be passed as fit for duty.

He follows the supremacists' trail to Boulder, where he is joined again by Kressler, and, with a team of black policemen led by Chief Dixon, they plan an assault on the group's nearby training camp. They surprise Gebhardt and his fascist "congregation," but can find to trace of Burns and his sidekicks until Beck stumbles on an underground hideaway and arms cache. In a running battle through the network of tunnels, Burns' henchmen are killed, but the dying Burns tells Beck that he did not commit the initial murders of the store owner and the patrolman. Beck and Kressler are then surprised by the crazed John Burns, who claims he committed the murders to prove to his brother that he had the requisite "fire and ice" to serve his organization. He is shot by Beck who—now more philosophical about his problems—bids Chief Dixon farewell after watching Kressler claim most of the credit at a press conference.

COMMENT

With *Dead Bang*, Frankenheimer is back in the political arena with a masterful film concerning the rise of neo-nazism in the United States. Timely, powerful and frequently frightening in its revelations and implications, it moves swiftly and dramatically from what appears to be just another brutal LA murder to the discovery of a nationwide, well-organized white supremacist conspiracy. The central figure is a real-life policeman, Jerome Beck, whose story this is, played with fierce pent-up anger and frustration over the failure of his marriage and the breakdown of his job, by the always credible Don Johnson. We are at once gripped by the authenticity of the locations, from the drab working class district where Beck lives under the thundering flight path to Burbank Airport, to the impressive open spaces of Oklahoma, Arizona and Colorado.

THE FOURTH WAR 1990

Director John Frankenheimer • *Executive Producers* William Stuart, Sam Perlmutter • *Producer* Wolf Schmidt • *Line Producer* Robert L. Rosen • *Production Company* Kodiak Films, Inc • *Screenplay* Stephen Peters, Kenneth Ross, *based on the novel by* Stephen Peters • *Camera* Gerry Fisher (Alpha Ciné color, DeLuxe prints) • *Editor* Robert F. Shugrue • *Sound* John "Doc" Wilkinson, Doug Turner, Grover Helsley • *Production Design* Alan Manzer • *Costume Designer* Ray Summers • *Music* Bill Conti • *Distribution* New Age Releasing, Inc., Canon/Pathé • *Classification* R • *Release* February 1990 • *Running Time* 91 mins • Working titles *Game of Honor, Face Off* • *Location* on location in Bragg Creek, city of Calgary, and the town of Canmore, Alberta, beginning in February 1989 • *Availability* VHS and LD.

CAST

Col. Jack Knowles •	Roy Scheider	*Red Privates* •	Garry Galinsky, Ed Soibelman, Garry Spivak
Col. N. A. Valachev •	Jürgen Prochnow		
Lt. Col. Timothy Clark •	Tim Reid	*Red Army Majors* •	Yefim Korduner, Brent Woolsey
Elena Novotna •	Lara Harris	*US private* •	Kent McNeill
Gen. Roger Hackworth •	Harry Dean Stanton	*MP* •	Brian Warren
Sergeant Major •	Dale Dye	*Czech guards* •	Roman Podhora, Joseph Vrba
MP corporal •	Bill MacDonald	*Innkeeper* •	George Scholl
Gawky soldier •	David Palffy	*Bavarian farmer* •	Gordon Signer
Needle-nosed soldier •	Neil Grahn	*Innkeeper's wife* •	Lilo Bahr
Knowles driver •	Ernie Jackson	*Frontier police captain* •	Claus Diedrich
Young US soldier •	Ron Campbell		
Defector •	John Dodds	*Villagers* •	Kyle Maschmeyer, Kurt Darmohray
Young soldier •	Richard Durven		
Dwayne •	Harold Hecht Jr.	*Czech tower guard* •	Igor Burstyn
Hannelore •	Alice Pesta	*Puppeteer* •	Matus Ginzbert
Communications corporal •	Gregory A. Gale	*Aide to Valachev* •	Boris Novogrudsky
Mayor •	Henry Kope	*Sports announcer* •	Tom Kelly

SYNOPSIS

The Czech-West German frontier, November 1988. Jack Knowles, a misfit Vietnam veteran, takes command of Camp Clayton. After a man is killed fleeing to the West, Knowles starts a grudge match by throwing a snowball at Colonel N. A. Valachev, his Soviet opposite number, a man embittered by the Afghanistan war. Reported by his second-in-command, Lieutenant-Colonel Timothy Clark, Knowles is ordered to Stuttgart for a reprimand from his friend, General Roger Hackworth. Later, after telephoning one of his sons at school in Vermont and learning of an injustice suffered by the boy's younger brother, a drunken Knowles secretly crosses the frontier and humiliates three Russian soldiers. Next day, Knowles' jeep is blown up by a Russian grenade; that night, Knowles destroys a Russian watchtower. While escaping under fire, he teams up with Elena Novotna, who claims to be a political dissident.

Back in Germany, Elena vainly begs Knowles to help her return to Czechoslovakia to collect her daughter. Hackworth flies to Camp Clayton and this time gives Knowles an uncompromising warning. Summoned to a guesthouse by Elena, Knowles is confronted by Valachev who insults the girl and warns Knowles that he will be killed next time he crosses the frontier. Knowles rises to the challenge only to be double-crossed by Elena, a Red Army captain. Knowles nevertheless turns the tables on Valachev and, after a car crash and a chase, engages him in hand-to-hand combat on a frozen river. Soldiers from the American and Soviet armies look on as the officers slug it out until weariness underlines the futility of their quarrel.

COMMENT

The Fourth War is a simple but strikingly effective moral tale set in the deep winter snows of the Czech-West German frontier in 1988. An American army post faces a Russian army post and each is commanded by officers disillusioned with a past war: the American with Vietnam, the Russian with Afghanistan. Going against all the rules (which in American motion pictures we accept as being entirely possible in the US Army), the American colonel finds an outlet for his anger and frustration by raiding the Russian outpost after its sentries have killed a defector trying to cross into the West. This brings him face to face with his Russian counterpart and following several stormy encounters they finally begin to discuss their lives and see the senselessness of their dislike of each other on both personal and national levels.

Based on Stephen Peters's novel about his military service on the Czech-German frontier this is an intellectual exercise for the questing Frankenheimer, who does not seek easy answers to the troubling contradictions of war, but to take us into the lives of two lonely men, once certain of the rightness of their calling but now finding the purpose of life blurred by uncertainties. The film recalls Einstein's comment that he did not know what weapons would be employed in the next war, but if there was a fourth war it would probably be fought with stones. This is symbolized at the closing of the film with the two colonels engaged in hand-to-hand combat on a frozen river, a struggle in futility from which neither emerges as the victor. For Colonel Knowles there is, it seems, no future contentment for a man embittered by the forces of war and in conflict with those who direct it. His one hope of happiness, with a Czech woman, is shattered when she turns out to be a spy.

There is nothing conventional about this war film if, indeed, it can be called a war film. There is a feeling of futility in the routine activities of both army camps, with their bored soldiers sullenly sitting out the Cold War. For once in a Frankenheimer film, dialogue is first expressed in voice-over thoughts following a typically gripping Frankenheimer opening scene (this time a tense escape across the border with a car driving across the snowy countryside). Notable moments arise in the conflict with the sergeant at the wedding— the close-up on the hat, now we see it at the foot of Roy Scheider, a good introduction to him, a part well-played; the Russian soldiers are seen riding horses, the Americans ride in their jeeps. There is much symbolism in this often striking study in impressionism. Harry Dean Stanton makes a convincing general, his comments about war are sensible, he is a figure with a commanding presence. What we are left with are the shadows of tanks and helicopters facing each other.

JF "When I was editing *Dead Bang*, two producers, Wolf Schmidt and William Stuart, called me to say they had Roy Scheider committed to a screenplay called *The Fourth War* and that Scheider wanted me to direct it. I read it and came back to them saying I liked the idea of two committed military professionals from opposite sides, unable to accept the changing world, who decided to make their own private war. The script needed a Robert Rosen—I called him and he became involved again, and we asked for Kenneth Ross who did *Black Sunday* for us, to rewrite the script. Stephen Peters, who wrote the novel, wrote the first draft. It took place on the German-Czechoslovak border and Wolf Schmidt assumed that we would go to Germany to shoot. I put it to him that, having spent a good time in Germany myself and going over weather figures, the snow we desperately needed for this picture was practically non-existent in Germany, especially around the Czechoslovak border. If it does snow, it snows for a very few number of days. Also, obviously anything around the border at that time would be watched, and filming there presented a huge danger. He then suggested that we go to Finland where we would get a lot of snow. But I knew that it would necessitate, to all intent and purposes, bringing in an entire crew. Then Bob Rosen came up with the idea of Calgary again. I'd worked up there on *Dead Bang* and we knew the facilities—so that's where we went. After that decision was made, the rest of it was an endurance contest. It was the coldest winter in Calgary for thirty years. We got all the snow we'd ever want, and with any other actor but Roy Scheider we would have never finished the movie.

"Gerry Fisher was an example for everybody on the location. It was twenty degrees below zero and he was out there, walking around. He never came in out of the cold. Roy Scheider never complained and the crew adapted magnificently to absolutely horrendous conditions. It was *so* cold making that picture! I never experienced cold like that! We were working in minus forty degrees centigrade only twenty minutes from Calgary, a location where we

They withdraw, and all goes quiet, with only the sound of the wind remaining. The film is full of haunting images such as this.

were at the center of everything and around us were about eight different locations. It was like the hub of a wheel. We went out and made this film very economically under these awful conditions. We used Alan Manzer, a Canadian production designer this time. He was Ken Adam's assistant on the last picture. He did a very good job but there really wasn't much design to do. We were out there in the snow almost the entire time. Snow presented huge obstacles for these soldiers to cross. Dramatically and psychologically the snow was a third lead in the picture creating the bleak landscape of a terrible isolation; the story would not have worked in hot weather.

"We cast Jürgen Prochnow whom I'd seen in *Das Boot*, and Lara Harris, a New York model whose accent was very good. Harry Dean Stanton was another of the many good actors I'd always wanted to work with. He played the General who represented the 'new military.' He stood by the Roy Scheider character, a military colonel who, in time of war, was desperately wanted on our side, but, in peacetime, was no longer required. He was like a loose cannon, or a grenade with the pin out of it—a modern Patton, but without his genius. The two army men were on a collision course—they could not accept the fact that life had changed.

"While we changed the script a certain amount, what we never could have foreseen—and if we could have, we would never have made the movie—was the fact that the border would disappear before the picture came out, so there was no Iron Curtain when this picture was released. This hurt us severely, obviously. We had made an historical piece without knowing it! I made no compromises and I was pleased with all the performances. And then Kodiak, the production company, made a distribution deal with Cannon— as a matter of fact, with the same distribution executive we had on *52 Pick-Up*! They didn't spend enough money opening it, but who can blame them? They were up against it with a subject which was no longer pertinent. But it's a movie I'm proud of and with the passing of the years it will be seen as an important part of its time."

THE YEAR OF THE GUN 1991

Director John Frankenheimer • *Producer* Edward R. Pressman • *Executive Producer* Eric Fellner • *Production Company* Edward R. Pressman Film Corp./Initial Films/Year of the Gun Productions • *Screenplay* David Ambrose, based on the novel by Michael Mewshaw • *Camera* Blasco Giuarto, (DeLuxe color/wide-screen) • *Editor* Lee Percy • *Sound* Bernard Bats • *Production Designer* Aurelio Crugnola • *Costume Designer* Ray Summers • *Art Director* Luigi Quintili • *Set Decoration* Franco Fumagalli • *Music* Bill Conti • *Distribution* Columbia Tri-Star/Triumph Releasing Corporation • *Classification* R • *Release* September 1991 • *Running Time* 111 mins • *Location* Cinecitta Studios and on location in Rome from October to December 1990 • Shown at the Toronto International Film Festival, September 1991 • *Availability* VHS and LD.

CAST

David Raybourne • Andrew McCarthy		*Questioner* • Maurizio Fardo	
Lia Spinelli • Valeria Golino		*Piero Gagliani* • Luigi Amodeo	
Alison King • Sharon Stone		*Round-faced man* • Lou Castel	
Italo Bianchi • John Pankow		*Cops* • Salvatore Billa, Natale Nazareno	
Giovanni • Mattia Sbragia		*Detectives* • Franco Beltramme, Cyrus Elias	
Pierre Bernier • George Murcell			
Lucio Spinelli • Roberto Posse		*Bearded man* • Fabio Traversa	
Marco Spinelli • Thomas Elliot		*Ben Gershon* • Dick Cavett	
Lena • Carla Cassola		*Bernier's wife* • Fiammetta Baralia	
Joe Bob • Darren Modder		*University woman* • Alessandra Marson	
Mattie • Carol Schneider		*Mattie's boyfriend* • Guiseppe Zarbo	
Lanky youth • Ron Williams		*Gunman* • Mario Novelli	
Man in café • Antonio degli Schiavi		*Guard* • Luciano Foti	
Aldo Moro • Aldo Mengolini		*Moro's interpreter* • Elena Cantarone	
Woman • Francesca Prandi		*BBC woman* • Cecilia Todeschini	
Men • Stefano Molinari, Pietro Bontempo		*University youth* • Maria Carolina Salome	
Terrorist • Luigi di Fiore			

SYNOPSIS

January 1978. American journalist David Raybourne returns to Rome as riots erupt around the militant activities of the Red Brigade. He resumes contact with his friend, Italo Bianchi, a teacher at the university, and the cousin of David's lover Lia Spinelli. David returns to work at *American News*, a newspaper run on the cheap by Pierre Bernier, an entrepreneur with supposed CIA connections. One of Italo's students, Piero Gagliani, is kidnapped—there are rumors that he is in league with the Red Brigade—but later he is found dead. David is reunited with Lia, who is divorcing her husband, but on leaving her flat he is attacked by two men and warned to stay away from her.

Alison King, a freelance photographer, is on the scene during a Brigade bank raid, and her pictures are published in *Time* magazine. David meets her at a party thrown by Bernier, which is raided by the Brigade. David embarks on a money-spinning writing venture, a novel in which the Red Brigade kidnap Prime Minister Aldo Moro. Alison confronts David with his past as a radical activist, and insists that they work together on his book about the Brigade. David denies all knowledge of such a book, and initially refuses her advances, but eventually they begin an affair. Alison searches David's flat and discovers the novel, which she takes to be a factual report on the Brigade. She mentions the book to Italo who, unknown to her and David, is working with the Brigade: he had become involved through his lover Gagliani, whose staged kidnapping ended in his accidental death. Under orders from his superior, Giovanni, Italo steals David's manuscript.

Finding his flat ransacked, David goes to *American News*, arriving just as Bernier is shot dead by the Brigade, having been implicated in David's book. David meets Italo, who tells him that Moro is really to be kidnapped. Giovanni arrives to interrogate David, but Italo intervenes and is shot dead. David rescues Alison from a Brigade trap and they escape. They contact Lia, but she is also a Brigade member and hands them over to Giovanni. While they are being interrogated, Lia is questioned about her commitment to the cause. After Moro is kidnapped in reality, David and Alison are driven away, apparently to be shot, but are released after Lia is executed in their place. David and Alison publish their book together, and David appears on American television to promote it, with Alison commenting by satellite from Beirut, where she is now working.

COMMENT

Here Frankenheimer takes up a difficult and engrossing subject, the struggle between politics and power, and expresses it with clarity, conviction and concern. Once again the director examines the paths of power, the devious ways of politicians and the havoc they wreak. This time this subject is set against the terrorism of the Red Brigade in Rome in the mid-1970s, leading to the assassination of Aldo Moro, the Italian prime minister. This is not, however, the intrusion of an American film-maker into foreign affairs, but a view of a nation in political turmoil as seen through the eyes and susceptibilities of two visiting Americans, a journalist and a photographer (somewhat similar to *The Challenge*, where contemporary Japan was seen through the eyes of an American brought in to participate in a "business" transaction).

Nor is the aptly titled *Year of the Gun* about the death of Moro. This takes place as an event that happened in real life. The coincidence is that the journalist, a somewhat weak and rather unprepossessing figure, a one-time activist back home, decides to write a novel in which he imagines Moro is killed (somewhat in the manner of Frederick Forsyth's imagined attack on De Gaulle in *Day of the Jackal*). Although the journalist, working for a Rome English-language paper, becomes aware of and involved with the activities of the terrorists he does not think events will culminate in such a horrible murder. When they do, his somewhat cynical attitude toward this turbulent political period changes into one of quiet resignation and despair. He realizes he knows almost nothing about the complexities behind their activities—their muddled political motives, their fanaticism or identity. Nor does the narrative go deeply into them. This is not a film about the Red Brigade, but about a writer and a photographer who deal with the surface of world events to gratify the media's need for instant copy. And, unlike many of Frankenheimer's films, the journalist, played by Andrew McCarthy, is not a figure of strength and determination; he is an ordinary, weak young man, representing the tide of disillusioned students who have graduated and cannot find positions.

The photographer is played in a likeable and practical way by Sharon Stone (before her provocative performance in Paul Verhoeven's *Basic Instinct*) and shows a deeper intelligence and determination than the writer. In a sharp ending, bringing in the Frankenheimer television touch, we see the writer back in New York. His book has been published, and he is enjoying his five minutes of fame on Dick Cavett's interview television program. The photographer joins the interview by satellite from Beirut, which is the latest trouble spot. They look at each other across the miles without really seeing each other—the past might never have been, except for his book accompanied by her photographs. Everything is superficial and exploitative, including the TV interview, briskly dispensed with to make room for the next guest.

This is Frankenheimer at his most pessimistic. There are very few static conversational scenes, the camera moves with the players, and the backgrounds are well-staged, effective and revealing, with the scenes of Italian family life having a neo-realistic quality to them. The pre-ending to the film, however, is a compellingly staged scene where the reporter and the photographer are taken into the countryside to be shot—in the same mountains where earlier they had happily relaxed over a picnic. Under gray skies, the leader of the Red Brigade tries to justify his actions, but instead of murdering them, he shoots Lia, the Brigade's undercover spy whom the reporter had made his friend and lover. This unexpected development makes a remarkably dramatic sequence, skilfully staged and edited, with an effective slow-motion shot of the photographer being ordered with grim irony to take pictures of the execution she was not, after all, a part of. This episode has a frightening, nightmarish quality to it. Conti's energetic and clamorous score is often intrusive, but a thoughtful touch by Frankenheimer brings in quiet choral music in the background as a "religious" counterpoint to the whole.

The camera work throughout captures the atmosphere of terror and deceit: in the riot scenes, the attack on the principals, a telling shot of the three of them, with McCarthy in the middle; the picnic in the mountains, the dark despair of street buildings seen from the ground looking up, the thunder in the air, the flight from a police force which is more interested in work permits than apprehending subversives. Everywhere the frightening face of terrorism is tellingly portrayed. For Frankenheimer this is tragic ground contaminated with the essence of evil.

PHOTO CHRISTOPHER BARR

JF "Edward Pressman called me about directing *Year of the Gun.* I had not worked with him before. I knew him to be a good producer. He gave me a script to read, and I didn't like it, but I did like the *idea* of the picture. It was from a novel by Michael Mewshaw, who gave me another scenario written by David Ambrose—a very interesting take on the book. Ed engaged Jay Presson Allen to rewrite, and she pared down that script to pretty well what we shot. It was a very good script. I liked the movie very much, although filming in Rome was not without annoying delays. When we arrived in Rome all the papers weren't signed, preventing us from securing the money to begin working. As negotiations continued, the lira kept going up against the dollar, and by the time the contracts came through we had less money to make the movie. Pressman, through his mother and his own resources, financed the picture—five weeks shooting with their own personal money. That's a brave undertaking. Ed Pressman is a man who puts his money into what he believes in—he walks like he talks, which is very important. We ended up with the deal signed, and, in spite of all the difficulties, we finished the picture on time.

"The difficulties were with the Italians. Permits were revoked, and while shooting in any big city is a continuous headache, on a location where individuals believe that the law is for everybody else but themselves, it was a nightmare. I don't speak Italian and the language barrier was an obstacle. Blasco Giuarto, who photographed *Cinema Paradiso*, spoke French, so I could talk directly with him—he's a good cameraman. I used the same Steadicam operator, David Crone, he worked with me on *The Fourth War*, who is very, very good. Ray Summers, the costume designer, has been with me since *Black Sunday*. A new film editor—Bob Shugrue wasn't available—named Lee Percy, who had done *Reversal of Fortune* for Barbet Schroeder, joined us, he's among the best film editors I've worked with. The Italian assistant

directors working with Tony Brandt, were terrific staging the crowd scenes and the riots. Tony, and Jerry Zeisman of *Black Sunday*, are the two best assistant directors for crowds I've ever had.

"We were lucky with the weather on that picture. Due to our financial delays we were not able to start shooting until October, and, by that time, the constant Mediterranean sun was not there. We shot mainly in bleak weather, and if the forecast was accurate, we'd go inside on bad days. Grey weather actually helped the mood, and we took advantage of the light. When I was a young director and critics and enthusiasts were talking about the fabulous look of European movies, I discovered when I went to France and lived there that pictures have that look because that's what it looks like! It's the old story—what comes out on the film is usually what's there to start with. It can be augmented to a degree, but usually we have to wait for the weather, and wait for the correct light. David Lean, at the height of his career, would not take an interesting shot at high noon, unless he wanted only unmitigated heat and no shadows. It's a waiting game requiring patience, and it's also expensive. David Lean once said that any director can shoot a movie, it's the really good director who knows when *not* to. And he's right. We waited for the weather, we rehearsed, we'd wait, the light would be right, we'd shoot.

"Sharon Stone was a pleasure to work with, a beautiful woman and an inventive actress. I first saw her on television in the mini-series *War and Remembrance*. When this film came along I knew she was right for the part. Andrew McCarthy was loosely connected with the Brat Pack media stuff going around at that time. He did well in *Weekend at Marty's* and was determined to get the part in *Year of the Gun*. I saw how Andrew would fit into the role—he had intelligence, vulnerability and caught the uncertain and deceptive nature of the character convincingly, I thought. Politics is a peripheral aspect of the narrative. It is not the subject. To me, this was a story of betrayal—truth, what is the truth—and it deals with the media and the media's responsibilities.

"Ending this picture offered several alternatives, and I decided to again use television. My background in early television influenced me here, as I did in *The Manchurian Candidate*, *Seven Days in May*, *Black Sunday*, and others. I used television in *Year of the Gun* to bring the writer and the photographer together—and to keep them apart. In other words, there she was in Beirut in the same shot as he was. Then there's that moment when they look at each other, but they are not really looking at each other, but it gives audiences that impression: she in Beirut, he in New York, that interchange of close-ups conveys an emotional distancing between the two former lovers. The idea of putting them on television at the end to be swallowed up by the on-rush of events seems to me to sum up much of life today. The original ending showed them signing copies of their book, but I couldn't dramatize an empty scene like that.

"The final sequence of events where they are taken to the mountains to be shot was complicated in many ways. The location was almost inaccessible, the weather was wet and cloudy, and I had to get that moment when Andrew McCarthy comes out not caring whether he lives or dies, where he becomes, for a moment, the hero of this picture. He had to have a moment of catharsis. That's what we worked for, and Andrew worked hard to convey it. He had hurt his knee falling on one of the rocks in the field and was in considerable pain, but he kept going in some of the worst weather. At times the stormy weather paralleled the cold of *The Fourth War*. Looking back, I don't know how we did it. Sharon Stone also broke her foot during the chase. She had worked with Nancy Ellison, an actual photo-journalist, for a month before coming to Rome—she did a lot of research for her part, and handled a camera most professionally. We shot the pictures she was supposed to be taking for normal screen in slow motion. We were very fortunate in our choice of Italian actors. Francesco Cinieri , who was my assistant director on *Grand Prix*, had become a casting director. He found some excellent actors and their faces gave this picture so much of its realism. Francesco died shortly after we finished the film. John Pankow. who played the professor, was American, but got the accent so right he passed as an Italian. I didn't want someone with a heavy accent doing the part because it had so much dialogue that needed to be clearly spoken.

"The scene of the kidnapping of Aldo Moro was very difficult. We did a tremendous amount of research looking at all the newsreel footage shot at the time. We looked at the actual location, where he was kidnapped, but the place had all been rebuilt. About three blocks away we found a matching location. For the Italians, the murder of Moro is very much like the Kennedy assassination. The Italian press was excited and worried about the fact that we were doing it. I tried to keep my interviews in Italy down to a minimum, but when the press said we were making an Aldo Moro picture, I replied 'No, we're not, we are doing a picture about a writer and his book, and Moro is one of the happenings during the course of the story.' I was in Paris and London when it opened and I was beseiged by the press, who seemed disappointed that it was not the Moro story. I think the Italians should make that picture.

"We didn't do huge business but did receive good notices particularly in Paris. Ed Pressman had problems with distribution too, just like the producers of my previous pictures. He raised his own print and advertising money and made a deal with Triumph, the distributing arm of Columbia for specialised films. They were not involved while it was being made and therefore didn't look upon it as one of their own to promote. This disappointment aside, I do believe I made a significant film tackling the political turmoil in Italy at that time."

FRANKENHEIMER ON CAMPUS

John Frankenheimer addressing film students at Bowling Green State University, Ohio, September 1992.

"Usually I start one of these discussions because although everyone wants to asks questions, I know that everybody's afraid to raise their hand the first time. I think it's wonderful that at an event like this every student gets a chance to meet those of us who make movies, and to have their own film classes. How different it is. When I was at Williams College and I was in your position, I was desperately trying to figure out what I was going to do with my life, how I was going to break into the theatre, and how I could realize my ambition to be an actor. I would alternate between terrific confidence and terrible despair. A lawyer from the Theatre Guild came up to Williamstown to talk to us, and if it had been Alfred Lunt it couldn't have been better. Here was somebody who was really in the theatre! Of course, when I stop to think of it, he probably had nothing to do with the theatre except to write a few contracts here and there because he was a lawyer; but it seemed real, meeting someone who had gone out there and accomplished something, instead of just theorizing about it.

"I find that, if I'm going to be of any help or assistance to you, it's by talking about things that actually happen in the field. I want to say to you first that I don't want to be negative, because you are going to get enough negativism when you get out of here, but being a movie director in the American system, or in the commercial movie world, has very little to do with what you are learning here in film school. Billy Wilder, I think, said it better than anyone else: 'I have been a commercially paid professional movie director for over fifty years of my life and, during that time, the camera has actually been turning less than two weeks.' A terrible comment. And it's true! So much of what we do is spending time trying to get certain films made, convincing people to make them, the preparation, the meetings, the editing afterwards, then going off and selling the movie. For those of you who want to be directors, you will find that it's a very lonely profession because most directors don't intermingle. You very seldom get a chance to see another director's work, you don't know how he or she works. I was lucky in that I was an assistant director in live television and I worked

with many directors on dramatic shows, most of whom you have never heard of and never would. But I ended up as Sidney Lumet's assistant director on a live show called *You Are There*, a recreation of historical events. Strangely, I learned much more from the bad directors, I really did. I learned much more from a bad movie than a good one—you learn what not to do. It's so easy to see the mistakes and you say—I don't want to do that, it's useful to see where the director went wrong because I'm not going to do that. On the other hand, it's very difficult to appreciate really great work. Sometimes you don't appreciate it until you are an adult.

"Obviously, what you really want to ask is: how do you do it? How do you get out there, how do you get a job, and how do you make a living at this? All I can tell you is that it's very, very difficult. The number of students being turned out by film schools, of actors who want to direct, of writers who want to direct, of editors who want to direct, is mind-boggling, it really is. The chances are slim. When I came along, live television was just beginning its ascendancy, and there were hundreds of live dramatic shows on from New York, and through a series of circumstances I was able to get a job as an assistant director in CBS. It was earn-as-you-learn productions in a strange kind of way. I learned about cameras, about cutting from one camera to another, about casting, by having to do it, I worked with incompetent directors where I had to go literally and put the show on the air. Yet that was wonderful because I had none of the responsibility. If it worked I was a genius and if it didn't, well, I was this idiot who didn't know how to do it. There was nothing to lose. I remember there was one live television show we did, a quiz show on Sunday nights. We used three cameras, one of them was on the contestant, another was on the panel and another was on the moderator. Every Sunday night this show was more or less the same thing, the same format—you cut to the guy over here who's talking, you cut to the panel over here, and so on—and the director was a kind of wild man who loved boats, and he'd just bought a new one. Now we go and rehearse this show for about three hours with the cameramen and so forth, and I remember I was there and the director wasn't. I kept going—this was live and we went on the air at eight o'clock. At seven-thirty there was still no director, and by this time the advertising representatives had started to panic. They were going crazy, they had no idea what was happening, they were climbing up the walls because to them this was very important. At ten minutes to eight the phone rang in the control room and it was the director. He always called me Kid—he said, 'Kid! how's it goin'?' I said, 'It's not going too good. They're very nervous about the fact that you're not here. Where are you?' He said, 'I'm on the boat. I've got the television set turned on. Now

you just do what I tell you. You got camera one on the panel, you got camera two on the contestants?' I said, 'That's right.' He said, 'You got camera three on the moderator.' I said, 'Yes.' He said, 'Now I'm going to watch the show on the boat and I'll call the cameras, how's that?' I said, 'Great.' So that's the way he directed the show, from his boat. That's what he did.

"Now, there was another time when I was Yul Brynner's assistant. I actually became a director because when Yul went on to do *The King and I*, I was promoted. But I was Yul's assistant and he and I were very close friends, and in those days they had us doing two dramatic shows a week with rehearsal in the morning, rehearsal in the after-

noon, one show was on Tuesday night, the other on Saturday night. Yul was under contract to CBS as was I, and he always had his own credit, and his credit, instead of saying 'Directed by Michael whatever-it-is' said 'Yul Brynner directed.' Part of my job was to carry this credit from show to show so that we could put it up on any camera. One of these dramatic shows went off the air. The CBS brass came to Yul Brynner and said 'You are going to direct the replacement.' He was very arrogant, they thought. Yul was Yul, he had great style, such class and nobody could ever penetrate that, particularly the CBS brass. They wanted to bring him down a couple of notches so they told him, 'You are directing Sunday night's *What's My Line*,' another quiz show. Yul was horrified at this. He said, 'I have never directed a quiz show, I have never seen this,' but they said 'Yes, but you are going to do it like everybody else because you're one of our contract directors.' He asked, 'What time does this show go on the air?' They said 'It goes on the air at nine-thirty, Sunday night.' And it was the top-rated quiz show in the country. He said 'I will only do it under conditions that I have my own assistant director, John Frankenheimer.' They said, 'You can have him.' He said, 'Fine, what time do you expect me there?' They said, 'Well, we start rehearsing seven o'clock' because they had Arlene Francis, and other celebrities on and it was a complicated camera show for a quiz program. And Yul said to me, 'John, get a limousine and pick me up at seven o'clock and make reservations at the Oak Room at the Plaza for dinner at seven-thirty.' I said 'Yul, we're supposed to be at this theatre over on Broadway at seven-thirty.' He said, 'Just do what I tell you.' So we did, we got the limousine, we were in dinner jackets and we had a great dinner at the Oak Room, and the show was going on the air at nine-thirty at night. At quarter past nine we arrived at the studio. Well, I've never seen bedlam like that—it was sponsored by Kraft Cheese, they probably had the President of Kraft Cheese there, it was hysterical. Yul—you've all seen him in the movies and he looked exactly the same then only not quite so bald—he walked in and said 'Where is the control room?'—he walked in like the King. They showed him the control room and he looked at this young woman over here and said, 'Young lady, what do you do?' and she said, 'I'm the script girl, Mr. Brynner.' 'What is your job?' She said 'I'm

supposed to time the show.' And he said 'When do you do the credits on the show?' 'At nine fifty-eight straight up we do the credits' which is a minute-and-a-half before the show ends. He said 'Very good. Now I'll tell you what I want you to do. Tell me when we're at nine fifty-four.' She said 'Yes Mr. Brynner, but why?' 'Just tell me.' So we went on the air, and it was obviously what we called a 'no-brainer.' Anyway, at nine fifty-four she said 'It's nine fifty-four Mr. Brynner.' He said 'Fine, roll the credits' and she said 'But it's six minutes early.' He said, 'Just do what I say' so they started to roll the credits, and he said 'John, where is my credit?' I said I had it. He said 'Camera one go on my credit, now camera two go on the audience. To camera three' he said, 'I want you to get close-ups of the audience. Now, cue them to applaud. The donkeys out there would do anything you asked.' He rolled through all the credits in about thirty seconds and we had five minutes of audience reaction! Do you really know what five minutes is really like on the air? 'Take two, cue them to applaud! Super my credit!' That's Yul Brynner directing, for five minutes, close-ups of the audience going—and they all know they're on television—hysterical, a standing ovation for five minutes seemingly for Yul. He was never asked to do that show again!

"That's what it was like then. There was a lot of fun, a lot of experimentation, a lot of skill and quick thinking. One more story and then we'll get on with questions—we were doing one of these half-hour crime shows, again, with the same director who phoned in the boat show. They gave him a crime show to direct because he directed the boat show so well! But he was the first director on U.S. television. His name was Johnny Kaiser and he's still directing. He directed the RCA Exhibit in the 1939 World's Fair. Totally insane, but you almost had to be a little mad to be a television director, and I qualified for that. But this was a crime show where Lee Marvin was playing a private detective, and we did it out of a converted movie theatre up on 105th Street and 5th Avenue. They took the seats out of the movie theatre and paved it over with concrete and took the balcony out, and they put the control room up there, and this became the studio where we did the whole show. When I tell you this you're going to know what happened, but the floor in this movie theatre was on a down grade. There were many attractive young women in this series, and the female lead was played by Connie Ford . In those days everybody just smoked, I mean, *smoked*. You were supposed to plan how actors moved from one set to the next, so that when the camera started on one scene I would run over to the next; it was live, you went from one thing to another, sometimes it was a lot more complicated than that. Lee Marvin was playing this scene with a police captain, and, in the next scene, Lee had to be on the telephone in a booth. This director didn't know how to get him from the captain scene to the phone booth. I said, 'Johnny, it's very clear, what you do is just move in to the captain and Lee will move out to the booth. 'No! I don't want to do that. I'm going to do something better!' I said 'What?' He said, 'Lee's smoking and as Lee puts his cigarette out, I'm going to move into the ashtray. That's a great shot!' I said 'That'll get 'em.' He said, 'That's what I'm gonna do.' 'But,' I said, 'Lee doesn't really have a chance to get out of the chair and get to the phone booth.' He said, 'Yes he does! Yes he does! We're gonna put the phone booth on a dolly.' So that's what he did. At dress rehearsal—the smoldering cigarette, the dolly, and Lee moving out and you can actually see his knee getting out of the shot, and so it doesn't work on dress rehearsal. The director comes down, 'Lee, you've got to wait a little bit longer before you get up.' 'Christ,' says Lee, 'I *am* waiting—and I've got to get to the phone for Christ's sake.' We go on the air without further rehearsal and, of course, the adrenaline is going and we dolly into the cigarette burning while Lee gets up. He was a big man, a strong guy, and he hit that phone booth going full speed. The camera's on the phone booth, Lee's dialing the number and suddenly the phone booth is moving. It goes right past Connie Ford who is changing her dress, it goes by all the women and past the crew, and Lee's talking the whole time! The camera pauses and the phone booth hits the wall because there's nowhere else to go. But we did things like that.

"After you've done all that stuff, there's very little they can throw at you in movies. In movies—with certain exceptions in films I've done like the train wreck in *The Train*, the Super Bowl in *Black Sunday* and the races in *Grand Prix*—it can be horrendous but you can do it again. But in live television you couldn't do it again, that was it. It was a great training ground but for me it wasn't a training ground, it was the be-all and end-all, that's what I wanted to do, I didn't want to be a movie director. I'm not going to go on about live television because none of you were around when all that happened. I'm sure you've got some questions you want to ask, so why don't we start the questions.

Question In those earlier films you did—*Seven Days in May* for example—it's very apparent that it came out of television. It plays very well on video, the camera shots are composed to work on television, whereas with something like *Grand Prix*, did you have a hard time bringing it down to size? How did you adjust to having bigger budgets for making films, and do you feel that perhaps now there is a trend to plan the shooting of them for the video conversion before actually starting a film?

JF The reason that *Seven Days in May* plays well on a video, is that it was shot in more or less the same format as television. I don't know how technically oriented you are—but I put a high mat in the camera of 1.75 for 1. Now that basically means that it gives me 1.75 times as wide as it is high—the television format itself is 1.33 to 1—in other words the television screen is 1.33 times wider than it is high. So that when *Seven Days in May* was converted to television, the idiots who do these things had nothing to play with. There was a hard mat in the camera, they had to make that picture fit on the television screen and, if you look at it carefully, there is a little bit of black up above and a little bit of black down below. Now, *Grand Prix* was shot in Super Panavision 65mm and on 35mm it was converted into Scope. Now Scope is 2.35 times as wide it is high, so therefore it is impossible to project it on television as we know it. What they do is what we horrifically call 'pan and scan.' Pan and scan simply means that if I have in Scope a shot of you and me and the camera is over where that camera is with a wide-angle lens shooting one way, you are on one end of the frame and I'm on the other. Now in a movie theatre that looks great because it is composed that way to use the whole screen. When they transfer that for television and video release it goes through a machine that focuses only on you, because you can't put the whole picture on, so they put on the half of the picture that you're in. Then they arbitrarily cut to me, whereas before it was one shot. That happens throughout the whole movie. A great movie like *Bridge on the River Kwai* which, in my opinion, is one of the best photographed, edited and acted movies I've ever seen, is turned on video into looking like a bad episode of *Gilligan's Island*. You don't see the great scenes between Alec Guinness and Sesuke Hayakawa when you saw both these men and their reaction; you see the back of one and then they cut to this someone over here and it's not the same. I hated the idea of my movies going on television and I tried to control a lot of them and the commercial breaks, as we all did, to no avail. It's criminal what has happened to a great many movies on video because you don't see it the way we shot it. On the other hand, laser disc is really quite wonderful because you do. There is a laser disc of *Grand Prix*, which I would advise you to get, which is the original way I shot it—they call it Letterbox format, and if you look at *Grand Prix*

on a big television screen with good sound, it's a pretty great experience. So it has nothing to do with my early work looking as though I came out of television and of my later work *not* looking as though I did. One of the reasons I stopped making films in Scope was the fact that they convert so badly to any other market. In Europe particularly, where I was making a lot of films in Scope, they didn't project them in Scope as they didn't have the facilities. Now all of that is changed and I almost prefer now to make my films in Scope, since we have the Letterbox format. As far as adapting to bigger budgets, I don't mean to be glib about it, but no director I've ever known will tell you he or she had enough time to make a movie. You never have enough time! So we are always fighting for time and control, and as you get more successful, of course, you get more time to do what you want. A brand-new director was about to start a movie, and

Frankenheimer with Evans Evans.

he was fighting for a ten-week's schedule. The studio gave him six weeks instead. Billy Wilder was asked what he thought of having six weeks instead of ten and Wilder said he wouldn't know what to do with a ten-week's schedule! That's true! The better you get at being a director, the more demanding you are—on yourself and everybody else. You don't want to settle for second best. You learn to use the camera and actors better, you learn to be a little more creative, more expressive. But there's no way you are going to see the new twenty million dollar budget film from United Artists versus a fifteen million dollar budget film from Paramount. You know what I mean? It's the content of the film that counts.

Question In *Grand Prix*, much of the story seemed to be sacrificed for some of the racing effects, and I was wondering if, when you get into a bigger budget project, are there are limitations on what you are allowed to do.

JF If I were talking to a group of the Sportscar Club of America, the complaint would be—Why do you have so much plot! They all wanted to see a lot more race footage. I was a racing driver, and my reason for making the movie was to exorcise my fantasy of being a Grand Prix driver. I was a club driver and, even given every opportunity in life, I would never have been good enough to be a Formula One driver, but by God I went into that movie about Formula One. I had all my Formula One cars and drivers, and so on. The object of the exercise was to make a movie about automobile racing—and that's what I did. I have to tell you that you happen to have hit on something very much a part of me. If anyone gave me the opportunity to do anything I wanted with this movie, I wouldn't change a thing. I love that movie. It is what it is, a movie that has a lot of reason in it, a perfect plot line, and I think the balance is just right. I'm sorry if you saw the film on television, because it's not your fault that you just weren't alive, or functioning, to see it on the big screen when it came out in 1966. I received letters from people who said they had been to it several times—one said eighty-five times—unbelievable. But it was really quite impressive on the big cinema screen. It was overwhelming—it really was.

Question Speaking of issues of control, how did you feel about *The Manchurian Candidate* being out of circulation for so long?

JF Well, actually, I was glad of it! We made that movie in 1962, and it was given a good release but not the kind of release we hoped for. The notices were good, especially in Britain where they were brilliant, and I think that much of its status as a classic came out of the English reviews. Then it kind of ran, as movies do, and became redundant, it was finished. Then President Kennedy was assassinated and certain people in the business wanted to take advantage of this by re-releasing it, which we didn't want—'we' being Frank Sinatra, George Axelrod, United Artists and myself. There were no ancillary rights then, there was no such thing as cable or video. It ran, went to television and that was that—it went to the boneyard of old movies. Then along came videos and cable rights, and I said, wait a minute, that was the movie everyone loved, a movie critics had called a masterpiece, so why don't we re-release it. Sinatra had cross-collateralised everything he had ever made and charged it against *The Manchurian Candidate*, so in a re-release there was no way we would have made any money. What they didn't realize was, after seven years, the rights to the re-release of the movie reverted to Sinatra, because it was in his contract. So Sinatra, George Axelrod and myself got together and said: 'They want to re-release this but we shouldn't let them do it because they are ten million dollars in debt.' We said to them: 'You give us a new deal, which means that we're even with the cost-sheet, in other words, not in profit, not in loss, and you can release the movie.' Well, the management kept changing at United Artists, as it does, and nobody was in tenure long enough to make a decision until about four years ago when there was a management in place long enough to say: 'Yes, we would like to do that, and we want to put it out on video.' Sinatra said: 'It's the best thing I've ever done and I would like it to go out theatrically again.' United Artists replied that they had already shown it theatrically and on television, and didn't think there was a market out there for it theatrically and it would cost at least two million dollars to re-release it theatrically and give it the necessary publicity. They were not willing to risk the two million dollars. I was sitting at the table when Sinatra took his checkbook out and wrote them a check for two million dollars saying 'There it is! I'll back it up. If you don't recoup your two million dollars, I'll pay for it.' Well, then it becomes very easy to be heroic, and they re-released the movie and it did very, very well. In fact, we all made a lot more in the re-release in 1989 dollars compared to 1961 dollars when it was first released. But it was strictly greed, all the figures that movie companies produce with their computer accounting methods to prove that money wasn't made. I was glad it was re-released and did very well. You always want what you can't get, as you well know; when the movie became unavailable, inaccessible, unseeable, then everybody wanted to see it. Had it been available to watch on late-night TV or video over the years it would never have generated the excitement that it did by not being accessible. I firmly believe that.

Question I found in *The Birdman of Alcatraz* a strong element of graphic design in the compositions but in *Year of the Gun* you are more interested in catching the action on a Steadicam. The conversation between Guido and his Italian friends is in long shot, you never cut into close shot, and it is not catching the action.

JF Very interesting. In the first place, in *Birdman of Alcatraz*, we were trying to use two different styles. I fired two cameraman on *Birdman of Alcatraz* because they couldn't get me what I wanted. We had one who had the shot of the bars on both floor shots, and I said, 'How did that happen? How does the sun go 180 degrees over there?' He said, 'Well, I just thought it would look nice' and I said, 'We are not out to make something that looks nice.' *Birdman of Alcatraz* was an intimate movie, very claustrophobic—we were in jail. *The Train* was a huge action movie, shot mainly on two lenses, my own 18mm lens, and on a 50mm lens—the 50mm lens on that picture was the close-up lens. Considering *The Year of the Gun*, I probably shouldn't have even mentioned to you that I used a Steadicam because I don't really think you can see where we use a Steadicam. You can see where we used the hand-held cameras, but the Steadicam movement is so good that I don't think you can really pick it out as opposed to a dolly on tracks. That was the work of a Canadian, David Crone. And as far as shooting something on a long shot, two characters talking in a long shot, what scene are we talking about?

Question They are sitting at an outdoor cafe in conversation . . .

JF Well, why do a lot of close-ups? There are too many close-ups in movies. Movies are not a close-up medium, that comes out of television, it comes out of the fact that you are used to seeing weekly television where they suddenly cut to watching over the shoulders and close-ups, with this and that and every other thing, and I think it's greatly overdone. I *dislike* it! I don't like to use a close-up unless I really have to use it for a reason. Many times close-ups are used to disguise bad acting. A close-up is actually a shot you can do with a non-actor and get some kind of a performance from him. For instance, if you really have a stiff actor, one of the things you can do is put a full magazine in the camera with a thousand feet and have that person sit there in close-up and repeat the line again and again and again, you can say 'No, do this' while the camera is running, you understand, and you can luckily sometimes get a pretty good line reading that way, as opposed to a shot where you have an inter-actor in the scene. Then you can't do that because you are affecting the other actor too, you are affecting his or her lines and how the actor plays the scene, and nothing's going to mesh. But in a close-up you can actually—if you have that kind of actor—pretty much control what they are going to do and what they are saying. You can talk to them while taking the close-up. I don't like to do it, but in a dire emergency I'll do anything. I try not to use close-ups unless it's a scene that warrants a close-up, because if you do it too much, it's like anything else, it just spoils the effect when you really want it.

Question I'd like to ask you, in *Grand Prix* you used a split screen process. This was used in another film, *The Boston Strangler*. Was it the style of those days or was it your own invention?

JF In the first place *The Boston Strangler* was made two years after *Grand Prix*, but I was not the first to use it by any means. Abel Gance did in *Napoleon* in 1927, and several other directors since then. I wanted to tell multiple stories at the same time, and the only way to do that on a huge screen was to split the screen and compose the shots specially for this purpose, often with the faces of the drivers heard in interviews and shown small in the corners of the screen. Anything that's successful, of course, is going to be copied. Today they call it a *homage*—in my days they used to call it imitation! *Manchurian*, *Train* and *Grand Prix* have been copied several times.

Question I would like to know if there are any interna-

tional directors that you admire and appreciate.
JF No matter how you answer that you're held suspect. You say you are influenced by a director; that means you copy his work, and if you say 'No,' then you are an arrogant hack! Forgive me for saying this, but I think to be a movie director you must be a rather sensitive person who can appreciate and be influenced by things you see in life, which influence your later choices. Naturally, I have been influenced by other directors' work; indirectly I may say. I've never set up a sequence like de Palma does in *The Untouchables*, where he copied a specific sequence from another director's film, in this case Eisenstein's Odessa Steps scene from *The Battleship Potemkin* with the baby carriage. That to me is unforgivable. But, yes, I have been influenced by other directors' work, and by many European directors, for instance, David Lean, Fritz Lang, Carol Reed, Réne Clément, Rossellini, de Sica, Kurosawa, and, in Hollywood, by Hitchcock, George Stevens, William Wyler, partly because these are the men who came before me. I love movies and ever since I was a child I lived in movie theatres. I used to go to five movies a week. I've seen an awful lot of movies and yes I've been influenced by many, but not consciously. You try and make it fresh, you try to do something your way and hope it works. I can't do it the way William Wyler did, or David Lean, it would be different. It's your own perception of what you see and how you want to express it.

Question Since you mentioned the new realists, do you record on-location sound? Did you do it for *Grand Prix*?

JF That's a very funny story. I'll preface it by saying that the sound man won the Academy Award. The enormity of having to do this movie really hit me about a month before I actually had to start shooting and I realized, 'My God! I'm going to shoot all these real races and I'm going to have to combine them with all my own sound and footage. What if something goes wrong, what if we have an accident? What if this, what if that? They're going to shut down the movie.' I worried about all these horrible things that can go wrong. I was in Monte Carlo about a week before we started shooting and I was having terrible pangs of anxiety, and an awful problem sleeping, knowing that nothing was going to go right. It was one of those things, I knew the first day we were going to kill somebody. It was the only movie I had ever done where it was possible that this might happen, because actors and drivers were going at speeds of 120 mph. There was a scene set in the tunnel from the old Hotel de Paris to the new Hotel de Paris underground—it was the only way to get from one hotel to the other during the race. To play the leads I had chosen Harriet Anderson and Jessica Walter. Harriet was a columnist for one of these big fashion magazines, and she was doing a story about racing and using models against the *leitmotif* of race cars. Then she became involved with one of the drivers. Well, this was the first scene and we brought down ten of the most beautiful models from London and everyone was 'doing' these girls' hair. We had this great show of fashion, with Harriet Anderson and Jessica Walter in fabulous dresses. We had devised a difficult dolly shot through the tunnel with the real photographers, Brian Guffy and Christian Marquand. It was a who's who of the fashion world, complete with photographers. I had this great cameraman, Lionel Lindon, with whom I had done several movies, he was so quick, and I said 'How long will it take to light this sequence?' and he says it will take some time because we've no ventilation. So he gets it lit, and we get the dolly ready to go—it's a Weston dolly—and we get them all there, we do a rehearsal and we're ready to go. I said 'OK' and then, 'Oh, wait a minute guv'nor! Wait a minute guv'nor!' and it's the sound man, one of our crew from London. I said 'What's the matter' and he said 'I can't hear it, the boom doesn't seem to be picking up the dialogue.' I got furious because this was the second day of shooting and I said 'Where the hell was the boom man during rehearsal, were you all having tea? You should have told me then.' He said 'Well, I can't help it, we must install radio microphones in the ladies' dresses.' Well, these radio microphones—even today I hate radio microphones, but in those days they were much bigger and such a drag—I leave it to your imagination, the dresses were very tight fitting and there was no place to hide the batteries. Finally after going up for air, we were ready to get the shot. I have to tell you that it was great and everything went well. I said to the cameraman, 'Have you got it?' and he said 'Yes' and I said 'Print it! and I thought Christ, we're on a roll! Then I heard 'One moment guv'nor! Not good for sound!' I said, 'What's the matter?' He said, 'It's not good for sound.' So we did Take 2—again, bril-

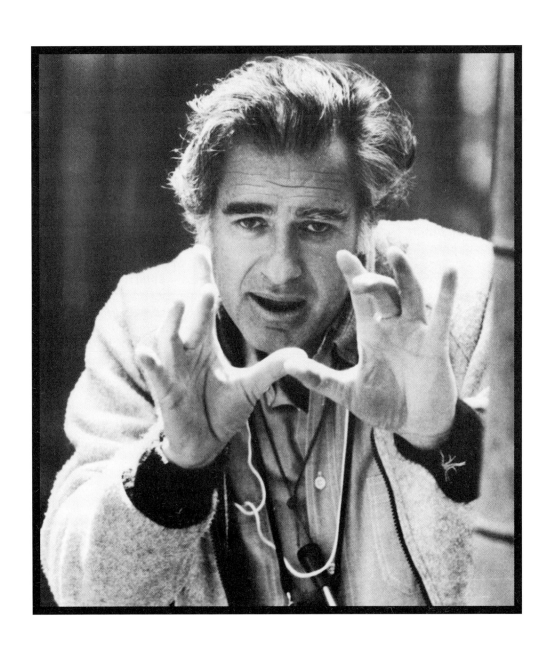

liant . . . 'Not good for sound!' Well, by Take 21, the girls' hair is down like this, they look terrible, sweat stains all over the place . . . 'Perfect for sound!' So I said to the script girl 'This guy is hopeless. Print Take 1 and Take 22.' On the day of the race we shot seventy-thousand feet of film, and we were looking at weeklies by the time it came back from the lab. But it took hours and finally on comes this shot, Take 1—the sound is pretty good, it's not great, but it's certainly a very good guide track that we could loop very easily, just a couple of lines. Then Take 2, it's a little garbled, then Take 22—the sound was absolutely perfect. You never heard such fabulous sound—except that it was two women from Radio Monte Carlo reading the news! He had picked up one of the radio stations on these radio mikes.

That sound man was on a flight the next day back to London. Then we got another sound man who wasn't much better. Finally, I just couldn't worry about location sound, and I shot a lot of the movie with hand-held cameras, with Arriflexes, with all the noise activity going on. We didn't even try to record dialogue along the way, yet he won the Academy Award for sound! He's been working ever since and he goes around saying—I won the Academy Award for *Grand Prix* for sound—and he didn't record one line of dialogue. That happened on *The Train* too with the French sound man—he didn't record one line of dialogue and we looped the whole picture, and he won the Academy Award. For most of my pictures I recorded with expert sound men and I've always recorded everything on location. For instance, on the picture you saw last night there was very little on the track that was post-synched, and anything that was post-synched I did for performance and not because we didn't have the sound. I believe very strongly in recording sound. I think it makes all the difference in the world.

Question How do you meet and choose your actors—what relationship do you establish with them?

JF Well, it depends on the actors. You never treat two actors the same way, at least I haven't. I believe in creating an atmosphere on the set which makes it possible for everybody to do their best work, I really do feel that. First, you have to give everyone confidence and freedom and try and inspire trust. Good actors know that it's permissible to make a mistake, you're not going to come down on them, you're not going to humiliate them. I think you have to give whoever it may be—a set designer, art director, the costumer—the freedom to carry out their best work because, after all, that's what you want. I would hope that an actor comes to me prepared, with ideas for his or her character, for me to see what they want to do. You just can't work in a vacuum, you talk a lot with the actors before they ever get to the set. I am a great believer in rehearsals. I think they really help, if nothing else, in getting the actors to know each other and they get to know you. It is all a matter of communicating with each other and being able to express to somebody else what you envision, and hope that they'll be able to accomplish it, and you must take advantage of any means that you have at your disposal to achieve this. For me, as I said, rehearsal is very important, I'm used to it and I use it, not to block out every scene, but certainly to read and talk about the script, the characters and their relationships. But you get different kinds of actors. You get an actor like Fredric March who comes in knowing every line and exactly what he has to do with the character, and you get other actors who are totally dependent on you, who really want to do what you want them to do, and really haven't any ideas of their own, leaving you to present different ways for them to do the scene. I think it helps if you, as a director, have been an actor. It certainly helps you to understand what their problems are and to be able to talk to actors. You have to be able to reach individuals if you want to motivate them, and I think having been an actor has helped me considerably. I don't know what I would have done if I hadn't been an actor, to tell you the truth, I don't know how I would have coped with most of the people I've worked with. But I think I do understand the actors' problems and certainly how to relate to them. I love working with actors, it happens to be something I like to do and casting them for films is terribly important. I think it's more than half of the battle. How many of you here have had acting experience? That's good! For those of you who haven't it wouldn't be a bad idea to enroll in an acting class, not with the idea of becoming an actor but with the idea of seeing what you have to go through to get the results you want. It's a very sensible step to take.

Question How involved in casting are you? How do you go about it? How do you make decisions?

JF I'm totally involved in casting. There are two types of casting that must be done. There is the casting to get the movie made in the first place which, for the purposes of this discussion, we will call the 'star casting,' and then there is the interesting casting to fill in the other parts. Now, today, to get a movie made, it is necessary to have a star or stars in it, and the star is someone whom the studio and distributor feels will draw people into the cinemas to see the movie. There are very few, in my opinion, *bona fide* stars today, but there are many performers who distributors think are stars and who command enormous salaries and who sometimes you have to use to get your movie off the ground. This is the way it works: you go through the script and you hopefully hire a casting director. I sit down and make a list of possible actors and actresses to play this or that role, star actors and actresses, people whose names we feel will get the movie made. Then you go to the person who's going to put up the money and you show them this list. They have a veto power usually and they say 'Well, I'm not going to make the movie with so-and-so and so-and-so,' and you say, 'I think so-and-so and so-and-so are terrific actors.' What they are really saying is that so-and-so's last picture didn't do any business, or the picture before that. And it becomes very frustrating because they won't make the movie with the person you really want for the part. So what happens is that we each compromise—I come up with another actor who will do the part well and who they feel will attract the money. Then what you are going to do is say, 'OK, now we just can't send the script to this actor without an offer of money to act in it, because they are just not going to read it without some idea of what they will be paid.' In other words, what we are trying to do is get the backers to spend as much money up front as possible, making it difficult for them to back out and not make the movie. Now suppose you get the leads you want, now you go ahead and cast around them. You have to get your leading actor first and then you hire the other actors. I knew in *Year of the Gun*, Sharon Stone was the actress I really wanted in that picture. I had wanted to work with her before, and it hadn't turned out, so I was determined that she was going to be in that movie.

But that's a rarity. Then you cast the remaining roles, you try and see many movies on television, and in theatres, to acquaint yourself with the work of the many actors available—both new and those who have been around for some time. You want to know who this or that person is, then if you don't know of a particular actor or actress, your casting director suggests someone very strongly for the part. You look at tape, video or films that he or she has done, you meet, and then in many cases you do a test. A test is done of a person playing the part with either, hopefully, the star, to see how they work together or with another actor playing the part. You look very closely at the test and base your decision on that. Then, of course, there are budgetary considerations. You have 'X' number of dollars to make the movie, so much for the star, and so much for the rest of the cast, and you have to cast your picture within the limitations of the budget, and some of that you can do by combining and making an actor's part run for a shorter length of time than you had originally scheduled. In other words, take this scene and that scene and do them closely together so that you don't have a big spread during which time you are paying an actor for not working. You make a more attractive deal with a well-known actor by hiring him for two weeks than if you hired him for the run of the picture, ten or twelve weeks, and you try and figure out how to do this. Then you get down to the smaller parts, the bit players. You might have a group of actors whom you liked working with, who worked well for you before, and you tend to go toward them. You bring people in, read them, you hold interviews, and you try and look at anything they've done before and you haven't seen. If you find talented people you usually have auditions. Then you send out calls for extras to come in and you meet them. It is very important to cast the extras correctly. The wrong extra can spoil a whole scene. You want a certain look, a certain type, depending on the movie you are making, and you go out of your way to try and find this. You hire local casting directors, you bring your own casting director in—and finally you look at those who have been weeded out. I have certain things that drive me crazy—like bad toupees on the top of their heads. You can spot them a mile away. You can never spot the good hairpieces, but the ones I can see I will not put in the movie. Then, for the extras' costumes, you have to tell them what to wear. I hate bright colors—anybody in a red dress automatically doesn't get the job because your eye goes to that person. It's very difficult with color movies to direct the focus of attention. It's so much easier in black and white. I will not have bright colors in my movies—unless they are for reasons of plot. In answer to your question; it's putting in a lot of time and effort and being able to make the decisions. In my movies decisions are made by me. I don't have to ask for anybody else's opinion. I do, but that's because I don't have to. As far as the star is concerned, as I said, that is usually done in conjunction with the producer.

Question You worked with Burt Lancaster several times—did you cast him?

JF It worked both ways. He cast me for *Birdman of Alcatraz*. He was already in place on *The Young Savages* and he insisted I do the picture. In *Seven Days in May* I cast him. For *The Train*, he cast me, and in *Gypsy Moths*, I cast him. But we were very good friends and we worked well together. Sadly he is now very ill.

Question Speaking of casting—during the past five years or so—among the first opening credits we read 'Casting By' with usually two persons named, or more. These people have become very powerful and wealthy—what is it that they do that you did or didn't do?

JF A good question! There are directors and producers in the movies today who don't have much of a background in the business, and they don't know the actors. So along came individuals who used to be agents, sometimes actors themselves, who have set themselves up as 'casting directors,' whose business it is to know almost any actor who is out there. They are hired to advise us and it has become a very lucrative profession. I also think it's a helpful addition. I've worked with some expert casting people and they've really helped me with actors whom I didn't know. I think it helps the actors too.

Question There seems to have been a decline in the depth of film criticism in the media in the last few years and it has become a show business with thumbs up and thumbs down, three stars, four stars. How do you feel about that yourself?

JF Hasn't everything come down to fast food? It's all Macdonalds and Wendy's, including the subject matter in many movies. People are looking for short cuts, they don't like to read, and we live in a very illiterate society brought up on television and music videos. They don't read any more, so short cuts get their attention. As far as film criticism is concerned, I always think when I get great reviews that film criticism is very astute, and when I get poor reviews that the critics don't know what they are talking about! I think it's improper of me to take off on film critics, there are an awful lot of them, some good and some bad.

Question Can I ask about two in particular. Everyone seems to think Andrew Sarris and Pauline Kael are the best among them all.

JF I think that in both Sarris and Kael we have two critics who really love movies and are, and were, very knowledgeable about them. I've come off well and I've come off badly from both, but I do respect them. But I must tell you this, when the critics have given you hell, been rude, sarcastic and often superficial in their opinions and judgements, and then the public doesn't respond to your movie or doesn't get the opportunity to see it, I can't help thinking was it something I had done wrong, and you wonder, have I lost the touch, the flair, the instinct, the ability to make a really good film, one that appeals to audiences?

Question Do you have a process you go through when you pick the projects you work on and how do you feel when some of them don't get made. Do you look for work?

JF Yes, there is a process. Sometimes I'm a director for hire and if somebody sends me a script or a book I really like I say 'Yes, I want to do that.' Sometimes I'll create a project—start off with an idea and have it written, or I'll find a book I like and want to do that. There may be a writer I want to work with who will come along with an idea. What I'm looking for is characterization, who are the characters? Is the story one I want to devote a year of my life to doing? Can I become involved in it? Most important, is it something that I believe in? I never like to make rules that I only do this and I only do that, because then something is going to come along and break them. But I like to portray interesting characters; that's what I like to do and that's what I look for.

Question How many films have you made in which you have had a financial stake, where you have not only been the director but the executive producer?

JF By executive producer, I assume you mean have I ever put up my own money to make a movie? No, I've never done that, and I have no intention of doing so. I am paid for what I do, I don't take the financial risk. I don't know very many producers that do, and most get their money from other sources. You have to be very rich to do what you are talking about, or very foolish. I feel that I'm a professional and I get paid for what I do. I take a risk with my own professional career every time I walk on the set, and it's very difficult doing this. You operate on intellect, emotion and instinct, and I don't think I should take a financial risk.

Question What is the difference between a director and a producer? Are we to believe the producer thinks only of money while the director is the artist?

JF I think that's more or less an academic's view, if you will forgive me! That's just not the way it's done. You may be a sensitive, articulate artist but nevertheless you have to know how much it costs, and you bloody well have to involve yourself in the deal, the budget, the money, and everything else. You may not want to do that, but it's part of the job. There's a very thin line between a producer and a director, especially since a director is supposed to be the person who, once everything is assembled, goes in and puts the camera where it's supposed to be, tells the actors what to do, where to put the writer, where to put the editor, and literally makes the movie. But it's not always the case. The producer in the ideal sense of the word, creates the project. He or she finds a book or a screenplay, they'll go out and negotiate with the author's agent and buy the rights. They will either at that time take it to a studio, or have a studio buy it for them if they are regarded highly like Richard Zanuck. They will then make a decision as to who they want to direct the picture, they will try and get this person interested at the entry level when the project is in its infancy, so that the producer and the director together can select a writer. On some occasions they don't hire a director right away, they'll hire a writer, and the producer and the writer will work on the project together and get the script to the point where they can take it to a studio, and the studio will say 'Yes, we want to do this,' and they give them a list of directors who will be acceptable, also a group of actors, and so forth. Sometimes the producer and the director will collaborate on the script together and take it to the studio. During shooting good producers are there to support the director. If there are any problems, they can usually solve them or try and solve them, they'll run interference for you with the studios, with the money people. They will be there to look at dailies, to tell you, 'I think you are wrong here,' 'I think what you are doing is not what we talked about,' 'you don't have enough coverage,' 'it's not working' or 'it is working', or 'we are spending too much money in this area and we will not have the money left to do that scene you really want to do over there,' and 'is there a way, there must be a way, since we are behind, that we can pick up here by doing less coverage or by trying to combine this scene with that scene,' and so on and so forth. Then when the movie is finished, when you as the director have your first cut, then the producer sees it and comes in and gives you notes that he or she has taken. Then you go on to the cut that you said you would deliver to the studio. In the meantime, the producer is working with all the marketing and advertising people on how this movie is going to be sold, where it's going to open, how it's going to open, when it's going to open, and will follow the movie right through. It's a very responsible position and good producers are very hard to find. My best work has always been done with producers. When I was a producer-director, I found that a really tough job to do, because directors frequently need help. A producer in the best sense provides that help. Where the confusion comes in about the responsibility of producers and their demands and decisions is a result of some trade publications confusing the producers with the studios. In other words, the production executives are called the producers because they are putting up the money. That has nothing to do with the individual who is actually producing the movie. I think the producers are a much-maligned group. There are certainly producers who put together a deal, walk away, and then come back for the cast party. And there are those who have nothing to do with the principal production, who help to put it together and then come around for post-production conferences. But that's not the kind of producer with whom I want to work. I need a hardworking person who is an active partner in the true sense of the word. You always go into a project hoping it's going to work, and, in some cases, it does, in others you have a lot of problems. I've fired producers, I've refused to go to the set if a producer is there, I've had terrible fights with producers, but at the same time I've had good relationships with producers and believe me, this is much to be preferred.

Question Which films are your own ideas, not based on a book, and what films have you made from your own scripts?

JF I am not a script writer myself and have never claimed to be one. Montgomery Clift was a very good friend and he said 'You know what you and I do best?' I said, 'What?' He said, 'You and I work best on dirty paper.' I said 'What do you mean by that?' He said 'After somebody else writes it, we're ready to criticize it.' And that's true. I am not someone who can put a clean piece of paper in the typewriter and say 'Fade in.' That's very difficult for me to do. I tried and it didn't work out very well. I knew there were writers out there who would do this a hell of a lot better than me. But what I do well is that I can read a script and say, 'I think this character should do this here instead of there, and I think we need more of this and less of that,' 'I think the story goes awry here and this is what we should do to change it.' I am valuable after the first draft and also sometimes in a conference before we ever begin to know how the story's going to proceed. This is the kind of movie we want to make, this is what we want, we have to know this. I have to know that the writer who's going to write the screenplay is writing the same movie that I want to direct. I've had a few surprises and it's not pleasant, believe me. When you get that script from the writer, the one thing you want most is for this film to be good. When you read it and it isn't, it's terribly discouraging and you usually have to start with another writer.

Question In a film like *Grand Prix*, how hard was it to get it made with the split screen effects?

JF *Grand Prix* was very easy to film because my previous films had been successes. Few at the studio knew what *Grand Prix* really was, because no picture like it had been done previously. I did a lot of tests before the movie ever started because up until that time no-one had really been able to convey the feeling of speed. If you watch a tennis match on television, it really doesn't look all that difficult to do until you're out there watching a tennis match, watching these balls coming at over a hundred miles an hour. It's absolutely astonishing, and you watch it and say, 'I can return volleys like this' and then you go out and actually see Boris Becker serve. Well, it was much the same with cars. You watch the Formula I races on television and the cars don't seem to be going that fast and it doesn't seem to be that difficult to be able to do it. You don't see where the danger lies, and you didn't see the skill involved. Now, I had been on the other end of that, because, as I said, I was a racing driver but not in their league. Nevertheless I knew what it was to drive very fast, and to go along a corner at my own ten-tenths. I knew the skill that was involved in driving a racing car and what I wanted to do was to convey that to the viewer. But, to be honest with you, I didn't really know how to do it, and we had to carry out an extensive series of tests between the camera and all the different locations, using different kinds of lenses, to arrive at the effects I really wanted to achieve. Now none of that cost very much, taking a couple of cars down raceways with about three or four people and so on. It did take a lot of time, however, by the time we went to shoot with about a hundred and eighty technicians, we knew pretty well what to do, where we should split the screen, what lenses to use and where. It's always difficult to get money to do this, but we managed. They always say, Well, you can always do these things later, but sometimes you can't.

Question Do you usually ask for more money?

JF No, I don't do that, I don't play games any more. I did at one time, you were expected to, but not under today's conditions. I go in with an honest budget to the best of my knowledge based on what I know. If the backers don't want to spend that kind of money, we just can't make the picture. I mean, we can't give you the quality that we want to give you if you are too tight on the budget. There are always cuts you can make here and there, really desperation cuts, but I usually try to avoid this—I don't pad a budget, but I always like to know that I've got a little pad because I always know that, no matter how I plan it, whatever I do, something is going to go wrong. I want to have some kind of insurance.

Question Did you ever go under a budget?

JF Yes, I've been under-budget because the budgets had been well-prepared, with some kind of contingency, and luckily it wasn't required, or

I've been able to go faster than I expected, or something didn't cost what I thought it would. Yes, I've gone under more times than I've gone over.

Question I'm a Popular Cultures study major, and one of the subjects we talk about is how certain objects affect culture through our time. I'm reading a book called *The Search for The Manchurian Candidate*, and it seems that your films, since people don't read as they used to, really convey the frightening nature of mind control and brainwashing on a level that every American of the following generation can understand. It's a fascinating book and was written because the Freedom of Information Act allowed the author to go into CIA files. Has *The Manchurian Candidate* become a millstone around your neck—do people want to hold you to that style of work?

JF Yes and no. I've done many interviews where people have come to me and said 'How do you feel having made one of the ten best movies ever made. Doesn't that inhibit you?' No, I'm just glad that I was able to make this movie, and some others, that are considered classics, and I don't give a damn if critics are comparing me to this, that, or the other one. I keep going back to Billy Wilder because I admire him and his work: he said that 'a director is as good as his best movie.' I like to believe that. If I always worried about exceeding what I had done before, I wouldn't get out of bed in the morning. I try and do the best I can with any movie or television film that I choose to make. I enjoy my work and the fact that some of them are among the most successful films ever made.

Question How much time do you usually spend on a film—from the very moment you decide to make the movie to its release.

JF About a year-and-a-half—on average.

Question And how much time is involved in the scriptwriting, the shooting and editing.

JF The shooting is the shortest part. The longest part is usually the preparation of the script and the editing. When I say the preparation of the script, I am also talking about raising the money, getting all the physical production ready, casting the players, and so on. The shortest part, the actual process of shooting, is also the most frustrating—you are dependent on so many people. The editing is really the best part of it if you've shot enough film. You're in there by yourself and everything you do leads you to believe you are a genius, because nobody's

seen it and you are your own master—it's a good time, it's before all the arguments begin and all that kind of stuff. It's a very comfortable time—I like that. What is so discouraging these days is that sometimes we make movies such as *Dead Bang*, *52 Pick-Up*, *The Fourth War*, and many more made by other directors, and they do not get sufficient publicity and marketing budgets, or the release they deserve. Today, it's come down to winning the battle twice; you have to make the movie first and then win the battle of getting the studio behind it and spending the amount of money it takes to release it to reach you in the cinemas. How many of you saw last night's movie, *Year of the Gun*, when it actually opened? None of you. I had the best reviews in fifteen years. If I tried to write them myself, I couldn't have done better! But the money wasn't there to advertise the picture, it didn't have the promotion budget to get it out there, to call it to your attention. It just wasn't marketed correctly. I went out on a cross-country tour for the picture. I think the movie should have been opened in what we call a showcase situation, in about 50 theatres, and built by word-of-mouth, because audiences who went to see it liked it. Especially with subtitles! The picture played very well but, with the limited amount of money we had to promote the picture, we had to spend it all at once, so we opened it in 800 theatres and that was it. I think we would have done much better. But that's yesterday's business, it happens with a great many good movies.

Question Speaking of *Year of the Gun*—what was the response from Italy?

JF It was a very sensitive situation. The Red Brigade was very active politically as a group and there are many people who still feel an affinity with the Red Brigade. Some people said, 'Well, you really didn't present both sides of the Red Brigade to make it an effective political movie,' but I said, 'No, I didn't do a political movie, I didn't do an attack on the Red Brigade, I made a film about people caught up in the Red Brigade.' But for the most part the film went over very well in Italy.

Question What kind of director are you?

JF 'I think there are two types of director: the company director and the director who is a filmmaker. There are a lot of directors who are hired by companies because the company knows these directors will do exactly what they tell them to do.

They'll use the actors they want used, they'll bring the picture in on the budget, on the schedule—in other words, they're studio hacks. There are certain actors who have director approval, who will hire a director, or will have the company hire a director, they know they can control. They will go and direct the movie and the director will stand by and let the actor do this. But then there are the directors who are serious about what they're doing and I would like to include myself among them. The companies—and by that I don't mean the high executives of the companies (not a man like Robert O'Brien who I feel very close to) but the production people at the studios—the companies really hate your guts because you are above them in a strange kind of way, because you don't do what they want you to do. And they are secretly hoping that you're going to fail. If you make a film the way you see it, and I think any good director would have to agree with this statement, you cannot completely schedule it on paper, everything cannot be that meticulously planned. If that were the case then you wouldn't really need the director. Anybody could do it, which I think the production people would like to think: that anybody could just go in and make movies. And my answer to all this is, 'Sure I can shoot the schedule. All I have to do is put the camera with a close-up lens on it and pan down the piece of paper and shoot it. And that's take one and I shoot the whole schedule.' Just put it up on a board and I'll shoot it. Make pictures of it. But that's not what the picture is about. So when you go your way with your work, which I think you have to do, you damn well better be right more than half of the time. I mean you can't continue making flop after flop, not really playing ball with what studio politics might be. You can go on making flop after flop, if you're the hired director who comes in and directs their trash. And if the picture doesn't make money it's not really your fault. But when you initiate the project as Edward Lewis and I did and you work hard to realise it, as for example, with *The Fixer*, *Grand Prix*, *The Gypsy Moths*, *Seven Days in May*, *The Manchurian Candidate* and *Seconds*, then you've got to be right. If you are wrong, they will be only too pleased to see that you do not get another chance. And everybody comes to the heads of the studio to say, 'I told you about that fellow.' Also, you are highly paid in this business if you prove a

successful director, and there are a lot of people who are not highly paid and that too has something to do with it. I'm not saying that money makes the difference, because if I found the right film I'd do it for nothing. Money is really not that important to me, and it never has been. My films are not cheap and I take a long time to make them and I insist on having the actors I want and the crew I want and the script I want and everything else. We are independents in every sense of the word; but we know as soon as we complete three flops in a row we've got to start thinking seriously about what we're going to do the next time because it grows harder and harder. Thank God I haven't been in that position, but I imagine it would be difficult to get things financed the way you want to do. This is what I was going to say about *Birdman*. Here I was, very young and very early in my career, with a lot of responsibility on my shoulders. It was not the sort of story that looks, outwardly, to have an appeal to a wide public. It was really a great responsibility because I went way over the schedule to achieve what I wanted. On release it did very well. It did fine.'

The discussion closed with a student thanking John Frankenheimer for taking the time to come and speak to them about his experiences in film-making.

JF How many of you here intend to pursue this and try to make a living at it? How many of you want to be directors? And how many cameramen? Actors? Producers? I wish you a lot of luck - it's really brutal! Tough. The main thing is to know how to start, to be willing to learn, to do anything you have to do to get in. Once you get your foot in the door, then it's up to you, but the problem is getting your foot in the door, and you have to dedicate yourself to going to where they hire people like you, which is California and New York. Just do anything you can to get into the business in any capacity whatsoever. A producer I worked with, Robert Rosen started by running a videographe machine at MGM. The chances of somebody coming along and handing you a blank check for a couple of hundred thousand dollars to make your first movie, and for that movie to then be seen by Mike Ovitz and to be signed to a multi-million dollar contract like John Singleton, are very remote. For every John Singleton there are maybe 200,000 would-be filmmakers, and you have to consider that the odds are over 200,000 and have to actively persevere in spite of it. If you have the talent to go out and try and get to see people, break down doors, do it, and just be persistent. A lot of people will give up, they know it's just not worth the effort. Then you should consider other areas, the fact that there's a terrific need for good editors, for great cameramen, secretaries, script girls, production assistants, producers. I would like to have a crystal ball and see, ten years from now, what's happened to you and how many of you are still in it and what you are doing. I expect that over half of you will end up producing, or trying to, because that's a very rewarding occupation. Being a producer means you don't have to wait for the telephone to ring, which is important. You are actually out there, perhaps flailing at windmills, but you are trying to get the movie made. You are not a secondary waiting for the 'phone to ring, with someone saying, 'Well, are you free to start work on October 12?' You are out there trying to create the situation, and for those of you who have been trying to raise money to get a movie made as a director, what you are really doing is being your own producer-director. No matter what you call it, that's what producing is and I think that of all the occupations in our business, this is the most gratifying. As I say, I have produced quite a few movies that I've directed, and I must say I liked that in spite of the extra work it entails. A lot of it I did at first out of self-defense, because I had certain needs, but I really like doing it and it's probably what I'm going to end up being. I'll let some of you younger ones go out there and get up at six o'clock in the morning, I'll take the limousine out at ten and find out how you're doing! [*applause*]

BACK TO TELEVISION . . .

John Frankenheimer returned to television work when HBO asked him to direct an episode of 'Tales from the Crypt.' The episode, entitled 'Maniac At Large,' was broadcast on August 19, 1992. The cast included Blythe Danner, Adam Ant, Clarence Williams III and Salome Jens.

"The period after *Year of the Gun* was a very depressing time—good scripts were not coming my way—until HBO asked me to make an episode in a television series called *Tales from the Crypt* . That was in 1992. I agreed to do it because I wanted to find out if I could work in that format within a shooting schedule of five days. They sent me an Edgar Allan Poe story with a script by Ray Woods, who used to be Walter Hill's associate, and I liked it very much. I thought it would be fun to do something like that requiring a small amount of my time, using my movie camera technique. I met this young cinematographer, John Leonetti. I had a very good cast—Blythe Danner, Salome Jens, who was in *Seconds*, Clarence Williams, and Adam Ant. It was the first time I had used electronic editing, which I found intriguing, and it was a change to do something different in the 23-minute format. We built the set at a studio they had in an old warehouse over in the Valley.

The plot, a rather surreal mystery, concerns Margaret, the librarian, who is working under a dominating head librarian. There is a maniac at large, a serial killer, but the head doesn't listen. Brady the security guard is drinking, but being a civil servant, he cannot be fired. Margaret is timid, hysterical, and thinks she sees the killer's shadow on the wall and a hand holding a knife. There is a close-up of a newspaper headline 'MANIAC AT LARGE'. There is some quick cutting to the faces of these characters, the emergency exit bell rings, there is a feeling of panic everywhere. Serial killers are usually always a man—could it be a woman? It is Margaret and she is mad. It's a suspenseful piece in dark tones with a nightmarish quality. We caught the audience, I think, and held them in this brief interlude of horror—without blood or violence. It was a journey into the imagination—if you will—and the way fear takes hold of the mind. I enjoyed the experience."

. . . AND INTO COMMERCIALS

Frankenheimer then directed commercials for Elizabeth Arden and AT&T.

"I had always wanted to work with Elizabeth Taylor. The agency approached me with the idea that they wanted some kind of thriller format to sell three fragrances of perfume, and Ron Hutchinson and I came up with the story of one of the great jewel thieves of all times, a true story taking place in the thirties. Customs officials and the FBI could never catch him even though they knew he was smuggling hundreds of thousands of dollars, in those days, in jewelry into the United States. They never found out how he was doing it. They finally went to him and said, 'Look, if you tell us how you do this, we'll let you off, because sooner or later we are going to find you.' He said, 'It's really very simple. I always take the same cabin on the boat coming back, and I always give myself this huge going-away party. I come in and I walk off the boat. I leave the jewels in the cabin and, at the going-away party, I take the jewels out and give them to my friend and he walks off the boat.' And that's more or less the story we used in the commercial, in sixty seconds! We filmed it with John Leonetti in California on the *Queen Mary*, and at the chateau in Pasadena. There was no-one else on screen.

With Elizabeth Taylor you don't need anyone else. The sponsor was Elizabeth Arden.

"Apart from my early days in TV, I had made only one commercial before this, in 1989, and that was the big AT&T commercial timed for the Bicentennial of Paris. It was huge—a television reporter who is sent over to cover the Bicentennial forgets that it is his parents' golden wedding anniversary. He discovers that they were married in Paris and they celebrated their marriage at a little restaurant fifty years ago. He finds the restaurant, he brings them over, he covers the Bicentennial, and gives them an anniversary party at the restaurant, in the meantime using all kinds of AT&T equipment—fax machines, telephones, and this, that and the other, to get it all done. We had three-minute, two-minute, a sixty second and a thirty second versions. It was a huge campaign for AT&T.

"The challenge of doing commercials is in compressing a sharply-told story into a just one minute. It gives you a terrific kind of discipline as a director, it makes you very inventive—and it's a chance to use a lot of the new high-tech stuff, and to keep up-to-date and really hone your craft."

Frankenheimer accepting the Emmy Award for Against the Wall, *September 11, 1994.*

AGAINST THE WALL 1994

Director John Frankenheimer • *Producer* Steven McGlothen • *Executive Producers* Jonathan Axelrod, Irwin Meyer, Harvey Bibicoff • *Production Company* Producers Entertainment Group • *Screenplay* Ron Hutchinson, *based on the reminiscences of prison guard* Michael Smith • *Camera* John Leonetti (Color/wide screen) • *Editor* Lee Percy • *Sound* Glen Trew • *Production Design* Michael Hanan • *Costume Design* Sylvia Vega-Vasquez • *Art Director* Sandra Cook • *Set Decorator* Cindy Coburn • *Music* Gary Chang • *Distribution* HBO Television • *Broadcast* on HBO, March 26, 1994 • *Running Time* 110 mins • *Location* in the Tennessee State Prison, Nashville, April–May 1993 • *Working titles* Attica *and* In the Line of Fire • *Cost* $M5.5 • *Availability* LD • John Frankenheimer won an Emmy as Best Director of a Dramatic Special for *Against the Wall.*

CAST

Michael	•	Kyle MacLachlan	Barber	•	Richard Cowl
Jamaal	•	Samuel L. Jackson	Bud	•	Bud Davis
Hal	•	Harry Dean Stanton	Kareem	•	Danny Drew
Chaka	•	Clarence Williams III	Willis	•	Jeffrey Ford
Weisbad	•	Frederic Forrest	Danny	•	Denis Forest
Oswald	•	Philip Bosco	Nunez	•	Juan Garcia
Ed	•	Tom Bower	Puzzled inmate	•	Al Garrison
Sharon	•	Anne Heche	Metal shop rioter	•	Vincent Harris
Mancusi	•	Carmen Argenziano	Reporter #1	•	Vincent Henry
Jess	•	Peter Murnik	Reporter #2	•	Scott Higgins
Cecil	•	Steve Harris	Trooper captain	•	Rand Hopkins
Kunstler	•	David Ackroyd	Scarred inmate	•	James Mayberry
Ken	•	Mark Cabus	Elderly inmate	•	James "Sonny" Moore
Yates	•	Bruce Evers			
Mrs Willis	•	Joey Anderson	Luis	•	Danny Trejo

ON LOCATION

Nashville, Tennessee, April 1993. The day dawned cold, wet and windy. For several days violent storms had lashed the East Coast of the United States; Tulsa, Oklahoma, had been devastated by a tornado. Planes were having a difficult time landing in low clouds and heavy winds at Nashville airport. In Waco, Texas, the evil leader of a fanatical religious cult burned down the fortress-like retreat killing men, woman and children alike; in Ohio, a terrible prison riot had taken the lives of prisoners and wardens leaving the building a smoking, dripping wreck. Here in Nashville, thirty years after *Birdman of Alcatraz*, John Frankenheimer is working in a vast, grim empty prison on the outskirts of the city re-staging the dreadful prison riot at Attica, New York, which had taken place nine years after he finished *Birdman*.

On June 26 last year all the clocks at the Tennessee State Prison in Nashville stopped at 9 o'clock. The iron doors clanged shut, the last of the prisoners filed out to be transferred to other prisons, and a deep silence settled over the long corridors and empty cell blocks once teeming with a thousand inmates. Today the clocks still say 9 o'clock, but the doors are open again and the place is alive with the familiar sights and sounds of a film crew on location. And director John Frankenheimer is at last in a prison!

When he made *Birdman of Alcatraz* he planned at first to shoot it there, but permission was refused and he had to settle for studio sets. This gave the film a 'too clean look' he admits, but it was justified in part as the story was self-contained, like a poem, about one man alone in his cell devoted to the study of birds. It was not about daily life of men in prison. But his latest film, *Against the Wall*, shooting in this immense and impressive Victorian-era castle-like building soon to be torn down, is about prison life gone mad due to appalling living conditions. The Attica New York State prison exploded in January 1971 with rage and riots, death and destruction. The response by Governor Rockefeller and the state troopers who clumsily and brutally put down the uprising left many questions unanswered.

Frankenheimer believes it is time they were. The official inquiry after the tragedy tended to be a whitewash. Working from a screenplay by the Irish writer Ron Hutchinson, *Against the Wall* is a partly fictional but otherwise true account of what actually happened seen through the eyes of Michael Smith. An ordinary warden at the time, he is adviser to the production staff. The then 22-year old Smith had just started work at Attica when the disturbance broke out and he was taken hostage along with other guards, inmates and prison staff. After four days of agony and indecision he was shot to pieces by the 'rescuing' troopers. His life was saved by a black inmate with whom he had become friends. Long months of healing in hospital followed before he could return home to a normal life—only to be plunged into a legal and bureaucratic nightmare over compensation; he never went back to work in a prison.

"Here was a young man whose life was changed forever" says the director, "whose beliefs and ideals in the decency of people, in the fairness of law and order and the rightness of justice, were shattered in both the emotional and physical sense."

This is a no-nonsense, no hanging around, five-week schedule on a five-million dollar budget. There are no huge salaries, no expensive trailers, no temperamental stars. Frankenheimer, always an economical filmmaker, prefers this and relishes the challenges; but they take their toll with long and exhausting hours of work and the constant demands of creativity under pressure.

Out in the compound more than five hundred raggedly dressed and 'injured' extras are playing prisoners. Fires are burning and smoking and rubbish is piled everywhere, broken furniture, boxes and beds, a camp of tattered tents for the dispossessed. Tall and bending slightly, Frankenheimer moves though the carnage giving directions. He is highly regarded by actors, crew and extras alike and is always greeted as Mr. Frankenheimer. When he speaks to the extras, all male prisoners, he addresses them as gentlemen, and the elderly as Sir. One was a former prisoner here.

Sitting down before the TV monitors under a large sun-shield he calls "are you ready, David?" and to his assistant, "where are my earphones." And a complicated sequence begins.

Producer Steven McGlothen observes, "he's really remarkable, he carries it all in his head; his visual imagination is unbelievable, he knows exactly where it will all cut and piece together. I find it fascinating and mystifying."

was a side issue to the war in Vietnam and the struggle for civil rights, it pointed out that incarceration should not be synonymous with brutalization. The penal system needed reform then and still does now. By and large prison guards have dirty jobs and they are not trained psychologists. After all, society only wants to know that they have criminals safe under lock and key."

```
17    CONTINUED:      (2)                                    17*

      Before the humiliated Michael can react, there's an
      explosion of violence the other end of the cell
      block among INMATES mopping out their cells.

A18   INT. CELL BLOCK - DAY                                  A18*

      Wiesbad slams Jamaal's cell shut, sees one of the
      inmates is still resisting as GUARDS baton on.  He
      reaches for a black can of mace kept under his cap.

                         WIESBAD
                Mace! Mace him!

      Pushes Michael towards the affray and watches as
      Michael tries to get a shot in with the can.

                         WIESBAD
                I said mace him!  In his eyes!

      Michael fumbles the can, recovers, then sprays the
      inmate full in the face.  The man screams, claws at
      his eyes and is subdued.

      Wiesbad walks up to the shaken Michael, grinning--

                         WIESBAD
                You did good, son.  Lose one cell,
                we've lost the tier.

                Lose the tiers we've lost the yard.
                Lose the yards we've lost the
                prisons.

                Lose them and we've lost America.

                Understand?

                We've got a civil war going on in the
                country, son.  This is where we're
                going to hold the line.

                Got it now?
```

THE BURNING SEASON 1994

Director John Frankenheimer • *Executive Producer* David Puttnam • *Producers* John Frankenheimer & Thomas M. Hammel (HBO Pictures Presentation) • *Screenplay* Ron Hutchinson • *Teleplay* William Mastrosimone, Michael Tolkin, Ron Hutchinson, *from a story by Mastrosimone based in part on* The Burning Season *by Andrew Revkin* • *Camera* John Leonetti (color/widescreen) • *Editor* Francoise Bonnot • *Sound* Glen Trew • *Production Design* Michael Hanan • *Costume Design* Ray Summeres • *Art Direction* Charles Lagold Theresa Wachter • *Set Decoration* Melo Hinojosa • *Music* Gary Chang • *Original Broadcast* on HBO, Saturday, September 17, 1994 • *Running Time* 120 mins • Shown at the Toronto International Film Festival September 1994 • *Location* Filmed in the tiny jungle town of Comoapan, in the state of Vera Cruz, Mexico, chosen for its overall similarity to Chico Mendes' hometown of Xapuri deep in Brazil's Amazon forests, March-May 1994 • *Cost* $8m • *Availability* VHS • John Frankenheimer won an Emmy as Best Director of a Dramatic Special for *The Burning Season.*

CAST

Chico Mendes •	Raul Julia
Regina De Carvalho •	Sonia Braga
Ilzamar •	Kamala Dawson
Estate Boss •	Luis Guzman
Steven Kaye •	Nigel Havers
Darli Alves •	Tomas Milian
Jair •	Esai Morales
Orlavo Galvao •	Tony Plana
Wilson Pinheiro •	Edward James Olmos
Euclides Tavora	Marco Rodriguez
Young Chico •	Jeffrey Licon
Francisco •	Tony Perez
Father Ceppi •	Jorge Vitezil
Alfredo Sezero •	Carmen Argenziano
Nilo Sergio •	Enrique Novi
Thomas Santos •	Jorge Zepeda
Darci •	Gerrado Moreno
Oloci •	Valentin Santana
Genesio •	Jonathan Carrasco
Helio •	Carlos Carrasco
Elenira •	Briana Romero

ON LOCATION

Comoapan, Mexico, April 1994. Vera Cruz brings back screen memories: seven years before Burt Lancaster appeared in the first of four films for Frankenheimer, leading to a firm friendship between them, Lancaster was here in 1954 filming locations for *Vera Cruz* directed by Robert Aldrich. In 1969 Frankenheimer came here to film *The Extraordinary Seaman.* Now Frankenheimer has returned, some seventy miles south of here in Comoapan, to film *The Burning Season.*

The once pleasant and picturesque city of Vera Cruz is an overcrowded and noisy place, and it is an hour's drive along the Pacific coast to Catamarca to reach the film location. It's a hot, dry day, and as we drive, the roadside changes from shacks and advertising signs, gas stations and fruit stands, to rolling landscapes with forests, and flowers of every color and variety. The dust-covered van which picked me up at the airport finally turned off the highway. Several miles along a country road we came to the village, sullen and silent in its poverty-stricken stupor. The faces of young children look sadly from windows and emaciated dogs slink across the road. Across the square, men sit drinking beer and tequila around tavern tables, while the women, carrying heavy jugs of water from the pump, walk home to continue washing clothes and sweeping floors. The stream running past a row of houses is stagnant and polluted. This is the village standing in for Mendes's Brazilian home.

The camera is set up across the road in front of a warehouse turned into the premises of the rubber-tappers Union, where Chico Mendes has his office. A police jeep comes racing around the square and slows down outside the building just long enough to throw out the badly beaten body of Mendes, who has been interrogated and tortured by the Brazilian police. After the shot has been taken to Frankenheimer's satisfaction, Raul Julia, shirt torn, face and body 'bleeding,' comes out of the building to lie down 'senseless' in the road to be discovered by two curious children. Frankenheimer gets down beside Julia, moves his position, and talks quietly to him about this sequence. As the jeep, in the previous scene filmed over an hour ago, had driven away in a cloud of dust, so the next scene should still have dust floating in the air. Even small scenes like this take up so much time.

After breaking for lunch, Frankenheimer, exp-

ressing his pleasure with the success of *Against the Wall,* seen by over two million viewers on the HBO network on its first showing, talked about the comparisons between Michael Smith and Chico Mendes—one is thrown into a demanding situation in which he barely escapes death, the other thrust into a cause for which he ultimately gives his life. "Mendes was a great yet simple man who took on the courageous and doomed struggle to save the rain forests." With the short lunch time over, filming resumed outside the same building showing the arrival, in his battered Land Rover, of the British newsreel cameraman Steven Kaye, played by Nigel Havers. After entering the building, the unit and the equipment also move inside. Mendes and his wife (Kamala Dawson) are working in their office. Havers enters and introduces himself as a filmmaker. Mendes tells him that Hollywood is in the opposite direction and turns away aloof and uninterested. A truck filled with rubber-tappers is brought up in front of the Rover. Mendes comes out with a bottle of beer in his hand and sits on the back of the truck listening to Kaye asking for his co-operation. The truck begins to move without Mendes replying, but he passes the beer to Kaye—the first indication of a friendship beginning between them.

The following day we are in the rainforest, and Frankenheimer prepares to shoot the encounter between the tree-cutters, the rubber-tappers and the army—more than 300 extras and the principal players. Pipes running unseen up the trunks of the trees surrounding the clearing provide the downpour of rain as reasoning fails and the brutality begins. Painstakingly staged, set and filmed, the director moves among the actors quietly talking to them and explaining exactly the action and responses required. The cinematographer, John Leonetti (who shot *Against the Wall*) moves as swiftly as the director, setting up and lighting complicated shots. Nothing however, is rushed, nothing escapes the director's eye, nothing will pass unless it is exactly as he envisions it.

Always keeping in mind the entire sequence, the individual shots are precisely laid out, the editing pattern clearly in mind.

Filming in Mexico was not without unexpected difficulties and given the short filming schedule and lack of official co-operation, the unit performed remarkable deeds: "We scouted locations in Costa Rica," noted co-producer Tom Hammel, "but we found Mexico had enormous potential and was closer to home." Still, the town needed to take on a different look. Production designer Michael Hanan was responsible for changing Comoapan into its Brazilian counterpart. The production had to remain faithful to the architecture and life of the original Portuguese-speaking settlement where Chico lived and worked. "In the town square, every building has been painted. I've added second stories and roofs to many buildings, and radically changed the look of the church, a focal point of the people," said Hanan. "In addition, all public signs had to be displayed in the Portuguese language, the native tongue of Chico's village."

Property master Steven Schalk said, "The toughest aspect is trying to make a movie in Mexico that's about Brazil. The cultural differences and nuances are very diverse." Schalk hired an assistant who was trilingual—speaking Spanish, English and Portuguese. His team had the difficult task of reproducing Portuguese-language newspapers, flyers, posters, official documents, land deeds and signs for vehicles, plus a variety of everyday appliances and consumer goods, and the tools of the rubber tappers' trade.

Weaponry presented another hurdle. Only the militia, police, and certain hunters are permitted to carry firearms in Mexico. Through negotiations with officials of the Mexican government, Schalk received special permits to rent the necessary pistols, rifles, automatic and semi-automatic weapons for use in the film. The ongoing rebel uprising in the state of Chiapas and the assassination of presidential candidate Donaldo Colosia made the Mexican officials extremely reluctant to deal with the filmmakers. They supplied far below the minimum number of weapons needed. "We had to scramble," recalled Schalk. "We rented from townspeople who illegally owned weapons. It was amazing that they risked coming forward to help us. Try asking someone in the U.S. to borrow his gun for a little while. Not likely! In the end we found some replicas, and many we made ourselves."

The movie's wrangler, Carl 'Cowboy' Mergenthaler, had to be aware of the needs of dozens of pigs, goats, sheep and burros, and hundreds of horses and cattle. "The pigs are very susceptible to heat—if you walk them too fast, they will pass out," noted Mergenthaler. The goats were another matter. "People in this region generally don't eat goat, so I had to import them from the mountain

PHOTO DOUG HYUN/HBO

areas about four hours away. Up there, they have an animal which is a cross between a goat and a sheep. Sheep are better suited to resist heat, whereas a goat is not." In controlling hundreds of cattle, Mergenthaler had to make certain they did not pose a danger to the other animals and the actors. "I walked around them in their pen to weed out those that were afraid of humans. Then I rode among them on a horse to look for that reaction. It's critical that cattle do not panic on the set." From the animals to the props, to the look of the people and the town, it was production designer Hanan's responsibility to ensure continuity. "It's very important that everything ties in visually so that we can film from one place to another without having to cut, which is essential to John Frankenheimer's style," Henan pointed out. "Working with John, I have to prepare the set to go 360 degrees because John covers that with his camera."

Director of photography John Leonetti agreed. "John is using a Steadicam more in this movie than in any of his previous films. As a result, lighting his sets required a lot more thought and creativity. You can't have any lights behind the camera because you'll end up having them in the shot," he added. "It's a very real challenge."

According to Raul Julia, Frankenheimer's approach to film-making is engaging and involving. "His use of the Steadicam helps the actor because while you're playing, the drama and the flow is not interrupted by stops and starts," Julia noted, adding that the director's style is a more natural approach, more like theatre direction. "He allows you to carry a scene from beginning to end in a progressive way. He is knowledgeable and very respectful of what an actor has to go through."

Although fellow actor Edward James Olmos had known Julia for twenty years, *The Burning Season* marked the first time they worked together. "I received a call from Raul and John, asking if I would help them make this movie," said Olmos. "I felt it was an honor." Olmos became the film company's ambassador and unofficial interpreter for the movie extras. During the filming of a key scene in the church of Comoapan, about two hundred extras playing rubber tappers were gathered for a meeting to be addressed by Olmos's character, Wilson Pinheiro. Just before filming commenced, Olmos noticed many puzzled faces in the crowd, and began addressing them in Spanish to explain in detail what was about to happen and how they were supposed to react. By the time the director called "Action," Olmos's dramatic speech had inspired the highly charged emotions demanded for the scene.

Of the director, Olmos added, "John Frankenheimer is one of the most intense directors I've ever worked with. His camera placement is superb, and he has a great rapport with actors." "I'm a very lucky man in many ways," said Frankenheimer. "I was born with the gift of very good visual sense. I have worked hard to perfect it. I don't ever want to be complacent and think that this is easy, because I've done it before. It never is, and there is never an end to what your imagination is capable of bringing to life."

SYNOPSIS

From his earliest boyhood experiences in the Amazon rain forest of Brazil, Chico Mendes witnesses brutality. Violence, even murder is committed against the rubber tappers who do not meet the demands of their wealthy estate bosses. Young Chico is aware that his father Francisco and the other tappers are grossly underpaid by the bosses for the latex they extract from the rubber trees. In the trading post at his village of Xapuri in rural Cachoeira province, Chico meets a man from Sao Paulo, Euclides Tavora who takes a strong interest in the young boy. He teaches him to read and write, and tells him about the outside world. Armed with this knowledge, Chico challenges the estate boss who has been cheating his father and the other tappers. He forces the boss to give an accurate weight and payment for the latex they have gathered. It is his first taste of the power of knowledge—a victory against oppression.

Twenty-five years later, the adult Chico, a union organizer in Cachoeira, struggles to unite the native Indians and the rubber tappers against cattle ranchers and land speculators who are cutting and burning the forest to create grazing land. Among his many admirers is Ilzamar, a young woman in her teens. Violence erupts between the two groups. One of Chico's supporters, Jair, is wounded by gunfire. Mendes implores the warring parties to engage in peaceful dialogue, and tensions ease. Within days, the Rural Worker's Union leader Wilson Pinheiro, and academician Regina De Carvalho arrive. Wilson has come to organize the rubber tappers; Regina brings educational materials and school supplies to educate the villagers. The three create a movement of passionate nonviolent protest. Wilson Pinheiro's activities anger ranchers Alfredo Sezero and Nilo Sergio, and Bordon Company executive Thomas Santos, whose company wants to clear the land. The businessmen are joined by politician Orlavo Galvao, who is backed by political and economic interests tied to clearing the land and cutting down the rain forest for a major highway through the Amazon.

Because he is a major obstacle to the forest clearings, Wilson Pinheiro is brutally shot down in a union office. Chico and his followers subsequently seize a radio station and broadcast the news of the murder. His plea is to "Unite and fight" —without weapons—not to give their enemies an excuse for wholesale murder. But Nilo Sergio is killed by unknown assailants in retribution. Chico is taken into custody and beaten by the police. Broken and bloody, he is nursed back to health by Ilzamar. Slowly regaining his strength— and steeling his resolve—Chico assumes control of the rubber tappers union.

The visiting filmmaker Steven Kaye petitions Chico to let him make a movie about his work. At first apprehensive, Chico warms to the idea, and agrees to the filming. Chico continues his nonviolent activity, but a group of chainsaw cutters draws blood when their foreman, Helio, cuts off the arm of a tapper. Finally, Helio and the cutters announce their decision to leave the area. Surprised and encouraged, Chico decides to run for the office of state deputy against the polished Galvao. Kaye films the campaign hoopla. However, the political process is a sham—votes are openly bought and sold, with Galvao's supporters trading chainsaws for votes. Galvao wins by a landslide, and Chico gets just 10 per cent of the ballots.

To keep Chico's spirits up, Regina and Kaye encourage him to go to Miami to lobby against multi-million dollar economic development loans to Brazil for building a major highway through the rain forest of benefit only to the land owners.

Arriving in the US he is mobbed by hordes of media and acclaimed as the savior the forest, which enables him to talk to statesmen and money men. Back in Sao Paulo, rancher Sezero, and beef executive Santos grimly watch Chico on national television as he wins wide support, sensing that he has been successful in his campaign to halt the flow of loan money to build roads and exploit the land for economic development. In retaliation for Chico's intervention, Sezero gives a huge tract of land in Chico's home province to the brutal Darli Alves.

Chico returns home a national figure and local hero, but now with more enemies than ever before. That night, bullets slam through the windows of Chico's family quarters. The next day, Darli Alves tells Chico of his plans to cut and burn his newly acquired acreage. In a show of solidarity and courage, dozens of tappers and Indians stage a sit-in on his land, only to be confronted by a paramilitary force. During the melee, a young native boy is shot dead. Days later, Jair is murdered while tapping latex in the forest. Half of Chico's tappers now advocate violence, despite his efforts to calm them. The police clamp a curfew on the town. Sezero and Galvao try in vain to persuade Chico to back off. The townsfolk gather outside the union hall and keep an all-night vigil. At daybreak, Galvao makes the surprise announcement that the government has, for the first time, designated a forest reserve that cannot be cleared by land speculators and ranchers such as Darli Alves. Chico is again the hero.

Back at his ranch, a seething Alves watches as his cutters are forced to leave under supervision of the police. Regina urges Chico to flee to safety in America, but he refuses. Chico gathers his infant son, Sandhino, in his arms and takes the boy into the forest, showing him the trees cut by generations of Mendes. It is a tender moment. But, later that night, with the family, Chico's daughter Elenira finds a severed goat's head on their doorstep, indicating a death threat. The following evening, as he opens his back door, Chico is struck by blasts from the shotgun of Darli Alves' son. Chico staggers back into his house. He dies in Ilzamar's arms. When Steven Kaye returns to Cachoeiria, it is to film Chico's friends and allies, numbering in the thousands, as they gather to lay him to rest.

COMMENT

After completing *Against the Wall*, a true-to-life event, Frankenheimer went on almost immediately to make *The Burning Season*, the true life story of Chico Mendes, the Brazilian rubber-tapper who led the peasant struggle and revolt against the corrupt Federal government and greedy landowners, who were (and still are) destroying the rain forests of the Amazon. After Chico Mendes was murdered in 1988, his life story suddenly became 'hot' property in Hollywood. Robert Redford and Ted Turner are known to have made bids for the screen rights. In 1989, Mendes' widow sold the rights to the story to a Brazilian production company JN Filmes, for $1m. Three months later, JN Filmes sold the rights to Warner Bros. for $1.8m.

Originally conceived by David Puttnam as a $35m production for Warners, *The Burning Season* was to be filmed over three months in Costa Rica with director, Chris Menges. Various actors such as Pacino, DeNiro, Tom Cruise and others, were being talked about for the role of Chico Mendes. Over $7m had been spent building sets on location in Costa Rica when a WB executive decided there was really no audience for a film about Mendes and cancelled the project. Time Warner, the owners of HBO, turned the screenplay over to the cable company for $50,000 and wrote the project off. With Puttnam still listed as the Executive Producer, the film went to JF who scaled down the screenplay and filmed it in five weeks on an $8m budget. It was filmed between March and May 1994 on location in the tiny jungle town of Comoapan, in the state of Vera Cruz, Mexico, chosen for its overall similarity to Chico Mendes' hometown of Xapuri in the Amazon forests of Brazil.

This is the kind of film that cynics enjoy taking to pieces on the grounds that its story is simply a thinly disguised Western with good against evil, and that, in a long-standing tradition of American movies, audiences will identify with the underdog, knowing full well that by the end, goodness and honesty will triumph. To a certain extent the screenplay by Ron Hutchinson and the director does seem to follow the old schematic and simplified form, but the fact of the matter is that such things did occur and still do. Here, Frankenheimer cannot escape what have become basic conventions because they are vital facts in this chronicle of real-life endeavors and sacrifices, including the crusading investigative journalist, here shown as a filmmaker. What Frankenheimer has done, with compelling artistry, is to charge all the characters and situations with a depth of feeling, honesty and complexity which, while necessarily compressing events, characters, time and place, restore true meaning to a noble and classic story of an individual who gives his life for a cause in which he believes. In this two-hour film for HBO, the director takes us into the heart of Mendes' life and holds the audiences' attention and concern throughout. With a feeling of dread and despair, we realize from the opening scenes, that we are witnessing a tragedy of treachery, deception and death.

The first hurdle the director had to overcome was, of course, the language barrier. In the original 'life', so to speak, everyone spoke Portuguese, the native tongue. From the beginning however, it seems perfectly natural that everyone should be speaking English because the cleverly chosen cast of almost entirely Mexican or South American players speak their accented English exactly as they would do if they were speaking in English to those of us who neither spoke nor understood Portuguese. This is seldom attempted in films. Usually English-speaking actors 'put on' foreign accents.

The opening scenes set us immediately in 1951 in the small Brazilian village where Mendes was born. The camera moves over the river, the homes, the oxen pulling carts, and comes to rest on a small boy, Pablo, who, with his father, take their rubber to the trading post. The father is cheated by the trader, and the living conditions we see are those of abject poverty. The score by Chang is quiet and sad, and the mood is one of despair and resignation. The credits appear singly and clearly, a few to a frame. Close-ups of the rubber flowing from the trees are in keeping with Frankenheimer's documentary style. A single lighted cigarette transposes into a flare. It is the end of the day, the villagers are assembled to watch a peasant being burned alive for the crime of attempting to start a trade union. Frankenheimer has set the scene for a complex sociological and political drama of international concern.

Within the close confines of the dense rain forest the time moves to 1983. Aerial views show the forests now burning, partially obscured by huge clouds of smoke. On the devastated land, the trees left standing are being felled and a rancher comments with satisfaction, "when I see fire, I see the future." The protests of the tappers are ineffective. They are shot and killed, and their cause seems hopeless. The figure who comes onto the scene to attempt to right the wrongs being perpetrated on his people is an ordinary man. He does not carry a gun nor believe in violence, who cannot be bought or dissuaded from his beliefs in social justice. But neither is he too good to be true. Perfectly played by Raul Julia, with his expressive eyes, distinctive voice and considerable emotional powers, his performance as the troubled Chico Mendes is subdued yet brilliant, rising to a peak of high expression in later scenes where he must hold on to his beliefs and speak out passionately when defending them to his detractors.

His foil here is the quietly determined film-maker, Steven Kaye, played by Nigel Havers, who represents the outside world and the means to make known the terrible devastation being wrought on the forests and its people and giving Mendes the support and encouragement he needs internationally. He tells Mendes, "I make films to educate people." A tracking shot takes us across the village square past the sullen police and into the cafe where Mendes talks of the need to inform the people. From this we cut to the company's glass and steel boardroom high above the streets of Rio de Janeiro. Here the agents of commerce consider their plans, because Mendes has become a nuisance. A sense of doom descends upon the film. Frankenheimer creates this atmosphere using naturalism rather than heavy dramatics. The matter-of-fact details in the narrative's development are chillingly rendered through lighting and acting, dialogue and symbolism. Mendes is horribly tortured, and the audience is forced to consider how a human being could survive this ordeal.

Every scene is cleverly conceived and developed. The story throughout contains an immense number of facts, and follows several relationships and character developments carefully woven together making a forceful whole. Different points of view and their justifications interplay with scenes of physical conflict, tightly expressed, well-staged and never sensationalised. When a chainsaw removes the arm of friend of Mendes, we see only the blood. The effect is more horrifying than an explicit depiction of the act. Frankenheimer also pays attention to domestic matters, for example Mendes's proposal of marriage, and the family scenes with the children The fact that the audience knows Mendes will die gives these moments a poignancy.

There are also sharp and satirical sequences. For example at the big United Nations conference in Miami on the future of the environment, the delegates are too busy eating to be interested in Mendes, this simple man from the rain forest. The Italians tell him his protests are "bad for business." In the washroom with Kaye, Mendes delivers a passionate statement saying that cutting down trees is progress in the wrong direction; he wants progress to help the people. He gave them faith and hope, yet the film makes clear the ambivalent nature of many of these same working people who could just as easily succumb to the greed and cruelty used against them. In a scene of chilling depravity, a developer brings in four prostitutes to bribe a rancher. The girls slowly undress and drape themselves around him as the developer talks calmly about the benefits he is offering. Except for nudity, nothing else is shown, but the scene's power of suggestion, the hypnotic close-ups of the girls' bodies seen from the angle of the sitting rancher, its deliberately slow rhythms, make this an unsettling depiction of depravity and evil.

Frankenheimer executes the final encounter between the tappers and the ranchers with his customary skill and imagination. It is just before dark, the ranchers on their horses appear through the trees to meet the peasants, all standing quietly blocking their way. Ironically, with the forests burning, the rain is falling. The encounter ends in violence. "Just because they are murderers, are we to become murderers?" asks Mendes, as the defeated peasants console wives and children, and attend to the dead and the dying. This scene shows forcibly why the oppressed turn to violence when opposing forces are utterly ruthless. In another scene, and one of sheer hypocrisy, the politicians and businessmen accuse Mendes of embarrassing his government and his country in the eyes of the world. Close-ups convey quite clearly that nothing is what it seems, every scene carries the undercurrent of resistance and every statement has a double meaning. In the final scenes the screenplay comes to grips with a continuing predicament: how to leave the audience with some hope after so much defeat. Mendes wins a Phyrrhic victory.

In some ways reminiscent of John Boorman's *The Emerald Forest*, *The Burning Season* is even more disturbing showing by implication that the world has other matters to consider, its own blemishes to hide, that we are powerless to affect changes and the rain forests and what they represent will continue to burn until none are left—not trees, not animals, not people.

Ultimately, of course, Mendes is killed, and at this tragic ending, Frankenheimer cleverly brings in once again his symbolic use of television. As Mendes is shot and lies dying he is seen in close-up on the screen of the small television on the kitchen table urging his followers to remain true to their cause. As his life slips away and he dies, his spirit continues to live on, his voice still heard, guiding the continuing struggle for change.

The Burning Season *received three Golden Globe Awards. From left* Mrs Raul Julia, *who accepted the award on behalf of her late husband, Frankenheimer, Mrs Edward James Olmos, Evans Evans, and Edward James Olmos.*

hole and the top is covered with a frame and turf to make it seem like original grass. They push this away as though they had completed their tunneling, climb out, and crouching down they run into the nearby woods. The rehearsals go well, the turf is replaced and the camera, low on the ground, is ready to roll. The director calls the familiar action in his powerful voice and we watch for the breakthrough from underground. But in spite of all the careful preparations by the special effects group, something goes wrong and cries of alarm are heard from below the heaving earth. Everyone rushes forward, filming stops, the crew desperately pull the ground away. The last thing Frankenheimer or Turner need is an accident, particularly if it involves a loss of life. But no one is the worse for the wear and the actors are rushed to their tents to recover from the incident. During the several hours delay during which the scene is once again set up, taking precautions against another cave-in, Frankenheimer drives to his trailer for hot coffee and sandwiches. The trailer itself is thick with mud and dirt, poorly lit, littered with boots and coats, and all the paper work associated with a film location from story board sketches taped on walls, call sheets and script pages. A small heater hums in the corner, Frankenheimer squeezes himself up to the small table and wearily relaxes, somewhat tense but confident; not for long however. A conversation begun is soon interrupted by an assistant director. Frankenheimer is needed back on the set.

YNOPSIS

About Andersonville

The Confederate prisoner-of-war camp Andersonville, or Camp Sumter as it was officially known, was built in late 1863 and early 1864 to house Union Army troops who had been confined in Richmond. The captive population there had grown so large that the Confederates could no longer feed them and feared that all those soldiers in one place would lead to a Union attack. Located in Sumter County, Georgia, between what is now Macon and President Jimmy Carter's home, Plains, Andersonville was a 26fi-acre pen, an open-air stockade ringed by a fifteen-foot-high wall of hewed pine with no permanent structures inside. Guard houses perched on the wall at thirty yard intervals. Inside, prisoners were forbidden on penalty of death to cross the "dead line," a twenty foot ring around the perimeter wall. A branch of Sweetwater Creek flowed through the prison yard.

The first prisoners were brought to Andersonville in February 1864. They arrived at a rate of about four hundred per day until June, when 26,000 men were confined to an area originally intended for 8,000. In August 1864, the population peaked at more than 32,000. The food shortage that had plagued Richmond soon settled on Andersonville, and the stream was quickly polluted beyond use. Hunger, exposure and disease were rampant; in seven months, one third of the prisoners died.

In the Fall of 1864, when General William T. Sherman's march to the sea brought him to Atlanta, and within striking distance of Andersonville, the Confederates began moving a majority of the prisoners to other camps in the South. Andersonville operated on a much smaller basis until the Civil War ended in May 1865. When word of what had happened at Andersonville reached the North, retribution was swift; Captain Henry Wirz, the camp's commandant, was arrested for violating the laws of war; tried and found guilty by a military tribunal. He was hanged in Washington, D.C. on November 10, 1865, the only soldier to be executed for war crimes during the Civil War.

In July 1865, with information from a Union prisoner, Clara Barton traveled to Andersonville on government orders to identify the graves of the Union dead. Only 460 of the original 12,914 graves were left marked "Unknown U.S. Soldier." Andersonville National Cemetery, established on July 26, 1865, today contains more than 17,000 interments.

The prison site was held in private ownership until 1890, when it was purchased by the Georgia Department of the Grand Army of the Republic, a Union veterans group that soon turned it over to the Woman's Relief Corps., the national auxiliary of the GAR. In 1910, the WRC gave the site to the people of the United States. Andersonville has been administered by the National Park Service since July 1971.

June 1, 1864, Virginia. Wounded Union Sergeant James McSpadden, young Corporal Josiah Day, and his men are captured and put on a train. The prisoners are jammed together so tight that those who die along the way continue to stand. After days of torturous thirst and misery the train finally stops, but this is just the beginning of their ordeal in the Andersonville prison camp, a field enclosed by walls made of logs. A putrid downstream swamp is the prisoners' only source of water, and the scarce food consists of moldy, rotten scraps. There is no medicine, no shelter, and four times too many men crammed into the available space. Starvation, disease, and wanton brutality are the order of the day as bloodthirsty, sadistic guards, some of them little more than children, shoot at the slightest provocation.

Devious inmate Munn welcomes the new prisoners but soon delivers the unsuspecting captives to the treacherous Raiders who lie in wait to kill and maim for food, clothing, and items of value. In the nick of time, Dick Potfer, an Andersonville veteran and old friend of Josiah Day, steps in and drives Munn off. Potfer details the horrors of Andersonville and warns Day to beware of the sadistic Captain Wirz, commander of the camp. Potfer takes McSpadden and Day to his lean-to called a Shebang, where they meet Union Sergeant John Gleason. Gleason and his men are "diggers" by trade from the coal mines of Pennsylvania. Their numbers are few and tunneling an escape route is difficult. McSpadden pledges his men to work with them. Meanwhile, the bullet in McSpadden's shoulder has caused infection and without warning he collapses unconscious. Gleason, Martin Blackburn, his second-in-command, and Josiah Day remove the bullet but McSpadden continues to suffer. Billy, almost a child still, keeps a watchful eye over his commander as Potfer and Day look for medicine. Young Patrick Shay finds some whiskey, the closest thing to medicine to be found. Fighting despair, Blackburn quietly sings along with his banjo, befriending Thomas Sweet, the large baby-faced farm boy from Massachusetts.

Suddenly, Collins, Curtis and Munn lead fifty drunken Raiders in a bloodthirsty assault on the unsuspecting and unarmed men from Massachusetts and Pennsylvania, who are robbed, bloodied and battered. Josiah Day cradles Dick Potfer's lifeless body in his arms. As a result of Potfer's death,

McSpadden's condition, and the realization of what it will take to survive this place, Josiah Day's demeanor has changed. He has fewer illusions, more determination, and more authority than when he arrived two days ago.

Unable to stand by idly as the Raiders conspicuously enjoy their spoils, Thomas Sweet goes after them with Blackburn, Day, Gleason, and company following closely behind. As the Raiders see them coming, a circle is drawn, and a fight between Sweet and a huge and menacing Raider ensues. It looks like Sweet is getting the worst of it, though with an unexpected maneuver he seems to reverse his fortunes, but then from behind, he is blindsided by a near fatal blow; and the Raiders continue their reign of terror. Strong and fearless, Limber Jim emerges from the crowd to help carry Sweet back to the Shebang. He promises his allegiance and support against the cut-throats. With this lesson behind them, Gleason drives the message home to Josiah that they can no longer waste time worrying about with the Raiders. Their only hope for survival depends upon digging an escape tunnel.

Several days later, while talking with other prisoners, Tobias accidentally lets the word slip out about their tunnel, prompting Gleason and the men to step up their operation and be on the lookout for a "tunnel traitor." Fellow prisoner Grundy, discovered to be the traitor, is held hostage by the group. Enraged, Tyce wants to slit his throat, instead Gleason mercifully carves two "T's" on his forehead. With the tunnel completed, Gleason leads the escape with Wisnovsky, Tobias, Benson, Billy, Tucker, Tyce, 2nd Wisconsin, 60th Ohio, Josiah Day with McSpadden, Blackburn and Sweet trailing behind. As the men attempt to cross to the woods, Sweet gets shot in the back and dies in Blackburn's arms. The rest are captured and held in the torture stocks outside the camp. After a few days, Wirz releases them in an effort to look benevolent to his visiting superior officers from the Department of War, Colonel Chandler and Lieutenant Dahlgren. Near death, Limber Jack and Young Patrick help to bring the men back to life.

Meanwhile, the relentless flow of new prisoners continues. The Raiders still reign and nothing has changed. Josiah and company are slowly regaining their strength but weeks have passed since their foiled escape and many have sunk into despair. Another group of prisoners arrives, and Limber Jim can no longer stand by as Munn baits the new arrivals. A cry for humanity rises up from the depths of his being—"Who is with me?" he demands. Alone, with only a rock for a weapon, he charges the Raiders. McSpadden struggles to his feet, then Josiah, Blackburn, and Tyce. Suddenly shouts of support ring out from every corner, and, within moments, ranks begin to swell as these men become an army once more, fighting for a cause. The Raiders at last are defeated and become prisoners within the prison.

Collins, Curtis, Munn and their gang are trussed and gagged. Limber Jim leads the call to hang them, then McSpadden's voice of justice gives them pause in their rage. Martin Blackburn proposes a fair trial, with the impartial new prisoners as jurors. It is an act of mercy in a merciless place. Compatriot Prosecuting Attorney, Horace Trimble, asks victim witnesses to describe their treatment at the hands of these perpetrators, while Defense Attorney, Jarred Hopkins, presents a compelling argument that the accused cannot be guilty of crimes when there is no law within the camp. Josiah Day passionately counters their attempt to justify murder and mayhem when he says, "The things they did, they knew to be wrong.

They're against every man's law and understanding . . . All men want to live, but there are some things men won't do just to live." The defense fails, the six ringleaders are sentenced to die and are hanged for their crimes.

With the threat of the Raiders gone, life remains in a state of daily deterioration. More Union prisoners arrive as the war continues to rage. At the Main Gate, Captain Wirz and Colonel O'Neil offer the prisoners the opportunity to "turncoat" and join the Southern army in exchange for freedom, clothing, food, cash and land. McSpadden promptly calls an "About Face". Although wracked, they are not ruined, and they march away defiantly refusing the offer.

As the war drags on, conditions at Andersonville worsen. Some of the Union soldiers do defect to the Rebels. In a startling turn of events, devious Wirz declares a Prisoner Exchange. As Josiah hobbles to Blackburn to tell him the good news, he finds his loyal friend dead. While fellow prisoners celebrate their liberation, Josiah and McSpadden sadly carry Blackburn to the Dead House. But the Prisoner Exchange was a lie—it was just a ruse to make the prisoners walk to the train that would only take them to other Confederate prison camps to sit out the war.

PHOTO DOUG HYUN/TURNER PICTURES

COMMENT

The credits appear over period paintings of the Civil War, thus establishing an authenticity which the film maintains throughout its length. The last painting comes to life and begins the film in a forest setting where Union soldiers are running from Southern forces. From here, the narrative unfolds quietly giving the audience time to become familiar with the setting and characters. Frankenheimer's imaginative power comes into full play as we enter the enormous, forbidding stockade. The gray, somber scene of deprivation and despair is relieved only by a flash of red in a flag flying over a sentry tower. The stillness of death lies like a pall over the scene, the silence broken occasionally by someone singing a ballad. Through the mud a group of weary men drag a huge iron ball behind them. They are chained to it as punishment for trying to escape. The atmosphere is filled with the smoke of a hundred camp fires.

The first fight with the Raiders is gripping in its horror and realism. The gunfire actually sounds like the weaponry of the time, and the characters' costumes, speech and behavior all suggest the carefully recreated period 'feel' of the drama. The presence of the weather is always with us. Close-ups of faces, worthy of Eisenstein, appear throughout the film—for example, in the trial sequence, "Murder was done here," Frankenheimer introduces a marvelous scene of close-ups of soldiers listening to the verdict transposed over a travelling shot of the assembled prisoners about to be hanged. Then the final struggle takes place between the soldiers and the Raiders, the camera slowly draws so far back, disengaging itself from the conflict, that the encounter between the hundreds of struggling men becomes miniaturized into a strange and jerking dance with death cloaked in the madness of hate itself. Then comes the rain, pouring down relentlessly and continuously—the weather plays an important part throughout the film. What is remarkable about the way this film has been conceived is that, while adhering closely to the detail of its subject, the events comes across with the truly broad sweep of drama. This is strengthened by the absence of well-known actors who have become associated with such stories and whose faces and mannerisms, had they been included, would have destroyed the honesty of this portrait of historical events.

This was Frankenheimer's third prison film and the most difficult to make. In *Birdman of Alcatraz* and *Against the Wall*, prison life was the setting, the backdrop, to other stories. *Andersonville* has no central character involved in anything other than the daily horror of keeping alive. Also, the two previous films were set indoors within the prison buildings. The prisoners were fed and watered and given sufficient care to make boredom and confinement the most trying elements they had to cope with. Staying alive was not the terrible struggle which formed the day-to-day existence of the prisoners in *Andersonville*. The other difference is, of course, that the inmates of *Birdman of Alcatraz* and *Against the Wall* were convicted criminals. The inmates of *Andersonville* were prisoners-of-war. In Spielberg's *Schindler's List*, the concentration camps were real but outside the main story line—that of Schindler's efforts to save his workers from the Nazis. We did not see the camp other than as a darkened mass of buildings, but we knew they were there, we felt their ominous presence. In *Andersonville*, the churning mass of humankind is constantly before us because there are no other forces within the story to set against them. They are the entire subject matter of the film and the director deals with this somewhat in the manner of war films where the conflict is enacted through the experiences of a particular group of soldiers. Frankenheimer's characters are all on the same level within the vast prison camp itself. Even the callous prison commander does not become a primary character. And so, in the long-established tradition of war films, where the participants cannot know what is happening far from their positions, life within the prison camp, comes to be represented by groups of friends through their behavior and response to the struggle for survival. This film is very much an ensemble piece where no single actor takes a role which puts him above another. As with dozens of past films in which a group of survivors meet and band together to save themselves from being attacked by others bent on taking from them whatever they have to support themselves, by murder if necessary, this film is about those who live and those who die under the conditions imposed upon them.

This is the longest film Frankenheimer has made to date (excluding *The Iceman Cometh*) and once again one can only marvel at his skill in making this film such a constantly living and compelling chronicle of history. His humanity makes him examine the appalling misfortune of men caught between warring sides with concern, horror and dismay. The director lets the situation speak for itself, and he never loses control of a narrative of immense detail and logistics. The passing of time, the familiarity of place, the atmosphere, and sense of reality are vividly and grimly created, but acts of gentleness and spiritual belief lighten the darkness of evil. The camerawork, the lighting, and the editing, in depicting the huge compound and its captives, is filled with stark and dreadful images. Nature, on occasion, provides some relief. There is little hope here, other than when the men finally depart for another camp where conditions may be better.

Yet this despair is not entirely unrelieved. There are touches of simple nobility in the behavior of the men. The film is more than a simplified portrayal of good and bad. "It is not," in Frankenheimer's words, "a four-hour descent into Hell. What I made is, I hope, a testimony to men who lived under deprivation and brutality and emerged with honor and dignity and perhaps as better and wiser human beings." This entire recreation of a period long past carries the stamp of Frankenheimer's documentary methods and style. It might well be considered as a documentary at its most realistic and alive. That hatred is not confined to any one side or nation is made quietly evident within the situation—this is a civil war. The brutality comes mainly from soldiers who set upon their own in much the same way as they would their enemy. Parallels between then and now inevitably arise, with conflicts in Rwanda and Bosnia. As the film ends we see a tag attached to the toe of the dead Martin Blackburn, with his name written on it. The image dissolves slowly into a headstone with the name again, this time engraved. The camera continues to pull back slowly and shows us 10,000 graves. The tune of 'The Battle Hymn of the Republic', heard earlier during the film, returns as part of this quiet and deeply moving closing.

PHOTO TURNER PICTURES

from left *Executive producer Ethel Winant, producer and screenwriter David W. Rintels, and Frankenheimer.*

JF "Simultaneously with HBO offering me the Chico Mendes project, my friend Ethel Winant from *Playhouse 90* and *All Fall Down,* called me and asked me if I would be interested in doing *Andersonville* for Turner. This was going to be 'their big event of all time,' their 'statement film,' a four-hour mini-series. I didn't know if I really wanted to do *Andersonville*. It was another prison movie—I had already done *Birdman of Alcatraz* and *Against the Wall*. Ethel talked me into it. The people at Turner were very complimentary about *Against the Wall* and many of my other films. It was going to conflict with the Chico Mendes project, so they held it for me until the fall. So we began filming in September outside Atlanta.

"Again, I worked with Michael Hanan. I didn't have John Leonetti this time, he was on another shoot, but a cinematographer named Ric Waite was very good. Many of the actors who were in *Against the Wall*, including Frederic Forrest and Denis Forest were with me. I enjoy working with the same actors who have proven their worth in previous films. Justin Henry, who was in *Kramer vs. Kramer*, came in to read. He auditioned like everybody else and I liked him. The screenplay was by David Rintels and the theme once again was that of courage, nobility, survival, the human spirit triumphing over adverse circumstances. It has been an integral part of my work over the years. In spite of the fact that we had a cast of exceptionally good actors, we did not have any stars. I thought that too-familiar faces would detract from the realism of what is, after all, historical. These soldiers lived and died, were known only to their family and friends. They weren't considered heroes, but they endured terrible suffering to win the war which created this country.

"Lacking star names, then, it might be assumed that it was a fairly inexpensive film but, on the contrary, it was the most expensive film I'd made since *Black Sunday*, although by today's standards that did not have a big budget. No, the money went into the immense set, designed by Michael, which we built from the ground up—the actual place is a small memorial park—and had to be demolished when we finished. We also had to pay the two-thousand-odd extras we used almost continuously throughout filming. David Rintels did a great deal of reading on the Civil War before and during the time he was writing the script. The National Park at Andersonville has kept all the records of what happened at the camp. I read up on the subject extensively, and I hadn't realized how far the brutality and suffering went in this camp. With the exception of Auschwitz and other concentration camps during the Second World War, Andersonville was the worst to be inflicted on mankind.

"The key figures were accurate, but we had to invent others and their dialogue. There was a man, Collins, who led the rogue prisoners, and the others did hang him and those who ran with him. Captain Wirz, of course, the camp commandant, was an actual person. Then we had advice from the re-enactors of the Civil War. They have preserved everything about the soldiers, their uniforms, guns and methods and maneuvers, and relive the war constantly, go on parade on special occasions and restage the battles. We had hundreds of them among the thousands of extras. I'm telling you the logistics on this film were staggering, but as a creative experience it was inspiring for me and the crew. We worked late into the night six days a week and shot the film in sixty days. It rained every day, it was cold, and physically we were always up against it. I did not make a single compromise and I believe it will be the most powerful film I have ever made. The long running time removed the constriction a director often feels when making a ninety minute film. I had more time to spend with the actors.

"I don't think Turner financed *Andersonville* because of the success of the recent films of the Civil War and Gettysburg. He has had a lifelong interest in the Civil War and this chapter about 'a concentration camp in the United States during the last century.' This isn't about Germans and their concentration camps in Europe, this happened here, happened less than 150 years ago in the country in which I live. The film was a brutal yet, I think, often poignant re-enactment of the way soldiers were treated and what war is like. It took all the so-called glamour and false patriotism out of it. You could read contemporary references into it—the fact that the prisoners were all packed into trains with long journeys overnight without food or water, and sent to a concentration camp commanded by Germans who were officers in the Confederate army. Put it this way, what they did during the last war wasn't new. Yes, we did that in our own country, to our own people."

SC. 108
8.
TIGHT ON
GUARD TOWER.
THEIR BACKS TO CAM.
OBVIOUSLY UNAWARE OF
THE ESCAPE.

SC. 108.
9. REVERSE. ON GUARDS
SEE ESCAPEES BETWEEN
THEM IN THE B/G.
GUARDS DON'T SEE
THEM.

SC. 110. 1A
C/U. ON BENTON
EMERGES FROM
HOLE . . .

1B
. . . OPEN UP MEDIUM
WIDE SHOT. SEE TOBIAS
PULLS BENTON OUT.

SC. 110
3. OPEN INTO A WIDE SHOT SEE TOBIAS + BENTON MAKING
FOR THE WOODS.

PRODUCTION NOTES

In the closing months of the Civil War, the Confederate forces were rapidly running out of men, munitions, medicine, food, clothing and every other kind of supply. The remaining rebel ranks endured tremendous deprivation. But some men suffered a far worse fate. They were the captured Union soldiers who struggled to survive in the deplorable conditions of Confederate prisoner of war camps. The most deadly of these was Andersonville.

Taking its name from the tiny Georgia town nearby, Andersonville was a 26fi-acre, open-air stockade enclosed by log walls standing fifteen to twenty feet above ground. Designed to detain 8,000 prisoners, at its peak the numbers swelled to more than 32,000. With no medicine or shelter, a food supply of scraps and a putrid downstream creek the only source of water, the Union prisoners lived on courage and will.

Re-creating Andersonville: building the immense set.
Production Designer Michael Hanan began by designing and building an accurate replica of the Andersonville stockade on a farm an hour outside Atlanta. Journals, diaries and drawings from pris-

oners, and a few existing photographs and illustrations from Harper's Weekly, guided the construction. "The stockage is a major character in the movie," says Hanan. "It's always looming in the background, representing the terror and oppression of the place." The stockade was made of logs procured locally. Three thousand feet of two-storey log walls surrounded the twelve-acre enclosure, with thirty-six guard houses perched at regular intervals.

Before the walls could be erected, Hanan's crews dug a trench establishimg the perimeter of the stockade. Each log was set into the ground four feet deep. "We operated two crews with about twenty-five men each and started a race between them," Hanan explains. "At first, they were averaging about ninety feet of wall per day. Because no one builds stockade anymore, we were reinventing the wheel. By the time we'd developed a system, we were doing about 250 feet a day, when the weather cooperated."

Another crucial 'character' in the film is the 1,000-foot stream that snakes through the compound. "The actual stream was badly polluted from waste of all sorts, yet prisoners cooked,

Contemporary photograph of the Andersonville camp.

PHOTO ANDERSONVILLE NATIONAL HISTORIC SITE

bathed and even drank this water," continues Hanan. Early discussions called for a site with a natural stream. But Hanan eventually opted for water he could control, hiding outside the stockade wall a water tank that pumped a gentle flow of water through the set. "It varied in depth from fifteen inches to four feet and was completely stable."

Hanan also oversaw construction of the nearly 2,600 'shebangs' (makeshift lean-tos) the prisoners built to protect themselves from the elements; the village outside the stockade serves as the headquarters of Captain Wirz, the commandant of the camp. The monumental task of making a film of such epic proportions called for some 2,200 people, including fifty-seven featured acting roles and eighty-two speaking parts. In addition, twenty-seven acres served as the primary set on which a camp with stockade, secondary critical structures, a locomotive train, cattle cars and tracks were built to scale during some of the worst weather in Georgia history. "My challenge as the director was not to let the physical aspects—the sheer scale—of the production overwhelm me and take me away from moving the story along" Frankenheimer continues. "I do that by surrounding myself with capable people who do first-rate work."

Dale Fetzer was responsible for the accuracy of period detail. "I'm proud to say that our characters look and act like Civil War Soldiers, not simply players in period clothing," he says. According to Fetzer, the Civil War was very specific in terms of military attire. Officers' uniforms were stylized and form-fitting. Regiments from so many states meant a great variety of insignias, ribbons, medals, buttons and belts. No detail was too small to be overlooked. "In terms of historical authenticity, *Andersonville* looks as if it were a documentary filmed there in 1864," says Fetzer.

For *Andersonville*. Frankenheimer estimates that he filmed 2,500 individual shots—an average of some forty-five set-ups per day. "So many actors in every scene required a tremendous amount of coverage," he explains.

Andersonville is one of the ugliest chapters in the Civil War. But while this story is told in a grey, semi-documentary style, with the director's imaginative use of the Steadicam and hand-held cameras, long tracking shots and close-ups with wide angle lens, Frankenheimer feels that his film is not intended to be a catalogue of horrors. "I wanted," he concludes, "to make a moral statement for our times." Not an easy objective to attain considering the content of today's films.

Recreation of the Andersonville camp for the film.

Ted Turner with Frankenheimer.

JF "There is no doubt that the HBO films, with the extraordinary press they have received, and with the enthusiasm that Turner had for *Andersonville*, have been instrumental in putting me back in the forefront where I want to be. They have also been very important in terms of my own self-confidence as an artist, as a director. They made me love what I do again after the, quite frankly, despairing times I had making *Year of the Gun*, *The Fourth War*, and, before that, *Dead Bang*. The three films which followed were inspirational for me because this was highly creative work with fine people both in front of and behind the camera. They really made a tremen-

dous difference to how I feel—at this point my life seems very clear and concentrated. I want to keep on doing work like this, with a core group of people with whom I enjoy working and in whom I believe in and who believe in me. The future looks relatively good.

"Yes, I hear it said that Frankenheimer has 'gone back' to television but the truth is that I have not 'gone back' to television. When I was in television I was doing live programs, now I'm making films which are going to be shown on television, made in the same way as though they were going to be shown in cinemas. It's simply a different means of distribution and exhibition. I've already spoken about the bad luck I had with companies who failed to market properly the films I made for them. Now I'm making films knowing they are going to have an immediate audience. In England, for instance, directors go between television, features, the stage, opera, commercials, with ease and accomplishment. They just do it. In America, it seems you must be compartmentalized—he's a feature director, a television director, a theatre director, a music director—which I think is wrong. I think of myself simply as a director and it doesn't really make any difference to me where my films are shown as long as they are shown well, in such a way that people know they are out there; and that the companies who produced them support them and spend some money marketing them.

"I think that cable, the medium I have been working in for these last three movies, is now what live television was back in the fifties. Then, not everyone had a television set so there was a rather elite audience looking at our programs. Today, there is a more selective audience, and we can deal with more demanding and controversial subjects on cable than in feature films made under the major studio system. I'm not saying that the studio system is wrong or anything like that, but it is easier to do a strong dramatic film on cable today because there is an audience for it, budgets are smaller, and the risk is not as great. That doesn't mean to say that I wouldn't love to go and do an important feature, but, for my present work there is this additional audience, which is very important for film-makers like myself.

"Certainly, I went into *Andersonville* for Turner knowing it would be interrupted by commercials, unlike those I did for HBO, so I would be hypocritical to tell you that it troubles me. It's not as if they have just sprung the news on me. There is a chance that it will be shown in cinemas in which case of course, there will be no commercials. I haven't structured the screenplay or the film to accommodate commercials, but there are natural act-breaks in the narrative and I think the movie is strong enough to hold through the commercials.

This is a very expensive movie for television; the budget was in excess of eighteen million dollars and it's very courageous of the Turner people to finance it. I don't know of anybody else who would. I can't see anyone else putting up this kind of money for this subject matter and I hope that it justifies their investment—I think it will. Looking at the movie you will see exactly where the money went to. There are thousands of people on the screen, the set itself is twelve acres in diameter. It's an epic production and the fact that we were able to do it for this amount of money is a miracle. Every day there have been over a thousand extras, we shot for over sixty days. It's a terribly difficult undertaking. There is no such thing as a simple shot on this movie, it's among the most difficult movies I've ever done. Had it been made for Paramount or Universal it would probably have cost twice as much or more. Yet there's really very little I would have done differently. I don't want to be critical of the major studios, but their budgets would have been much higher above the line for the actors, for me, for the writer. Using stars in the public sense of the word, would have cost more.

I don't think this movie will look compromised at all either on a small or a big screen. I think it will go theatrical without any of us thinking: If we'd meant to do it this way we would have spent more money. Because I don't think we would have. If I hadn't done the other movies I might never have done this in the first place, because I would have said: It's impossible to shoot it in sixty days. But again, because of an extraordinary crew and actors, we have succeeded. Theoretically however, there is not a major studio around that would have sunk even 30 million dollars into this subject matter. It would be foolish. If a major studio had made this movie the budget should have been no more than we made it on, otherwise they wouldn't have made it, it's that simple. I mean, the individuals running the major studios are not fools. They have a good idea of what their audience wants and what is going to succeed, and I don't think they would say: 'Well, great, we're going to spend 30 million dollars on *Andersonville*, this picture about a prison camp.' I really commend Ted Turner for saying: 'This is what I want to do.' And he has not asked me to make change s of any kind. I think Turner is one of the bravest figures around in this business today, and I just hope that I've made a movie that will justify his faith in me. And no, it's not 'another action movie' as some critics have said. I don't think I've ever done an action picture except for *The Train* and *Grand Prix*. You might call them action pictures, but they are the only two; but like my other films, they are also dramas."

GEORGE WALLACE 1997

Director John Frankenheimer • *Executive Producer* Mark Carliner • *Producers* John Franken-heimer, Julian Krainin • *Co-Producer* Ethel Winant • *Screenplay* Paul Monash and Marshall Frady *based on the latter's book* Wallace • *Camera* Alan Caso • *Editor* Tony Gibbs • *Production Designer* Michael Z. Hanan • *Art Director* Charles Lagola • *Costume Designer* May Routh • *Special Effects* David Dion • *Makeup* Jamie Kelman, Patricia Ross • *Music* Gary Chang • *Sound Recordist* Mike Le Mare • *Production & Distribution* Turner Television Pictures • *Running Time* 3 hrs 20 mins • *Cost* $13 million • *Broadcast* August 24 and 26 in two parts, August 29 and 31, September 3 • *Location* filmed entirely in and around Los Angeles during January 1997; post-production in March and April 1997 at the Post Film Studios, L.A. • *George Wallace* won the Cable Ace Award as Best Mini-Series (November 1997), and the Golden Globe Outstanding TV Film of the Year Award (January 1998).

CAST

George Wallace •	Gary Sinise	*Guitarist* •	Kent Houseman
Lurleen Wallace •	Mare Winningham	*Demonstrator* •	Ron Jeremy
Cornelia Wallace •	Angelina Jolie	*Eddie* •	Mel Jackson
Archie •	Clarence Williams III	*General Graham* •	Jan Johannes
Big Jim Fulsom •	Joe Don Baker	*Jamison* •	Frank Jones
Billy Watson •	Terry Kinney	*Man in Church* •	Robert Jones
T. Y. Odum •	William Sanderson	*Demonstrator* •	Kathleen Kane
Ricky Brickle •	Tracy Fraim	*James Hood* •	Bobby Kirby
Gerald Wallace •	Mark Rolston	*Klan Member #1* •	Clancy Imislund
Al Lingo •	Skipp Suddeth	*Wallace Girl* •	Sabrina Mance
Nicholas Katzenbach •	Ron Perkins	*Reporter* •	Jim McHugh
Bobby Kennedy •	Mark Valley	*TV Commentator* •	Jonathan Mumm
Demonstrator •	Charles Bartlett	*Vivian Malone* •	Ketema Nelson
Demonstrator •	Terrence Beasor	*Cornelia's Trooper* •	Race Nelson
Convention Speaker •	Chuck A. Bernard	*Choir Leader* •	Kaye Phillips
Arthur Bremer •	Scott Brantley	*Cornelia as Child* •	Briana Romero
Girl at Party •	Kathryn Craig	*Wallace Girl* •	Chanel Ryan
Demonstrator •	Tim Dowling	*Velma* •	Tiffany Salerno
Demonstrator •	Miata Edoga	*Demonstrator* •	Vernon Scott
Mrs. Folsom •	Kathryn Erbe	*Reporter* •	Liam Sullivan
Reporter •	Julian Forbes	*Stunt Coordinators* •	Dennis Scott
Klan Member #2 •	Francis Guinan		Charles Croughwell
Mass. State Trooper •	Randy Hall		Bud Davis
Doctor (Maryland) •	Michael Harrington	*Loosh* •	Don Blakely
Neal •	Steve Harris	*Dr. Jeff McKinney* •	Cliff De Young
Cornelia's Trooper •	Michael Haynes	*Demonstrator* •	Beau Billingslea
Reporter •	Vincent Henry	*Alabama State Trooper #1* •	Rob Roy Fitzgerald

SYNOPSIS

This film is a biography of George Wallace, the avowedly segregationist Governor of Alabama in the early 1960s, who was propelled into national prominence until an assassination attempt ended his 1972 run for the United States presidency and left him permanently confined to a wheelchair.

PHOTO: JIM McHUGH/ TURNER PICTURES

COMMENT

At a time when American motion pictures made by the major studios and companies associated with them have slipped into superficiality and sameness, in stories, style and special effects, whatever cinematic qualities certain directors possessed making their films notable have all but wasted away. John Frankenheimer is an exception. Over the years he has remained true to himself and has refused to fall into the present pattern of vulgarity, stupidity, sex and violence. Much of his work has gone unappreciated by critics and unseen by a wide public. Critics who pounce on his work can do little more than refer to *The Manchurian Candidate* as being his last important film and when he does receive good notices, as those for *George Wallace* turned out to be, he again gets *The Manchurian Candidate* brought up as though nothing in between was significant. None of this however seems to overly dismay or concern Frankenheimer. He believes in what he has done; recognises the validity of some aspects of negative criticism (not every film turns out the way the director envisioned it) and continues on undeterred making original and disturbing movies. Such a film is *George Wallace*, a triumph in all but a few aspects of its portrayal. It has become a commonplace these days to compare towering tales of present-day corruption and struggles for power with the great tragedies of Shakespeare. In the case of *George Wallace* such a comparison is appropriate; here we have a man, small by nature, who became a great power in the land, cruel and corrupt, but who lived to see the error of his ways and to seek redemption. All that is missing is the language, but the speeches spoken in the Southern dialect, have about them the ring of Caesar and the slyness of Richard. And the crowds roar as they did in Roman times, with politics twisted and duplicitous, punishments meted out with cruelty and vengefulness among events staged and manipulated to serve the grasping ends of those in power.

More than any other filmmaker in America Frankenheimer has consistently shown in his films a deep social awareness and undiminished political concern and he is at his best when dealing with figures such as George Wallace. This compelling drama takes him back to familiar territory and once again reveals his remarkable feel for documentary which combined with his deep understanding of how to obtain performances of depth and conviction from his actors, makes his films to be both important and continuingly inspiring. In many ways both openly or by suggestion, they have always reflected his views and philosophy on society, both past and present, and, as he has frequently remarked here, his continuing fascination with the indomitability of the human spirit. *George Wallace*, filmed with imagination and feeling, and adeptly scored, is powerfully acted and cleverly edited. Sinise is not added to newsreel sequences. These scenes were re-staged. Under the drab cloak of political activity, always at one with all weather and containing touching private moments, alternating with the hysteria of little men playing out large roles; the whole comes together to bring to life a tragedy which the Bard would have taken up with the same motives and enthusiasm as did Frankenheimer.

JF "When I finished *Andersonville*, Ted Turner asked me to think about filming a comprehensive biography of George Wallace. He already had a screenplay which I liked. The problem with all films dealing with famous or infamous people is 'who should play the role?' We simply could not, at that time, think of an actor we felt was suitable to play the part. I put it aside when Edward Pressman asked me to fly to Australia to take over *The Island of Dr. Moreau*. After that I was supposed to make *The Long Rains*—it didn't get made! During that time I met Gary Sinise who was going to play the lead in this film. I thought to myself that he could play Wallace and I asked him if he would be interested. He said that he was going into rehearsals for a stage production of *A Streetcar Named Desire* and wanted to do a film before the play. I gave him several books on Wallace to read, and some documentary films and finally convinced him to do it. We shot it on fifty-five locations in Los Angeles in forty-one days. My daughter, Kristi Frankenheimer Davis, was the location manager. She was a tireless marvel with the locations she came up with. The present Governor of Alabama wanted nothing to do with us making a film about Wallace there, so the Governor's mansion was an old mansion in downtown LA. Its exterior was a building in Pasadena. There were no studio shots; you know I always try to avoid them. I cannot remember when I last went into a studio. Paul Monash structured the script, Marshall Frady wrote it from his biography of Wallace. I liked what we did with time, with flashbacks; and the quadruple dissolves—which I haven't had an opportunity to use since *All Fall Down*. It was complicated devising a way of going through the years when he ran for Governor, his many election campaigns, his constant travelling, his various relationships with other politicians and people around him. It was a frenetic life to put on film, and by far one of my most difficult pictures. There were occasions when we left the book and turned to other sources available about Wallace.

"I know that many people were surprised and possibly dismayed when they heard I was going to make a film about Wallace. Well, if he were just a bigot, I would not have made this movie. This life is about forgiveness and change. With his unexpected charisma he evolved into a political and social force for the people of his state and in his later years for the nation. He is the Faust of our generation, a tragic hero who sold his soul. In his deal with the devil he became a blazing symbol of the most shameful era in American history. He was a fiercely intense and intelligent man in his time. He knew what he wanted and the fact that he chose to be wrong is what this picture is all about. The film either will or will not speak for itself, and people may well criticise it after they see it. But whether the audience is for or against George Wallace, I'm certain they will be emotionally moved. Like Roosevelt and Churchill, he had the unique ability to make people think he was speaking directly to each of them. An interpretation of Wallace as a one-dimensional villain would be inaccurate, because there was a side of him that was charming. But he decided to wrap himself in the race issue to get elected. That was his most important goal in life, and he is alive today to regret deeply what he did to accomplish this."

IN CONCLUSION: *some afterthoughts*

"The year that Wallace was first elected Governor of Alabama in 1962 was the year that *Manchurian Candidate* came out. My first political film you might say, and Wallace's first grasp of real political power. As I said to you more than thirty years ago I didn't have the same ideas at 39 as I did when I was 29. And since then I have changed again. I think that unless you accept change you will die. But I try to remain true to the principles I always held. As an artist, as a moviemaker, I cannot compromise.

"I have mellowed somewhat in how I accept other people; I am a lot different now in this respect. Back during the tragic days of the Kennedy assassinations and the first racial unrest under Wallace in Alabama, I remember telling you that I feared for America and my depression over those years was deep. Filming scenes for Wallace at the Ambassador brought back memories of the times I was there with Bobby Kennedy, which ended in tragedy; but looking at America today I think that considerable progress has been made from the '60s. Certainly race is still a tremendous issue here but the situation has greatly improved. We survived the Nixon years, we still have a lot of pressing problems in this country, but for the most part, I think we have a President who is doing his best to solve them. And I can tell you that my interest in making political issues an important part of my work is not going to lessen and I believe that television today provides greater opportunities to do this rather than the cinema."

Turner Television Studios, Atlanta,
September 3, 1997

PHOTO JIM McHUGH / TURNER PICTURES

RONIN 1998 (in production)

Director John Frankenheimer • *Producer* Frank Mancuso Jr • *Associate Producer* Ethel Winant • *Screenplay* J. D. Zeik and Richard Weisz • *Photography* Robert Fraise • *Editor* Tony Gibbs • *Production Designer* Michael Z. Hanan • *Costume Designer* May Routh • *Sound* Bernard Bats • *Production and Distribution* United Artists • *Location* filmed in Nice, Arles, Provence and Paris, November 1997–February 1998.

CAST

Sam •	Robert de Niro
Vincent •	Jean Reno
Deirdre •	Natascha McElhone
Gregor •	Stellan Skarsgard
Larry •	Skipp Sudduth
Seamus •	Jonathan Pryce
Spence •	Sean Penn

SYNOPSIS

When six mercenaries meet in a dimly-lit Paris bar, their adventure of friendship, love and betrayal has just begun. Like the honored Japanese warriors of hundreds of years ago, these modern-day Ronin are embarking on their final covert mission. They are hired for one purpose, to recover a mysterious briefcase. Their employer's identity is unknown, but these men and women hold dark secrets of the Cold War that could topple governments in a tragedy culminating in death and finally redemption.

FRANKENHEIMER ON FORM AND TECHNIQUE . . .

Los Angeles, Summer 1995 .

"Cameras are lighter, lenses are faster and film emulsion is faster, so that now one is able to shoot with available light, especially at night. Night shooting with fast film and fast lenses has become much easier than it was. When we were doing nights with the old film we would use big arc lights—practically lighting up the sky! I must say I used to love coming to a movie set where these huge arc lights were all over the place. I would come up there at night and it was magic. That's all changed. It's a hell of a lot easier to light and tremendous improvements have been made in the diaphragms resulting in very good quality from these new fast lenses. Film stock is much better, both Kodak and Fuji. We now have these remote-controlled camera heads for use on cranes, long boom arms and even for slinging cameras from cables. With the help of radio remote controls, the camera operator can start/stop, focus, zoom, set the diaphragm, pan and tilt. With the help of miniature video-assist cameras, he can even watch a TV monitor and see what is going on to the film without actually being right out there physically where the camera is. We do more intricate shots in ways easier to arrive at. Still, nobody's done an opening shot like Orson Welles in *Touch of Evil*, and still no one has shot a movie as well as David Lean.

"It's all toys, but the toys have improved. They now include Steadicam (which won an Oscar for technical achievement), a man-held camera, mounted on a 3-axis gimbal and Iso-Elastic arm attached to the operator's harness. This eliminates the shake and vibration of the old hand-held camera. It provides a very smooth movement, and at the same time walks with the actor. It's very useful. It eliminates dolly tracks over long and difficult terrain, it enables you to go up and down steps, in and out of houses, and other difficult movements much quicker and easier than we used to do by setting up all the long dolly tracks, with endless rehearsing with the grip pulling the dolly. There are good and there are bad Steadicam operators—David Crone is the best operator in the business—and there is good and bad use made of the Steadicam. As with all of these advances, it's how they are employed which makes the difference. It's not always easy to decide when it would

be better to lay tracks and use a dolly shot or to use the Steadicam.

"With the semi-documentary type of movie I do, like *52-Pickup*, where I didn't want the shot to be absolutely perfect, where the audience had to see in close detail this or that particular thing, and the movement was more-or-less all at eye-level, I would use the Steadicam. If I wanted to do a shot establishing locale and I had to stop and see this object, I would crane up and see this, down here to see this, come across, very tight across a person's face, then dolly with that person to somebody else, and the whole scene depended on that shot—I would lay tracks and do it on a dolly because I would have more control over it, and I'd have exactly the result I wanted. Think of that long Steadicam shot in the yard of *Against the Wall*. I love to move the camera around when such movement is called for. I managed to get several shots like this in *Andersonville*. One is six minutes long and goes halfway around the camp in the stockade, taking in about three acres. The Steadicam operator walked around four hundred yards to shoot this very complicated sequence. We can see his picture by looking into a little video monitor, but it's not the same as having control of the dolly. Certain directors who used to be beside the camera when directing are now quite a long way away watching it on video. This raises the issue of how to get the sense, on video, of how actors are playing their scene the way we want them to.

"In live television I was used to blocking. Most of the directors we are talking about never did live television—there are very few of us around who worked in live television and are still going. There's Robert Mulligan, Lumet, Petrie, Delbert Mann, Arthur Hiller, and me. What I used to do was block, on the floor with a television monitor next to me, so I could see the actors at work and watch what was happening on the television screen. In movies, depending on the shot—if it's a complicated dolly shot or something like that—I will watch it on the television monitor, because that's the only way I know if I'm getting it. If it's a close-up or a two-shot where the camera doesn't move there's not that much to it—the actors are in place and it's a question of performance. Then I will watch the actors. That's just my way of doing it.

"Super Panavision is another name for Scope—a 225 to 1 aspect ratio. I like it for certain subjects and I don't like it for other subjects. In the ancillary market, it's a rough go because, until the advent of laser discs, the pan-and-scan method was used. This means that on home video you do not see the movie we made—that's all there is to it. It's a difficult aspect ratio to compose for but I like to use this size of picture—although I haven't done it in a while. There have always been techniques which now have new names. Foley is mostly footsteps, with other little things, named after the man who created these sounds. Sound effects are different sounds. We call it 'at the foley stage' when sounds like a door slamming or drinks being poured into a glass are recorded on the stage. They don't exist exactly the way you want them on the disc or digital tape. Other sound effects including bullet heads and guns are put in by sound effects editors. None of that has changed. ADR is nothing in the world but looping—it's just done a different way. Instead of having the loop of film going around, it's done digitally, easier than putting up another loop.

"It's the same with editing methods. There's no doubt that electronic editing is absolutely terrific. I did it recently on a *Tales from the Crypt* drama, but while the technique itself is great, I haven't yet found someone to operate it who does for me what an editor like Lee Percy or a Fred Steinkamp or a Henry Berman, the great editors I've worked with, will do for me, which is to help me create my final vision. A good editor is so important. I've found that the really great editors don't like working with the electronic stuff, because they weren't brought up doing it. Yes, it's fine to bring up four takes and look at them in a line from each tape, the same line, but if you only have a technician operating it, it's not the same as an editor taking a series of shots and assembling them in a way that sharpens the sequence. With their eyes and instinct you've got real artists working with you. That's what I want an editor to do for me and until I find such a person who uses electronic techniques as well as our existing methods, I'll continue to do what I have been doing, which is to work with editors in the traditional way. I've always been an independent-minded person, and nobody has ever told me what methods to use. I've always had choices, either I do it or I don't do it at all.

"I say this as a person who made the first cut on videotape on *Playhouse 90*. Videotape had never been cut up to that point. We did it with a straight-edge razor blade. We cut the master and we patched it together with a piece of scotch tape and ran it through the system. If we had a video balance movement, we cut a little bit more off. We've come a long way since then, but I'm the first person who ever did it. Yes, I think that we are definitely going into an age of video editing, because the young editors coming along know how to work with these techniques. The editors of my generation and the generation before me don't know how to work it, and don't particularly want to, but the new young people do. There's no doubt about the fact that the benefits in time and costs alone are tremendous, it's just finding the artist to work it. No doubt in the years to come I will use it because I am sure I will find somebody I have the confidence to work with. I know it's quicker and saves money, and it's the way filmmaking is going.

"It's the same with sound recording. That's gone digital with Dolby—good and bad—and competing systems. When I'm shooting I do think in terms of sound. For as along as I've been doing movies, since 1959, we've had stereo sound. We won the Academy Award for *Grand Prix*'s stereo sound track. It's simply a matter of it being better now. There are technicians now who specialize in sound design, and are sound engineers. I rely a great deal on sound, and I hate looping on location. There's a great deal of difference between the production mixer and the post-production crew responsible for the final mix. The production mixer's job on the location or in the studio is to record the dialogue in a very usable state and to be able to record all kinds of effects for you to use later in the mix. I've seen the really great production mixers spend hours walking around trying to get crowd sounds, loudspeakers sound, at airports, cars going by, off-stage lines, wild lines, material that helps you later when you are mixing the film. The final sound effects and dialogue effects editor, the post-production editor, is the person who decides with you how it will be used. You must spend time with the rough cuts talking about the effects you want, what you think you can get, and miscellaneous noises. But in order to get any of this you've got to have a good production track, otherwise you have to post-sync everything. Some of the design of the final mix is done with the post-production sound editor, but much of it is done with the post-production mixers in your pre-dubs. In other words, you start off with a hundred or more different tracks, maybe more, and you bring those down into something like fifteen tracks, which you are finally working with, but that's all done in the pre-dubs. Then even in the dubs, and this takes days and weeks on the dubbing stage, in your final mixing dubbing, if you want to get more to the left, more to the right, you can do that, to go more to the surround speakers, all of this is possible with patient tracking and mixing. So when audiences talk about not being able to understand or hear the actors dialogue, either you are seeing it on a bad system because, up until recently and even now, many theatres have had really terrible sound systems. Or you have a badly mixed picture, which can happen—a lot of technicians and producers rush through it as fast as they can— but if you have a good, well-mixed pre-print, and if you have a skillful mixer—and there are about four or five of them in Hollywood today—you have the possibility of doing really good work. Thanks to George Lucas, sound systems in cinemas are being inspected and more exhibitors are caring about the sound. He has been a great influence on improving the sound in the theatres and we have much to thank him for.

"We also have to thank him for improving visual effects. These are really unbelievable today. I look at what Industrial Light and Magic did in *Terminator II*, and I don't know how they did it. It seems that anything written or imagined can be done. It's just a question of finding the right artist and having the money to spend. There seem to be no limits. Directors today, and I include myself, try and keep as much abreast of what is going on and to use these technologies and computers to your own advantage and not be so in awe of them, that you are put off using them. You have to understand them and be technically knowledgeable enough to incorporate them into your work when needed, not become a slave to them. There are ways you can save a lot of money if you know how to employ these processes. Visual effects are just absolutely startling. The fire sequences in *Back Draught*, for instance, were just extraordinary. The technicians worked very hard, and spent a lot of money on it, and they got it right. Some of the stories and the acting are not up to the special effects, but that's always been the case."

ON STUDIO POLITICS AND PERCEPTIONS . . .

"It's harder to make a personal movie than ever before; there are too many people around who want to have a voice in the shaping of it. If you want to make small personal movies, you apply for grants from arts organizations or companies or individuals to finance them. Distribution and exhibition is limited and that's it. If you want to join the mainstream of American movies then you play by the rules, and if you don't, you get out. If I take millions of dollars from a studio or company to make a movie, I believe that movie should appeal to an audience large enough to recover its costs and show a profit, otherwise how could we continue as film-makers? Critics are always talking about 'personal films' usually made by non-American directors. Every movie I've made has been a personal movie. I have believed in the content, I have never sacrificed substance for style. It comes down to a close-up of a character saying the key lines, not on the huge canvas, but right down to a human being saying something very personal. I shape my scripts to my view of the subject matter, it becomes a part of me. With most of the so-called personal films the director often writes the script, at times the writer, or the actor, becomes the director. This movement is flourishing here. Sundance is an excellent place for beginners. Under the old system, new directors would make 'B' pictures at the studios. That was their training ground. As a friend of mine once said, when talking about the film business, art is a delicatessen.

"When you've got a number of studio executives involved in the decision-making process, particularly before and after the movie is made, it is very difficult to pull away from it and still have the feeling it's the movie you want to make. You must hold firm to this belief though, that's the secret, that's when you have to fight, you have to cut a swathe through all kinds of opposition, criticism, damn stupidity, and foolishness. It can wear you down. With marketing and advertising, you have it in your contract that you are entitled to a consultation. They want to know what you think, and they want to hear everything you have to say. Many producers want you to go out and sell it, and you can't do that if you feel everything's wrong about marketing and advertising and they have ruined the movie. Most studios give a great deal of thought to putting out a film.

"If you put yourself out there as a director for hire, it's difficult, yes, to break away from stereotype. But the object of the exercise is to set out to form relationships with producers and writers enabling you to create and control your own material, and to be locked into it. It then becomes a question for the studio, whether they should make the movie or not. But if they do make the movie, I am going to be the director because it's material I control. More and more, that's what I've been doing. If I put myself on one of these studio laundry lists as director for hire, that's a very precarious way of making a living. It's precarious enough, but that's really being in the wind, and it's always out of your control. They hire you or they might not hire you. This doesn't mean that I don't ask my agents to put me up for various films if I know of a story that I think I might want to do, or if I read a script that I like which is controlled by a studio. But studios have their own agenda, and I'm either part of it or I'm not. I've been part of it and I've not been part of it, and I have every reason to believe that I am part of it. But I like to have more control over my own destiny than that.

"I think the actual process of making a film hasn't changed that much. There are still people in high positions in studios who make decisions and say, 'Yes, we are going to make this film, we are going to try and get so-and-so to star in it, and we are going to try and get this name or that name to direct it.' If you have a marvelous script, a great director who wants to do it, and you present it to an actor who is interested, you can go out and 'package' it. But that's a very rare occurrence because usually scripts are developed by the studios, or they are sold to the studios, and then studios come and make the offers, or the independent producers do. The fact is, you can't get a movie made these days, and you never could, unless you had a star. And unless you can make an offer to the star, you can't get the star, because people won't read on spec. And I don't blame them. But you must have a source of finance behind you in order to make the play for or the pay offer to the actor. These actors will not seriously read scripts coming from nowhere.

"The world, has become much more complicated that it used to be. You've got buy-outs, junk bonds, mergers, the accessories and music markets, the residuals, the up-fronts and down-sizings, all of which has little to do with movie making. When I was working for CBS, and even when I was doing pictures for MGM, when life was simple, I would finish a season at CBS and an entire movie at MGM without a contract. But that's all changed. A contract is only useful when you disagree—if everybody agrees all the time, you don't need a contract. That's why I didn't need one with the CBS or the old Metro pictures, because we agreed. It was a straightforward understanding—CBS let me make my television shows, and Metro let me make my pictures. Later on, when you disagree, you'd better have a piece of paper. Lawyers are everywhere. And as soon as you become better known and more in demand, your compensation goes up and your life becomes more complicated. You become involved in profit participation, in gross, all matter of issues to be defined legally as to what they are, because we all know what the Hollywood accounting system is like. Take the case of *Grand Prix*—*Grand Prix* was sold by Metro to television in a package with 11 other movies, none of which you ever heard of! They were all allocated equal shares of the sale so that *Grand Prix* would not reflect the profits they would have to pay us.

"It's always been very difficult to get pictures made. It never was easy. If you have a run of successes then it's easier. The crop of bankable actors changes, and you may be close to some of them and you may not be. In my case, I was very close to Burt Lancaster, Fredric March, Angela Lansbury, Rock Hudson, Sinatra, and many others whom you've seen in my pictures. I don't know some of the bankable stars today. That's my problem, not theirs. But the only difference I can see is that the moguls, like Jack Warner, Daryl Zanuck, L. B. Mayer, Harry Cohn whom I worked under, are all gone. The only man that I really had anything to do with was William Paley at CBS, one of the great men in the history of television. They were in the movie business to make money, there's no doubt about it, but they believed in their pictures, and Paley was in the television business to make ratings, but he believed in *Playhouse 90*. Every once in a while a story or play came along they wanted to make and to be proud of having made it. Today, the big studios are run by conglomerates—a conglomerate does not make anything to be proud of having made, a conglomerate only makes things to make money—so today there are few pictures being made because they are worthy of being made. Most pictures are made today as commercial enterprises to make money—quality is a secondary consideration. That's the big difference between the old and the new. There are many fewer movies of quality being made, and the costs of marketing have become almost prohibitive. Marketing and opening a movie correctly today costs more than making the movie—somewhere around a minimum of $10 million to do it properly. It gets more expensive because as the networks start losing their viewing audience, it's not enough to buy television only on the networks. Many of the viewers you want to reach are on cable channels, like HBO, ESPN, CNN, cable sports channels, cable movie channels like Turner and American Movie Classics. You have to buy time on these places. And yes, newspapers and magazines are horrendously expensive. It costs more and more and more, and the demographics of audience attendance in cinemas is dropping because with the improvement of home video, the laser disc, big screen TVs with the sound systems you can buy for the home now, it's getting extremely difficult to get people to go to a movie theatre. Very soon, in the next five years, high definition television is going to radically change everything with the screen size being in the same format as the motion picture screen.

"Now the foreign market is becoming more and more important. With big action pictures the foreign market accounts for maybe 55% of the revenues. But we don't know what's going to happen with Europe becoming a united entity, with big broadcasting satellites carrying hundreds of films and programs. It's very simple to take movies and put them on to satellite, on to various channels in countries with different soundtracks on them. I have no idea where we're going—and yet perhaps I do. I see events that are happening and I see the possibilities are endless.

"Up until now, the financial remuneration for all of us making films for cable and video has been very limited, but it's starting to change. They are television movies, more in the British way than MOWs. The latter I would never make. But I'm not contemptuous about television. I love television, it's just that the shooting schedules are very short and the money's very short compared to what you are paid on feature films. Yet, if the subject matter is right, I would sacrifice the money, accept shorter schedules, to be able to do the material I believe in. We are in a complicated arena. It's not that the Philistines have taken over—the Philistines always were in charge. Louis B. Mayer was not a paragon of culture, nor was Harry Cohen, nor was Jack Warner, let's not forget that.

"Everybody talks about the *Golden Age of Television*, but they forget that we were involved in the black list. My God, that was horrendous—what the *Golden Age of Television* did to an important group of actors, directors and writers in this country. It's so easy to remember *Playhouse 90* and the good plays we did—but let's not forget that we had to call an extension at CBS, read off the list of actors we wanted, and wait a day to get a call back and we never knew who was at the other end of the extension and who made those decisions. We don't have that any more. We've got some pretty enlightened men and women running the studios today—Jeffery Katzenburg knows a great deal about movies. Sherry Lansing is no fool, and has produced some very good ones. Likewise, Mike Medavor and Joe Roth. These are responsible and intelligent people running studios—they are not to be confused with the owners. Several of the older studio heads I knew were personal friends. Unfortunately I don't have this relationship with anybody running a studio today, with the exception of Sherry Lansing. I don't know too many other directors, except to say Hello at Directors' Guild meetings. Martin Manulis is still a friend—that's a friendship that's survived many outbursts and disappointments—not directing *Days of Wine and Roses* among them. Somebody said 'I have a feeling that so many people are against me.' A friend replied 'they're not against you, they are for them.' And that's what it is about. This is a highly competitive business, and individuals are looking out for themselves. In that kind of situation it's very difficult to be friends. Yet the movies and the television business have given me a life that would have been impossible anywhere else."

ON THE SATISFACTIONS OF A CREATIVE CAREER . . .

"In the sixties, with the release of *Birdman of Alcatraz*, *All Fall Down*, *Manchurian Candidate*, *Seven Days in May*, and *The Train*, I was considered to be among the most important directors internationally. But you can only stay up there that long. I am often asked how it feels to have directed one of the ten best movies ever made—*The Manchurian Candidate*—how could I ever hope to improve on that? I have to say that I feel pretty good about it because only nine other filmmakers have ever done it, and most of them are dead, while I'm alive and working. It's rewarding to have done it in the first place. What I've done can never be taken away from me, and that's a satisfying feeling. Every time I start a new movie, I don't think that it's got to be better than *Manchurian*, or that I've got to improve on previous pictures, I just try and do my very best with every film I make. I stay out of all that talk of the past and the fear of the future and just spend my time right here, right now, doing what I believe in.

"*The Manchurian Candidate*, I suppose, became a point of reference, if you will, with my newer films almost always being compared to it. Now, when we made *The Manchurian Candidate*, we certainly didn't know we were making a classic. We knew we had an excellent script, we had a hell of a good time making that picture, and I shot the whole movie in forty-one days—working with Frank on the first take. And it wasn't a question of Frank refusing to do any other takes, he would have done all the takes I wanted, but he is better on the first one. We were relaxed and we enjoyed making that movie. It was based on good source material—Richard Condon is a clever writer—and George Axelrod wrote a brilliant script. We were a group of people getting together at a certain moment in our lives and doing the best work we were capable of. Who's to say it isn't going to happen again?

"But the only way it's going to happen is for me to continue making movies. It's not going to happen by sitting back reminiscing about the good old days. It's not going to happen by spending time at film festivals, or by sitting back and waiting for something to happen. You have to be active, to go out and try and put pictures together and be optimistic that all this will be the basis for

your best work still to come. I feel optimistic about the future. I feel I am capable of doing better movies than I have done before, and let's hope I get the opportunity to do so. And I've got an awful lot to be grateful for. I'm able to go out there on that tennis court at sixty-five years old and hit a tennis ball at over a hundred miles an hour. I feel exhilarated and very proud of that. I feel better than I've felt in years. But sooner or later everything goes full cycle. Then the bystanders start to cheer for you to keep living! When you come to a certain age, they say, 'Isn't it marvelous, he's ninety years old and he's still doing this!' That's what I hope to reach.

"Movie-making is a highly competitive business, and individuals are looking out for themselves. In that kind of situation, friendships have always been borderline. I find that your friends in this business are the people who you have worked with, and who you *are* working with. It can get difficult to maintain friendships because, somehow, the personal relationship gets into the work ethic—if you have a best friend who's an actor, and you don't use that actor in a particular picture, the friendship becomes strained and *vice versa*, if the actor becomes a huge success and doesn't put you on his or her preferred list of directors, you're upset. I find that my friends continue to be my friends whether my latest film is a success or a failure.

"My best friend is my wife, she really is. We've been together for thirty-two years. She is the person I care about, she is the person who makes life real for me. She is one of the most beautiful women in the world, and she's loyal and devoted to me, what more can one want? She keeps me from being too depressed at times. She's a very positive person and her parents are very positive about life. She pushes me in the right direction. I have a few good friends, and many tennis-playing friends. I play tennis frequently. I was once a very good tennis player when I was a kid, highly ranked in the juniors, won tournaments, played for my college tennis team, and I gave it all up in my late twenties, when my first marriage, with Carolyn, broke up and I moved back to New York. I played a few times in my early thirties, but nothing very seriously, and then I gave it up—threw it away. I started playing again when I was fifty-seven, and like most things that I do, it was all or nothing. It became all and I eventually sold my house in Malibu, bought a house in Beverly Hills, up in the hills with a tennis court, and I play every day. Even when I'm shooting I manage to play at night and in the morning. I'm back to playing senior tournaments now, and it is another form of life for me. I still like to cook. I like to build miniature cars and planes. I have a huge collection of miniature cars. And I'm a voracious reader. I love thrillers, I love biographies and non-fiction. I watch masses of movies, older movies sometimes. I have a big collection of tapes and laser discs.

"Yet the movies and the television business have given me a life that would have been impossible anywhere else. Like David Lean, I've lived places, gone to places, traveled widely, lived rich and roughed it poor. I would never have done this in any other profession. I've had experiences I would have never been part of elsewhere. I have seen the faces of the world and learned so much about life. I've made money—lots of it—much more than I could ever imagine, and I've spent most of it, but nevertheless, I made it. I've had tremendous artistic satisfaction—I've had some of the greatest happiness that you can possibly imagine. I've also plunged the depths of despair. Knowing that I was using myself to the fullest of my capabilities and doing the best I was capable of has brought me continual satisfaction. I've had feelings like that—how many people can say that? Very few. I have never lived what Thoreau called 'a life of quiet desperation.' It's been a great life. I've had great triumphs and I've had failures, but out of it all, I think what's happened is I've become a fulfilled and better person.

"But you have to be resilient as well. If you are not strong in this business you cannot survive. I've seen too many people go down. A friend of mine, Jerome Hellman, was a very good producer—he did *Coming Home*, and *Midnight Cowboy* among others—and we are about the same age. We were talking the other day and he said, 'Do you realize how many friends we knew who have either died too soon or are out of the business? It's like an invasion on a beach. The doors of the landing craft are open and you're running to get to the dunes. The enemy is firing, and guys are going down all around you, but you keep going until you hit the dunes. That's what we're doing. We are running through a constant fusillade of bullets, if you will, and you hope you don't get hit. We're still running for the dunes.' That's the only analogy I can give you.

"As a director, you are the person who takes charge, who knows what you want, and knows how to get it. Even then you can still make mistakes. It requires a lot of work to be a movie director. It's very important too that you keep yourself in good physical shape and realize that what you are about to embark on is a marathon. It's not a sprint, and you must be in terrific shape at the end, because most of the mistakes in movies are made towards the end when everybody's tired. I think filmmaking is full of individuals who are experts at the fifty yard dash, but there is no such event—we're in it to run the hundred yard dash!

"I want my movies to emotionally involve the audience. I want the audience to feel moved when they leave a movie of mine, to feel and think the experience was worthwhile. The audience places its trust in me by buying a ticket. I have a responsibility to give them something important for their money, not something that's going to make them lesser people leaving the movie theatre, but hopefully something that will enrich their lives. That's what I have always tried to do. There are many good subjects in life. I want very badly tŏ do a love story again. I like good dramas and there are comedies that are fun. I'm not tying myself down to a particular subject matter, I don't want to get more typed than perhaps I already am. I would like to branch out, but I seem to be grouped into what are loosely termed the action, suspense, and thriller pictures. I'd like to get back to dramas. I don't want to do work that's irresponsible and immoral. I try and choose material from what I like and what I react to, and if I respond well to it, I have to believe the audience is also going to react well to it. I've got to be right more than half of the time, otherwise I'm out of the business."

AND ON THE FILMS THAT WERE NEVER MADE.

"I made *The Challenge* in '81, and *The Holcroft Cov-enant* in '83. 1982 was spent trying to get a racing picture put together at Universal called *Flat Out*. We had Derek Washburn write a preliminary script, and then we brought in Dan Jenkins. Actually we had several scripts including one by Oliver Stone, and from Oliver Stone it went to Robert Garland, who did *No Way Out*. It was a very good project and we practically had a 'go' on it when Universal's management changed again. Ned Tanen resigned, and the new management came in and decided not to make a racing picture. That was a year's worth of work out the window! It was heartbreaking, and a terrible blow to one's beliefs and self-confidence.

"I then became involved in another movie with Michael Phillips, a Robert Parker project called *Wilderness*, from his novel, with Richard Dreyfuss participating. I spent about six months trying to get it done and that didn't work. The money didn't come through. It was a very interesting story about an ordinary man who is forced through circumstances to fight for his life in the wilderness. Parker's a good writer. I might do that movie some time in the future. I liked the brief association I had with Dreyfuss—he is an intelligent actor. I had Paul Newman in mind for *Flat Out* in a father and son relationship. Gene Hackman could have played it too, but it never reached the point where the studio would make a firm offer to one of these actors.

"Among several films I was about to make but didn't was one of my favorite Hemingway stories *Across the River and Into the Trees*. It was critically panned as a self-parody of the author when the book was published in 1949, and is now one of the few remaining Hemingway novels yet to reach the screen. The story concerns a colonel's adventurous love story. This was one of those pictures that went through many people and was never made mainly because of problems with Robert Haggiag. He is a very wealthy man who years ago secured the rights to Hemingway's book. He is multi-national—Egyptian or Syrian by birth, I think—and spent years in Egypt amassing a fortune in various ways. He then went into the movie business with a studio in Rome. He acquired theatres and was the Italian distributor for United Artists in Italy. I first met him when I was filming *Impossible Object* in France. He became a very powerful man in European movies, one of those legendary movie moguls of the sixties, producing some very fine pictures. He made an awful lot of money one way or the other, was handsome and charming, but I don't think he ever wanted to make this movie. We all met Haggiag in Venice, we had a splendid screenplay by the English writer, Alan Scott, but for unknown reasons Haggiag was afraid to proceed. At least, Gene Hackman, who was to be in it, and I were partially paid for our work. Altman of course, came before us and John Huston before him. Quite a saga of sorts—eight years of effort!

"Then there was *Endurance*, later changed to *Speed*. It was the story of a racing car driver at Le Mans and other Grand Prix circuits in Europe. The film would not have been another *Grand Prix*. With that film I had the choice of making it either as a *Grand Hotel* style of picture or as a *Test Pilot* kind of film. I chose to make it *Grand Hotel*. *Speed* was to have been my *Test Pilot*. I'm a speed buff myself and I sensed that the time was right for such a picture. So did Universal—at first. Racing has always been a popular subject in Europe but now I feel, in fact, I know, that North Americans are equally interested in it. All filmmakers face the same problem of trying to predict what the public will want to see in two years time when a movie is finished and opens. And although I say I think the time may be right for a picture, when it comes right down to it that cannot be the deciding factor. What decides me is—do I want to make this film? Does it excite me? The possibility of making this one did!"

Note: see Appendix, page 284.

CONCLUSION

As another year begins, John Frankenheimer and Evans Evans are returning home from France where they have been on location filming *Ronin*. Once more there have been *Ten Best Lists, Reviews of the Year*, opinions expressed about Hollywood's prospects and profits, and predictions of yet more mergers and take-overs in the aftermath of Universal-MCA by Seagram from Matsushita; Capital Cities/ABC-TV by Disney; CBS-TV by Westinghouse Electric Corp.; Turner Broadcasting System by Time Warner; and Cineplex Odeon by Loew's Sony Cinemas.

John Frankenheimer, crossing the divide between CBS's live television years and HBO's present day television films, won the 1994 Emmy Award for Best Direction with *Against the Wall*, and again in 1995 for *The Burning Season*. Despite all the obstacles frustrating film production today and the shortage of screenplays appealing to him, he continues to find his way with significant work through the monolith of Hollywood's mass communications machine. His work is about passion, beauty, and about life itself. His best movies combine a thematic complexity with psychological depths. His cameras have a fluid grace combined with a deep and natural realism and cinematic flow rare among today's major film-makers. He knows their lenses, has embraced widescreen techniques and made imaginative use of improved film stock. He understands the visual nature of his medium so well that his images keep us transfixed. His instinct and knowledge of what constitutes an effective screenplay bring his narratives constantly alive, and his empathy with actors, his skill at drawing out remarkable performances from them, puts motion and humanity into his films.

The founding of his career in the early days of television is unique in the history of American film-making and by moving into films for cinemas he found the perfect means of linking up the first with the future technologies. Apart from minor lapses during his painful period of deep depression in the late seventies and early eighties, his choice of subjects has been unerring. Always willing to try different styles and narrative forms, he has been knowing and perceptive when exploring interior family drama and community violence, and broadly imaginative and even startling in his exterior adventures. His stories have within them an irresistible moral force combined with a poetic imagination and dramatic intensity. His well-chosen and impressive casts of characters come from all walks of life, from the hypersensitive to the deceptively ordinary, and always remain true to their lives.

He is uncompromising when it comes to obtaining what he requires to achieve his vision in his work leading his close colleagues to comment, on more than one occasion, that his creed has always been "If it suits my purpose, I'm going to have it," carried out with a fierce determination and unflagging energy. In his films he never raises false hopes or offers sentimental solutions. He has no illusions about the world of film-making and nothing dampens his unquenchable spirits. There is little about the desperate nature of life that he is not aware of, and his interest and concern in his country's social and political affairs remains constant.

In March, Frankenheimer and Evans celebrated his 65th birthday with a quiet candle-lit dinner at their home in Beverly Hills, with Nanette Siegert, Robert Rosen, and other close friends. He was himself the chef; it was am evening of delicious food, fond memories and lively conversation.

John Frankenheimer's quiet sense of humor has helped considerably in seeing him through the changing years. Called upon recently to meet new studio executives, he was asked: "What's your track record?" Frankenheimer replied with equanimity, "What's yours?"

Dhiegh, Khigh, in *The Manchurian Candidate*, 35; in *Seconds*, 55
Diggstown, 160
Diller, Barry, 166
Dillman, Bradford, in *The Iceman Cometh*, 137, 140, 141; in *99 and 44/100% Dead*, 145, 147, 149
Dillon, Laurie, 153, 156
Dillon, Robert, 145, 153, 156
Dion, David, 269
Divorce, Italian Style, 96
Dobbins, Bennie, in *99 and 44/100% Dead*, 145
Dobtcheff, Vernon, in *The Horsemen*, 109
Doctor Zhivago, 79
Donovan, Tate, in *Dead Bang*, 197
Donforth, Dick, in *The Gypsy Moths*, 83
Douglas, Kirk, in *Seven Days in May*, 43, 45, 46, 47, 93; 58
Douglas, James B., in *Dead Bang*, 197
Dowling, Helen, in *The Fixer*, 75
Dozier, Robert, 13, 15, 16
Dozier, William, 9, 16
Dresner, Hal, 69, 72
Dreyfuss, Richard, 281
Drought, James, 83, 86, 88
Duggan, Andrew, in *Seven Days in May*, 43
Duggan, Pat, 19
Dunaway, Faye, in *The Extraordinary Seaman*, 69, 71
Duncan, Kirk, in *Seconds*, 55
Dunn, Beverley, 265
Durning, Charles, in *I Walk the Line*, 101
Dye, Dale, in *The Fourth War*, 203
Dynam, Jacques, in *French Connection II*, 153
Dysart, Richard, in *Prophecy*, 169

Eames, Charles, 64
Eastwood, Clint, 148
Easy Rider, 112
Edmondson, Joe, 35, 43, 55
Edwards, James, in *The Manchurian Candidate*, 35, 36
Eisenhower, Dwight D., 46, 72–73
Eisner, Michael, 166, 171
Eliot, T. S., 157
Elliot, Thomas, in *The Year of the Gun*, 207
Elliott, Peter, in *The Island of Dr. Moreau*, 265
Ellis, Don, 153, 157
Ellison, Nancy, 211
Ely, David, 55, 56, 58, 121
The Emerald Forest, 248
Emick, Jarrod, in *Andersonville*, 251
Emilfork, Daniel, in *Riviera*, 187
Evans, Evans, 1; in *All Fall Down*, 29, 31, 32;

93; 123; in *Impossible Object*, 125ff, 135; in *The Iceman Cometh*, 137; 151; in *Prophecy*, 169; 189; in *Dead Bang*, 197; 279, 282
Evans, J.C., in *I Walk the Line*, 101, 105
Evans, Robert, 159, 163, 166
Evanson, Edith, in *The Young Stranger*, 13
Evers, Bruce, in *Against the Wall*, 233; in *Andersonville*, 251
Executive Suite, 32
An Exile, 101, 104, 106
The Extraordinary Seaman, **69**, 92, 115, 242, 249

Face of a Hero, 11, 32
Fair, Jody, in *The Young Savages*, 19
Fangio, 64
Farrel, Bernard, 49
Faulkner, William, 8
Fehmiu, Bekim, in *Black Sunday*, 159, 160, 164
Fellini, Frederico, 98, 126
Fellner, Eric, 207
Fetzer, Dale, 261
Field, Betty, in *Birdman of Alcatraz*, 23
Fiermonte, Enzo, in *Grand Prix*, 61
Fifth Column, 8
52 Pick-Up, **191**, 199, 227, 274
Finch, Jon, in *Riviera*, 187
Fitzgerald, F Scott, 8, 27
Fisher, Gerry, 157, 183, 184, 185, 197, 199, 200, 203, 205
The Fixer, 25, 36, **75**, 92, 94, 95, 96, 112, 121, 128, 129, 156, 228, 238
Floersheim, Patrick, in *French Connection II*, 153
Flon, Suzanne, in *The Train*, 49
Fluellen, Joel, in *The Young Savages*, 19
Fonda, Jane, 27
Fonteray, Jacques, 153
For Whom the Bell Tolls, 8, 116, 120
Ford, Constance, in *All Fall Down*, 29, 31; in *99 and 44/100% Dead*, 145; 215
Ford, John, 96
Fordney, Alan, in *Grand Prix*, 61
Foreman, Carl, 71, 98
Forrest, Frederic, in *Against the Wall*, 233, 236, 238; in *Andersonville*, 251, 258
Forest, Denis, in *Andersonville*, 251
Foster, Robert, 197, 200
Forsythe, William, in *Dead Bang*, 197
The Fourth Protocol, 188
The Fourth War, **203**, 210, 211, 227, 262
Foxworth, Robert, in *Prophecy*, 169, 171
Frady, Marshall, 269, 271
Fraim, Tracy, in *George Wallace*, 269
Fraise, Robert, 273
Fraker, William A., 265
Frank, Richard H., 179

Frankenstein, 57
Franklin, Tommy, in *Grand Prix*, 61
Fraser, Elizabeth, in *Seconds*, 55
Fredericks, Ellsworth, 43
French Connection, 151
French Connection II, 128, 130, 134, 151, **153**, 163
Fresson, Bernard, in *French Connection II*, 153, 155
Frick, Bill, 65
Friedkin, William, 129, 151, 154, 156, 157
Le Front de l'Art, 49
Fuin, Christian, in *The Train*, 49
Fujikawa, Jenny, in *The Extraordinary Seaman*, 69
Fukasaku, Kenta, in *The Challenge*, 173
Fumagalli, Franco, 207

Gaddis, Thomas E, 23, 25
Gardner, Ava, in *Seven Days in May*, 43, 45, 46, 93
Garland, Robert, 281
Garner, James, in *Grand Prix*, 61, 62, 63, 64, 65–66, 120
Gary Moore Show, 7
Gates, Larry, in *The Young Savages*, 19
Gazzo, Michael V., in *Black Sunday*, 159
Geer, Will, in *Seconds*, 55, 59
Gibbs, Tony, 269, 273
Giuarto, Blasco, 207, 210
Glenn, Scott, in *The Challenge*, 173, 174, 176, 177
Glick, Michael, 55, 69
Globus, Yorman, 191, 195
Glover, John, in *52 Pick-Up*, 191, 193, 195
Godard, Jean-Luc, 96, 126, 135
Godfather II, 157
Goldsmith, Jerry, 43, 45, 55, 173, 174
Golan, Menahem, 191, 194, 195
Golino, Valeria, in *The Year of the Gun*, 207
Golon, Georges, 153
Gordon, Scott, 149
Gotell, Walter, in *Black Sunday*, 159
Govons, Marica, 179
Grace, Henry, 29, 69, 83
Gracie, Ian, 265
The Graduate, 38, 96
The Grand Illusion, 96
Grand Prix, 38, 52, 56, 57, 58, **61**, 70, 72, 92, 113, 115, 118, 120, 123, 129, 163, 164, 165, 174, 176, 211, 215, 216, 217, 218, 219, 221, 226, 228, 263, 275, 277, 281
Grant, Clare, in *The Island of Dr. Moreau*, 265
The Grapes of Wrath, 94
Gray, Charles H., in *Prophecy*, 169
The Greatest Story Ever Told, 65
Green, Martyn, in *The Iceman Cometh*, 137